MANAGING THE ECONOMY, MANAGING THE PEOPLE

Managing the Economy, Managing the People

Narratives of Economic Life in Britain from Beveridge to Brexit

JIM TOMLINSON

OXFORD
UNIVERSITY PRESS

OXFORD
UNIVERSITY PRESS

Great Clarendon Street, Oxford, OX2 6DP,
United Kingdom

Oxford University Press is a department of the University of Oxford.
It furthers the University's objective of excellence in research, scholarship,
and education by publishing worldwide. Oxford is a registered trade mark of
Oxford University Press in the UK and in certain other countries

First Edition published in 2017

Impression: 1

Published in the United States of America by Oxford University Press
198 Madison Avenue, New York, NY 10016, United States of America

British Library Cataloguing in Publication Data
Data available

Library of Congress Control Number: 2017936086

ISBN 978–0–19–878609–2

Printed and bound by
CPI Group (UK) Ltd, Croydon, CR0 4YY

Acknowledgements

I am grateful to the Carnegie Trust for the Universities of Scotland for several small grants that helped finance research in the Public Record Office at Kew. Thanks also to the University of Glasgow for a period of study leave in which I was able to complete this book.

I have been working on some of the themes of this volume for a long time (with several interruptions and deviations along the way). During this period I have talked about some of the issues raised at a number of conferences of the Economic History Society, and seminars at York, New York, and Columbia Universities. I have received helpful comments, direct and indirect, from colleagues at Glasgow, especially Catherine Schenk, Neil Rollings, and Jim Phillips, and from my collaborator in research going back to our days in Brunel University's Department of Government, Ben Clift, now at the University of Warwick. None of these, it should be emphasized, bears any responsibility for any statements made here.

Some material in this volume draws upon three articles published in the *Economic History Review* (*EcHR*): 'British Government and Popular Understanding of Inflation in the Mid-1970s', vol. 67, no. 3 (2014), pp. 750–68; 'Managing the Economy, Managing the People: Britain circa 1931–1970', vol. 58, no. 3 (2005) pp. 555–85; and 'Inventing "Decline": the Falling Behind of the British Economy in the Post-War Years', vol. 49, no. 4 (1996), pp. 734–60. I am grateful to Wiley-Blackwell for permission to use this material, and likewise for their permission to cite data from: N. Crafts, 'The Golden Age of Economic Growth in Western Europe. 1950–1973' *EcHR* 48 (1995) (Table 2.1), and S. Broadberry and N. Crafts, 'UK Productivity Performance from 1950 to 1979: A Restatement of the Broadberry–Crafts view' *EcHR* 56 (2003) (Table 7.4). All rights to this material are reserved, and it may not be reproduced, stored, or transmitted in any form without prior permission from the copyright holder.

I am grateful to the Margaret Thatcher Foundation for permission to quote from the Margaret Thatcher papers, to NatCen Social Research for the use of data from the British Social Attitudes survey (Table 3.2), and to James Alt for his data (Table 8.2).

Data from the ONS and OBR is used under the Open Government Licence (OGL), and I affirm that the volume contains public sector information licensed under the OGL, version 3.0.

Acknowledgements

Contents

List of Figures

List of Tables

List of Illustrations

All images courtesy of the National Archives.

List of Abbreviations

AACP	Anglo-American Council on Productivity
BEQB	*Bank of England Quarterly Bulletin*
BJPIR	*British Journal of Politics and International Relations*
BOUIES	*Bulletin of Oxford University Institute of Economics and Statistics*
BPC	British Productivity Council
BSA	British Social Attitudes
CBH	*Contemporary British History*
CBI	Confederation of British Industry
CIPU	Counter-Inflation Publicity Unit
Cmd./Cmnd./Cm.	Command Paper
COI	Central Office of Information
COPPI	Council on Productivity, Prices, and Incomes
CPS	Centre for Policy Studies
CRESC	Centre for Research on Socio-Cultural Change (University of Manchester)
DEA	Department of Economic Affairs
EcHR	*Economic History Review*
EEC	European Economic Community
EHR	*English Historical Review*
EIU	Economic Information Unit
EJ	*Economic Journal*
EPA	European Productivity Agency
ERM	Exchange Rate Mechanism
FBI	Federation of British Industry
FDI	foreign direct investment
FIS	Family Income Supplement
FS	*Fiscal Studies*
GATT	General Agreement on Tariffs and Trade
GDP	Gross Domestic Product
HC	House of Commons Papers
HMT	His/Her Majesty's Treasury
ICT	information and communications technology
IEA	Institute of Economic Affairs
IFS	Institute for Fiscal Studies
IMF	International Monetary Fund
IPPR	Institute for Public Policy Research
JPC	Joint Production Committee
JRSS	*Journal of the Royal Statistical Society*
JSP	*Journal of Social Policy*
MNC	multinational corporations
MRC	Modern Records Centre (University of Warwick)
MTFS	medium-term financial strategy
MTFW	Margaret Thatcher Foundation website

NBPI	National Board for Prices and Incomes
NEDC	National Economic Development Council
NEDO	National Economic Development Office
NICE	non-inflationary continuous expansion
NIER	National Institute Economic Review
NOP	National Opinion Polls
NPE	*New Political Economy*
NUCUA	National Union of Conservative and Unionist Associations
OBR	Office for Budget Responsibility
OECD	Organisation for Economic Co-operation and Development
OEEC	Organization for European Economic Co-operation
OMH	output per man hour
ONS	Office for National Statistics
OPEC	Organization of Petroleum Exporting Countries
PEB	Production Efficiency Board
PESC	Public Expenditure Survey Committee
PQ	*Political Quarterly*
PS	*Political Studies*
PSBR	Public Sector Borrowing Requirement
PSNB	Public Sector Net Borrowing
RPI	Retail Price Index
SJPE	*Scottish Journal of Political Economy*
TCBH	*Twentieth Century British History*
TNA: PRO	The National Archives: Public Record Office
TUC	Trades Union Congress
UNECE	United Nations Economic Commission for Europe

Introduction

'It's the economy, stupid', like most clichés, both reveals and conceals important truths. The slogan suggests a hugely important truth about the post-1945 politics of the advanced democracies such as Britain: that economic issues have, for most of that period, been crucial to government strategies and political arguments. But what the cliché conceals is the need to examine what is understood by 'the economy', a term which has no fixed meaning, and which has been constantly reworked and reinterpreted. Starting from those two points, the aim of this book is to provide a distinctive new account of British economic life since the Second World War, focusing upon the ways in which successive governments, in seeking to manage the economy, have sought simultaneously to manage popular understanding of economic issues. In doing so, governments have sought not only to shape expectations for electoral purposes but to construct broader narratives about how 'the economy' should be understood. This book analyses the conditions surrounding the narratives governments have tried to propagate, and also asks how successful they have been in persuading the population, which is inherently much harder to determine. But, with varying degrees of enthusiasm and focus, governments have sought to understand popular opinion on economic matters, including, periodically, the effects of their own propaganda, generating lots of material for the historian to work with. More broadly, opinion polling by all manner of organizations, the growth of which has been such a feature of the post-war world, provides us with data which, used with care, can yield useful results.[1]

The idea that a government's electoral prospects are linked to the performance of the economy is a well-established theme of political science literature, one strand of which identifies a 'political business cycle', in which economic management is used to try to maximize electoral benefit. However, such attempts have had limited success, partly because it is not clear which aspect of economic performance must be manipulated in order to gain popularity. For example, would maximizing growth or minimizing inflation and unemployment be most advantageous? In terms of the historical record, the existence of these types of cycles is contested.[2]

But the issue of economic narratives goes well beyond the electoral cycle. Of course governments in a democracy have regard to the electoral consequences of their economic policies and how those policies are presented. But what they do and say is also shaped by longer-term ideological positioning, by the changing

[1] For the explosion of political opinion polling in particular: Bartle et al., 'Post-war', p. 210.

[2] Mosley, *Making*, pp. 17–43, 183–201; Middleton, *Government*, pp. 576–7; Lewis-Beck, Nadeau, and Belanger, 'General', pp. 279–90.

events and circumstances with which they have to grapple, and by the framing of the issues by economists, civil servants, advisers, the press, and other external voices. So economic narratives, the public stories or propaganda governments tell about the economy, are always constructed from a variety of sources, with complex origins and underpinnings.[3]

Governments have not taken popular economic understanding as given; they have sought to be, in the language of political science, 'preference-shapers'. In pursuit of that shaping they have deployed a very wide range of strategies, tactics, and means of propagating the message(s). This book is more focused on the 'message' than the 'medium', though it emphasizes the variety of means used, which in modern Britain have varied from ministerial speeches and broadcasts, parliamentary statements and debates, and detailed government white papers, through to press advertising, mass 'popular' leaflet distribution, and factory-wall newspapers. Much effort has gone into designing this economic publicity, to worrying about its audience; and a significant amount also into seeking to gauge its effects.

All these activities have been aimed at constructing particular understandings of 'the economy'. The term 'constructed' is the right word to use. 'The economy' is not a natural object, but a socially constructed one: as Adam Tooze puts it, '"the economy" is not pre-existing reality, an object which we simply observe and theorise about. Our understanding of the "economy" as a distinct entity, a distinct social "sphere" or social "system", is the product of a dramatic process of imaginative abstraction and representational labour'.[4]

Thus, unlike much political science literature on popular responses to economic conditions, we do not assume a 'real' economy, which electors may 'misunderstand'.[5] Rather, all economic understandings are treated as constructed, without seeking to claim that some are based on incontestable truths about the economy. This allows us to follow arguments made in the literature on the public understanding of science, which suggests that people develop understandings of the world which are best appreciated in their own terms, rather than their degree of conformity with expert knowledge (knowledge which, especially in the case of economics, is often itself contested, even by the experts).[6] Unsurprisingly, those who have sought to persuade the public of a particular view of the economy have often presented their actions as purely 'educational', as when in the 1940s the Labour Minister, Herbert Morrison, talked of a campaign to overcome 'national economic illiteracy'.[7] But

[3] The word 'propaganda' is used in this book as a non-pejorative term for attempts to shape public debate; while these attempts are necessarily normative in character, the term is used without any suggestion that this activity was ill-intentioned or illegitimate.

[4] Tooze, 'Imagining', pp. 213–14.

[5] For example, Sanders, 'Real'. While Sanders recognizes that politicians may seek to change the electors' evaluation of the 'real' economy, he treats the official statistics of inflation and unemployment as simply 'reflections' of that reality.

[6] Michael, 'Ignoring'. The diversity of economic understanding even at the highest professional level is well brought out by the award of the Nobel prize in economics over the years to practitioners with often wholly conflicting theories: Offer and Soberberg, *Nobel*, pp. 107–48.

[7] Cited in Crofts 'Attlee', p. 453.

'education' in economics is never innocent of ideological and political purposes, implicit or overt.

One of the striking features of the efforts at persuasion employed was the frequent use of *moral* language, often a language of 'fairness' and 'just deserts'. The astute economist Barbara Wootton observed that 'the public is always better at ethics, which are warm and real, than at economics, which are cold and abstract', and this perception seems to have informed many official propaganda efforts.[8] Notions of distributive justice, however inchoate, influenced the framing of all four of the economic 'problems' that are analysed in Part II.[9]

This book argues that the process of 'imaginative abstraction and representational labour' in constructing 'the economy' took on a radically different shape from the 1940s in the context of British economic policy, because governments in this decade took on major new responsibilities for the performance of the national economy. Simultaneously, these new responsibilities made governments much more anxious to shape popular views of the economy in order to secure support for government policy, and to make it more likely that economic policy aims would be achieved.

This introduction analyses how the preconditions for the management of the national economy built up in the years before the 1940s and how 'management of the people' developed roughly in parallel, concluding with a summary of the structure of the book.

I

What came into being in the decades before the Second World War was a notion of a national economy as something which, at least within limits, could be managed; hence we can talk of the twentieth century as seeing the emergence of national economic management. Such management emerged from the 'unmanaged economy', which had its heyday before 1914, and which rested on three pillars: the gold standard, free trade, and low and balanced budgets. Taken together, these arrangements served to minimize the role of government.

In principle the gold standard was an automatic mechanism, in which gold flows stabilized the economy without intervention.[10] In practice the Bank of England acted as orchestrator of the system, but in this role the Bank was effectively politically unaccountable, and neither did it seek to persuade the populace at large about the desirability of its policies, let alone aim to change their behaviour.[11] Apart from a brief flurry about bimetallism, adherence to the gold standard was never politicized, and was never the object of popular political debate.[12] In many ways the gold standard was the ultimate laissez-faire arrangement in which institutional

[8] Wootton, *Social*, p. 100.
[9] This particular dimension is assessed in more depth in Tomlinson, 'Re-inventing'.
[10] Eichengreen, *Gold*, pp. 1–23.
[11] Kynaston, 'Bank', pp. 19–55.
[12] Green, 'Rentiers'.

rules were established within which self-seeking individuals were best able to pursue their own interests with no need for any 'political' involvement.

Free trade might be seen as on a par. After all, the classic case for free trade is that it establishes a mechanism by which the workings of comparative advantage in the marketplace will maximize the economic welfare of all. But unlike the gold standard, free trade was the object of political struggle. Indeed, a large part of British politics in the first half of the nineteenth century, and again in the early years of the twentieth, was organized around free trade versus protection.[13] As recent accounts of free trade have emphasized, far from being an ideology of 'rootless cosmopolitanism', free trade versus protection became an issue around which conflicting versions of the identity of Britain were organized, and both sides found wide popular resonance.[14] However, as with the gold standard, the antagonists in the trade debate were struggling over the kinds of national rules that should govern commercial relations. The protagonists attempted to persuade the populace about their case, and deployed economic arguments as an important part of their armoury, but they were not attempting to change the *behaviour* of the population.

Like free trade, taxing and spending was the object of major political struggles in the pre-1914 period, culminating most obviously in the battle over the People's Budget of 1909.[15] These struggles, like those over free trade, were deeply entwined with broader cultural and political issues, and debates over the nature of Britain. But like free trade, the struggle over taxation and spending was, in one dimension, a struggle over the character of incentives, not an attempt to change behaviour. The arguments were about how people would respond to particular patterns of tax, and the economic and social consequences that would flow from these (alleged) effects.[16]

Thus, while in the unmanaged economy economic policy was far from wholly depoliticized (except in the case of the gold standard), the political struggles were largely organized around the institutional framework of policy, *not* around active management of the economy. In this world, the government established the 'rules of the game', but did not usually attempt to directly shape popular economic understanding or behaviour (but see exceptions noted in Section III).

If there was no national economic management, there was also only a very limited sense of a 'national economy'. The gold standard and free trade, in principle, built on and encouraged indifference to national boundaries. Both gold and goods flowed internationally without help or hindrance by national governments. Budgetary policy, on the other hand, obviously does have a national aspect, even though until the First World War a large part of the fiscal system was locally based. But the national role of the budget was heavily circumscribed; the Treasury seeing itself as 'the national housekeeper not the national breadwinner'.[17] And even if central government *had* sought to use the budget for economic purposes, it was too small a proportion of national income to have a significant impact.

[13] Howe, *Free*. [14] Trentmann, 'Wealth'. [15] Green, *Crisis*; Murray, *People's*.
[16] Daunton, *Trusting*. [17] Clarke, 'Treasury's', p. 173.

The unmanaged economy eventually gave way to national economic management as the lack of government action became increasingly politically unsustainable. One force behind this was the political changes which even before the First World War had put the 'Condition of England' question at the centre of domestic policies. The complex of arguments around that 'Condition' particularly focused on the labour market, and a long-running battle had opened about the degree to which government both could and should take responsibility for the state of that market.[18] Before 1914 that responsibility was very limited, the belief in a self-equilibriating market for labour remained very powerful, and the perceived dangers of intervention were emphasized. However, the state, in the form of the Board of Trade, had started to take a formal role in measuring changes in the labour market.[19]

A second force at work of great importance, and one reason why the 'Condition' question had become so prominent, was of course the rise of labour as a social and political force, symbolized but by no means wholly represented in the growth of the Labour Party. Before the First World War, and indeed for some time afterwards, Labour was by no means a simple proponent of national economic management, a point made clear if we note Labour attitudes to the 'three pillars'. First, Labour was a supporter of free trade, although the grounds for that support were by no means simply a reflection of the classic Cobdenite free-trade case.[20] Second, Labour seems to have developed no hostility to the gold standard before 1914.[21] Third, while Labour had fought for greater government responsibility for the state of the labour market, this was by no means a corollary of attacks on the low and balanced budget convention. Many in Labour's ranks were suspicious of the role of the state, as had been graphically illustrated at the time of the 'New Liberal' welfare reforms.[22] Furthermore, the idea of using the budget as a macroeconomic instrument did not exist before the First World War, little of 'Keynesian' fiscal proposals being evident in the discussions of public works in the Edwardian period.[23]

Another force undermining the unmanaged economy was the war itself. It led to the suspension of the gold standard, and the first chipping away at free trade (the McKenna Duties of 1915).[24] More broadly, the war undermined many of the assumptions on which the 'culture' of free trade had rested.[25] The wartime budget expanded beyond all precedent, and was never to return to its pre-war scale.[26] The state's responsibility for the economy was greatly enhanced, as total war made unprecedented demands on production. One result of this enhancement was a new level of scrutiny of the economy by government, yielding a whole new knowledge of economic failings previously hidden.[27] Better known is the impact of wartime economic problems ramifying into a wide range of controls of economic life. In the long run the most important of these controls related to labour, because here the controls were only one part of a new 'compact' between labour and the

[18] Harris, *Unemployment*; Harris, 'Transition'; Stedman-Jones, *Outcast.*
[19] Davidson, *Whitehall.* [20] Trentmann, 'Wealth'.
[21] Snowden, *Labour*; Tomlinson, 'Labour', pp. 47–50.
[22] Thane, 'Labour'; Thane, 'Working-class'. [23] Winch, *Economics*, pp. 58–61.
[24] Tomlinson, *Public*, ch. 3. [25] Trentmann, 'Strange'.
[26] Middleton, *Government*, pp. 88–9, 330–8. [27] Supple, 'Official'; Tomlinson, *Government.*

state. While the direct level of responsibility of government for the labour market was long to remain a battleground, the government's *concern* with the labour market (in what was, after all, the most proletarianized country in the world) was now to be central to political debate for the rest of the century.[28]

The war did not immediately usher in the age of economic management. The gold standard was reconstructed.[29] Despite the policy of Safeguarding, free trade remained dominant (the McKenna Duties being abolished by the Labour Chancellor Snowden in 1924).[30] While the budget was markedly larger than before the war, the aim of budget balance was central to policy in the 1920s.[31] But the political climate in which these restorations took place had shifted. The defence of the return to gold now had to embrace the employment effects.[32] Free trade no longer enjoyed such deep support across the social classes as in the Edwardian era.[33] The size of the budget laid down a key foundation for the argument that government had acquired, if 'accidentally', an instrument with which the state of the economy could be manipulated. Politically, the main casualty of the war was the Liberal Party, the party of the unmanaged economy. In the 1920s Labour, a beneficiary of Liberal decline, was led by men (Ramsay MacDonald, Philip Snowden) who in large part remained wedded to Victorian 'rules of the game', even though ideologically they were not true believers in the underpinnings of those rules. When these 'rules' were swept away in the debacle of 1931, the much more statist views which had been bubbling away in Labour circles in the 1920s came to the fore.[34]

More immediately important in the politics of economic management was the Conservative Party. The war had greatly enhanced the retreat from support of the 'Victorian pillars' within the party, already evident in the tariff reform battles of the Edwardian period. While still supportive of the gold standard, the Tories in other respects were in full-scale retreat from laissez-faire, with a markedly declining faith in the capacity of a free enterprise system to deal with the problems of the staple industries and mass unemployment.[35] The events of 1931 enabled them to seize the initiative in largely rejecting this legacy, though their alternative was one which emerged from responding to the unexpected, rather than imposing a clear, pre-existing alternative vision.

If the roots of national economic management were diverse and complex, it is reasonable to argue that an important turning point came in 1931 when, as so often, a crisis crystallized a range of forces into a shift which marked the beginning of a new era. The abandonment of gold, the introduction of protection, and the pursuit of industrial 'rationalization' after that year meant the beginnings of a new relationship between state and economy, and hence state and people.

Historical accounts of economic management in the 1930s have been overly dominated by arguments about the impact (or lack thereof) of Keynesianism. In

[28] Lowe, *Adjusting*. [29] Boyce, *British*, chs 2, 5; Moggridge, *British*.
[30] Tomlinson, *Public Policy*. [31] Howson, *Domestic*, chs 2, 3.
[32] Boyce, *British*, ch. 2; Sayers, 'Return'. [33] Marrison, *British*.
[34] Tomlinson, 'Labour'. [35] Boothby et al., *Industry*.

fact fiscal policy, usually seen as crucial to Keynesianism, was the most 'orthodox' of policy stances of governments in the 1930s, at least on the surface.[36] This is wholly unsurprising, given that the huge Conservative majorities of the 1930s originated in the events of 1931, a political battle won by the Conservatives as they successfully constructed it as a battle to defeat fiscal extravagance and disaster.

What governments clearly did do in the 1930s was to make a conscious attempt to manage the economy by trying to raise the price level and hold down real wages, so stimulating higher profits and investment, and eventually employment. To this end they introduced tariffs, held down the exchange rate (whilst keeping interest rates low), and encouraged cartelization in industry.[37] Capital and trade flows were much more tightly controlled, and while Britain remained by international standards a very open economy, the degree of insulation of domestic economic activity from external influences gave a plausible underpinning to the idea of *national* economy which could be successfully managed.

This regime was, of course, radically changed by the onset of war in 1939. From an economic management point of view, the key challenge of the war was to keep prices under control whilst allowing a huge shift of resources from peacetime to military purposes. No single instrument was adequate for this task, but a combination of rationing, controls, and a new approach to fiscal policy was employed both to make immediate wartime management successful, but more broadly to inaugurate a new era in that management. Ironically, the approach to understanding the national economy, and the means to its management, that Keynes had invented to try and underpin policies to combat unemployment was now deployed to defeat inflation.[38] The 'first Keynesian budget' of 1941 is rightly seen as a key moment, moving the economic agenda well beyond the rather ad hoc policies of the 1930s, to one underpinned by governments believing that they had the means to control economic events to a previously unimagined extent.

More broadly, the war brought about a political shift to the Left, symbolized above all by the widespread support for the Beveridge proposals of 1942.[39] While the National Insurance principle that the *Report* promised to generalize across the field of social welfare was politically centrist rather than socialist, the assertion of the scope of government responsibility, extending to the five giant evils of Want, Disease, Ignorance, Squalor, and Idleness, symbolized a new dispensation. Some form of management of the economy was now politically inescapable.

II

The 'national economy' which governments sought to manage in the decades after 1931 is an artefact, a constructed entity of the mind through which governments sought to understand and manipulate the world. Under the governments of the 1930s there was no new overarching theory to inform action; indeed policymakers

36 Middleton, 'British'. 37 Booth, 'Britain'.
38 Stone, 'Use'; Tomlinson, *Employment*, ch. 3. 39 Cmnd. 6404.

and their advisers explicitly repudiated the theoretical approaches suggested by many of the proponents of more active management. In particular, the kind of fiscal activism starting to be suggested by Keynes and his allies was attacked from the perspective of long-established arguments about the dangers of debt, loss of confidence, and flight of capital.[40]

But new understandings were not just being put forward by Keynes. The parallel but separate development of national accounting was also of enormous importance. It was from a combination of both of these strands that a new discourse of macroeconomics was constructed.[41]

Integral to this new construction of the economy was quantification. Modern Britain has been characterized by a statistical explosion crucially, but by no means exclusively, in the economic sphere. At its broadest, this explosion can be seen as part of modernity: as Badiou notes, 'The ideology of modern parliamentary societies, if they have one, is not humanism, law or the subject. It is number, the countable, countability'.[42] 'Countability' has certainly been central to the economic imagination. As Tooze remarks, 'Today, statistics define our knowledge of the economy'.[43]

The national economy as it emerged by the middle of the twentieth century was imagined as a relationship between a limited number of statistical aggregates. These encompassed national income and output, employment and unemployment, the balance of trade and payments, and the price level. Each of these statistics has its own complex history and developed according to forces having little to do with 'national economic management'. It was really only in the 1950s that they finally came together to form the fully articulated notion of 'the national economy', in line with newly established international conventions, and linked to what emerged at roughly the same period as the major responsibilities of governmental economic management: growth, low unemployment, balance of payments equilibrium, and low inflation.[44]

Concern with growth or the wealth of nations is central to the classical economists from Adam Smith onwards, and their vision of 'commercial society' can be seen as linked to maximizing consumption in the national economy.[45] But the core of their arguments was an organized scepticism about the ability of (national) government to directly deliver such a goal, as opposed to providing a framework within which private agents would so deliver.[46] Their work developed largely separately from that of the tradition of 'political arithmetic' which is commonly seen as the precursor to modern national accounting. This school can be traced back to William Petty in the seventeenth century, and onwards through a variety of non-economist figures.[47]

This latter tradition was concerned with establishing the 'wealth of the Kingdom', an endeavour which could be deployed for several purposes but was particularly

40 Peden, *Keynes*.
41 Laidler, *Fabricating*; Tribe, *Economy*, pp. 89–107.
42 Badiou, *Number*, p. 3; Rose, 'Governing'.
43 Tooze, *Statistics*, p. 1.
44 Tooze, *Statistics*, p. 6; Winch, 'Economic'.
45 Brewer, 'Concept'; Robbins, *Theory*, pp. 10–11.
46 Robbins, *Theory*.
47 Studenski, *Income*.

linked to judgements about taxable capacity in the context of international political and military rivalry.[48] In the later nineteenth and early twentieth centuries such unofficial enquiries multiplied, spurred by new concerns about the distribution of income, and often underpinned by income tax data. But it was the two world wars, as in other areas of economic statistics, that were to give a major impetus to estimates of national income, and brought government (in Britain and many other countries) into a direct role in their compilation. Much of this new interest in national income stemmed from a concern with income *stabilization* following the upheavals of the First World War and the post-1918 period. A key moment was the publication in 1940 of the first official National Income estimates, designed to underpin wartime anti-inflationary policy.[49] These then became a staple part of measuring the national economy in the era of post-war macromanagement. But then from the 1950s, and linked to the efforts of a range of international agencies, they became part of international comparisons of income per head, and all the paraphernalia of growth league tables.[50]

Official estimates of national output date from the first British census of production, which was in 1907 and was occasioned by the contemporary protectionist debate and arguments about the impact of free trade on the structure of production. The focus was on *industrial* production, though the boundaries between industry and the rest of the economy varied between censuses (the first Census of Distribution did not follow until 1950). These official efforts were supplemented in the interwar years by the efforts of private bodies, especially the London and Cambridge Economic Service.[51] As in so many areas, the Second World War gave a major boost to production statistics, a key requirement for wartime planning.[52] After the war, production statistics (especially industrial production) became another part of the statistical armoury when governments sought to persuade the public about how well or badly the economy was performing.

A key aspect of the imagining of the national economy in the interwar period came when these income and output figures were supplemented by expenditure estimates: 'it now became possible to picture the economy, in statistical terms, as a self-contained "circular flow" of production, income and expenditure. The image, first made real in the interwar years, has since occupied the first pages in every textbook in macroeconomics.'[53]

Because the regulation of trade so long figured as an important government function, trade statistics are the oldest form of national economic numbers, traceable back to the thirteenth century, but initially codified in the seventeenth.[54] The reliability of this data, at least until the late nineteenth century, is low, but more important in the current context is its incompleteness—it covered only visible trade. It was only in the 'fair trade' debates of the 1880s that the key role of invisibles was established, and the initial estimates of these were extremely crude.[55] The

48 Studenski, *Income vol. I*, pp. 26–40.
49 Stone, 'Use'.
50 See Chapter 2.
51 Devons, *Introduction*, pp. 122–6; Leak, 'Censuses, pp. 1–4.
52 Cairncross, 'Development', pp. 14–16.
53 Devons, *Introduction*, pp. 239–40; Tooze, *Statistics*, p. 42.
54 Maizels, 'Overseas'.
55 Giffen, 'Use'.

tariff reform debate at the beginning of the twentieth century led to a great expansion of data on the payments position, much of the debate being highly, if inconclusively, statistical in character.[56] But comprehensive official data were not published in Britain until after the Second World War, official data before that time having little reliability outside the visible items.[57]

Politically, employment and especially unemployment data were to be crucial to economic management in twentieth-century Britain. Official statistics about the labour market in Britain began as part of the growing concern with the 'Condition of England' question in the late nineteenth century, and especially with the contribution of unemployment to the social problems of the day, particularly poverty and its perceived correlates in immorality and social disorder.[58] A crucial moment in the development of national economic management was when this public administration conception of unemployment was displaced by an *economic* understanding of the issue, a process which arguably began before the First World War but only gained political force in the unemployment crisis of the 1920s and 1930s. This economic notion of unemployment meant that the previously 'technical' issues of monetary and fiscal management were now linked with a pressing political concern.[59]

Unemployment data were initially derived from the National Insurance data, following the 1911 Act. In the long run, tying the statistics to benefit entitlement was bound to make the numbers highly contested, and by the 1970s the Insurance figures were no longer generally accepted as a reliable guide to the state of the labour market. By the end of the century the Labour Force Survey was in widespread use as a superior alternative, but this source continued to seriously underestimate the scale of the unemployment problem, even in the good years of the 'Great Complacency' before 2007.[60]

Employment data, reliable only after World War Two, were important in making possible another statistical measurement of the national economy—productivity. Once production and employment data were available, it was possible to make systematic estimates of labour productivity, and these formed the basis of the new discourse of productivity levels and 'gaps' with other countries, another staple of national economic management from the late 1950s and the 'declinist' notions that afterwards developed.[61]

Finally, inflation data began to inform policy. The technical possibility of measuring inflation rates had to await the development of index numbers, first systematized in the late nineteenth century.[62] Policy concern with inflation was, as with unemployment, initially a product of the 'Condition of England' question, the first official wholesale price indeces being produced in 1903, as rising prices

[56] Rogers, '"Naked"'.
[57] Allen, 'Official'; Carter and Roy, *British*, pp. 79–93; Devons, *Introduction*, pp. 157–67.
[58] Davidson, *Whitehall*; Harris, *Unemployment*; Walters, 'Discovery'.
[59] Tomlinson, *Problems*; Winch, *Economics* and 'British'.
[60] Beatty et al., *Real*; see also Chapter 6.
[61] Devons, *Introduction*, pp. 54–66; Tomlinson, 'Inventing', pp. 740–3.
[62] Tooze, *Statistics*, pp. 7–8.

succeeded the fall of the late nineteenth century.[63] The policy importance of the working-class cost of living very much increased in the context of the inflationary pressures of the First World War and arguments about the distribution of the burdens of war. The first official cost-of-living index was produced in 1914, and government concern with and management of the inflation index was significant throughout the war.[64]

The cost-of-living issue was revived as a major policy concern in the Second World War, when managing the wage/price relationship was crucial to the development of both 'Keynesian' economic management and the systems of price control and rationing. The wartime government manipulated rationing and price controls to minimize the rise in the index, and hence limit pressure for wage increases. Official wage indices were themselves the product of the First World War, and were to become a key variable in the campaigns over wage inflation which were to be such a feature of the post-1945 years. In the 1950s the explicit focus on working-class cost of living gave way to a broader focus on all-consumer price indices, but these served the same function in governmental and popular economic discourse: to measure 'the' rate of inflation of the national economy as a way of underpinning stories about how economic behaviour should change.[65]

This sketch of the statistical basis of the invention of the national economy emphasizes the incremental and contingent nature of these figures. Most were developed for specific administrative and political purposes quite separate from economic management. Economic management did not have to await the elaborated and comprehensive national economic data which arrived, at its earliest, in the 1950s. But that management in its early stages could draw upon pre-existing data, and in turn gave impetus to further data development.

Much of the discussion of economic data has a functionalist, technocratic tone, a common theme being the bemoaning of the inadequacy of statistics for the technical tasks of economic management (rather than persuading the people). Almost thirty years ago, Alec Cairncross asked: 'Why is there no history of economic statistics? Why has one of the most important changes in human affairs passed almost without comment and analysis?'[66] His view of the importance of the statistics was based precisely on this technocratic view, and in his own career he had been a major supporter of the view that statistics needed to be improved as they were lagging behind the requirements of policy; the 'deficit' model of economic statistics.[67]

But the drive for data improvement came from those concerned with policy presentation as well as policy formulation. If the economy was imagined statistically, governments were concerned to shape that imagination in ways that would convince the public and persuade them to see the economic world in a particular way. Managing the people meant trying to construct compelling narratives, and numbers were often central to those narratives.

[63] Devons, *Introduction*, pp. 173–4.
[64] Flux, 'Measurement'; Searle, 'Is there?'
[65] Devons, *Introduction*, pp. 184–5, 194–9.
[66] Cairncross, 'Development', p. 11.
[67] O'Hara, 'Towards'; Wilson, 'Statistics'.

III

Governmental attempts to shape popular understanding of the economy pre-dated the rise of national economic management. Perhaps most famously, the protectionist debate from 1903 onwards saw the Liberal government deploying enormous efforts to pursue a party political dispute, but making a great deal of use of official data, much of this freshly minted. As already noted, many new statistics on the balance of payments, prices, and real wages were produced to provide evidence (or one might say ammunition) for this debate. But while having enormous consequences for both policy and statistics, this propaganda activity was exceptional in the 'unmanaged economy' years before 1914. Above all, it was propaganda about an economic policy stance, but not aimed at changing popular *behaviour*; in that respect, it remains a long way from the propaganda of the post-1945 years.

The First World War brought both an enormous enlargement in the economic role of the state, and a huge governmental propaganda effort. Most importantly, as noted above, statistics about the cost of living, aimed at reducing wage pressure, were a key element of anti-inflation policy in the war. The Cost of Living Index thereafter became embedded in British wage bargaining, though in the interwar years this was not part of any formal attempts by government to manage changes in wages; the introduction of peacetime 'incomes policies' had to await the aftermath of the Second World War.[68]

In the 1920s one important government-backed attempt to change economic behaviour was the Empire Marketing Board, set up by Conservatives who had been thwarted in their attempts to establish systematic imperial preference. Particularly by the use of powerfully evocative posters it encouraged consumers to buy from Empire sources.[69] Much less well known is the brief 'Buy British' campaign of 1931, claimed by one Minister as 'the biggest campaign ever undertaken by a government in peacetime'.[70]

So, prior to the new era of economic management, British governments, even outside wartime, had tried periodically to shape economic understanding. But these attempts were episodic and could not be part of an overarching attempt to link managing the economy to managing the people, as managing the economy was not yet happening.

Even after 1931, when such management began, it relied primarily on policy measures that did not seek to change the economic beliefs or behaviour of the population. Exchange rate management was a classic form of monetary management, conducted by the Bank of England as a 'technical' operation with little input from politicians and none at all from the citizenry.[71] Its efficacy in no sense relied on popular consent or support.

In large part the same was true of tariffs and the management of trade in the new protectionist regime, where an independent body, the Import Duties Advisory Council, had no remit to propagandize for protectionism and trade discrimination.

[68] Searle, 'Is there?' stresses the multiple uses of the Cost of Living Index in the 1920s and 1930s.
[69] Constantine, 'Bringing'. [70] Constantine, 'Buy British'. [71] Howson, *Sterling's*.

Indeed, insofar as the tariffs of the 1930s involved imperial preference, they replaced the propaganda of the Empire Marketing Board with an incentive to buy imperial produce (relative prices), and that Board was abolished.[72]

However, the tariff regime, apart from being about managing trade, was also used as part of the government's attempts to rationalize British industry by amalgamations and the closing of plant. The success of this has been much debated, but what is important here is that the policy did involve governments attempting to directly change the behaviour of at least some of the population.[73] By methods which have been aptly described as 'industrial diplomacy', the government sought to negotiate with employers in the major staple industries to get them to rationalize, often with the suggestion that such efforts would be rewarded by protection of the industry concerned. The aim was to avoid a directive role for government, given both civil service and industry worries that this would involve the expansion of the state's role.[74] These efforts can be seen as a microeconomic part of an overall strategy of trying to raise profits and investment. They are not commonly regarded as having been very successful, but they did, to a degree, involve a new, if persuasive rather than directive, role for government in the economy. However, they were directed at a small number of employers, not the masses.

As regards the mass of the population, the main policy aimed at changing behaviour in the 1930s was based on manipulating incentives in the labour market to encourage the unemployed into work. This, of course, was nothing new, such efforts being in direct descent from the Poor Law Amendment Act of 1834 and much subsequent Victorian legislation.

If national economic management as it actually developed in the 1930s was largely 'management without the people', it is worth noting that the largely untried 'Keynesian' alternative would have been similar. It is well known that what Keynes was advocating was very much 'hands-off' management, with the focus on macro aggregates and minimum interference by the state in individual agents' decisions. In this sense Keynes was very much a liberal and not a socialist. The only area in which, before 1939, he seems to have envisaged government acting to change popular behaviour was in the advocacy of encouraging spending, especially on holidays, as a way of getting the employment multiplier increased.[75]

IV

The First World War was important not only in beginning the undermining of the 'unmanaged economy', and enhancing the role of the state, but also shifting the relationship between state and citizen. One aspect of this shift was the emergence of substantial state propaganda aimed at the public. Institutionally, most striking

[72] Grant, *Propaganda*, pp. 41–5, 50–3. On the impact of the tariffs: Capie, *Depression*, chs 7–10; Foreman-Peck, Hallett, and Ma, 'End'.

[73] Garside, *Unemployment*, pp. 209–25.

[74] Roberts, 'Administrative', pp. 93–104.

[75] Harris, 'Society', p. 87.

was the Ministry of Information, which was created in 1918. Wartime propaganda evoked much unease in the aftermath of the hostilities, but as in so many other areas, post-war cutbacks in state activity did not restore the pre-war status quo. While the Ministry of Information was abolished at the end of the war, several ministries continued with, or indeed expanded, their own publicity organizations.[76]

The scale and scope of wartime propaganda reflected the 'total' character of the Allied battle with the Central Powers, involving as it did mobilization not only of an army of immense size, but a civilian labour force to supply munitions on an unprecedented scale. This mobilization involved not only coercive measures, but also measures to persuade workers to intensify their efforts. Sustaining morale became central to the propaganda, which had to be designed for a mass audience if it was to achieve its purposes.

Between the wars state propaganda expanded, Grant suggesting that the cost of government staff in press and public relations roles increased around seven-fold between 1930/31 and 1937/8, albeit from a low level.[77] When war came there was a partial centralization of these efforts in a re-created Ministry of Information.

In the Second World War, as in the First, the government was forced to seek consent from the population for a policy of wage restraint, and to persuade the mass of workers to produce more with little hope of immediate reward for their efforts in the form of higher consumption. The war thus saw unprecedented efforts on the part of government to persuade the population at large and the industrial workforce in particular on economic issues. Much of this operated through the efforts of the Ministry of Labour to develop new attitudes at workplace level in return for better conditions, welfare provision, and consultation. By comparison, the much more public efforts of the Ministry of Information were, in the economic field, relatively limited.[78]

In parallel with the changing relationship between state and citizen through the growth of state propaganda there was a shift in the relationship between political parties and the electorate, the trebling of that electorate in 1918 ramping up the desire by the political parties to find more effective ways of communicating with those who might be persuaded to vote for them.[79] This was partly about new technology, notably 'wireless' and cinema, though the interwar period was also the 'golden age of the public meeting', helped by better amplification and relaying. Coupled to this, party propaganda became increasingly focused on the uncommitted 'silent majority', and for them printed material was deemed most effective. Part of the response to a new, much larger, electorate was propaganda targeted at specific groups of electors.[80]

Between the wars both the Conservatives and the Labour Party invested heavily in their publicity activities. Labour, seeing itself as disfavoured by the attitudes of

[76] Grant, 'Propaganda', p. 35; McLaine, *Ministry*.
[77] Grant, *Propaganda*, pp. 5, 225.
[78] Bullock, *Life*, chs 2, 3, 6; Inman, *Labour*; McLaine, *Ministry*.
[79] Beers, *Your Britain*, pp. 1–10.
[80] Lawrence, *Electing*, pp. 103–20.

most of the press and the BBC, was particularly innovative in the 1920s.[81] In contrast, the Conservatives were able to draw directly on wartime experience by employing many of those who had previously worked for the state propaganda and intelligence agencies.[82] But all these efforts were undertaken by the parties with very little knowledge about what the opinions of the electors actually were, or how they might best be persuaded.[83]

The first opinion polls did not arrive in Britain until 1937, and initially were not taken seriously by the parties.[84] For the Conservatives the shock of defeat in 1945 pushed the party into taking opinion research seriously.[85] Labour had an early experiment in using opinion research in the Fulham by-election of 1938, done by the newly created organization Mass Observation, but thereafter the party neglected this approach until reluctantly persuaded of its efficacy in the 1950s.[86]

But such scepticism about opinion research was not characteristic of the state during the Second World War. Public and parliamentary opposition thwarted the creation of a Wartime Social Survey under the aegis of the Ministry of Information, a hostility grounded in a (partially justified) belief that such polling was part of a left-wing agenda to mobilize opinion against the status quo.[87] But despite this hostility, the wartime state did engage in unprecedented attempts to survey and understand popular opinion. Wartime propaganda became, at least in principle, guided by evidence as to what the public actually believed, and therefore what might sway their views.[88] As in so many other areas, wartime innovations of this kind were carried into the immediate post-war years. The culminatory episode of this concern with public views in the area of economics came in the extraordinarily detailed 'Survey of knowledge and opinion on the economic situation', carried out between 1948 and 1951.[89]

So, in the 1940s, a whole new approach to economic management, underpinned by new conceptual and statistical constructions of the national economy, came into being. This was combined with a radical extension both of government efforts to persuade the population on economic issues, and the deployment of the new 'technologies' of opinion surveying to judge the effectiveness of that persuasion. Thus a new era in both managing the economy and managing the people was opened up.

V

Part I of this book analyses the dominant economic narratives in British economic life in successive periods, from the wartime shift in citizen–state relations symbolized by the Beveridge Report of 1942 to the Brexit decision in 2016. 'Dominant' is not a precise quantitative term, and it is not suggested that in each of these

81 Beers, *Your Britain*, pp. 27–138.
82 Cockett, 'Party', pp. 548–9.
83 Lawrence, *Electing*, p. 120.
84 Abrams, 'Public', pp. 9–10.
85 Taylor, 'Record', p. 82.
86 Beers, 'Whose?'; Hinton, *Mass*, pp. 93–6.
87 Beers, 'Whose?', pp. 185–7.
88 Zweniger-Bargielowska, *Rationing*, pp. 60–98.
89 TNA: PRO RG23/92–117.

periods only one economic issue was discussed. Rather, the narratives are chosen as the ones which had most significance in shaping the economic policy debate of the years concerned, and within which government actions, both in policy and propaganda, can best be understood.

This does not mean, of course, that governments are the *only* source of economic narratives. All sorts of bodies, such as newspapers, pressure groups, and think tanks, have also tried to shape public economic understanding.[90] Sometimes these bodies have reinforced government stories, sometimes contradicted them. In looking at the construction and dissemination of government narratives we cannot ignore these other influences. But the primary focus here on government derives from the view that the post-war period saw a new and distinctive *combination* of economic policy actions and propaganda that deserves to be focused upon.

Both contemporaries and later commentators on post-war economic policy have identified four key objectives (low unemployment, growth, low inflation, and a 'satisfactory' external position) and assessed governments' success or otherwise in achieving these goals. As one Prime Minister, Harold Macmillan, put it: 'Full employment, an expanding economy, stable prices and a strong pound; these were the balls which the Chancellor of the Exchequer, like a new Cinquevalli, was expected to keep in the air.'[91]

Each of these four objectives is examined in detail in Part II, focusing on periods when they were of particular prominence in public debate. So the account of employment policy deals especially with the 1940s and 1980s; for productivity the emphasis is on the 1940s and 1960s, and for inflation the 1970s. The final chapter, on the balance of payments, says a lot about the 1950s and 1960s, but is above all concerned with a rather bigger temporal question; the 'disappearance' of the payments problem from the 1970s on. By narrowing the focus in Part II's chapters, it becomes easier to combine an analysis of the narrative in play, the means of its dissemination, and the popular response evoked.

[90] The focus here is on the *public* face of economic argument. Behind the scenes, civil servants and academic economists were also hugely important in shaping what public actors said.

[91] Macmillan, *Riding*, p. 3. Paul Cinquevalli (1859–1918) was a famous circus performer, known as 'the greatest juggler in the world'. The standard economics textbook of the 1960s refers to 'four major aggregate variables that economic policy seeks to influence: the level of unemployment, the price level, the balance of payments and the rate of growth of the economy': Lipsey, *Introduction*, p. 829.

PART I

CONSTRUCTING THE NARRATIVES

1

Austerity to 'Never had it so Good'

The Attlee government spent more money than any other, before or since, on propaganda aiming to shape public understanding of the economy and bring about 'appropriate' beliefs and behaviour.[1] The underlying notion of this propaganda was that Britain's legacy from the war required a policy of austerity until the economy was put back in balance. From 1945 until 1951 the strategy of austerity was rigorously pursued and influenced almost every aspect of government policy.[2] But the attempt to shape popular economic opinion and behaviour was at best only partially successful, and increasingly the government's policy options were constrained by the unwillingness of many voters to support the austerity strategy. Ultimately, the discrepancy between government hopes and what some groups in the population were willing to support greatly contributed to the loss of the 1951 general election, and opened the way to the anti-austerity policies of the Conservative governments of the 1950s. By the middle of that decade a whole new public political economy was opening up, with the constraints of austerity being displaced by the beguiling prospect of prosperity and abundance; an expectation of an unending rise in living standards and levels of consumption.

This chapter charts the intricacies of the Attlee government's austerity strategy, the attempts to shape opinion around this strategy, and the obstacles faced. Central to persuading the public in these years was a notion of 'fair shares', a particular version of equity which was crucial to the politics of the 1940s. The chapter then outlines the grounds for success of the alternative, anti-austerity message from the Conservatives, and assesses who responded most strongly to this stance. Third, it analyses how a new politics of 'affluence' emerged during the 1950s, and how this related to public understanding of the economy.

I

Austerity in the 1940s meant something very different from its meaning in the post-recession years after the crash of 2007/2008. In the years after 2010 the core aim of austerity was to reduce public sector borrowing by cutting public spending; in the 1940s it meant holding back the growth of private consumption (of both

[1] Crofts, *Coercion?*; Moore, *Origins*. There was also extensive publicity on the related topic of the expanded welfare state: Wildy, 'From the MOI to the COI'.

[2] Kynaston, *Austerity*; Zweiniger-Bargielowska, *Austerity*.

home-produced and imported goods) so that resources could be transferred from the war effort to civilian uses, with most of those resources flowing into exports and investment. In his first budget under the 2010 Coalition, George Osborne asserted that 'Our policy is to raise from the ruins of an economy built on debt a new, balanced, economy where we save, invest and export'.[3] But whilst 're-balancing' became something of a feature of public economic debate for a while, it was a 'shifting and more or less vacuous trope', a footnote to policies and propaganda which focused on debts and deficits as the defining problem.[4] By contrast, 're-balancing' in the 1940s was indeed the key policy aim, but one which the government recognized would require some hard selling to persuade a war-weary public.

In macroeconomic terms the austerity strategy flowed from an economy suffering from immense excess demand. The fully employed wartime economy had put purchasing power in the pockets of the population, but the needs of war had meant the state could not allow this money to be spent. High taxes and rationing and controls kept consumption low to allow resources to flow into the war effort. At the same time, resources had been diverted from producing exports, and across much of the economy investment was neglected and there was widespread physical destruction, especially of the housing stock.[5] So for the post-war government the problem was how to persuade the people to allow the continuation of tight controls on consumption, how to limit imports and channel resources into exports to correct the payments deficit, and how to expand investment in order to rebuild the country's productive capacity and physical infrastructure, especially its housing stock.[6]

The propaganda effort to support this strategy was, by previous standards, enormous. Expenditure on 'Home Information' rose tenfold compared with 1938/9. This funded activity in a wide range of media. At the campaign's peak, one in five poster sites was occupied by government advertising; more official films were made than ever before; 9,000 talks were delivered in works canteens; 'popular' pamphlets and versions of government documents, such as the *Economic Survey*, were published in volumes ranging from a few thousand up to several million.[7] All this went along with hyperactive speech-making by government representatives, both in the traditional format of public meetings and on the wireless.

Much of this effort was aimed at driving home a story about the general overstretched state of the economy, and hence defending the continuation of rationing and controls. But it involved a simultaneous effort to spread the message that the constraints would be lessened if more was produced; hence the focus on production and productivity (see Illustration 1). Part of this was a big campaign to recruit workers to into key industries, especially coal mining, agriculture, and textiles.[8] Also involved was a publicity drive on improving the balance of payments, to persuade people why this should be given such high priority. Finally, from 1948, it involved propaganda to support an incomes policy, on the grounds

[3] *Hansard* (Commons) vol. 512, col. 167, 22 June 2010.

[4] Froud et al., 'Rebalancing', p. 36.

[5] Howlett, 'New'.

[6] Cairncross, *Years*, pp. 3–46.

[7] Crofts, *Coercion?*, pp.11–12, 41, 48–9.

[8] The last of these is considered in great detail in Crofts, *Coercion?*, pp. 91–167.

Illustration 1 1940s graphics for a popular narrative of key economic aims (1947).
Source: Image courtesy of the National Archives.

that rapid growth of wages would be inflationary and worsen the payments position, and so further delay the time when more resources could be put into home consumption.

Underpinning all Labour's campaigns was a notion of 'fair shares'. This moral message was a crucial aspect of how previous wartime restrictions and rationing had been defended. Although there were always those sceptical about whether the burden of consumption cuts was indeed 'fair', and perceived unfairness led to individual grumbling along with avoidance and evasion of controls, whilst hostilities continued these responses were kept in check by an overall sense of 'we are in it together'. There was no immediate delegitimization of restrictions at the war's end, but it was clear this legitimacy rested upon claims about the unavoidable and temporary nature of shortages, and support would be eroded if some degree of decontrol was not forthcoming.[9]

Labour also brought to this task of persuasion about 'fair shares' a belief in propaganda as a way of 'making socialists'—of bringing out what many Labour leaders thought of as the latent desire of most of the population to behave collectively and responsibly. This belief had informed Labour's propaganda in the run-up to the 1945 election, and was carried forward into the years in office.[10] Thus Labour had far fewer inhibitions than the Conservatives about the deployment of state agencies (after 1946, mainly the Central Office of Information (COI), plus the Economic Information Unit (EIU) of the Treasury) to shape popular understanding. Alongside this was a belief in 'democratic planning'. Labour in 1945 was strongly committed to a planned economy, believing this to be the only way to prevent a recurrence of unemployment, and develop the national economy.[11] But it was keen to make the distinction between totalitarian and democratic planning, as spelled out in the 1947 *Economic Survey*:

> the former subordinates all individual desires and preferences to the demands of the state.... But in normal times, the people of a democratic country will not give up their freedom of choice to their Government. A democratic government must therefore conduct its economic planning in a manner which preserves the maximum of possible freedom of choice to the individual citizen.[12]

Hence the Prime Minister's foreword to the same document proclaimed: 'The Government alone cannot achieve success. Everything will depend upon the willing co-operation and determined efforts of all sections of the population'.[13]

Democratic planning meant politically contentious decisions about how national needs were to be defined and met. These needs were defined by the government as fivefold: defence, payment for imports, additional investment, increased personal consumption, and public services.[14] But prioritizing amongst these uses of resources was the crucial challenge for the government, above all, of

[9] Roodhouse, *Black*, pp. 259–61; compare Zweiniger-Bargielowska, *Austerity*, pp. 258–9, 262–3.

[10] Beers, 'Labour's', pp. 685–95; Fielding, Thompson, and Tiratsoo, *England Arise!*, pp. 93–7; Nuttall, 'Labour', p. 669.

[11] Brooke, 'Problems'; Tomlinson, *Democratic*, pp. 124–46.

[12] Cmd. 7046, para 8. [13] Cmd. 7046, Foreword. [14] Cmd. 7046, para 3.

how rapidly personal consumption could be restored, given the major reductions in wartime. Consumption is usually the largest component of demand in the economy, but in wartime Britain it had fallen from around four-fifths in 1938 to about half in 1944.[15] This reduction had only been sustainable in times of war because of the extent of popular commitment to the war effort combined with a policy of fair shares, which meant that all classes shared (if not exactly equally) in the privations of war.

The core aim of the government's post-war strategy was to only slowly relax the rigours of wartime constraint on consumption, and to try and sustain support for this policy by continuing with rationing and controls (and food subsidies) as a way of ensuring 'equal misery'.[16] Because it was recognized that such a stance could only succeed if there was clear progress in easing limits on consumption, the government organized what it called a 'Prosperity campaign' which was initially aimed at getting back to pre-war consumption levels by the end of 1946 and dealing with the balance of payments by the end of 1947, after which 'the national income and standard of living should steadily rise to levels higher than the bulk of the people have ever before enjoyed'.[17] In this way austerity was presented as a passing phase, after which the suggestion was that the 'sky was the limit' for future consumption; this prospect, set to become the core of the economic narrative in the 1950s, was already present in nascent form in the 1940s.

As Ina Zweiniger-Bargielowska shows, this popular expectation of a rapid return to pre-1939 standards of consumption was evident even before the war ended. And this was not just a matter of the middle classes looking for a restoration of their lost comforts of the 1930s; *for those in work*, the 1930s had also seen significant consumption gains for many workers (perhaps two-thirds of the total class).[18] This breadth of remembered pre-war affluence underlines how difficult it was likely to be for the government to secure popular acquiescence in keeping the lid on consumption once the war ended.

Because of the ubiquity of the term in post-war economic policy narratives, the Attlee government's productivity campaign is looked at separately and in detail in Chapter 8. But, linked to this specific focus on productivity, the government attempted to create a new, and politically pivotal, politics of production: in the words of a contemporary slogan, to make *Production the Bridge to Socialism*. A pamphlet with this title was published by the Labour Party in 1948 and called upon all 'active public-spirited citizens' to make every effort to raise production. In particular, it urged party members to play a leading role in increasing efficiency.[19] This emphasis was hugely important for Labour politics and ideology because it

[15] Hancock and Gowing, *British*, p. 199.

[16] Food subsidies were a very big item in public spending in the late 1940s, costing more than the NHS in 1948: Rollings, 'British'.

[17] TNA: PRO INF 12/14 D Jay, 'Prosperity Campaign', 13 May 1946.

[18] Zweiniger-Bargielowska, *Austerity*. It is a useful perspective on the 'consumerism' of the 1950s to see it as a return to the trends established in the 1930s: Obelkovich, 'Consumption'; Sandbrook, *Never*, pp. 106–7.

[19] Labour Party, *Production*.

pointed to the emerging key social democratic strategy; to make the pursuit of higher spending on social security and welfare politically possible by ensuring that the 'cake' from which this spending was cut got bigger, so that no one got a smaller absolute share. This approach can be seen as constituting a 'strategy of equality' which was increasingly at the core of much post-war Labour thinking.[20]

But alongside this appeal to already existing socialists, and those who might be won for the cause, Labour recognized that increased production had to be promoted as beneficial even for those with different views about priorities. In the 'popular' pamphlet *Productivity Pays* the reader was invited to note their personal priorities against a checklist of possibilities as production increased. The list had five elements: 'jobs for all'; homes for all'; 'lower prices and more goods in the shops'; 'social services'; and 'a strong, secure nation'.[21] In this way, production propaganda accepted that the audience might have different priorities from those of the government, but believed they could be persuaded that output growth was the way to achieve those ends.

This way of posing the issue of production was much more positive than the emphasis in an earlier phase under the heading of 'We work or want'.[22] In that campaign it was unsurprisingly found that when asked 'Do you think it is important that Great Britain should produce more goods?' only 2 per cent answered negatively (with 6 per cent 'don't knows').[23] But this was combined with less than one in ten believing there was anything they could do *personally* towards increasing output. Four out of five said they were doing all they could. We have no good evidence on whether the more unambiguously positive message of the later campaign evoked a greater sense of ability to make a difference.[24] But the suggestion that all good things were possible if output grew shows the important shift from propaganda, much of which evoked the continuation of wartime necessity, to one which suggested future expansionary possibilities.

An important component of the Attlee government's production campaign was the aim to encourage women to continue in or enter employment, especially in traditionally important sectors of women's employment such as cotton textiles. The terms of such campaigning reveal the complexities of governmental attitudes to women's (especially married women's) employment, and also the limits of propaganda.

At the highest level of government there were tensions about how far women with children should be asked to participate in the labour market at all, with longstanding notions about the harmful impact of mother's employment on their children asserted by some elements, for example in the Ministry of Health. The Ministries more directly concerned with the labour market focused attention on what they saw as the likelihood that in the post-war years many women would exit the labour market in order to marry, catching up on the backlog of marriages

[20] Le Grand, *Strategy*; for an assessment of this strategy: Tomlinson, 'Distributional'.

[21] *Prosperity Pays*, p. 6.

[22] Though, as always, there was not a single message universally adhered to. Talk of future 'prosperity' can be found in ministerial speeches as early as 1946: Crofts, *Coercion?*, p. 36.

[23] Crofts, *Coercion?*, pp. 38–9.

[24] See discussion in Chapter 7.

caused by the war. This perception accounts for a lot of the propaganda aimed at women presenting the need for their labour as temporary, to help deal with the production crisis, rather than as a permanent shift.[25]

This combination of concerns fed into the Minister of Labour's broadcast setting out the aims of this campaign. On one hand, it emphasized he was not appealing to those with very young children 'although for those who wanted to volunteer, and who had children a little older, there were in many places day nurseries and creches'. On the other, he argued that the labour shortage was temporary, and 'women were being asked to take a job only for whatever length of time they could spare, whether full-time or part-time'.[26]

The campaign began and was particularly intense in Lancashire, where women had traditionally made up a large proportion of the cotton workforce.[27] Its success was constrained in part by the shortage of childcare availability, following the closure of many publicly funded nurseries as central government support for them was cut back and local authorities had to bear more of the cost. However, although this issue is highlighted in discussions of the period, such nurseries could only ever have played a minor role in provision, given the scale of the hoped-for re-employment of women, where the government had a target of 60,000, of whom perhaps 10 per cent had nursery-age children.[28]

The Ministry of Labour faced local medical opposition in Lancashire and national newspaper criticism of its encouragement of married women to go back to work.[29] A striking slogan deployed in this campaign was 'Britain's bread hangs by Lancashire's thread'. But one of the problems faced was the belief that while a revival of cotton might be important in the short run, the long-run prospects of the industry were a return to the depressed conditions of the 1930s. While the campaign in Lancashire could well argue that the current condition of cotton was much better than in 1930s, there were widespread expectations that unemployment would return.[30] The local Labour MP, Barbara Castle, reported opposition to overtime in cotton: 'they see no evidence of any basic reorganization or re-equipping of the industry and the call for overtime to get us out of a mess seems to them to be an old Tory expedient'.[31]

A wide variety of types of propaganda were used in the cotton industry. In the later, most intense, phase of the Lancashire campaign in 1948 there were, for example, striking invocations of Stakhanovism and Soviet-style 'socialist competition' in

[25] Tomlinson, *Democratic*.

[26] *Ministry of Labour Gazette*, 55 (June 1947), p. 183; for discussion of the campaign: Crofts, *Coercion?*, pp. 91–9.

[27] Crofts, *Coercion?*, pp. 110–48.

[28] TNA: PRO BT 190/4 NPACI Ministries of Health and Education, 'Day nurseries', 3 April 1947.

[29] TNA: PRO LAB 26/168 Isaac to Bevin, 9 May 1946; LAB 8/1283 'Employment policy: part-time employment', 1946.

[30] TNA: PRO CAB 134/474 Labour (T1) Committee, 'Public opinion in Lancashire cotton towns', 24 January 1949.

[31] TNA: PRO CAB 134/472 Labour (T1) Committee, report by Barbara Castle on visit to Lancashire, 6–10 January 1948.

what was labelled the 'status-creation' aspect of the propaganda. Crofts argues that the (imperfect) surveys of the response to all this activity suggest some positive effects, especially where propaganda about how different the industry had become since the 1930s was coupled to actual improvements in wages and working conditions in the mills.[32]

More generally, Carruthers has noted that much of this propaganda was aimed at getting women back into occupations where they had a traditional presence, so did not aim at sustaining the advances women had made into new sectors during wartime 'dilution'. However, the evidence suggests that while the aggregate number of women in the workforce fell back from its wartime peak, the appeal to older married women to return to work was in line with the long-run trend for the participation rate of such women to rise.[33]

The cotton campaign in Lancashire was the first to highlight a balance-of-payments constraint that was to become a hardy perennial of post-war British economic narratives. Chapter 7 deconstructs the shifting ways this 'problem' was framed and deployed from the Attlee years through the 'golden age' and beyond, but it is worth noting briefly the particular terms around which 1940s propaganda on this issue was framed.

The 'Britain's bread' slogan emphasized the importance of exports in funding the supply of basics, and given the contemporary problem of dollars to pay for food imports this appeal was wholly unsurprising. This neglected entirely the use of foreign exchange both for government expenditure overseas and for foreign investment, which was such a striking feature of the Attlee years. Rather than dealing with the complexities of defining a balance-of-payments 'deficit', the problem was presented as one largely concerning the balance of *trade*. The key document in the popular representation of this issue was the 1946 pamphlet *We Live by Exports*. This started with the need to import, looked at the sources of finance for these imports, noted how invisible sources of earnings had been hard hit by the war, and went on to show how increased exports were the answer. In setting out the targets for exports the clear message is that it is exports of *goods* that are at issue: 'the quicker we reach every target we set ourselves, the easier it will be to reach our next target. The markets are crying out for our goods now'.[34]

That the trade issue was framed in this very particular manner doesn't of course tell us what message, if any, was taken on board by the audience. One of the problems of this type of propaganda is whether the audience is familiar with the basic terms of economic argument; do words such as 'productivity' or 'inflation' convey the meaning usually taken for granted by those who routinely deploy such terms? In the case of trade there does seems to have been this basic congruence; 88 per cent of those asked knew that exports were items sold abroad (while in the same survey, for example, only 65 per cent were able to give any meaning to the term 'social services').[35]

[32] Crofts, *Coercion?*, pp. 149–51.
[33] Carruthers, 'Manning'.
[34] Board of Trade, *We Live by Exports*, especially p. 16.
[35] TNA: PRO RG23/115, 'Survey of knowledge and opinion', July 1949 to February 1951, Table 12.

Table 1.1 Percentage of those surveyed believing it is desirable to increase exports, 1947–51

December 1947	42
March to May 1948	50
June to August 1948	48
September to November 1948	52
March 1949	52
May 1949	38
September 1949	46
March 1950	42
July 1950	37
November 1950	34
March 1951	31

Sources: RG23/92 'Survey of knowledge and opinion' Table 16; RG23/105 Table 4; RG23/116, p. 10.

Having said that, if people knew what exports were, they were not all persuaded that increasing their volume was desirable. Table 1.1 shows that, at its peak, support for increasing exports reached only just over half of those surveyed, and much of the time was significantly below this level. This may partly be explained by evidence that, while people knew what exports were, they hadn't absorbed the government's key message that the reason for exporting more was to be able to import more.[36] Or perceptions of the issue may have been shaped by the estimation people made of the proportion of domestic production going for export, perhaps a paradoxical consequence of the government's efforts to raise 'export consciousness'. The evidence was clear that many greatly overestimated this proportion, and that the more people made this overestimation, the less enthusiastic they were about increasing exports.[37]

Table 1.2 shows how, the higher the occupational ranking, the more enthusiastically the export message was embraced. This was recognized to be a serious problem by the government, given its belief that persuading those directly involved in production of the need to understand the export issue was crucial. Much effort went into trying to put economic propaganda into terms deemed appealing to a working-class audience, but Table 1.2 suggests there were clear limits to the success of this endeavour. Absorption of the government's message might have been increased at times of events which acted to drive it home, such as the Marshall Aid debates in 1948 or devaluation in 1949, but, this aside, the evidence was of considerable 'stability in ignorance' amongst the audience.[38]

[36] At the time of devaluation in 1949 it was found that 46 per cent of those surveyed 'didn't know we were not selling enough exports to pay for all we import': TNA: PRO RG23/109, 'Survey of knowledge and opinion', November 1949, p. 4. That said, when asked directly what was the purpose of exporting, 80 per cent said 'to pay for imports': TNA: PRO RG23/95, 'Survey of knowledge and opinion', March 1948, Table 12.

[37] TNA: PRO RG23/95, 'Survey of knowledge and opinion', March 1948, Table 16.

[38] TNA: PRO RG23/115, 'Survey of knowledge and opinion', February 1951, pp. 4–6.

Table 1.2 Support for increasing exports, by occupational groups, 1949

Occupation	Percentage saying 'we should increase our exports'
Managerial	80
Professional and technical	64
Higher clerical	74
Inspectional and supervisory	57
Routine clerical	52
Skilled operatives	51
Unskilled operatives	35
Other	53
Housewives, retired, and unoccupied	33

Source: RG23/112 'Survey of knowledge and opinion', Table 3.

Any government pursuing a policy of exhortation and persuasion on economic issues is going to be faced with the question of how far it wants and is able to use market mechanisms to support its objectives. This question was particularly acute under the Attlee government, with its overarching faith in planning rather than price mechanisms. Wages were a particularly important policy area where there were major questions about the relation between the ideological commitment to planning and finding effective policy instruments. Part of the government's strategy aimed to 'man-up' industries seen as crucial for exports (such as cotton) or overall economic recovery (such as coal). This led to a big debate on 'wage planning': how far government could and should intervene in the labour market to change wage relativities to encourage inflows into these favoured industries.[39]

The debate on this issue pitched the strongest advocates of economic planning, usually on the Left of Labour, against those on the Right who feared that such a policy applied to labour would politicize every wage bargain as well as undermining the 'free collective bargaining' that many saw as a foundation of British Labour's strength. In the end the opponents of wage planning won the argument, and the shift of labour had to rely largely on exhortation, though there were some small shifts in the relative wages of the 'undermanned' industries.[40] This seems to have been in line with popular opinion, which combined a hostility to controls over the labour market with support for incentives to draw workers in to the 'undermanned' industries. In 1947 only 9 per cent of respondents believed 'direction of labour' was the best way to get more workers into the shortage occupations, whilst almost half supported incentives of various kinds.[41]

A more successful policy endeavour, at least in the short run, was the government's incomes policy, the first of its kind.[42] How was this sold? Strikingly, and in contrast with later attempts at such policies, the focus was not primarily on notions

[39] Tomlinson, 'Labour'. [40] Flanders, 'Wages'.

[41] TNA: PRO RG23/92, 'Survey of knowledge and opinion', December 1947, Table 15.

[42] Jones, *Wages*, ch. 4. Ideologically this led to something of a reversal of positions: where the Left had generally supported wage planning, they generally opposed what was seen as an attempt to hold down wages.

of distributive justice, but, in line with the outcome of the 'wage planning' debate, on the need to provide incentives to attract workers to particular industries. In this way incomes policy, while having a macroeconomic, anti-inflation aspect, was also intended to be a *substitute* for full 'wage planning' in encouraging labour into shortage areas by allowing exemptions from overall limits on wage increases where workers could not be attracted in any other way.[43] The policy also allowed exceptions for productivity increases, though this clause did not play a central role in this incomes policy, unlike those in the 1960s.

The characterization of this period as one of austerity jars with our sense of the Attlee government bringing a fundamental expansion of the welfare state, especially by implementing much of the Beveridge social security plan and creating the NHS. This seeming contradiction is largely resolved by recognizing that what was created in the 1940s can rightly be called an 'austerity welfare state', in two different senses of 'austere'.[44]

First, Beveridge's proposals for expanding National Insurance, while hugely ambitious in scope, were designed to minimize the Exchequer contribution to the cost by emphasizing the centrality of contributions from employees and employers: this was to be no 'Santa Claus' state.[45] While the Attlee government then went beyond Beveridge in extending pensions to those without a significant contribution record, the level of pension payments and other National Insurance benefits was set very low, so that the means-tested National Assistance system expanded to supplement Insurance benefits, rather than contracting as Beveridge intended.[46] In this way, the public spending costs of the new social security system were kept down, an outcome also much helped by the savings in unemployment benefit from the very low levels of post-war unemployment (see Table 1.3).

Second, the key constraint on welfare state expansion in the 1940s was not primarily public spending or borrowing; total spending was falling as a result of the end of the war, and budget balance was quickly regained. Rather, the problem was shortage of physical resources, either human 'manpower' or materials such as timber, iron, and steel. As these resources were also required for exports and investment, the

Table 1.3 The austerity welfare state, 1945/6–50/1

	1945/6	**1950/1**
Public spending on welfare state, including transfer payments	£900 million	£1,265 million
Spending on welfare state as share of GDP	10 per cent	14 per cent

Source: Tomlinson, *Democratic*, p. 253.

43 Cmd. 7321. The notion of 'justice' was still employed in, for example, encouraging recruitment into coal mining, but in the form of 'just desserts' for work done, rather than distributive justice.

44 Harris, 'Enterprise'. This evidence wholly undermines Corelli Barnett's claims about an insouciant liberal elite fatally saddling Britain with an unaffordable welfare state in the 1940s: Barnett, *Audit*; Barnett, *Lost*.

45 Harris, *Beveridge*.

46 Deacon, 'End?'

government seriously economized in their use in expanding the infrastructure for welfare provision. Thus, the NHS saw the building of almost none of the local health centres which had been seen as integral to the new service, and none at all of the district general hospitals, also intended as core features of the NHS.[47]

In the short run these austerity measures did not seem to arouse much popular opposition. In health the huge surge in demand for the newly available provision could mostly be satisfied within the physical infrastructure the NHS inherited. In education, the school-building programme focused on areas where the growth in demand was most significant, such as the new towns. But much more politically problematic for the government were the constraints on housebuilding imposed by the shortage of manpower and raw materials, especially timber. In housing, where construction was overwhelmingly concentrated in the public sector, the numbers built were impressive, reaching around 200,000 per annum, but the targets of 1945 were not achieved, and after 1947 the programme was cut back in order to release labour and timber for other uses.[48]

It is difficult to know how damaging for its support was this failure of the government to build as many houses as promised. The evidence certainly supports the view that housing was a key concern of the electorate in 1945.[49] The surveys of opinion on the economy from late 1947 asked respondents to identify the main 'national problems'; initially housing came second to food shortages, but by spring 1948 it came top of the list and it remained there or thereabouts for the life of the surveys.[50] The extent to which the government was blamed for the problem is much less clear, but there is some evidence that by 1950 housing issues were being linked to the extent of controls, and that attitudes to housing were becoming more 'recriminatory' as part of a general trend for the identification of specific agents as responsible for economic problems.[51]

Was housing part of a general pattern whereby shortages were increasingly blamed on the government? Was austerity the policy which, whatever its economic consequences, ultimately led to Labour's loss of power?

Almost throughout the 1945–51 period the government was on the defensive on the issue of consumption controls, with the Conservatives consistently claiming that the failure to relax these much more quickly was due to socialists' love of state control, rather than stemming from any macroeconomic necessity. More than this, the Conservatives increasingly complained that the controls prevented free enterprise from bringing about a much more rapid expansion of output.

The government's response to this argument was twofold. Within the narrative of austerity as a temporary necessity the government combined propaganda making the case for austerity with a policy of easing controls when circumstances were deemed to make that viable. The most famous easing came with a 'bonfire of

[47] Tomlinson 'Why?' [48] Cairncross, *Years*, pp. 451–2.

[49] Fielding, 'What did "the people" want?'

[50] RG23/92 'Survey of knowledge and opinion', Table 4; RG23/95, Table 1; RG23/110, Table 1.

[51] RG23/110 'Survey of knowledge and opinion', March 1950, Table 17; RG23/114, November 1950, p. 8 noted that 'the tendency to recriminate over the housing shortage tended to increase'.

controls' in 1948/9.[52] The government's stated line was that decontrol would proceed as quickly as the balance of payments allowed, subject to a policy of retaining controls where needed for economic recovery, industrial efficiency, and full employment.[53] But there is no doubt that most Labour leaders saw no prospect of a complete ending to controls. Partly this was because they saw continuing threats to post-war economic buoyancy and full employment, but also because of an ideological attachment to control as a necessary counterweight to market forces.[54]

There is no direct evidence on popular attitudes to austerity; this was not a word that was used in opinion surveys. But there is evidence on attitudes to controls from the 'Survey of knowledge and opinion' covering the period up to the general election of February 1950. Table 1.4 shows a small shift in anti-control sentiment in the run-up to the election. But this is quite small and of itself does not provide strong support for the view that 'set the people free' was shifting many people's votes.

A broader sense of shifts in opinion is given by the 'Survey':

(i) a gradual shift of emphasis onto money problems as the main ones affecting people in their everyday lives;
(ii) a marked decline in the importance of food problems, together with;
(iii) a decline in emphasis on the importance of production as a means of solving everyday problems: high prices, food and housing;
(iv) a slight increase in the numbers favouring a relaxation or abandonment of controls as a means of solving each of these everyday problems.

Table 1.4 Attitudes to controls, 1949–50 (percentage of those surveyed)

Issues	May 1949	September 1949	March 1950
Question: 'Main things to be done to end shortages and ration' Proportion agreeing with answer: 'end controls; free markets'	4 per cent	4 per cent	7 per cent
Question: 'Ways to bring down prices' Proportion agreeing with answer: 'take off controls and restrictions'	5 per cent	4 per cent	9 per cent
Question: 'How to end the housing shortage' Proportion agreeing with answer: 'End restrictions on private enterprise'	17 per cent	17 per cent	22 per cent

Source: RG 23/110 'Survey of knowledge and opinion', Tables 6, 10, 17.

[52] This bonfire had more ideological than practical significance. Only thirty to forty jobs were saved in the Board of Trade as a result, because many licences were issued almost automatically, and their issuance was often the by-product of other administrative arrangements. That said, 125,000 out of 200,000 licences were abolished before the 'bonfire'. TNA: PRO T222/215 Co-ordinating Committee on Controls, Johnston to Woods, 11 November 1948; TNA: PRO T222/215 Woods to Bridges, 2 December 1948.

[53] Wilson in *Hansard* (Commons) vol. 457, cols 113–14, 4 November 1948.

[54] Rollings, 'Reichstag method?'. Concerns about a likely return of mass unemployment were common amongst the populace, a fear which made for scepticism about the government's talk of manpower shortages: for example TNA:PRO RG23/97, 'Survey of knowledge and opinion', May 1948, Table 23.

The 'Survey' went on to suggest that:

> the appearance of more, and more varied, goods in the shops—although partly the result of rationing by the purse—had made people more inclined to resent rationing by the purse. This has contributed to increasing uncertainty about the wages issue, and to the steady shift of emphasis onto process and the cost of living. The reasons for retaining controls have become less apparent as the existence of shortages has become less obvious, and this has resulted in an increase in suggestions for decontrol.[55]

This subtle analysis plausibly suggests the interplay between changing circumstances and popular attitudes, and how these together could be used effectively to strengthen the Conservatives' anti-austerity narrative.

II

In the 1950 and 1951 general elections the Conservatives' central claim was that recurrent economic crises were due to the failures of socialist planning and government mismanagement, with only a return to free markets able to bring lower prices and a wider choice of consumption goods. Their 1950 election broadcasts 'had "anti-socialism" as their dominant theme, defined sometimes as opposition to nationalisation, but more often in terms of general hostility to controls, bureaucracy, expansion of State power and interference with economic liberty'.[56] The underlying theme a year later was very similar, though this time there was more emphasis on the rise in the cost of living and how far 'socialist mismanagement' was responsible for this.[57]

A version of this claim had been the thrust of Conservative argument going back to 1947, when in response to the King's speech Churchill declared the Conservatives' aim to be to 'set the people free'.[58] Churchill also frequently defined socialism as 'queuetopia', a term, as Kynaston notes, clearly aimed at the 'housewives' vote'.[59] These arguments attacked the 'fair shares' underpinnings of Labour's claims about the need for austerity by suggesting that the policy was one of 'equal misery', and that such misery could be greatly lessened by allowing market forces a much larger role in encouraging the expansion of supply. This posture, it should be emphasized, was perfectly compatible with the Conservatives accepting full employment as a key goal of policy; in that limited but important sense they accepted the emergent post-war 'consensus'. Having said that, the rhetoric of 'Set the people free' links to the broader ideological attack on the expanding role of the state, epitomized in the 1940s by Hayek's *The Road to Serfdom* which had considerable resonance in Conservative circles.[60]

[55] TNA: PRO RG23/110, 'Survey of knowledge and opinion', March 1950, p. 18; Zweiniger-Bargielowska, *Austerity*, pp. 86–7.

[56] Nicholas, *British General Election of 1950*, p. 129.

[57] Butler, *British General Election of 1951*, pp. 105–10.

[58] Zweiniger-Bargielowska, *Austerity*, p. 220.

[59] Kynaston, *Family*, p. 33.

[60] Cockett, *Thinking*, pp. 57–99; on the tensions in Conservative thinking, Francis, 'Set the people free?'

In 1951 the Conservatives regained power. This was despite Labour polling a quarter of a million more votes than the Conservatives and their National Liberal allies, and indeed getting both their highest vote share (48.8 per cent) and highest number of votes (13.9 million) ever. This disparity between votes gained and seats won emphasizes the perennial difficulties of using general elections as a measure of popular opinion, let alone as a verdict on the impact of any particular policy narrative. However, it seems clear that the 'set the people free' message had considerable resonance amongst voters in the suburbs, and above all amongst women—both groups that moved away from voting Labour compared with 1945. Ina Zweiniger-Bargielowska has argued persuasively that much of the burden of the rationing and controls system fell upon women, who took most responsibility for shopping and providing food and consumables for the family. They, encouraged by well-aimed Conservative propaganda which effectively mobilized a housewives' vote, turned disproportionately against Labour.[61]

More broadly, Zweiniger-Bargielowska plausibly links Labour's loss of support amongst women to the party's 'productivist' ethos, which linked expanding output to a primary focus on the role of men in bringing this about. In turn this can be linked to the predominantly male world of trade unionism which underpinned the party.[62] But, as Matthew Hilton has argued, it might have been different, given that there was an emergent consumer politics in the Labour Party in the late 1940s, at odds with this 'productivist' approach. He points out that Labour had a long-standing concern with the price and quality of necessities, and this had been reflected in Labour's history of support for free trade before the First World War, and arguments about, for example, milk supplies between the wars.[63] There was also a tradition on the Left of attacking cartels and monopolies in the name of protecting the consumer against predation, a theme which was strongly present in Labour's 1945 manifesto.[64] But while the latter impetus led to the pioneering Monopolies and Restrictive Practices Act of 1948, the overall thrust of Labour policy in the 1940s was to defend the interests of producers.

The point is not just to indicate an alternative 'road not taken', because there was one policy of the period very much concerned with consumers: food subsidies, an underemphasized feature of the economic policies of the 'austerity' era. There was huge expenditure on these subsidies, at its peak greater than was spent on the NHS. The scale of this expenditure was partly to do with supporting incomes policy by holding down the price of basic commodities.[65] But the subsidies were also seen by most Labour figures as integral to a policy of 'fair shares', subsidizing the necessities of the working class. But these subsidies were in turn strongly attacked by advocates of 'liberal socialism', who regarded them as both expensive

61 Zweiniger-Bargielowska, *Austerity*.
62 On this broader issue: Black and Brooke, 'Labour'.
63 Hilton, *Consumerism*; Trentmann, 'Bread'.
64 Mercer, *Constructing*, p. 87.
65 Whiteside, 'Creating'.

and ill-directed, leading to distortions in the efficient allocation of resources.[66] However, for most Labour policymakers these were not the main issues affecting the significance of subsidies. Rather, the problem was that subsidies could only be justified ideologically when they concerned the price of 'necessities'.[67] Above all, they were *not* tied to notions of expanding working-class horizons of consumption, an expansion which was increasingly at work as scarcity diminished and the economy stabilized. As Hilton notes, 'Consumption remained an ideological problem for the party, especially in this crucial period of austerity overshadowed by expectations of affluence'.[68]

III

Initially very careful to emphasize their support for major elements of the post-war settlement (especially full employment, the principles of the NHS, and co-operative relations with trade unions), slowly, in office, the Conservatives evolved a new narrative around economic growth and a rising popular standard of living. David Kynaston identifies 1953 as a breakthrough year 'in terms of moving away from austerity and towards improved living standards and even a measure of affluence'. He highlights sharply increasing expenditure on food, clothes, shoes, household goods, and new cars.[69]

At the 1954 Conservative Party conference Butler, the Chancellor, held out the prospect of a doubling in the standard of living within twenty-five years, albeit only if there was a substantial increase in investment.[70] This beguiling prospect became something of a Conservative catchphrase over the next few years, and was repeated in the Conservative manifestos in both the 1955 and 1959 elections.[71]

This prospect rested on several foundations. First, it reflected an undoubted improvement in the economy's situation, in part because the end of the Korean War in 1952 brought about a marked fall in world commodity prices and an improvement in the British terms of trade and balance of payments. This allowed the termination of wartime controls and the end of food rationing in 1954.[72]

Second, it was linked to a new international discourse of 'economic growth', resting on the spread of statistics of GNP and in a global context of the Cold War, where higher living standards were promised by both sides. Domestically, economic growth offered a resolution of distributive conflicts, with the promise of a bigger 'cake' meaning all demands could be met.[73] Above all, for a Conservative

[66] Tomlinson, *Democratic*, pp. 218–19, 228–9.
[67] Hilton, *Consumerism*, pp. 137–64. [68] Hilton, *Consumerism*, p. 162.
[69] Kynaston, *Family*, p. 317; for a quantitative summary of the consumption expansion of the 1950s, Hall, 'Consumer'.
[70] National Union of Conservative and Unionist Associations (NUCUA), *Conference Report 1954* (1954), p. 66; such an increase in investment was a striking feature of post-war Britain, as emphasized by Matthews, 'Why?'
[71] Craig, *General Election Manifestos 1918–66*, pp. 163, 189.
[72] Zweiniger-Bargielowska, *Austerity*, pp. 236–8.
[73] The rise of economic growth is discussed further in Chapter 2.

government this would seemingly allow the nirvana of lower tax rates whilst at least maintaining public spending.

Third was recognition in some quarters of the potential political benefits to the Conservative party of this argument. The Conservatives had started doing systematic opinion polling in 1949, and by the early 1950s this was picking up on the idea (later to be central to political analysis) that an affluent working class might have views that would detach them from a Labour allegiance.[74]

The Conservative official Brendon Sewill reported after the 1955 election that 'the main division between the parties in the field of economics was between prosperity and fair shares. Neither side denied the other's accusations. Socialists said prosperity is not being fairly shared, while Conservatives just said people were better off and left it at that.' This theme dominated the party's election broadcasts.[75] This time the Conservatives secured a plurality of votes and an increased majority.

Decontrol was accompanied by faster inflation after 1953, and this, in the context of attempts to return the pound to convertibility, worried Conservative policymakers. This worry was reflected in a 1956 white paper on the inflationary consequences of full employment, and its popular accompaniment, entitled *Must full employment mean ever-rising prices?* Both of these asserted that inflation would be socially and economically detrimental; an old argument. But a new note was the emphasis on the threat to 'the possibilities of economic progress' or, in the starker language of the popular version, inflation 'could lead to rising unemployment and falling living standards'.[76]

The concern with inflation led to the setting-up of the Council on Prices, Productivity, and Incomes in 1957, whose main focus was on wage inflation, though its impact was very limited.[77] This concern also framed the famous speech by Macmillan at Bedford which gives this chapter its title. The relevant passage is worth quoting in full:

> Let's be frank about it: most of our people have never had it so good. Go around the country, go to the industrial towns, go to the farms, and you will see a state of prosperity such as we have never had in my lifetime—nor indeed in the history of this country. What is worrying some of us is 'Is it too good to be true?' or perhaps I should say 'Is it too good to last?' For amidst all this prosperity, there is one problem that has troubled us... ever since the war. It's the problem of rising prices. Our considered concern today is: can prices be steadied while at the same time we maintain full employment in an expanding economy? Can we control inflation? This is the problem of our time.[78]

[74] Taylor, '"Record"'. [75] Ramsden, *Making*, p. 176.

[76] Cmd. 9725, p. 9; His/Her Majesty's Treasury (HMT)/COI *Must?*, p. 12. The publication of this popular version was the source of much debate in government circles, with many ministers believing that their speeches were the most effective way of shaping the debate on inflation and the threat to the value of the pound: TNA: PRO 230/453, 'Economic publicity', 1955/6 (see Chapter 7).

[77] TNA: PRO T 267/10 Treasury Historical Memoranda 'Government and wages 1945–60' vol. III, 1956–60.

[78] *The Times*, 22 July 1957.

Many government advisers and economists would have concurred that inflation was 'the problem of our time', but the message taken by most from this speech was something very different: that a rising standard of living for the mass of the people was now the central concern of government. While in this speech Macmillan carefully counterbalanced the evidence of prosperity against the threat of inflation, the central message was that the Conservatives embraced prosperity and implicitly promised its continuation. It was undoubtedly, as Sampson stresses, 'a boast'.[79]

As noted, this shift had been building up before Macmillan's speech so vividly encapsulated it, but it was not a message that all Conservatives readily embraced. Many in the party thought it made 'a vulgar appeal to materialistic instincts' rather than traditional conservative values. Others were already worrying about the impact of prosperity on the morals and behaviour of the people.[80]

Equally, there were those Conservatives who thought that the control of inflation should not be sacrificed to this promise of affluence. Five months after his Bedford speech, Macmillan was telling the Cabinet that inflation was the 'most pressing problem' and calling for a consistent line on this from ministers.[81] The next year, 1958, there was a major dispute in the government about how far public spending should be cut to aid a reduction in inflation. But the eventual outcome was the departure of the ministers who had wanted to take this tough line, a line which Macmillan feared would undermine the expansionary trend of the economy, especially in the light of rising unemployment and the prospect of a general election in the near future.[82]

For the 1959 election the Conservative slogan was 'prosperity and peace'. The manifesto was very clear about the centrality of this promise: 'The main issues at this election are therefore simple:... Do you want to go ahead on the lines which have brought prosperity at home?' Later on the promise of 1955 was reaffirmed: 'Conservative policy is to double the British standard of living in this generation and ensure that all sections of society share in the expansion of wealth'.[83] The result of the election was a resounding defeat for Labour, with the Conservatives increasing their majority. As always, it cannot be said that one issue decided the election. But the Conservative focus on prosperity, and Labour's parallel emphasis on the standard of living, helped to shape an election debate in which 'vulgar materialism' seems to have played a very large part. A Gallup poll at the time of the dissolution found 44 per cent of those interviewed thought the Conservative Party the one best qualified to increase production and prosperity, while only 26 per cent thought Labour best; 86 per cent of Conservatives had confidence in their party on this issue, while only 62 per cent of Labour supporters believed Labour could handle it best.[84]

This evidence is backed up by the opinion research done in the wake of Labour's defeat and published under the title *Must Labour Lose?* One of the most striking

79 Sampson, *Macmillan,* p. 167.

80 Jarvis, *Conservative*, pp. 2, 11; Lindsay and Harrington, *Conservative*, p. 203.

81 TNA: PRO CAB 129/89 Prime Minister 'Explaining the economic situation', 5 October 1957.

82 Green, 'Treasury'.

83 Craig, *General Election Manifestos 1918–1966*, pp. 188, 189.

84 Butler and Rose, *British General Election of 1959*, pp. 69–70.

findings of this survey was that even amongst Labour voters there was thought to be little to choose between the parties on 'who would make the country more prosperous'. Amongst non-Labour voters, 67 per cent thought the Conservatives would have the advantage on this, and this was the largest lead given to the Tories on any topic.[85]

Because so many commentators (especially on the Left) thought it was the promise of prosperity that had defeated Labour in 1959, this issue had a chapter devoted to it in *Must Labour Lose?* Survey material showed that ownership of new consumer durables was unrelated to working-class voting behaviour in 1959, but that house ownership was correlated with Conservative voting. The conclusion drawn was that 'general prosperity and security are not themselves the determinant of working class politics: within the working class both Labour and Conservative supporters seem to have enjoyed their prosperity of the past decade'.[86]

Most subsequent analysts have agreed that there is not necessarily any relationship between prosperity and voting Conservative. But all have agreed that Labour had great *ideological* difficulties in coming to terms with this new affluence, especially as represented by the acquisition of new consumer durables, central to most understandings of affluence in the 1950s and 1960s. All sorts of attitudes seem to have been at play in creating this difficulty; a tradition of socialist asceticism, a distrust of the perceived individualism and domestic focus of this affluence; a distaste for 'vulgar materialism' very similar to that voiced in many Conservative circles. These cultural and political predispositions meant that Labour struggled to make sense of the changes in popular consumption.[87] The spread of home ownership was, as suggested by *Must Labour Lose?*, a particularly difficult aspiration for Labour to come to terms with, but here too there are good grounds for refusing any automatic relationship between tenure and voting. For example, as Nick Tiratsoo argued in his pioneering work on Coventry, when, in the early 1950s, the association between home ownership and voting was first commented upon, 'Labour seemed to have accepted this as an almost natural state of affairs, which it could do little to alter', rather than, for example, getting itself involved in ratepayers' associations.[88]

IV

In economic terms the austerity policy was very successful; as Table 1.5 shows, between 1946 and 1952 consumer spending rose only about a third as fast as Gross Domestic Product (GDP), as the bulk of increased output went into investment and exports. Politically the consequences were problematic for the Labour government. The holding back of consumption, and the rationing and controls which accompanied this holding back, allowed the Conservatives to mount an effective campaign to free the people from the shackles of socialism.

[85] Abrams, *Must?*, pp. 14–16. [86] Abrams, *Must?*, p. 45.
[87] Black, *Political*; Tiratsoo, *Reconstruction*. [88] Tiratsoo, *Reconstruction*, p. 116.

Table 1.5 Austerity, 1940s-style

Expenditure category	Change 1946 to 1952 (percentage)
Consumers' expenditure	5.9
Public authorities' current expenditure	−12.4
Gross domestic fixed capital formation	57.9
Exports of goods and services	77.3
Imports of goods and services	14.5
Net property income from abroad	24.5
Gross domestic product	15.0

Source: HMSO, *National Income and Expenditure* (1957).

Contemporary arguments about the balance of payments focused on the private sector and the current account, the slogan of 'export or die' obscuring the extent to which foreign exchange was flowing into overseas military spending and foreign investment (see Chapter 7). But within this framing of the issue, policy was highly successful, with the payments position corrected, until the onset of the Korean War brought further problems. The improvement in the current account was greatly aided by the inability of the devastated economies of Germany and Japan to fully compete in expanding world markets, and by devaluation of the pound in 1949. While conditions were favourable, the political commitment to correcting the payments position, despite the consequential starving of the powerful demands of the home market, is striking.

The emphasis on a rise in investment flowed from a strong sense in the Labour leadership that their commitment to full employment and expanded welfare provision in the post-war settlement was only politically feasible in an expanding economy.[89] Some of the investment was itself part of delivering on that settlement, most notably in housing. But the biggest increase in investment was in plant and machinery, and the sectors that benefited most from the government's priorities were manufacturing and construction.[90]

1940s austerity was driven by a macroeconomic problem of demand outrunning supply, and therefore the need to restrict consumption in order to prioritize exports and investment. This excess demand accounts for the low unemployment levels, and also for the government's supply-side initiatives, in areas such as subsidies for research and development, expansion of technical education, and a drive to import what were perceived as the superior techniques of American industry for achieving high productivity. This excess demand was countered not only by rationing and controls, but increasingly by tight fiscal policy, so that for most of its years

[89] The share of investment in GDP also rose sharply in the late 1950s, so that post-war Britain came consistently to invest a much larger share of GDP than before 1939: Little, 'Fiscal', p. 292. This is one reason why, notwithstanding the rise in consumption levels, the epithet 'consumer society' should be used with caution about the post-war decades.

[90] Cairncross, *Years*, pp. 451–2, 456; Chick, *Industrial*, pp. 16–24.

in office the Attlee government was running a budget surplus, and reducing the national debt.[91]

Labour's moral economy of fair shares was undermined by the ending of the shortage economy. In its great propaganda campaigns to raise production and productivity Labour had already held out to the population the prospect of growing prosperity once the immediate crises were over, most unambiguously in *Labour's Plan for Plenty* in 1947. So when, as the economy boomed in the post-Korean-war period, the narrative of a prospective continuous rise in the standard of living was not a new invention. But now, in the 1950s, unlike in the late 1940s, benign international economic conditions, coupled to an investment boom at home, made this prospect credible. In this environment the Conservatives could easily deliver on their promise to 'set the people free' whilst presiding over a continuously expanding economy. Whilst ministers and advisers fretted over the balance of payments and inflation—and occasionally tried to get the public to share their fears—growing consumption of new items, especially consumer durables, spread down the social scale. While economic advisers were only starting to think of 'growth' as an issue applicable in rich as well as developing countries, politicians and their advisers were beginning to see the possibilities of a whole new politics based on promises about the standard of living of the mass of the population.[92]

The Conservatives after 1951 largely eschewed the intensive propaganda efforts of Labour.[93] These efforts were seen by many Conservatives as part of the excesses of an intrusive state that needed to be halted. This did not mean a complete withdrawal from attempts at persuasion, for example on productivity, where Butler and Gaitskell (the latter Labour's last Chancellor of the Exchequer before the party lost office) appeared together in a 1953 film exhorting improvement. But even on this topic the government soon adopted a much more 'hands-off' attitude. 'Productivity Year' in 1959/60 was largely under the control of the British Productivity Council (BPC, successor to the Anglo-American Council). Occasional 'popular' pamphlets on economic issues, a striking feature of the Attlee years, were produced by the Conservatives. Following the pattern seen under Labour, a 'popular' version of the Economic Survey was published in 1952.[94] Most notable was the pamphlet in 1956 on the impact of full employment. There was a similar example in 1955 on the balance of payments.[95] But these were largely isolated efforts, rather than part of Labour-style structured and intensive programmes of persuasion.

In a broader sense, of course, the Conservatives were engaged in an almost continuous effort to shape the electorate's views on the economy. The most obvious manifestation of this was the innovation of using the budget to provide

[91] The debt: GDP ratio in 1945 was 235 per cent, but had fallen to 164 per cent by 1951: Allen, *Monetary*, p. 4. This was much higher than ever again—much higher than in the 'austerity' period from 2009, when the figure was 80–90 per cent.

[92] Cairncross, *Roberthall*, pp. 256–7; Hall, 'Reflections'.

[93] The 'Survey of knowledge and opinion' was abolished, so we have nothing like that source for trying to understand the impact of economic narratives after 1951.

[94] *Where We Stand This Year. An Official Account in Popular Form of the Economic Situation and Prospects for 1952.*

[95] Discussed in Chapters 6 and 9, respectively.

short-term boosts to economic activity in the run-up to general elections, so that contemporaries increasingly referred to a 'political business cycle'.[96] This approach carried the clear implication that government was responsible for the state of the economy—a double-edged weapon if the economy was perceived to be performing badly. This strategy paid some dividends, but was no guarantee of electoral success. Most strikingly, the huge boost given to the economy by Maudling's 'dash for growth' in the run-up to the 1964 election failed, albeit by only a small margin.

Interwoven with this pattern of 'stop-go' macroeconomic management, in the 1950s the Conservatives discovered, partly by accident, that unleashing the expansion of popular consumption could pay huge political dividends. From around 1954 this possibility seems to have been recognized amongst at least some elements of the party's leadership, and promises of future growth and prosperity became a staple of ministerial and other party pronouncements. However unevenly this prosperity was spread, however much it left behind substantial pockets of poverty, and however much it relied on increased consumer indebtedness, increasingly it was *the* economic narrative.[97] Political argument was both shaped by and helped to shape understandings of this prosperity, and while initially its appearance favoured the Conservatives, in the longer term Labour forged a critique of Conservative performance in this regard which gave them back the initiative.

Consumerism and affluence created a complex politics across the political spectrum. Most has been written about the Labour side.[98] But it also posed problems for Conservative politics and ideology. 'Setting the people free' suggested an assertion of laissez-faire attitudes whilst in many other respects the Conservatives were adjusting to the more collectivist politics of the post-war settlement. The battle over the budget in 1958 partly reflected this tension within the party. But, on a longer timescale, 'setting the people free' to enjoy the new consumer choice and affluence locked the Conservatives into a politics of delivering prosperity.[99] When their record in delivering on this prosperity came under challenge at the beginning of the 1960s, their response was a programme of 'modernization' which involved *expanding* the role of the state, a paradoxical consequence of 'freeing the people'.

[96] Oppenheimer, 'Muddling', pp. 120–1.

[97] Todd, *People*, pp. 199–211.

[98] In addition to works already cited, see Thompson, 'Conceptualising'; more broadly, Offer, 'British'.

[99] Girvin, 'Affluence'.

2

'Decline' to Modernization

In the late 1950s a new narrative, of Britain's economic 'decline', was invented and widely propagated. This narrative suggested that Britain suffered from profound, chronic deficiencies in a wide range of institutions and attitudes, and that these deficiencies showed themselves in a failing economy. The immediate consequence of the widespread adoption of this narrative over the next few years was that the political debate of the early 1960s became dominated by arguments about how to *reverse* decline—how to 'modernize' the economy. This chapter examines the underpinnings of this 'declinist' turn in public economic argument; while there had been previous notions of economic decline at work in Britain, none had the force, significance, and longevity of that which began to be produced in this decade. The chapter then goes on to look at the emergence of 'modernization' narratives as a response to the broad agreement on the evidence of decline, and a belief that economy had to take a new direction.

I

Modern concerns about British economic decline originated in the late nineteenth century, with Britain's seemingly poor response to the growth of German and American competition and the simultaneous development of a problem of unemployment. These initial concerns were then expanded to embrace related issues such as the weight of manufacturing compared with services in the industrial structure.[1] Once established, these approaches to economic performance were to echo through the next century of discussion of decline, but this continuity is in many ways misleading. Declinism has *not* taken a constant form, but rather has been reinvented periodically in relation to differing current concerns and ideological positioning. For example, the debate analysed by Supple, which began in the 1880s, is qualitatively different from the debate around the time of the Boer War, analysed by Friedberg.[2] While the earlier arguments were quite narrowly economic in focus, the debate stimulated by the war in South Africa was linked directly to inter-imperial rivalry, and to broad strategic and military issues. Similarly, the notion of decline prevailing between the world wars was different again, 'as disappointment with the country's industrial performance came to be focused on the organisation and efficiency of the staple and traditional industries'.[3]

[1] Supple, 'Official', pp. 330–1. [2] Friedberg, *Weary*. [3] Supple, 'Official', p. 340.

Not only were notions of decline different at different times in the past, but the concern itself was episodic rather than continuous. The idea of a continuous '100-year decline' is the product of retrospective judgements, not a reflection of contemporary debate throughout this period; the preoccupation with failure has been intermittent as well as differentiated. While historians, it should be emphasized, did not invent declinism, they have been a major source of its generalized use, projecting current diagnoses and prescriptions onto the past.[4]

So the meanings of decline have varied through time according to prevailing economic and political concerns. The pervasiveness of the idea of decline was also much less pronounced before 1939 than it came to be in post-war Britain. Writing in the 1990s, Supple noted the long history of ideas of decline, but accepted that, 'Admittedly, it is only really over the last generation that economic and political debate has come to be dominated by the idea that Britain is in such serious decline that it is heading for national ruin'.[5]

Elements of a new declinist mood can be found at work even before the Suez crisis of 1956, a huge shock to British thinking, encouraged a bout of national soul-searching, not least on Britain's global standing.[6] Kynaston sees it as 'well under way by 1955–6', and cites a number of examples of contemporary expressions of concern about Britain's economic performance.[7] These were sufficiently prominent for the Chancellor to give a public address, 'the main purpose of which was to disabuse those present of the idea that Britain is in economic decline'.[8] But as yet these arguments were largely on the margins, and dominance of the public narrative didn't arrive until close to the end of the decade. As Campbell rightly argues:

> 1964 was the first General Election at which modernisation was the central issue. The notion of Britain's relative decline—the realisation that in terms of economic prosperity, social services, and the 'quality of life' Britain was falling behind other industrialised countries—had struck the previously complacent public consciousness quite suddenly within the previous five years. It was to be the staple assumption of every subsequent election over the next three decades.[9]

In this period from the end of the 1950s declinism was reinvented, largely around the specific idea that Britain was lagging behind the growth in living standards taking place in other Western European countries. There was a wider context, not least in doubts about Britain's declining international role post-Suez, but it was the linkage to growth and living standards that was to prove especially powerful and enduring. This notion of decline was highly political, as Budge rightly emphasizes.[10] He stresses the *party* political aspect, where political parties or groups out of power use 'decline' as a stick to beat the government. This was certainly true in

[4] Pollard, *Wasting* is a classic example of this genre. See also Supple, 'Fear'; Supple, 'British'.

[5] Supple, 'Fear'. Also Supple, 'British', pp. 318, 326.

[6] Sandbrook, *Never*, pp. 76–7.

[7] Kynaston, *Family Britain*, pp. 616–17.

[8] TNA: PRO T230/453, 'Outline of points for statement by the Chancellor of the Exchequer' 16 May 1956.

[9] Campbell, *Heath*, p. 163.

[10] Budge, 'Relative'.

the late 1950s, where the opposition Labour Party took up decline as a basis for attacking the Conservative government, with the latter belatedly responding, and this important party political aspect will be returned to later. But in a broader sense the idea of living standards as a major concern, which underlies the new declinism, can be understood as going beyond party politics, as marking a change in widely shared ideas about the extent and nature of government responsibility for economic performance.

If decline in this period was about relative economic performance, it was a narrative that crucially relied upon new statistical assessments of that performance. This was a period when the production of both national and international economic statistics exploded, and the second of these was especially important in underpinning *comparative* measures of performance. Decline, in other words, was seen as a *measurable* failure, and this suggests that the developing means of calculation are an important element in understanding the underpinnings of the doctrine of decline. All these issues will be treated in turn.

II

The Second World War inaugurated a major extension of government responsibility for economic life, symbolized by the White Paper on *Employment Policy* of 1944, with its commitment to a 'high and stable' level of employment.[11] This commitment assumed not only that governments had the techniques to secure full employment, but that they would be punished politically if they did not deploy those techniques effectively. In this way governments assumed a new responsibility for the economic welfare of the mass of the population.

In the 1940s and into the early 1950s the major threat to this welfare was perceived to be from a recurrence of interwar mass unemployment.[12] However, once the US recession of 1953 passed without serious consequences for the British economy, this threat no longer seemed plausible. Now economic welfare was increasingly seen to depend not on sustaining full use of resources, but on increasing the efficiency with which those resources were used—in other words, it depended upon the rate of economic growth. In 1954 R. A. Butler, the Conservative Chancellor of the Exchequer, made his famous speech holding out the prospect of a 'doubling of the standard of living in twenty-five years', which reflected the beginnings of a major shift in political rhetoric, as economic growth in the sense of rising living standards came to replace full employment in the political debate about economic improvement.[13]

At this stage the shift was largely rhetorical, the Conservatives having few clear ideas on how to influence the growth rate.[14] But there was a straightforward logic

[11] A theme returned to in Chapter 6.
[12] Peden, 'Old Dogs'; Rollings, 'British'; Tomlinson, *Employment*; Winch, *Economics*, ch. 13.
[13] NUCUA, *Conference Report, 1954*, p. 66.
[14] Harris, *Competition*; Tomlinson, 'Unfortunate?'

to this development. Politically, the Conservative government was engaged in electoral competition where consumption standards had become a key issue, as it had successfully realized in 1951.[15] This shift in focus had been predicted in 1951 by the pioneer growth economist Colin Clark, when he suggested that 'the main issue in the next decade is not going to be full employment at all... but the long-run problems of production and distribution of real income'.[16] His insight reflected the inherent logic of 'solving' the employment problem and then moving on to expand the output produced from fully employed resources.

The rise of growth as a policy objective had a multitude of causes, and was not confined to Britain.[17] In the US there was a strong Cold War element; a concern with growth rates relative to the USSR, and the idea that success in the growth race would be crucial for the underdeveloped countries' choice between capitalism and communism. But while there are echoes of this kind of geopolitical debate in Britain, the concern with growth was generally more parochial, linked to the domestic political concerns noted above, and focused upon changes in the British 'standard of living'. This notion could, of course, be given a number of meanings but in the initial public debate at least it came to be linked to two measured quantities—the rate of consumer price inflation, and the rate of money wage increases brought about by the annual wage round. The rise in the standard of living was the gap between these two magnitudes.

Both of these figures emerged only in the post-war period as significant aspects of public understanding of the economy. Consumer price indices first became important just before the First World War, as part of the tariff reform debate, but were then taken up as part of the government desire to demonstrate its commitment to controlling inflation, in order to maintain working-class support for the war effort.[18] The same cause produced the same effect in the Second World War, though this time the effort to control price inflation (at least as registered in the index) was more intense and more successful.[19] Under the Attlee government the retail price index continued to be employed in the first attempts at a peacetime incomes policy, which led to a policy of subsidizing food and other commodities in order to hold the index constant.[20]

On the wage side, the attempt to limit wage inflation was linked to the emergence of a *national* wage pattern, an annual bargaining round in which nominal wage claims were highly sensitive to changes in the consumer price index. This national 'going rate' for wages never, of course, embraced all aspects of wage bargaining, either during the war or afterwards.[21] But it did mark a sharp break with the pre-war experience where the great bulk of wage bargaining had never assumed this *national* form.

The idea of the standard of living was not invented in the 1950s. What was new was the belief that it should be the clear aim of economic policy to raise that standard, underpinned by measurement of general price and wage movements which

15 Chapter 1, above. 16 Clark, *Conditions*, p. vii. 17 Arndt, *Rise*.
18 Searle, 'Is there?' 19 Hancock and Gowing, *British*, pp. 552–5.
20 Rollings, 'British', pp. 286–90. 21 Roberts, *National*; Turner, 'Wages'.

could be used to give plausible meaning to that aim. By 1956 the Conservative government was proclaiming in a major statement on economic policy: 'This government is pledged to foster conditions in which the nation, if it so wills, realises its full potentialities for growth in terms of production and living standards'.[22] The emergence of the standard of living, and its growth, as a political issue provided the starting point for the rise of declinism in the later 1950s.

Just as political talk of the standard of living in the 1950s was grounded in newly conceived forms of economic measurement, so the rise of declinism can only be understood against the background of new forms of economic calculation and statistics. The key statistics were those which placed British performance in an international context, because declinism drew upon *relative* measures of that performance. The 1940s and 1950s saw a veritable statistical revolution, both in national data and in international comparisons. For the latter a key role was played by the UN and Organization for European Economic Co-operation (OEEC), as they produced a wide range of comparative data. Four types of data seem to have been particularly important for the emergence of declinism; those for national income, industrial production, productivity, and shares of world trade. Each of these had its own trajectory of development, linked to the role of emergent international agencies in producing comparative figures. Each was then taken up in the British debate.

From 1952 the UN published *Statistics of National Income and Expenditure*, and, crucially, by the late 1950s the UN *Economic Survey of Europe* was producing regular league tables of growth rates, destined to become a staple statistic of economic narratives of relative performance and decline.[23]

In parallel, in 1952, the OEEC published a standardized system of national accounts, and in 1954 a major benchmark work by Gilbert and Kravis, comparing the national products of the US, the UK, France, Germany, and Italy. While this methodology remained controversial, the study in many ways marked the coming of age of comparative national income work.[24]

By the early 1950s these comparisons of growth registered with British officials and politicians. For example, in 1954 a briefing prepared by Board of Trade officials for ministers drew explicitly on the 'standard of life' comparisons in Gilbert and Kravis, especially to emphasize the scale of the gap with the US (estimated by Gilbert and Kravis as between 40 and 70 per cent, depending upon the basis of the calculation). Publication of this study roughly coincided with Rab Butler's 'doubling the standard of living' speech cited above. In the subsequent official discussions of the plausibility of this doubling, use was made of the emerging UN and OEEC data to suggest how fast the economy could grow in the period up to 1960.[25] At the same time, and drawing on such material, ministers were telling the

[22] Cmd. 9725, para. 25. See also Cmnd. 827, para. 58.

[23] United Nations Economic Commission for Europe (UNECE), *Economic Survey of Europe in 1949*; UNECE, *Economic Commissioner*. The first league table of growth rates produced by the UN seems to have been in the UNECE, *Economic Survey of Europe in 1957*, ch. 2, p. 3, which shows Britain fourth from bottom in a table of 17 countries.

[24] OEEC, *Standardised*; OEEC, *Statistics*; Gilbert and Kravis, *International Comparison*.

[25] TNA: PRO, T230/284, 'Long-term survey of the income of the UK'; T230/285, 'Long-term survey', 1956.

public that the evidence of the recent growth in Western Europe, while subject to special considerations, suggested that 'the differences in pace of movement are clear'.[26] So these new statistical productions were becoming important underpinnings of British public debate.

These figures showed, and were seen to show, the ambiguity of the British growth position, namely the quite rapid increase in historic terms, but its slowness in comparison with other Western European countries. Paradoxically, while so much of the discussion of Britain's economic performance, especially in the late 1940s and early 1950s, extolled the virtues of the US model, US growth was at a rate similar, or in some calculations even below, that of Britain. This pattern can best be explained as a result of processes of 'catch-up and convergence'.[27] This means that within a set of rich countries such as that of the advanced capitalist countries of Western Europe in the post-war period, all with access to the technologies and production systems of the richest country in the world, the USA, there will be strong tendencies towards convergence. Those countries which at the end of the Second World War lagged a long way behind the richest had the motive, means, and opportunity to catch up, and that is what they did. In this context Britain was, for most of the 1950s and 1960s, like the USA, a 'leader' being caught up by Western European laggards, while itself catching up a little with the USA. Table 2.1 shows the generally inverse relationship between Western European countries' absolute starting point in 1950 and the rate of growth thereafter. While the relationship isn't perfect, with countries such as Norway and especially Ireland doing particularly badly, the broad pattern is clear.

Crafts, who assembled this data, argues there is still something to be explained—Britain's rate of growth 'should' have been faster on purely statistical grounds. Nevertheless, this data and the 'catch-up and convergence' narrative act as a hugely important qualification to declinist stories. While the data in Table 2.1 could only be assembled in retrospect, some commentators in the Golden Age recognized that it would be implausible that Britain should have a permanently higher standard of living than her neighbours, as would be the result if her growth rates had matched theirs. Thus in the *Report* of the Conservative Party's Policy Committee on Economic Growth in 1962, the faster expansion of Britain than the USA was noted, and it was suggested that

> the most striking contrast lies with the rates of growth by the three main countries of the EEC: Germany, France and Italy. Indeed, in some ways the phenomenon that needs explaining is not so much the relative stagnation of the British economy during this period as the exceptional rate of growth of the Continental countries.[28]

In the long run, data on relative growth rates, and league tables derived from them, can be seen as both one of the most important statistical innovations of the 1950s, and one of the most enduring staples of declinist claims. However, important as their development was, in the 1950s national income estimates were still widely

[26] TNA: PRO, BT64/4896, 'Briefing for ministers on UK productivity', 1954.
[27] Abramowitz, 'Catching up'. [28] Conservative Party, *Report*, pp. 7–8.

Table 2.1 'Catching up' in Western Europe, 1950–73

	Ranking in 1950 (GDP/head)	Ranking in growth rate of GDP per annum, 1950–73
Switzerland	1	12
UK	2	16
Sweden	3	12
Denmark	4	12
Netherlands	5	10
Belgium	6	9
France	7	8
Norway	8	11
West Germany	9	4
Finland	10	7
Austria	11	5
Ireland	12	12
Italy	13	5
Spain	14	2
Portugal	15	3
Greece	16	1

Source: Crafts, 'Golden Age', p. 435.

seen as problematic, especially by non-economists, and in the attempts to gauge the path of aggregate output recourse was commonly had to figures deemed more reliable, notably total industrial production.

While national income data took a number of years to produce because of the conceptual difficulties, comparative data on industrial production were available from the beginnings of regular post-war publication of economic statistics by the UN. The first UN *Economics Bulletin for Europe* in 1949 published comparative figures on this topic, and used them as the basis for its discussion of Europe's economic performance. In fact industrial production remained the basis for most UN comparative economic commentary right through the 1950s, even after comparative national income data were devised.[29] The same point is true of OEEC publications, where industrial production was again the staple of comparisons, for example in the *Statistical Bulletin*. The tendency to focus on industrial production rather than national income fitted in with prevailing ideas about the centrality of industry to economic performance. The 'productionism' of the Attlee government was notably centred on raising industrial output, with the service sector being regarded as secondary if not actually parasitical upon industry.[30] While the Conservatives in the early 1950s backed away from Labour's interest in industrial modernization, they still usually (if implicitly) regarded industrial growth as the key to economic performance. Thus, for example, in the 1956 version of the *Economic Survey*, the major official publication on economic policy in this period, a figure is given for the growth of industrial output in Britain compared with

[29] UN, *Economic Bulletin for Europe*, 1949; see also *Economic Survey of Europe* published annually from 1949.

[30] Tiratsoo and Tomlinson, *Industrial*, ch. 4.

Germany.[31] Industrial output growth (though not usually in a comparative context) remained the staple of those surveys throughout their period of publication which ended in 1961. By contrast, no figure for national income was ever published there.

If the government tended to treat industrial production as the key measure of economic expansion in this period, so too did the critics. Shonfield, for example, in his foundation text of declinism, cites comparative GDP figures, but then goes on to say that these give too rosy a picture, and a truer (worse) position is revealed if the comparison is made in terms of industrial production.[32] Similarly, Shanks, in his influential text, treats the comparisons of industrial production as central, though he goes on to give national income figures as well.[33]

The Labour Party, in the emblematic *Twelve Wasted Years*, starts its indictment of Conservative policy with the figures for the comparative growth of industrial production. The following year (1964) Labour's general election manifesto focused on industrial production deficiencies in making its case in favour of policies for faster growth.[34]

Another measure of relative economic performance increasingly deployed from the 1940s and 1950s on was that of productivity, at this time almost always defined in terms of labour productivity in the industrial sector. A much broader notion of productivity, measured simply as national product per head, has as long a history as national income accounting. But the idea of industrial productivity as a measure of efficiency seems to have been stimulated by the peculiar conditions of wartime.[35] In the last years of the war and immediately afterwards the government's concern was still mainly with the need to raise output, but the problem was increasingly put in an international context, largely by comparisons with the US. At this time the American economic model was commonly seen, at least by the government and quasi-government bodies such as the Anglo-American Council on Productivity (AACP), as the one to which Britain should aspire, and many unfavourable comparisons with US productivity were made. In fact, such Anglo-American productivity comparisons had a long history, predating the First World War. However, in the 1940s such work changed from being of largely academic interest to contributing to a major reorientation of British economic policy towards seeking to improve industrial efficiency.[36]

The Anglo-American focus of early comparative work on productivity had an important institutional focus in the OEEC. From the beginning, one of the key aims of this body was to raise productivity, and this was reflected in the early

[31] Cmd. 9728, p. 2. This was part of a broader, cultural, phenomenon in which 'industry' was seen as the core of the economy; see, for example, COI, *Fifty Facts*, which discusses the role of industry (and agriculture) but makes no mention of the service sector.

[32] Shonfield, *British*, pp. 14–15.

[33] Shanks, *Stagnant*, pp. 24–6. Shanks's approach was affected by his desire to compare Britain unfavourably with the USSR as well as with Western Europe, when the USSR did not produce national income figures on a basis readily comparable with those used in the West.

[34] Labour Party, *Twelve Wasted Years*, p. 1; Craig, *General Election Manifestos 1918–1966*, p. 231.

[35] See Chapter 7.

[36] For interwar and early post-war comparisons see Broadberry and Crafts, 'Explaining'; Tomlinson, 'Failure'.

establishment of a 'productivity group', one of whose tasks was to provide a standardized terminology for productivity in an international context.[37] More practically, the OEEC, through the European Productivity Agency, embarked on a series of initiatives aimed at spreading good practice, through such methods as document exchange, technical assistance programmes (especially the continuation of the team visits, initially organized by the AACP in Britain, and parallel bodies in other European countries), a technical information service, encouragement of national productivity centres, and stimulating expert discussions under the aegis of the OEEC. Much of the work on productivity focused on productivity in industry, though the OEEC did finance a major study of whole economy productivity at the end of the 1950s.[38]

The impact of the OEEC on the British debate on productivity was different from that of the same body and the UN on the discussion of national income. First, as noted, the British already had a well-established concern with, and administrative apparatus to pursue, the issue of raising productivity as well as considerable domestic expertise before the OEEC was established. Rostas, an adviser to the Board of Trade, was already an acknowledged expert on the subject and had published a benchmark comparative study on the issue, as well as work on Britain.[39] He was to become a major figure in the European Productivity Agency (EPA). Richard Stone, by contrast, though later to receive a Nobel prize for his pioneering work on national income, and very important in the deliberations of both the OEEC and UN, never occupied the same policy-oriented role that Rostas had as a British civil servant. Rostas's role symbolizes the 'fit' between the practical concerns of the British government in the late 1940s and OEEC initiatives.[40]

At the same time, (labour) productivity appeared a much more straightforward measurement of economic performance than comparative national income. In principle at least, calculating total output relative to labour inputs had a precise statistical meaning, and at the same time served to embody an everyday notion of efficiency, so that, as a civil servant noted in 1953, productivity 'has really simply taken the place and absorbed the mantra of the earlier term "efficiency" or "productive efficiency."'[41] In fact, of course, the calculation of a satisfactory measure of productivity is beset with all sorts of difficulties, both of measurement (the valuation of output, the exact measurement of inputs, even if these are confined to labour) and of interpretation. Most obviously, the focus on *labour* productivity has all too often served to bias political and public opinion towards labour *effort*, however much the experts generally decried such an approach.[42]

American enthusiasm for raising productivity operated not only through the OEEC and EPA but directly through the Conditional Aid programme under the 1952 Mutual Security Act. Under this programme Britain was given £3 million to

[37] OEEC, *Terminology.* [38] Paige and Bombach, *Comparison*; Frankel, *British*.
[39] Rostas, *Comparative*; Rostas, *Productivity*.
[40] TNA: PRO, BT258/602, 'Report of productivity and conditional aid committee', 1953.
[41] TNA: PRO, BT258/602, 'Report of productivity and conditional aid committee', 1953.
[42] Kravis, 'Survey'. This issue is returned to in Chapter 7.

study the issue, and this financed many pieces of academic work which tended to bring out the productivity problems of British industry.[43]

Pessimism about Britain's productivity performance based on international comparisons is evident in official circles from at least 1953. The *Policy and Programme* of the BPC (the body created in 1952 to replace the AACP) contrasted British performance not just with that of the USA but with 'some other countries', and went on to argue that 'our position will grow relatively worse until we reverse this trend'. The first report of the productivity and conditional aid committee in 1954 compared trends in Britain with those in Western Europe and the USA for the period 1948 to 1953, and concluded that

> the general moral to be drawn from them is that if the tendencies they reveal were to continue, the relegation of the UK to the 2nd division in the industrial league would not be far off. At the moment there is not much visible reason for optimism, and a certain amount of rather disquieting evidence.[44]

This report triggered off a substantial ministerial debate about how far the government should go to try to alter this state of affairs, but there was little dispute that there was a serious problem to be addressed.[45] The Conservative response to this critical view of Britain's productivity performance was conditioned by a broad political strategy, and will be returned to below, but it is worth noting at this stage the clear ministerial recognition of the links between productivity and the emerging Conservative emphasis on prosperity in their appeal to the electorate. In December 1954 Thorneycroft, the President of the Board of Trade, wrote: 'what matters is where we are going, how fast we are moving, and, in particular how our performance compares with other people! This is the connection between prosperity and productivity.'[46]

Enthusiasm for productivity measurement in the 1950s was not just a result of the new-found concern with growth and standards of living, but also followed from the largely separate issue of wage bargaining. As part of the growing concern with inflation in the 1950s, the government sought to establish the idea that wages should not rise faster than productivity. Thus, the Committee on Productivity, Prices, and Incomes (the Cohen Committee) established in 1957 was wholly concerned with productivity in that context, not at all with productivity in the context of the growth of the national economy.[47]

Also in the 1950s, comparisons of productivity came increasingly to focus on Britain's position relative to that of other countries in Western Europe. Until the 1940s almost all comparisons were with the USA, and only a very few with other countries, notably Germany.[48] But from the 1950s, as comparative European data

[43] For example, Burn, *Structure*; Carter and Williams, *Industry*.

[44] PRO, BT64/4742, 'Report of the productivity and conditional aid committee', 1953; BPC, *Policy*.

[45] PRO, CAB 134/851, Economic Policy Committee, 'Report by productivity and conditional aid committee' 6 March 1954; CAB 134/850, Economic Policy Committee minutes, 18 March 1954.

[46] PRO, BT64/4896, 'Briefings for ministers on UK productivity', 1954.

[47] Council on Productivity, Prices, and Incomes (COPPI), *1st to 4th Reports, 1958–1961.*

[48] Broadberry and Fremdling, 'Comparative Productivity'.

became available, this encouraged the movement to view these countries as the natural comparators for Britain. This tendency was, of course, greatly strengthened by the movement towards economic union in Western Europe, and the possibility of Britain's attachment to that union. Increasingly, in the 1950s West Germany became the country favoured for comparisons with Britain. After 1960, France too achieved prominence, especially because of the belief that its planning system had brought a superior growth performance.[49]

While data on national income, industrial production, and productivity had a long history prior to their development and promotion by international agencies as measures of relative economic performance in the 1940s and 1950s, calculations of shares of world trade were a new development of the post-war years. While the Anglo-German trade rivalry of the late nineteenth century had given rise to a debate on British trade performance, it does not seem to have led to systematic comparative assessment. The League of Nations had initiated some major studies of long-run trends in trade, but these appeared only after the Second World War. This work led to academic assessments of long-run trade issues in the 1950s, especially concerning the role of industrialization in encouraging the growth of trade. This concern provided a major stimulus to the compilation of new data in this area.[50] Most important from a British perspective were the calculations of world manufacturing trade, derived from the OEEC *Statistical Bulletins* and first published in 1951. These were fed directly into the deliberations of the Working Party on Export Trends established in 1953, whose existence signalled growing worries at both official and ministerial level about Britain's trading performance, especially in comparison with West Germany. Successive reports of this Working Party supplied evidence to ministers of the decline in Britain's share of world trade in manufactures evident from 1950.[51]

The significance of this decline was disputed amongst the government's economic advisers. The Economic Section argued that unduly pessimistic conclusions were being drawn about Britain's competitive power from such figures. Its staff pointed out that the evidence suggested the decline had been occurring throughout the twentieth century; that the figure had risen in a necessarily temporary fashion in the 1940s because of the disablement of Germany and Japan; and further that it had no direct implications for the balance of payments.[52] Having said that, the Board of Trade stressed that the share of world trade was a measure of competitive performance, and that if total world trade expanded more slowly, Britain's declining share could translate directly into a balance of payments problem. The Board of Trade also pointed out that one of the key questions asked by the Working Party

[49] O'Hara, 'Use', pp. 11–27.

[50] League of Nations, *Industrialisation*; League of Nations, *Growth*; Cairncross, 'World Trade'; Tyszynski, 'World Trade'.

[51] TNA: PRO, CAB 134/848 Economic Policy Committee, memoranda, 1953; CAB 134/1228, 1958, 2555–7, Reports of Working Party on UK Export Trends, 1953 to 1959. For discussion of the Board of Trade's assessment of the export situation, see Milward, *European*, pp. 352–7.

[52] TNA: PRO, CAB 134/2555 Economic Section, 'Export performance and prospects' 26 March 1957.

was how far Britain's export problems were due to an adverse pattern of geographical or commodity composition, and that its analysis showed that these factors had a small and declining part in any explanation. In other words, in the view of the Board of Trade, Britain did seem to be suffering from a general loss of capacity to compete. The Board concluded, 'it would appear to be unwise for a country so dependent on its export trade not to pay attention to the danger signal afforded by a decline in its share of trade so widespread over different markets and commodities'.[53]

This kind of pessimistic analysis of Britain's declining share was carried by OEEC publications themselves, in the *Board of Trade Journal*, and found its way into the *Economic Surveys*.[54] In the 1954 *Economic Survey* a chart was published showing Britain's declining share, and this became a recurrent theme of later *Surveys*.[55] It was also referred to in the key statement of government economic policy in the 1950s, *The Economic Implications of Full Employment*, and was a theme of ministerial speeches by the mid-1950s.[56] This focus on a declining share of world trade was pressed by the Board of Trade precisely because they recognized its ready appeal to a wide audience.[57]

Overall, relative decline emerged in the early 1950s as a problem in terms of all four of the measures so far mentioned. But they did not all have equal prominence in debate. The declining share of world trade was taken up quite widely by officials, academics, and ministers because of the contemporary concern with the balance of payments. It was precisely the link between this latter problem and the trade share that the debate in the 1950s focused upon. However, the sharp improvement in the terms of trade after the end of the Korean War eased worries about competitiveness, even though payments problems continued to dominate economic policy debates because of the vulnerability of the pound to crises of confidence. Productivity emerged as a major dimension of debate because it could plausibly be linked to the trade share and payments problem: as the 1954 *Economic Survey* put it: 'The return of buyers' markets abroad has two particular implications for the home economy; productivity in industry must be increased, and costs and prices must be kept down.'[58] But more broadly, the focus on productivity built on an already established set of debates and concerns which could now be redeployed. Whereas in the 1940s the concern with increased productivity had been largely a matter of maximizing output from more or less given inputs, and for mainly short-run macroeconomic purposes, in the 1950s it increasingly came to be seen as the means to generate higher living standards in the long run. Productivity performance thus became both a promise and a threat to the emergent project of a sustained rise in such standards. As the comparative data on Britain's lagging

[53] TNA: PRO, CAB 134/2555 Board of Trade, 'Export performance and prospects' 27 May 1957, p. 3.

[54] UNECE, *Bulletin*, Nov. 1955; Board of Trade *Journal*, 27 March 1954, 18 Aug. 1956.

[55] Cmd.9108, para. 79; Cmd.9728, paras 44–5.

[56] Cmd.9725, para. 21; PRO, BT64/4896 'UK Productivity: Ministerial Briefs and Background papers' 1953–4.

[57] TNA: PRO CAB 134/2555 Working Party on Export Trends, minutes 30 May 1957.

[58] Cmd.9108, para. 106.

performance in this measure gained increasing prominence, it became perhaps the key calculation underpinning declinism. Productivity also seemed to have a propaganda aspect absent from such large abstractions as GDP and world trade. As the quotation from Thorneycroft given earlier suggests, productivity could be linked to individual attitudes and behaviour in a manner which was much more difficult for other measures of performance (see Chapter 7).

III

The Conservative relationship with declinism can best be seen against the background of two aspects of the party in the 1950s. First, as outlined in Chapter 1, the party adopted popular 'affluence' as central to its electoral appeal; second was the fact that the party was in government rather than in opposition. The emphasis on high mass consumption partly followed from the electoral strategy of 1951, which attacked Labour's austerity programme and its restrictions on personal consumption. This rhetoric was reinforced after the election victory of 1951 by the congenial international economic environment following the end of the Korean War, making possible a rapid rise in living standards from improvements in the terms of trade. When at the 1954 Conservative conference Butler held out the prospect of a doubling of the standard of living in twenty-five years, this rise was *not* seen as something that could be achieved only with great difficulty, or that required great changes in British society, but as something either already happening or readily attainable.[59] Macmillan, of course, emphasized the former aspect, when in 1957 he made his 'never had it so good' speech. But the reception of that speech made it clear that this line was not without problems for the Tory Party. As Ramsden notes, 'many in Parliament and the press were openly hostile to the arrival of mass affluence in the later 1950s, as the outcry that greeted "never had it so good" makes clear'. This hostility came not just from the supporters of the opposition, but also from Conservatives who regarded this pitch as a vulgar appeal to materialism, a view Macmillan went out of his way to respond to.[60]

As well as the ideological problem of popular affluence, the Conservative government also had to contend with the economic policy implications of this line of thought. In the early 1950s the rise in the standard of living via the terms of trade was a gift from the gods rather than being linked to policy. The Conservatives in this period did try to develop policies to encourage growth, focusing largely on encouraging competition domestically and reducing trade barriers. However, such a stance was far from universally approved by the party or its supporters, as Harris

[59] The key requirement for this ambition to be realized was maintaining the level of investment: hence the slogan of the 1954 Conference was 'Invest in Success': NUCUA, *74th Conference* (1954), pp. 65–6.

[60] For the context of this phrase, see Sampson, *Macmillan*, pp. 155–67. See also Horne, *Macmillan*, pp. 64–5, 146; Ramsden, 'Churchill', pp. 450, 455. Hornby, 'Conservative' suggests that between 1955 and 1957 prosperity was played down by the Conservatives in favour of emphasis on freedom and anti-inflation. Output was stagnant in those years.

emphasized. Freer trade raised all sorts of problems vis-à-vis the empire, while more competition at home in the form of anti-restrictive practices laws, and later over Retail Price Maintenance, created fierce arguments in Tory ranks.[61]

Apart from the emphasis on competition, the main advice from the economists on growth was the desirability of raising aggregate investment.[62] Aside from the question of how to achieve this, it was necessary to bear in mind that, for any given level of income, higher investment meant lower consumption. Attlee's government had been willing to make that sacrifice, but it was more difficult politically for the Tories to do this because of their emphasis on personal consumption as a key goal. (This emphasis was not without its ambiguities. Macmillan's housing boom of the early 1950s was presented as a boost to the 'consumption' of housing, though in national income terms, of course, it involved allocating more *investment* expenditure to housing.)

The Conservative commitment to the growth of personal consumption was not an acceptance of declinism. Initially, it was more or less the opposite—a vista offered of achievement, not failure. This initial stance in part reflected the favourable external forces at work in the early 1950s, alongside the resources made available by the reduction in military spending after the end of the Korean War. But whatever the pre-election rhetoric in 1950 and 1951, Conservative ministers from quite early in the 1950s knew that Britain's growth performance was falling behind that of other countries. This perspective was reflected in some government statements after the 1955 election.[63] But declinism was difficult for the Conservatives to publicly embrace, since they had been in power for some years and the problem could thus be seen as their responsibility. Hence, despite their growing awareness of evidence of Britain's relative deficiencies, they did not generally take the initiative in articulating declinist views. This didn't mean an absence of economic reform. For example, they did take some action in the area of manpower, where from 1956 a significant effort was made to reform technical education, and in 1957 the same concern was strongly reflected in the defence White Paper, with its call for a nuclear strategy, whose primary purpose was to free trained manpower for the civilian sector. (This concern continued in the early 1960s, most noticeably with the establishment of the Robbins committee on higher education in 1963.) Overall, up to the 1959 general election, while Labour made explicit use of the comparative data on Britain's poor economic performance, the Tories continued to stress the *positive* prospect of a doubling of the standard of living as long as they retained power.[64]

[61] Campbell, *Heath*, pp. 150–5; Harris, *Competition*; Mercer, 'Monopolies'. The Conservative Party's own inquiry into economic growth made much of the need for greater competition, but also argued that this should come via entry into the European Economic Community (EEC), rather than by any change in domestic rules on competition. Conservative Party, *Report*.

[62] For economists' views on how to increase growth, see Middleton, 'Economists'.

[63] Kynaston, *Family*, pp. 616–17.

[64] Cmd.9703; Cmnd.124, esp. paras. 40–6, 67, 72; Craig, *General Election Manifestos 1918–1966*, pp. 189, 197. The first league table of growth referred to at Conservative conferences was in 1961: NUCUA, *80th Conference* (1961), p. 90.

IV

How did Labour's relationship with declinism develop? Contrary to assertions that historically Labour has focused upon distribution rather than production, the issue of economic efficiency was an important part of the party's policy agenda in the 1950s. Industrial efficiency and especially labour productivity had become particularly important in the Attlee years, in the context of the compelling need to expand output with a constrained workforce and capital stock. However, the emphasis on industrial modernization in the 1940s was not based, primarily, on a belief in the secular decline of the British economy. The arrival of declinism at the centre of Labour's agenda can be registered by two milestone publications by the party: that of *Plan for Progress* in 1958, and, more importantly, of *Signposts for the Sixties* in 1961. The production of these documents originated from the 1955 election defeat, and the policy reviews that followed.[65]

The *Plan for Progress* was produced in 1958 for discussion at that year's party conference, and has some notable features.[66] It is the first Labour Party document to contain comparative data on Britain's economic performance, showing the country's poor relative performance in respect of both the growth of industrial production (1953–7), and cost of living indices. The starting point of the document was the slow growth of industrial production since 1955, and it set out more clearly than any of the party's previously published documents why expansion deserved its place at the top of the agenda. The aims were to provide employment, to meet the demand for a higher standard of living, and to strengthen Britain's international position. At the 1958 conference Wilson introduced the document with a speech which emphasized the *short-run* stagnation of the economy, but suggested that Labour's approach would also deal with *long-run* weaknesses, not least the weakness of the pound as an international currency.[67] This was certainly not full-blown declinism, though many of the strands were there.

The response to the document and to Wilson's speech was both supportive and diversionary. While there was little overt opposition, speakers tended to pick up on one particular theme rather than on the overall expansionary rhetoric. Some focused on the idea of growth as a solution to unemployment, which, in its regional variant especially, was currently re-entering the domain of economic problems exercising both government and opposition. The broad implications of Wilson's rhetoric were most explicitly endorsed by a key figure on the Right of the party, Roy Jenkins. He deployed it to support standard revisionist positions, such as the need not to quarrel over 'irrelevant' issues such as public ownership, and the need for income restraint. Interestingly, he also linked this rhetoric to key themes of Crosland's *The Future of Socialism*, by referring to the expansionist position

[65] More detail on evolution of Labour's debates in this period in Tomlinson, 'Inventing Decline'.

[66] LPA, Research Department memorandum, RE155, Control of industry study group, draft report, April 1957.

[67] Labour Party, *Annual Conference Report 1958*, pp. 141–6; Wilson's position at this time is summarized in his Fabian pamphlet of the previous year, which focused on the government's sacrifice of production to the fight against inflation: *Post-war*.

helping to free Labour from its association, 'with drabness, with rationing, and with restriction'.[68]

Prior to the 1959 election, then, many of the themes of declinism had been articulated in Labour documents and speeches. The possibility of a rapprochement between the revisionists and the left wing can be seen in the position taken by people such as Jenkins. But, on the evidence of conference discussions at least, declinism was not widely embraced within the party. It took the shock of the loss of the 1959 election to bring that about.

The key document showing this shift was *Signposts for the Sixties* (1961). This set Britain's economic performance in an explicitly comparative context, contrasting unfavourably the country's share of world trade and growth of industrial production with that of other Western European countries. The first symptom of decline was said to be 'private affluence and public squalor' a term deployed by Galbraith in his much-cited *Affluent Society.* The second was the 'growth of new forms of privilege and the rapid concentration of economic power which has taken place since 1951'. Thus decline was not only registered by the now widely available comparative economic statistics, but also linked directly to the 'functionless shareholder' analysis deployed in *Industry and Society*, another key document from the policy review.[69]

By 1961 declinist rhetoric had captured the high ground of Labour politics. This capture represented a kind of compromise between revisionist and left-wing positions. For revisionists declinism was attractive because it meant an acceptance by the party that the electorate's changing character had to be responded to, in particular its increasing affluence. Declinism suggested the need to embrace affluence as a desirable feature of British society, a shift in position which revisionists had long sought to extract from the left wing. Secondly, declinism seemed to offer an escape from the perceived sterilities of the debate over public ownership.

But declinism was not without its difficulties, at least for some revisionists. In particular, it meant giving priority to increasing economic growth which was seen, by Crosland especially, as both unnecessary and undesirable. In 1956 in *The Future of Socialism* he had argued that while growth was desirable, the current level 'may be almost sufficient for all reasonable purposes', and explicitly attacked those who would give too high a priority to raising the rate of growth on the basis of unfavourable international comparisons.[70]

But Crosland's position seems to have changed as his modernization rhetoric, which emphasized 'a dogged resistance to change' as the defining British characteristic, was extended to embrace the economy, so that by 1960 he could claim that 'the performance of the economy, and the efficiency of the average enterprise, are both shameful by international standards'. Also, declinism pushed aside equality as the key objective of Labour policy, by offering more to the poor through growth rather than a more egalitarian distribution of income.[71]

[68] *Annual Conference Report 1958*, pp. 157–9; Crosland, *Future*.

[69] Labour Party, *Signposts*, p. 9; Labour Party, *Industry.*

[70] Crosland, *Future*, pp. 379–80.

[71] Crosland, 'On the Left'; Crosland, 'On Economic Growth', pp. 65–8.

For the Left declinism seemed to offer an economic programme, where one had been so strikingly absent in the 1950s, without any explicit retreat on public ownership. In addition, it provided a rich vein of egalitarian rhetoric for attacking parasitism in the name of efficiency. However, it glossed over the whole issue of who controlled industry which had been the starting point of the rows over public ownership that had accompanied the policy reviews, especially over *Industry and Society*. More broadly, the diagnosis of decline underpinned Labour's focus on modernization, a term which was put at the centre of Labour's appeal to the electorate, especially after Wilson became leader of the party in 1963.

This modernization rhetoric was most famously expressed by Wilson at the 1963 Scarborough conference, when he talked of the need to promote the 'white heat of technology', to embrace technical change, in order to expand the economy. This was not just a rhetorical flourish, but reflected a long period of development in Labour ranks of what has been called a 'centre-left technocratic' agenda, with Wilson playing a key role.[72] In the 1950s Wilson, at Gaitskell's behest, had been drawn into extended discussions on science and technology policy, notably with the Nobel Prize-winning physicist, Patrick Blackett, and this had pushed his already existing enthusiasm for 'supply-side socialism' in an even more technocratic direction. (In power, Wilson's commitment to these ideas was most evident in the creation of a very powerful Ministry of Technology.)[73]

But while rooted in very specific understandings of the economy and the sources of economic growth, this focus on modernization was also very much an electoral strategy. Like almost all Labour leaders, Wilson recognized that the key electoral issue was not whether the party should seek to attract the support of parts of the middle classes, but on which part attention should be focused. His answer was the white-collar, technically competent salariat, seen as those who most embodied the computer technologies and the automation that the technocrats thought would define the future.

This positive appeal was linked to well-established declinist themes, not least the notion that Britain's economic decline had been caused by the country's rulers being dominated by an anti-technological dilettantism.[74] Labour's modernization promised new rulers who would understand and embrace these new technologies, a stance which the Conservatives were portrayed as wholly unfitted for. Labour's modernization narrative embraced a strong commitment to economic planning. But this term, always ambiguous, needs to contextualized with care. While ideas of modernization dominant in Britain from the 1960s into the early 1970s were usually linked with talk of planning (even under the Conservatives), this term, while broadly suggesting a greater role for government, is best understood to refer to something both much more and much less than a full-blown national economic 'plan'. Rather, it suggested the need for a new sense of national purpose; a 'will to

[72] Favretto, '"Wilsonism"'. [73] Edgerton, *Warfare*, pp. 230–69.

[74] This genre of declinism is best represented by Thomas, *Establishment*, many of whose contributors were Labour supporters (and many of whom later became right-wing declinists): Harvie, 'Liturgies', p. 20.

modernize'. Wilson epitomized this with his recurrent emphasis on 'purpose'; his collection of speeches for the early 1960s years was entitled *Purpose in Politics*.[75] As we shall see, Conservative planning for modernization had very similar connotations.

V

Despite the great success of the Conservatives in the 1959 election, they were soon put on the defensive by Labour's claims about the failings of the economy. According to Samuel Brittan, 1960 was the year which saw the beginning of the 'great reappraisal' of British economic policy, as a post-election 'stop' succeeded the pre-election boom and another period of slow growth, as had characterized the 1956–8 period, threatened.[76]

This great reappraisal was encouraged and underpinned by a number of forces. There was pressure from the Conservatives' friends as well as their political enemies, notably when the Federation of British Industries, Britain's biggest employer's organization, took up the modernization issue. This came to a head in October 1960, when the Federation of British Industry (FBI) conference publicly pressed for a more active growth policy.[77] There was pressure from within the government machine, including the Treasury, where the persistent failure to combine faster growth with a satisfactory balance of payments suggested the need for a new departure. The Chief Economic Adviser to the government noted in his diary in January 1961, 'One thing that would be interesting is to look at work on a policy for growth *which has been anathema since about 1951*'.[78] Also important were the administrative pressures for the government to take a more active role in at least analysing economic trends, especially because of the desire to plan and control public spending more effectively.[79]

But, above all, the Conservatives' embracing of declinism and the need for them to present themselves as the party of modernization were based on an understanding of the mood amongst the electorate, a mood the Conservatives had increasingly come to grasp more effectively through their use of public opinion polls. These polls suggested that support for the party relied heavily on their promise to deliver prosperity, and doubts about their competence to do so underpinned their electoral problems in 1961 to 1963.[80]

This electoral polling suggests that the narrative of decline had gained wide resonance amongst the public, though *direct* evidence of support for this belief is hard to come by. No contemporary polling organization seems to have used the precise term in framing its questionnaires, the closest being where respondents were asked:

[75] Wilson, *Purpose*.

[76] Brittan, *Treasury*, pp. 204–45; Pemberton, *Policy*, p. 46.

[77] Pemberton, *Policy*, pp. 66–7.

[78] Cairncross, *Roberthall*, pp. 256–7, emphasis added; on the Treasury more generally, Pemberton, *Policy*, pp. 69–76.

[79] A new Public Expenditure Survey Committee (PESC) system was introduced in 1961, which planned public spending in relation to prospective future resources.

[80] Taylor, '"Record"'.

'Is Britain nowadays moving towards prosperity, or away from prosperity?', the pessimistic answer being given by 53 per cent (with 26 per cent saying 'towards' and 21 per cent don't knows) in March 1963.[81] So, generally, we can only infer public perceptions from indirect evidence.

The enormous breadth of journalistic declinist commentary can be seen as an important part of the mechanism for spreading declinism, and it is difficult to believe that its scale would have been sustained without finding an accepting audience (as well as some dissentients).[82] Similarly, not only were there many books about decline, but some of these sold very well indeed, with Shonfield's *Stagnant Society* selling 60,000. This book was a 'Penguin Special', part of a wide-ranging series which up until 1961 covered especially issues of foreign affairs, but thereafter was particularly strong on critical 'state-of-the-nation' works, including Penguin's 'What's Wrong with Britain?' series (though Shanks's *British Economic Policy Since the War* was published by Penguin in 1958). No doubt much of this literature was both written by and sold to a particular segment—those on the Left—but its existence does suggest something about the broader public appetites of the period, at least the appetites of the book-buying public.[83] As Blackburn has argued, this literature for a while embodied a 'conventional wisdom' about the failings of the British economy which was supported by lots of Conservatives as well as many in the Labour Party; it was, to a considerable degree, a 'consensual' narrative.[84]

As suggested already, the Conservatives believed by the early 1960s that 'declinist' notions *had* impacted upon the electorate, and it was in response to this understanding that modernization to reverse 'decline' and deliver faster growth became their watchword.

Modernity and modernization are of course highly ambiguous terms. It has been persuasively argued that there was a drive for modernity in Britain in a broad sense from the late 1950s, including the beginnings of modernizing legislation on 'moral' issues by the Conservatives in the run-up to the 1959 election.[85] Many of the changes associated with the 'swinging sixties' find their roots at the end of the previous decade.[86] Equally, economic 'modernization' always has ambiguity attached; above all, how is it to be achieved: by unleashing market forces, or harnessing the power of the state?

In the Conservative party of the early 1960s there were many who believed that the first of these would be the route to faster growth. The party's Policy Committee on Economic Growth (chaired by Paul Chambers of Imperial Chemical Industries), which reported in 1962, focused much of its attention on the shortcomings of the nationalized industries, and called for cuts to industrial subsidies and more competition.[87] It also argued that 'Planning in the sense of a controlled economy can

[81] Gallup, *International*, p. 677; this question seems to have been a one-off, though there were many others asking something about 'prosperity'.

[82] Fairlie, 'Comforts'.

[83] Grant, 'Historians'.

[84] Blackburn, 'Penguin Specials', pp. 159–61, 166–76.

[85] Jarvis, *Conservatives*, p. 1.

[86] Kynaston, *Modernity Britain*.

[87] Conservative Party, *Report*. Greater competition was seen as a key benefit of the hoped-for entry into the EEC, and this was emphasized rather than any change in domestic rules on competition.

only impede growth. The emphasis should, on the contrary, be on the further reduction of controls which impede the conduct of business in the most efficient way.' However, it went on to suggest, 'Planning, in the sense of some machinery to enable plans to be concerted and establish a consensus of aim at higher rate of growth, may be useful'.[88]

Macmillan was inclined to give planning a rather less grudging place in modernization. When he came to offer his agenda to the Cabinet in 1962, he invoked his own 1930s book, *The Middle Way*, to suggest a more robust critique of the working of market forces than many Conservatives were comfortable with.[89] This was a theme some in the party supported: in early 1961 a Research Department memorandum had argued that 'we have virtually exhausted the neo-liberal seam in economic policy. The existing armoury of economic weapons... is admittedly deficient.... Yet... we have done nothing visibly to examine the problems and search for new ones.'[90] It is this desire to present modernization as embodying novelty and a distinctive departure from existing policies that is most important in understanding the new policy agenda. The amount of 'planning' involved was very limited; it involved mainly the creation of the National Economic Development Council (NEDC) (and Office) and a National Incomes Commission, neither of which deserved to be treated as major expansions of state intervention. Indeed, the high level of publicity given to these 'modernizing' bodies overshadowed less high-profile but at least potentially more significant changes in contemporary economic policies, such as on tax and the labour market.[91]

The *active* pursuit of higher economic growth via modernization by the Conservatives implicitly meant an acceptance of declinism—only if there was a problem in achieving the desired growth rate with existing policies were the claims about the need for a significant change of direction justified. There was a strong presentational and 'educational' element involved in this modernization narrative. The complexity of the government's attitude is well summarized by two quotations from the Chancellor of the Exchequer when discussing the new initiative on growth and the creation of the National Economic Development Office (NEDO). First,

> There appeared to be a growing weight of public opinion that the economic direction of the country suffered from the lack of suitable machinery for long-term forecasting. He hoped that the machinery he had in mind would be of value in creating a climate of opinion in which the economic facts of the country were better understood.[92]

The following year he suggested that the 'positive idea of growth is a valuable means of presenting many politically difficult decisions, emphasising that such decisions are a means to enrich people and not to impoverish them'. The 'politically

88 Conservative Party, *Report*, p. 5.

89 TNA: PRO PREM11/3930, 'Remarks made by PM at Cabinet on 28 May 1962' 28 May 1962; Ramsden, *Winds of Change*, pp. 158–73. The previous year he had told his Chancellor of the Exchequer, 'I think we could devise something on the French basis which could be Conservative or "Middle Way" planning and would dish the Whigs': TNA: PRO PREM 11/3294 Macmillan to Selwyn Lloyd 14 August 1961.

90 Horne, *Macmillan*, p. 347.

91 Pemberton, *Policy*, pp. 74–5.

92 TNA: PRO, CAB 134/1689 Economic Policy Committee, minutes 10 May 1961.

difficult decisions' related to the Treasury concern to restrict the growth of public spending and secure an incomes policy.[93]

These highly political calculations were to a considerable extent reactive to shifts in the political climate, but were underpinned by the kind of changes in the ways of calculating economic performance already outlined. The supply of comparative economic data was very important. As a somewhat disgruntled senior civil servant (and economist) remarked in 1961, 'If it were not for the activities on an international scale of the economic statisticians, it is doubtful whether the present agitation would be anything like as noisy'.[94] Alongside this international data was the increasing volume of other evidence of Britain's problems which ministers had long had brought to their attention. Maudling at the Board of Trade, for example, had clearly spelt out the many failings of British business in a memorandum to Macmillan in 1960.[95] These international comparisons and evidence of British failings were the staple of the the economic journalists, who produced so much of the more popular declinist literature of this period—from the pioneering work of Shonfield in 1958 through to that of Shanks and Macrae over the next few years.[96]

The Conservatives lost the1964 election (albeit marginally), but the theme of modernization continued to be at the core of their politics, symbolized by the election of the modernizer, Edward Heath, as the new leader in 1965. Heath was 'modern, meritocratic, class-less, exuding an air of competence', and his election reinforced the party's commitment to a 'reformist and modernizing agenda'.[97] This posture was not without its difficulties, not least because of the ambiguities of 'modernization'. However, as Evans and Taylor argue, whatever the Conservative Party's unsuitability for bearing the gospel of modernization, it was a message it could not ignore. 'Heath projected himself as the face of Conservative modernisation but found... that while there was a broader agreement on the need for modernisation specific proposals generated massive opposition.'[98]

Heath's own political career as leader of the Conservatives illustrates the tensions of 'modernization'. In the 1970 general election the Conservatives offered a declinist analysis with a modernizing agenda. The declinism was clear:

> Our economy has expanded more slowly than that of any other comparable country in the world. Almost everywhere in Western Europe and North America the standard of living grows faster than in Britain. International experts are predicting that if these trends are allowed to continue Britain will soon be the poorest major country in the West.[99]

[93] TNA: PRO, CAB 134/1696 Economic Policy Committee, 'Economic growth', 28 June 1962. On incomes policy, see Jones, *Wages*, ch. 5. Conservative enthusiasm for an incomes policy was muted in the early 1950s because the party's slim parliamentary majority led to the avoidance of policies which might antagonize the trade unions. The electoral successes of 1955 and 1959 reduced this concern.

[94] TNA: PRO, PREM 11/2973, correspondence with Roy Harrod; TNA: PRO, T230/579, B. Hopkin to P. Vinter, 5 June 1961.

[95] Porter, 'Downhill', p. 25.

[96] Macrae, *Sunshades*; Shanks, *Stagnant*; Shonfield, *British*. See also Craig, *General Election Manifestos 1918–1966*, pp. 216–18.

[97] Taylor, '"Record"', p. 103.

[98] Evans and Taylor, *Salisbury*, p. 131.

[99] Craig, *General Election Manifestos 1959–1987*, p. 114.

The answer to this decline was a modernizing agenda, with a distinctly more free market tone than that put forward by Macmillan and the modernizers of the early 1960s. An increase in 'planning' did not figure in a programme associated with 'Selsdon Man', represented (at least by his opponents) as an advocate of more competition as the sovereign route to better economic performance. In truth the message of 1970 was more ambiguous than these hostile assessments suggested, but there is no doubt that the tide of anti-statism, always strong amongst the Conservative rank and file, was a growing influence in the party. This meant that the reversal of the Conservative government's policy in 1972, which combined reflation and interventionism, can be seen in retrospect as the last gasp of early 1960s-style 'modernization'.[100] The insurgent pro-market politicians in the party now eschewed the word, it connoting too much, in their view, of the failed statist policies of the past.

For all the reasons outlined, a powerful and distinct narrative of declinism rose to prominence in the 1950s and early 1960s, and it underpinned the rhetoric of modernization which dominated the politics of the 1960s and early 1970s. Declinism was thereafter reinvented in relation to a new, radical Right, politics. As a result, 'modernization' lost most of the connotations it had acquired when taken up by the Labour Party, and later by the Conservatives under Macmillan, Home, and Heath. Modernization now meant a wholesale assault on post-war economic institutions and policies; above all, it meant a project of 'rolling back the state'—the subject of the next chapter.

[100] This policy reversal crucially included the abandonment of a fixed exchange rate, rightly seen as a crucial part of the underpinnings of the post-war settlement: Blackaby, 'Narrative', pp. 62–76.

3

Rolling Back the State

Public expenditure was 'at the heart of Britain's economic difficulties' according to the new Thatcher government's White Paper on the topic in 1979.[1] This echoed the broader claim in the 1979 election manifesto that Labour 'by enlarging the role of the state and diminishing the role of the individual, [have] crippled the enterprise and effort on which a prosperous country with improving social services depends'.[2] In this way the Conservatives stressed their adherence to a key part of the anti-state narrative which had been rapidly growing in prominence since the mid-1970s, though of course it was given much greater political impetus by the accession to the Conservative party leadership of Margaret Thatcher in 1975, and the party's election victory of 1979. Scepticism about public expenditure and its growth had always been an element in Conservative politics, but historically views had been mixed, part of a complex and evolving attitude to the role of the state in the ideology of modern Conservatism.[3] But by the end of the 1970s 'rolling back the state', including especially cutting spending, had come to have a defining role in Conservative politics that it hadn't had since the crisis of 1931 or the 'Geddes Axe' years after World War One.[4]

Much of the Conservative anti-statism of the 1970s was ultimately grounded in a moral story about the damage inflicted on individual conduct by excessive growth of the state, and the consequent erosion of personal responsibility. This impetus was particularly evident in the framing of social policy, but it can justifiably be seen as foundational for Thatcherite ideology as a whole.[5] This underpinning explains why so much of 'Thatcherism' between 1975 and 1979 was 'defined more by what it was against than by a specific set of policies'.[6] The focus of this chapter is on how this ideological positioning played out in economic policy and the 'rolling back the state' narrative.

The immediate background to the rise of this narrative lies in the responses to the 'stagflationary' effects of the Organization of Petroleum Exporting Countries (OPEC) crisis of 1973/4, when the quadrupling of the oil price unleashed both

[1] Cmnd 7746, p. 1. But note that despite the strength of this assertion, the White Paper proposed only to stabilize public spending in volume terms, the cuts proposed being only relative to the previous government's plans; statement by John Biffen, Financial Secretary to the Treasury, *Hansard* (Commons) vol. 972, cols 1450–63, 1 November 1979.

[2] Craig, *British General Election Manifestos 1959–1987*, pp. 267–8.

[3] Green, *Ideologies*, pp. 240–79.

[4] Geddes was the most radical cutting exercise in modern Britain: Hood and Himaz, 'UK Geddes Axe'. For an important conceptualization of these issues, Offer, 'Why?'

[5] Sutcliffe-Braithwaite, 'Neoliberalism'.

[6] Saunders, 'Thatcherism'.

inflationary and deflationary effects on oil-importing countries like Britain. The Labour government of 1974 had great difficulties in dealing with the serious problems posed for macroeconomic management by this crisis, but more broadly it presented a major challenge to social democracy and its understanding of the effects of state activity. This put much of the Left on the defensive in the 1970s, while the Right was able to go on the attack, taking advantage of the crisis to propagate a version of post-war Britain and its economic performance, and use this to underpin the electoral victory of 1979. Central to this narrative was connecting the specific problems of the 1970s (not least inflation) to a *right-wing* version of the 'declinism' which the Centre-Left had invented from the late 1950s (see Chapter 2), which recast the whole of Britain's economic history since 1945 as a story of 'government failure'.

The *political* strength of Thatcherite attitudes to the state lay not only in taking advantage of the events of the 1970s by linking them to a narrative of long-run decline. It also drew on the long-standing hostility to the post-war settlement in the rank and file of the Conservative party.[7] As the most acute of historians of the party has argued, 'Thatcher*ism* existed long before Margaret Thatcher became leader of the Conservative party, and 1975 was as much the occasion as the cause of the "Thatcherite Revolution"'.[8] Thatcher was the first leader of the party who came to wholeheartedly reject the post-war consensus.

In office after the 1979 victory, the new government was able to pursue many of the aspects of 'rolling back the state' that it had committed to in Opposition. But translating an anti-state narrative into effective policy action ran up against considerable obstacles. While some elements of the anti-state agenda were attained, others were aborted or deflected, and overall important components of that 'rolling-back' proved far more difficult to achieve than 'Thatcherite' ideologues had hoped, or the general election victories of the Conservatives might have suggested.

This chapter begins with the economic crisis of the 1970s, OPEC 1 and Labour's responses, and the broader ideological challenge presented to social democracy by the economic problems of the mid-1970s. The second section looks at the broad growth of anti-state notions amongst a variety of elements in 1970s Britain, including academics, journalists, and think tanks, and how these notions related to the Conservative Party's developing positions. The third section looks in a more focused fashion at the development of the 'rolling back the state' policy agenda as applied to public spending after 1979. The fourth section looks more broadly at the successes and failures of the attempt to roll back the state down to the end of the Conservative government in 1997. In conclusion, the final section looks at the links between the Conservatives' agenda and public opinion.

I

The 1970s did not see a serious crisis of *output*. The recession of 1974/5 was a mild one in comparison with either those of the interwar period, or the three that have

[7] Moore, *Thatcher*, p. 56. [8] Green, *Ideologies*, p. 238.

occurred since.[9] Average growth of GDP during that decade was little different from preceding or succeeding periods, though there were sharp cyclical movements, involving a period of clearly unsustainable expansion in 1972–4, followed by a short-lived recession.[10] Of course, to contemporaries the recession was a major shock after twenty-five years of almost uninterrupted expansion, which had come to be assumed to be the 'new normal'. Contemporaries were also much exercised by the rise in unemployment. This passed the one million mark in 1972, stimulating a policy'U-turn, and the recurrence of that figure in 1975 was also a major basis of criticism of the Labour government's policies.[11]

The key distinguishing economic events in the crisis of the 1970s were twofold. First, the *combination* of higher unemployment with much higher inflation. Most of the 'Golden Age' of the 1950s and 1960s had seen inflation running at between 2 and 3 per cent per annum, but after the 1967 devaluation there was a notable upward shift, accelerating in the boom of the early 1970s, before reaching a peak at 26 per cent in 1975. Second was the growth in the public sector deficit, driven largely by the automatic stabilizers responding to the recession. Again, the contrast with the Golden Age was stark. In those good years there was normally a public sector current account surplus, with an overall deficit typically around 2 per cent of GDP, whereas in the 1970s Public Sector Net Borrowing (PSNB) peaked at 6.7 per cent (the Public Sector Borrowing Requirement (PSBR), the figure used at the time, peaked at 9.6 per cent). Note, however, that the debt: GDP ratio declined in the 1970s, largely as a result of inflation reducing the value of outstanding debt.[12]

The Labour government was elected with a majority of just three in the second, October, general election of 1974. The context was the breakdown in industrial relations caused by conflict over the Conservatives' incomes policy which was part of the post U-turn policy package. This had led to a miners' strike and the imposition of a three-day working week to reduce electricity consumption. The key Labour policy to attempt to resolve the tension between unions and government was the Social Contract, which sought to bargain policies desired by the unions against their acceptance of wage restraint. No formal agreement on such restraint was achieved until union leaders 'stared into the abyss' of accelerating inflation in 1975, when a deal was agreed to limit wage rises to £6 per week.[13]

The macroeconomic context which formed Labour's inheritance was one of accelerating inflation brought about by the expansionary policies of the Conservative government (only reversed in November 1973) combined with a world commodity price boom and the OPEC 1 oil price rise.[14] Domestically, the most important legacies from the previous administration were extraordinarily rapid monetary growth of 20–30 per cent per annum, and the pay threshold system. This latter guaranteed pay increases to match inflation, and thereby built

[9] Dow, *Major*, pp. 14–15; Faccini and Hackworth, 'Changes'.

[10] Artis and Cobham, 'Background'.

[11] And in 1979 the Conservatives famously deployed 'Labour isn't working' as a major slogan at the centre of their election campaign.

[12] Allsopp, 'Macroeconomic'; Office for National Statistics (ONS) database.

[13] Ormerod, 'Incomes'.

[14] Britton, *Macroeconomic*, pp. 13–17.

in a mechanism which made reducing inflation very much harder. While some have seen maintaining the threshold policy as the major error of the new government, any repudiation would have been directly contrary to Labour's desire to achieve a rapport with the trade unions.[15]

Almost from the beginning of its period of office Labour started to shift the focus of its macroeconomic policy from reducing unemployment to combating inflation. Whilst the fiscal stance was broadly neutral in 1974, by the budget of Spring 1975 the Chancellor, Denis Healey, was explicitly rejecting the possibility of an expansionary fiscal policy to expand employment:

> I fully understand why I am being urged by so many friends both inside and outside the House to treat unemployment as the central problem and to stimulate a further growth in home consumption, public or private, so as to start getting the rate of unemployment down as fast as possible. I do not believe it would be wise to follow this advice today.... I cannot afford to increase demand further today when 5p in every pound we spend at home has been provided by our creditors abroad and inflation is running at its current rate.[16]

This was against the background of the growth of public borrowing resulting from the automatic stabilizers. To combat this, Healey moved to cut spending, and, very importantly, introduced a new policy of 'cash limits', which meant departmental budgets were no longer automatically increased in line with inflation, but were fixed in monetary terms. This had a big impact on spending, with cuts falling particularly heavily on capital items, especially housebuilding.[17]

By late 1975/early 1976 the government appeared to have got a grip on the crisis. The rate of inflation and the PSBR were falling and monetary growth was diminishing, though unemployment was still rising.[18] But despite these improvements, the exchange rate, which had been falling since the pound had been floated in June 1972, continued to decline and did so at an accelerated rate from March 1976. This acceleration was partly stimulated by a government desire to see a further fall to improve competitiveness, but quickly got out of control. It was this fall which drove the government to seek a loan from the International Monetary Fund (IMF), and a long autumn of political dispute resulted over the terms of the deal to be agreed in return for borrowing from the Fund.[19]

The negotiations with the IMF have formed a key aspect of most accounts of the Labour government's period in office. In part this emphasis rightly reflects the political traumas which accompanied these negotiations, which sharply divided opinion in Labour circles and brought the party to a crisis point. Yet in terms of the impact on the trajectory of the economy the loan deal is of limited importance (see Figure 3.1). The myth that it was only after the IMF deal that public spending was seriously cut has become entrenched in many accounts of the 1970s. In some cases this narrative is based on obvious political partisanship, such as in the official biography

[15] Artis and Cobham, 'Summary', pp. 269–70.
[16] *Hansard*, (Commons), vol. 890 col. 282, 15 April 1975.
[17] Burk and Cairncross, *'Goodbye'*, pp. 184–8. [18] Burk and Cairncross, *'Goodbye'*, p. 215.
[19] Artis and Cobham, 'Background', pp. 12–14; Britton, *Macroeconomic*, pp. 28–33.

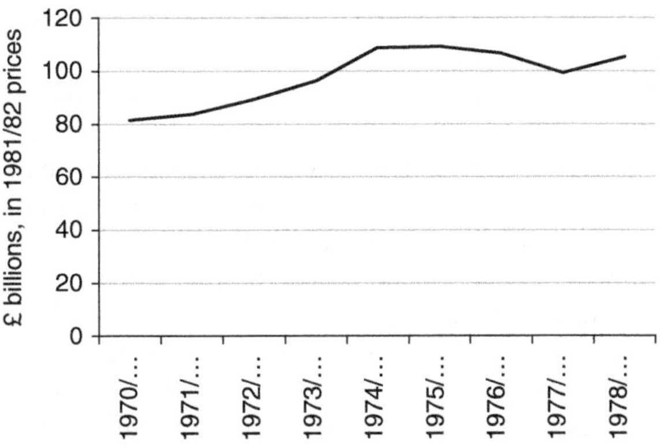

Figure 3.1 Public expenditure, 1970–9
Source: ONS database.

of Thatcher.[20] But in other cases there seems to be no such obvious motive for ignoring the historical evidence.[21] In fact, as already noted, the stance of policy had been tightening since 1975, with public spending cuts and the stabilization of PSBR: public spending peaked before the deal had come into effect. Monetary targeting also pre-dates this episode.[22] The significance of the loan deal was, more than anything, to give a 'seal of approval' from the IMF to the government.[23]

In the event, public spending fell faster than envisaged by the deal, largely as a result of the cash limits system; 1976/7 and 1977/8 turned out to be the only years in post-war Britain after the demobilization of the late 1940s that saw a significant fall in public spending. Only half the offered loan was taken up. The settlement of the discussions with the IMF initiated a notable rally in the exchange rate, aided by the discovery and exploitation of North Sea oil. Through 1977 and well into 1978 most of the evidence suggested an improving economy, with output expanding, unemployment and inflation falling, and the balance of payments improving. Policy helped support this by some fiscal loosening.[24]

But the problem of industrial relations and wage inflation continued. The £6 agreement had been followed in 1976 by an agreement to limit increases to 5 per cent, and the following year the figure was 10 per cent. But in 1978 the government sought to reduce inflation further by a 5 per cent agreement, which was not accepted by the Trades Union Congress. In the autumn of 1978 a strike at Ford led to a 16.5 per cent agreement. In response, the government sought to impose sanctions on the Ford Company but was defeated in the House of Commons. The impact of the 5 per cent ceiling thereafter fell almost entirely on the public sector, where government controlled the budgets. This meant, with inflation running at 8–10 per cent, that low-paid public sector workers faced a further fall in their real wages, and it was

20 Moore, *Thatcher*, p. 338. 21 Thompson, 'Thatcherite', p. 49.
22 Ludlam, 'Gnomes'; Needham, 'Britain's'.
23 Burk and Cairncross, *'Goodbye'*, pp. 225–6; Needham, '"Goodbye"?'
24 Artis and Cobham, 'Summary'.

resistance to these cuts which underpinned the 'Winter of Discontent' of 1978/9, and the subsequent Conservative election victory.[25]

Up until 1978 the Labour government could be said to have managed to overcome with some success a combination of an appalling economic legacy and external buffeting. But even if such a verdict on the immediate policy position is apt, the crisis exposed major problems for the party. At the most pragmatic level it exposed the fragility of the links between the party and the unions, which were crucial to its claim to be a governing party; the claim that it alone could offer a peaceful resolution of industrial conflict. Some saw this breakdown of relations as fundamentally undermining 'the forward march of Labour'.[26]

At a more ideological and strategic level the crisis was profound because by focusing so much on the level of public spending (especially around the IMF conflict) it laid bare a core tension in British social democracy as it had developed from the 1950s. In his key doctrinal text, *The Future of Socialism*, Anthony Crosland had attacked the notion that public ownership was the key to socialist advance, and instead argued that an aim, greater equality, should be the defining feature of socialist politics. In pursuing this aim, he saw public spending as crucial.[27] As a result of the subsequent capture of the party leadership by those who, in effect, sided with Crosland on this matter, 'the policy of public spending through the agencies of the existing state now reached its apogee as the distinguishing mark of reformist socialism, because it no longer shared place with the earlier demands for the structural transformation of society'.[28]

Public spending did indeed expand unprecedentedly rapidly under the Labour government of 1964 (though the upsurge began in the last years of the previous administration). But even during that government there was questioning within party circles of how far such spending could continue to expand. The key problem, identified by Crosland, was that higher spending would only be politically sustainable if it was pursued on the back of a reasonably fast-growing economy; otherwise the higher taxes required would stimulate opposition, including amongst Labour's own supporters.[29]

By the early 1970s Crosland was reflecting on these problems, by reiterating his belief that public spending was crucial to social democracy, but stressing the growing constraints. In the wake of OPEC 1 he emphasized that resistance to higher taxes in a slow-growing economy was now showing itself in higher inflation, and proponents of higher spending needed to be hard-headed about which areas of spending increase should be prioritized to achieve egalitarian goals.[30]

Given this background it is unsurprising that in the debates about public spending surrounding the 1976 IMF deal Crosland emerged as a leading resister to the scale of cuts initially proposed, even if eventually he gave way.[31] But by then support for his position was eroding fast, as the arguments for higher spending as a key aim

[25] Brown, 'Industrial'; Hay, 'Narrating'.
[26] Hobsbawm, 'Forward'.
[27] Crosland, *Future*, pp. 51–3, 62.
[28] Crouch, 'Place', p. 165.
[29] Whiting, *Labour*, pp. 214–58.
[30] Crosland, *Socialism*, pp. 26, 55–6.
[31] Burk and Cairncross, *'Goodbye'*, pp. 85–9, 98–107; Jeffreys, *Crosland*, pp. 179–86.

of Labour policy weakened even in its own ranks. A particularly striking example of this was an interview given by Roy Jenkins, the Labour Home Secretary, in February 1976, when he claimed that public expenditure had increased rapidly to reach 60 per cent of GDP. At this level, he asserted, Britain was approaching the 'frontiers of social democracy' where the ability to 'maintain a plural society with adequate freedom of choice' would be threatened.[32]

This apocalyptic view, based on the same figure for the scale of public spending, was strongly endorsed in an article by Milton Friedman later that same year.[33] It says a great deal about the febrile atmosphere of these years that the 60 per cent figure was based on a variety of statistical mis-specifications, and when Britain's official data was brought in line with new international conventions in 1977 the figure fell to 45 per cent.[34] Nevertheless, a Labour government cutting spending was now politically acceptable to a degree previously absent. The political calculation underlying that shift is nicely evidenced by Healey's budget of 1976, which alongside putting forward a programme of expenditure cuts suggested a bargain with the trade unions in which they reined in their wage demands in exchange for tax cuts. Clearly, this proffered bargain suggested the government's willingness to reduce the 'social wage' as a response to tax resistance amongst its working-class supporters.

In sum, in the crisis of the 1970s, the core notion of British social democracy, that a prosperous and expanding industrial economy would provide the resources for a relatively painless expansion of publicly funded social welfare, came under severe challenge. The perception of a tax revolt amongst its supporters, combined with a profits crisis in 1973–5, which Labour was forced to respond to by concessions on corporate tax, gave weight to the argument that without some mechanisms for guaranteeing future economic growth, the dividend of continuous social improvement and pursuit of greater equality would have to be curtailed.[35] Partly because of the key role that issues about public spending had assumed in its ideology, it is right to see the 1970s as the high watermark for British social democracy—without suggesting that the tradition was entirely exhausted.[36] Conversely, Labour's problems on this front help to explain how 'rolling back the state' became such a central part of the radical Right's agenda.

II

On the Conservative side, the key moment was, of course, the election of Margaret Thatcher as leader in 1975. The overarching rhetorical strategy relating to the

[32] David Wood, 'Chancellor of Labour's apocalypse' *The Times* 16 February 1976.

[33] 'The line we dare not cross'.

[34] Pliatzky, *Getting*, pp. 156–63.

[35] On the profits crisis, see Glyn and Sutcliffe, *Profits*. For the general argument about social democracy, Przeworski, *Capitalism*.

[36] Sassoon, *One Hundred Years*, pp. 647–90 argues that by the 1980s social democracy faced major challenges across Western Europe from both structural changes such as de-industrialization and ideological shifts, especially regarding the welfare state, full employment, and trade union rights.

economy that soon emerged under her leadership was twofold. First was an emphasis on the enormous dangers to economic, political, and social stability brought about by inflation. Second was the argument that inflation, along with all other of Britain's problems, were the result, not of conjunctural circumstances, but the culminatory effects of the whole of the post-war settlement; part of the manifestation of British 'decline', which only a radical reversal of policy could effectively address.[37] Here we focus on the second of these, the issue of inflation being returned to in detail in Chapter 8.

The 'declinist' trope was politically polymorphous. As shown in Chapter 2, it began on the Centre-Left as a critique of the Conservative government in the late 1950s and early 1960s, and soon spread across the political spectrum; but it was deployed especially by the Right in the 1970s.[38] While not inherently politically Conservative, declinism provided British radical Conservatives with an important and widely resonant starting point for the critique of the alleged failures of the post-war settlement.[39] While no doubt sincerely believing in declinism, Thatcher clearly recognized the electoral advantage of talking up 'the national decline theme'.[40]

One sign of the potency of this new version of declinism was the way it was taken up by those who moved from the Left and Centre-Left of politics to embrace 'Thatcherism', especially when linked with anti-trade unionism.[41] The most famous example, perhaps, is Paul Johnson, editor of the *New Statesman*, whose journey to the splenetic Right was announced in an editorial in that paper on 16 May 1975, saying British trade unionism 'has become a formula for national misery'.[42] Another example is the economist John Vaizey, ennobled at the end of the Wilson government, but soon denouncing Labour's 'slavish subservience to trade unions'.[43]

Thatcherite Conservatism melded declinism with elements of neo-liberal thinking. Neo-liberalism as a doctrine is complex, and its impact in British policy-making even more so. The most persuasive accounts of the genealogy of neo-liberal ideology suggest its roots in three strands of argument: neoclassical economics, ordoliberalism, and Austrian Economics. Its origins lay especially in the critique of the growth of economic planning in the 1930s and 1940s, dominated by the belief that such planning was a threat to democracy, and its various strands came together in the founding of the Mont Pelerin Society in 1947.[44] As Jackson has persuasively argued, the neo-liberalism of the 1930s and 1940s was significantly different to that of the 1970s and 1980s.[45] The most important changes were threefold. First, it retained a visceral dislike for trade unions as coercive monopolies, whilst its

[37] Cannadine, 'Apocalpyse?'; Green, *Thatcher*, pp. 55–82.

[38] A pioneer example of this political migration of declinism is Hutton, *Politics*. But 'centrist' declinism could also be apocalyptic: Jenkins, *Anatomy*, pp. 49–85.

[39] Tomlinson, 'Politics'.

[40] Cited in Lawrence and Sutcliffe-Braithwaite, 'Thatcher', p. 140.

[41] Saunders, 'Thatcherism', p. 34.

[42] Cited in Taylor, 'Scapegoats', p. 79.

[43] Letter to *The Times* 3 December 1980. Vaizey went on to systematically attack the legacy of social democracy: *Breach*.

[44] Plehwe, 'Introduction'.

[45] Jackson, 'Origins'.

parallel critique of large companies had almost disappeared.[46] This dislike was a long-standing feature of British conservative politics, but became especially virulent in the 1970s, when trade unions were central villains in the Conservatives' 'declinist' account of Britain.[47] However, Conservative claims about the relationship between unions and inflation were more complex, a point returned to below.

Second, hostility to the welfare state was much more wholehearted in the 1970s and 1980s than in the previous decades. In the earlier period neo-liberals were somewhat divided on this issue, but even Hayek, for example, was willing to support a social safety net, while others saw a much more extensive provision as an important way of sustaining worker support for free markets, and as a quid pro quo for breaking up trade unions.[48] By the 1970s the welfare state was on a much larger scale in all Western countries than thirty years earlier. More generally, the state's role in economic and social life had expanded. In response there had emerged a very significant new strand of argument, called public choice theory or 'the economics of politics', which focused on the inherent shortcomings of government action in comparison with markets in delivering popular demands. This offered a much more thoroughgoing critique of the state and the workings of democracy than had been available in the 1940s, and was enthusiastically embraced by neo-liberalism.[49]

The relationship between Thatcherite Conservatism and the state was ambiguous. On one hand they deployed argument from the public choice school to unfavourably contrast political decision-making with the workings of the market. On the other, their conservative politics favoured strong state action in areas such as 'defence' and law and order. Andrew Gamble long ago captured this duality in his pioneering book on Thatcherism, *The Free Economy and the Strong State*.[50] In 1979 Thatcher herself pithily summarized it as 'tax cuts and order'.[51] As Jackson notes, such a combination was evident in the arguments of the ordoliberals in the 1940s, but for them the strong state was not to be used for classic conservative purposes of coercively maintaining social order, but to rigorously sustain a competitive order, including against the machinations of large companies; this was not part of Conservative politics in the 1970s.[52]

The third shift in neo-liberalism of great importance was the much greater role given to macroeconomics, something much less focused upon in the 1930s and 1940s. In those earlier decades there was some division of opinion amongst

[46] Jackson, 'Origins', pp. 142–5; on the union aspect, see also Jackson, 'Ideology'. The approach to companies is discussed in Van Horn, 'Reinventing'.

[47] Joseph, *Reversing*. A notable feature here is how neo-liberals whose background was not in conservative politics were amongst the most virulent in such anti-unionism: notably Samuel Brittan and Peter Jay: see Cockett, *Thinking*, pp. 184–8.

[48] Jackson, 'Origins'.

[49] As Bosanquet points out, the origin of these ideas did not lie in neo-liberalism: Bosanquet, *New Right*, p. 62; Anthony Downs, a key founder of this approach, had originally used the framework to argue why public spending was too *low* in democracies: see Bosanquet, *After*; Tomlinson, 'Economics'.

[50] Gamble, *Free*.

[51] Moore, *Thatcher*, p. 403.

[52] Jackson, 'Origins', pp. 134, 151.

neo-liberals on macroeconomic issues, especially how far they supported Keynesian remedies for unemployment. Their attitude was by no means one of wholesale rejection, with even Hayek objecting more on 'technical' grounds than to the spirit of Keynes's proposals.[53] But the notable point is how unfocused on macroeconomic issues most neo-liberals were until the late 1960s.[54] From that decade onwards the work of Milton Friedman was crucial. He advanced claims about the macroeconomy that were to be crucial to British politics in the 1970s. First, he argued that, in anything but the very short run, the level of unemployment was determined by 'real factors', including the operation of the labour market, not by macroeconomic policy, and therefore that, at best, activist fiscal policy was ineffectual. Second, that inflation was 'always and everywhere' a monetary phenomenon, and could only be effectively addressed by control of the money supply.[55]

Obviously, these kinds of arguments became much more politically significant when inflation rose sharply, and as the Conservatives put its reduction at the core of their politics. 'Monetarism' thus became a core feature of Thatcherism. The significance of monetarism did not lie in its specific, instrumental recommendation of controlling the 'money supply' as a way of limiting inflation; instrumentally monetarism in this narrow sense was a resounding failure when applied after 1979, and Friedman strongly rejected the Conservative government's approach to monetary control.[56] But the broader significance of monetarism was as a form of 'statecraft' which enabled Conservatives to detach themselves from negotiating with interest groups, unions, and employers, in pursuit of counter-inflationary goals. It gave them a freedom of manoeuvre which earlier post-war Conservative ideology had lacked.[57]

Monetarism also posed ideological and policy challenges for British conservatism. As a doctrine it undermined the long-standing view that one of the problems caused by trade unions was inflation, given that inflation was deemed a wholly monetary phenomenon. In the mid-1970s this analysis was, from a Conservative Party view, ironic, as the Labour government predicated its policies on the belief that unions *were* key to inflation, and the eventual failure of the Labour government to persuade the unions to agree to lower wage increases was of course the basis of the Winter of Discontent and the triumph of the Conservatives in the

[53] Jackson, 'Origins'. As Jackson points out, it is ironic that two of the British members of the Mont Pelerin Society, Lionel Robbins and John Jewkes, had been major contributors to the 1944 White Paper on *Employment Policy*, commonly seen as a key foundation of post-war Keynesianism (even if its formulations were in fact much hedged about with 'neoclassical' caveats); on the 1944 White Paper, Middleton, *Charlatans*, pp. 92–3.

[54] Cockett, *Thinking*, p. 145.

[55] Friedman, 'Role'. As Peter Clarke points out, this foundational statement of monetarism was strikingly vague in its policy recommendations, suggesting that the authorities might target the exchange rate or the price level rather than the money supply itself: 'The Rise and Fall of Thatcherism', p. 311.

[56] Friedman, 'Memorandum'. This attacked the government's focus on the PSBR within its 'Medium Term Financial Strategy' and argued for direct control of credit creation through monetary base control.

[57] Bulpitt, 'Discipline'.

following general election.[58] A monetarist analysis of inflation was, however, reconciled with anti-unionism by ascribing to unions both an indirect role in the causing of inflation, and responsibility for a whole range of other ills in the declinist framing of Britain's condition.[59]

The conclusion from this discussion is that, while neo-liberalism was an important element in Thatcher-period conservatism, the latter was by no means simply derived from the former. It is equally important to note that the growth of neo-liberalism in these years was by no means just a matter of a few senior Conservative politicians being converted by the doctrine, and then carrying the ideology into policy on achieving office. Important in spreading the neo-liberal message were the think tanks, the most important of which was the Institute of Economic Affairs (IEA), founded in 1957, along with the Centre for Policy Studies (CPS, 1974) and the Adam Smith Institute (1977). Early historians of these bodies tended to give them an exaggerated, 'heroic' role as outsider institutions battling against the odds to get a hearing.[60] But this is by no means the whole story. Rollings shows how closely the IEA was tied ideologically and practically to employers' organizations back into the 1960s.[61] Jackson points out how much financial support large firms gave it, and how extensive were its 'Establishment' connections, as he concludes: 'While it may have been useful to the IEA and British neo-liberal activists to present themselves as maverick outsiders, this claim is overstated'.[62] Up until the 1970s it is true that neo-liberalism made little headway amongst British university economists, and this is why bodies like Mont Pelerin were so important as a mechanism for importing such ideas into Britain.

The IEA (unlike the CPS) was never a Conservative Party body. Its aim was a Fabian-like desire to permeate its free-market ideas amongst any who would listen, and this included a number of Liberals as well as a few Labour party mavericks. It saw its role as a mobilizer of opinion aimed at 'opinion-formers' such as lecturers, teachers, and journalists. This mobilization was especially aimed at shaping media opinion, and a key feature of the political economy debate of the 1970s was the role played by economic journalists in the serious press.[63] Figures like Samuel Brittan, Peter Jay, and David Butt drew heavily on American academic economists, not only macroeconomists like Friedman and Phelps, but also the public choice theorists like Buchanan and Tulloch, and older figures like Schumpeter.[64] This latter strand of literature was especially significant in the debates about the public sector, offering a root-and-branch critique of the notion of the state as a beneficial actor and thus greatly broadening the attack on the 'post-war consensus'.[65] These journalists had influential roles as commentators at *The Times* and *Financial Times*, as well as contributing to IEA publications, and, especially in Brittan's case, publishing books and academic journal articles. Cockett plausibly suggests that 'Most Conservative and Labour MPs learnt more about economic liberalism from

[58] See Chapter 8. [59] Jackson, 'Ideology'; Tomlinson, 'Thatcher'.
[60] Cockett, *Thinking*. [61] Rollings, 'Between'.
[62] Jackson, 'Think-tank', p. 60. [63] Parsons, *Power*.
[64] Lee, *Public*. [65] Skidelsky, 'Thinking'; Thompson, 'Hollowing out'.

the journalism of Samuel Brittan and Peter Jay than they did from their own party "research" organizations or from the universities'.[66]

Brittan and Jay were especially important in constructing the problems of the mid-1970s not as passing, conjunctural, challenges of dealing with 'shocks' to the economy, but as indicative of profound problems of representative democracy, drawing their approach in part from the public choice literature. For them, the inflationary and fiscal pressures were the result of a combination of exaggerated expectations and over-powerful interest groups which threatened all liberal states with ungovernability.[67] In the mid-1970s this message undoubtedly fell on fertile ground because of the pre-existing declinist narrative along with the contemporary fiscal and inflationary crises. As Brittan later remarked of one of his key articles 'declinism gave my paper a currency it might not otherwise have had'.[68]

This journalism provided intellectual firepower for the Thatcherites in the Conservative Party, though neither Jay nor Brittan was a Conservative or a paid-up member of the New Right. Jay came from a Labour background, while, as Roger Middleton stresses, 'Brittan was a resource for the New Right: he was not a member of the New Right'.[69]

As well as their general role as what Hayek called 'second-hand dealers in ideas', these journalists were very important in shaping opinion in financial markets, and hence feeding directly into judgements about the 'credibility' of British fiscal policy. In a context, in the mid-1970s, of great leverage for such markets because of the scale of public borrowing in an inflationary environment, these anti-Keynesian ideas undoubtedly reduced governmental room for manouevre.[70] Chancellor Healey's understanding of this episode became very important in framing the next generation of Labour leaders' obsession with policy 'credibility' and their emphasis on financial market globalization as a major constraint on future Labour governments (see Chapter 4).[71]

III

The ambivalence of Conservatives on the role of the state and their advocacy of a 'free economy and strong state' fed directly into the immediate practical issues of curtailing public spending when the new government came to power in 1979. Whilst in opposition, the party had devoted relatively little attention to precise changes in public spending, with a much greater focus on tax changes.[72] But it had strongly committed itself to increasing spending on the military and law and order. As Thatcher emphasized in a lecture in 1979: 'We do not ask for a feeble state; on the contrary we need a strong state to preserve both liberty and order'.[73] Alongside

[66] Cockett, *Thinking*, p. 325. [67] Middleton, 'Brittan'. [68] Brittan, 'Time', p. 61.
[69] Middleton, 'Brittan', p. 75. [70] Keegan and Pennant-Rea, *Who?*
[71] Exchange rates, Healey asserted, were now determined by 'the faceless men who managed the growing atomic cloud of footloose funds': Healey, *Time*, p. 412.
[72] Conservative Party, *Right Road*. [73] Cited in Marquand, 'Twilight', p. 62.

these what we might call traditional Tory commitments was also a slightly more ambiguous pledge to maintain spending on the NHS.[74]

How then was the (qualified) rolling back of the state to be argued for? One important aspect was the linkage to declinism. In the new government's first budget the growth of public spending was presented as a key element in Britain's 'decline'. The peroration by Geoffrey Howe entitled 'The Years of Decline' asserted that:

> Only a quarter of a century ago—within the memory of almost every Member of this House—the people of the United Kingdom enjoyed higher living standards than the citizens of any of the larger countries of Europe. Amongst the free nations of the world, Britain was then second only to the United States in economic strength. It is not so today. For example, France and Germany's combined share of world trade in manufactured goods, which in 1954 was almost the same as Britain's alone, is now more than three times as large as ours. The French people now produce half as much again as we do. The Germans produce more than twice as much, and they are moving further ahead all the time.... But in the last few years the hard facts of our relative decline have become increasingly plain, and the threat of absolute decline has gradually become very real.[75]

Containing public spending was a key part of the new Conservatism's 'moral revolution', aimed at persuading the population of the desirability of replacing reliance on the state with much higher levels of individual responsibility. By 'rolling back the state' such a policy would not only reduce the sphere of government activity, but also by reducing taxation it would gave back to individuals more resources to deploy as they saw fit. Tax-cutting was crucial because this individualism was firmly linked with the key ideological-cum-electoral strategy of the Conservatives, which was to deny the reality of social class in the name of appealing to all 'hard-working people and their families', again with an implication of emphasizing individual/family responsibilities rather than those of the state.[76]

The link made between public spending and freedom which had accompanied the debate over an alleged spending level of 60 per cent of GDP was, unsurprisingly, seized upon by Thatcher. The link was made especially through the issue of taxation. In 1976 she wrote an article for *The Sun* titled 'The hand in your pocket' which cited the 60 per cent figure, and urged that 'the hand which takes most money from your pocket should be your own'.[77] Earlier that year she had said that 'the more heavily individuals are taxed, the more difficult it is for them to move house, to acquire new skills and experience, to set up their own business, to give their children a better start, to help out their elderly parents, or to plan their own retirement'.[78] Geoffrey Howe's memoirs make it clear how important the tax issue was to the party in the late 1970s; in 1978 he saw his key aim at the Annual Conference as 'to convince the party that we had a detailed and workable response to their central anxiety, most notably on taxation'.[79]

[74] TNA: PRO PREM 19/18 G. Howe to M. Thatcher, 'Public expenditure' 11 May 1979.
[75] *Hansard* (Commons) vol. 968, col. 237 12 June 1979.
[76] Lawrence and Sutcliffe-Braithwaite, 'Thatcher'.
[77] *The Sun* 13 September 1976.
[78] Speech to Exeter Conservatives 20 February 1976, MTFW 102963.
[79] Howe, *Conflict*, p. 102.

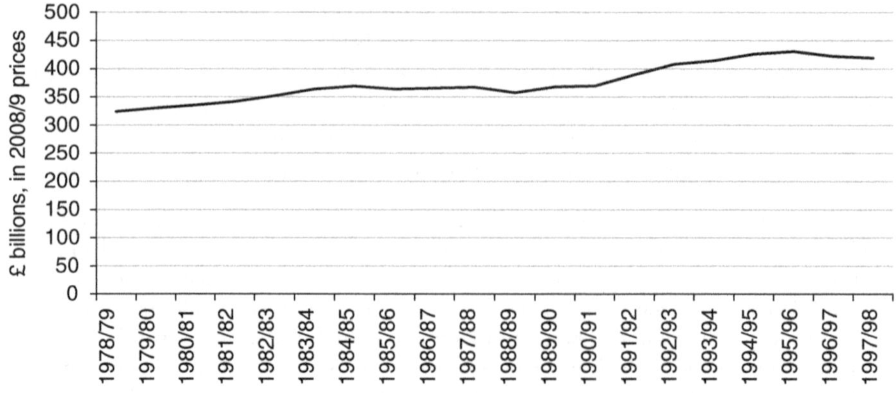

Figure 3.2 Public expenditure, 1978/79–1997/98
Source: ONS database.

But for all this ideological commitment the Conservatives in office struggled to reduce the overall level of spending (see Figure 3.2). In part we can see what happened in the early1980s as a partial replay of the lessons of the late 1950s and early 1960s, when an earlier generation of market enthusiasts in the Conservative Party (and the Treasury) had aimed to roll back the state, but been defeated by perceptions of public opinion on social welfare.[80] However, this time the Prime Minister was in the 'roll-back' camp, so some areas were indeed subject to significant cuts—all the larger because of increases and ring-fencing elsewhere. The nature of the problem was spelt out very early on in the life of the government when it was already being disputed whether cuts of 15–17.5 per cent to non-protected programmes were realistic.[81]

The outcome in the first Thatcher government was serious cuts, but to only a small number of programmes. Between 1978/9 and 1983/4 only overseas aid, trade and industry, and housing showed any reduction, whilst total spending in constant prices rose by 8 per cent. Initial cuts focused especially on capital spending on housing, where the fall in this period was 34 per cent. Alongside defence and law and order, big increases were recorded in energy (largely assistance to coal), and employment measures, as unemployment was responded to by emergency measures (see Chapter 6).[82]

Martin Daunton offers the following summary of the Thatcher years: 'Public expenditure was 42.2% of GDP when Mrs Thatcher came to power, and 42.3% in 1995/6. *Mrs Thatcher did not roll back the state*'[83] (see Figure 3.3).

The difficulties of reducing spending relative to GDP were compounded in the immediate period after 1979 by the Conservatives having to contend with the impact of the 'automatic stabilizer' of increased spending deriving from higher levels of unemployment raising the demand for social security, even while

[80] Lowe, 'Modernizing', pp. 39–42.
[81] TNA: PREM 19/18, 'Note by PM's private secretary' 21 May 1979; K. Berrill (CPRS) to PM's private secretary 'Review of expenditure programmes' 23 May 1979.
[82] Jackson, 'Perspectives', p. 56.
[83] Daunton, *Just*, p. 338, emphasis addded.

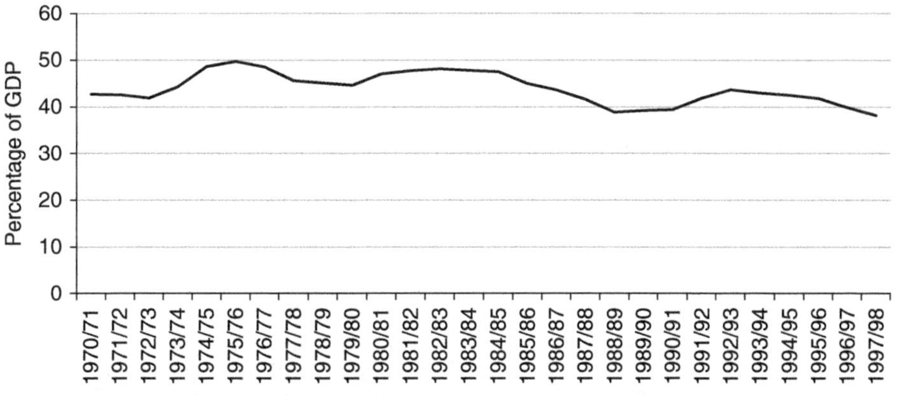

Figure 3.3 Total public expenditure as a share of GDP, 1970/71–1997/8
Source: ONS database.

for the unemployed individual benefits were squeezed, whilst GDP was falling. This spending ratio did fall in the late 1980s as the economy recovered from the slump at the beginning of the decade, but the absolute level of spending continued to grow. When the economy returned to recession in the early 1990s, the ratio again rose.

Breaking down the data emphasizes how much of the cutting of the early 1980s focused on capital spending (continuing a trend begun under Labour in the mid-1970s).[84] Indeed, taking the long view and ignoring cycles, one could say that the most important feature of public spending in the 1970s and 1980s was the collapse of public capital spending, with the gross figure falling by two thirds over those decades, the net figure by even more, amounting to only well under 1 per cent of GDP at its nadir of 1988/89 (see Figure 3.4).

A distinctive feature of the Conservatives' approach to economic policy after 1979 was the focus on the PSBR. Cutting this was made a crucial element in the medium-term financial strategy (MTFS) because of the belief that its trajectory was closely tied to the favoured measure of monetary growth, Sterling M3, which included bank deposits as well as the note circulation. The strength of commitment to cutting public borrowing meant that when public spending was not cut as hoped, recourse to borrowing rather than taxation to fund this expenditure was ruled out, and overall tax levels had to be sustained. Because of the commitment to cutting 'headline' income tax rates, there followed a major switch of tax revenue from direct to indirect taxes.

This political commitment to cut direct taxes was of such crucial importance to the Conservatives that a start was made immediately to deliver on this pledge, though only after much agonizing about the revenue consequences. The initial strategy was to offset cuts in income tax rates by failing to index (and therefore lowering) the thresholds, coupled to raising National Insurance contributions (income tax by another name, but with different distributional aspects) alongside

[84] Clark, Elsby, and Love, 'Twenty-five Years'.

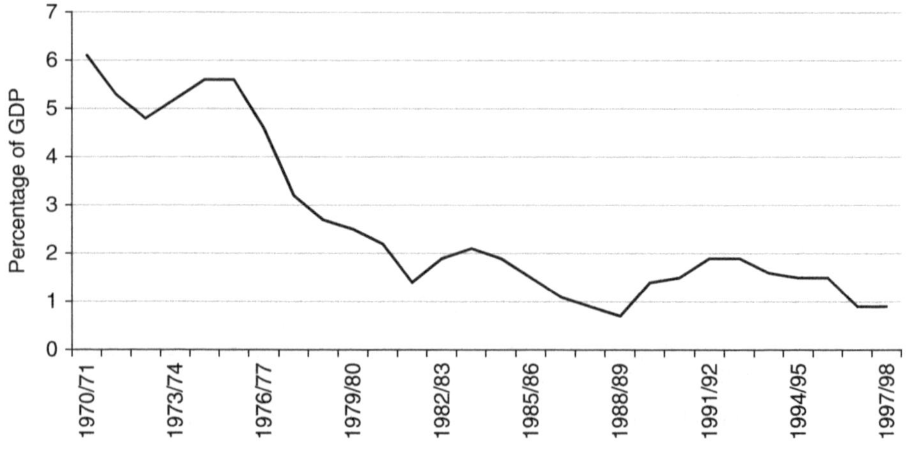

Figure 3.4 Public sector net investment as a share of GDP, 1970/1–1997/8
Source: Office for Budget Responsibility (OBR) database.

raising indirect taxes, especially VAT.[85] These changes had big distributional impacts in contributing to sharply increasing inequality.[86] Alongside tax changes, most benefits were increased in line with prices rather than incomes, at a time of significant inflation. Overall, Clark and Leicester calculate that tax and benefit changes contributed half of the total increase in inequality in the 1980s.[87] To a degree Thatcherites welcomed this trend, as they celebrated the benefits of inequality. In a speech in 1975 Thatcher had characteristically argued that, 'the pursuit of equality is itself a mirage' and linked this directly to the distributional ambitions of an over-mighty state.[88] But it is doubtful if she or anyone else envisaged how big an increase in inequality there was going to be as a consequence of the correlates of trying to roll back the state.

The focus on the 'headline' rates of income tax set a political agenda which endured. This focus obscured the fact that changes to income tax allowances partly offset these rate cuts, but the overall shift away from income tax in total revenue is clear. 1975 was the peak year, and as Figure 3.5 shows there was an almost continuous decline from that date until the Conservatives left office in 1997.

It is ironic that while so much of the long-standing impetus beyond advocacy of cutting spending came from Conservative hostility to the welfare state, long the

[85] Moore, *Thatcher*, pp. 464–5, 534, 625–7; also important, though much less remarked upon, was the collapse in the central budget contribution to the National Insurance Fund, which in the decade after 1979 fell from 18 per cent of total receipts to zero, significantly reducing the progressive element of NI: Glennerster, *British*, p. 178.

[86] The step change is summarized by the Gini Coefficient which went from 0.23 in 1978 to 0.34 in 1990 (an increase of 50 per cent).

[87] Clark and Leicester, 'Inequality'; this is against a benchmark of benefits rising in line with incomes.

[88] Thatcher 'Let Our Children Grow Tall' 15 September 1975 MTFW 102769; see Hickson, 'Conservatism'; Joseph and Sumption, *Equality*; Letwin, *Against*. For a critical assessment, Walker, '"Don't Cut Down"'.

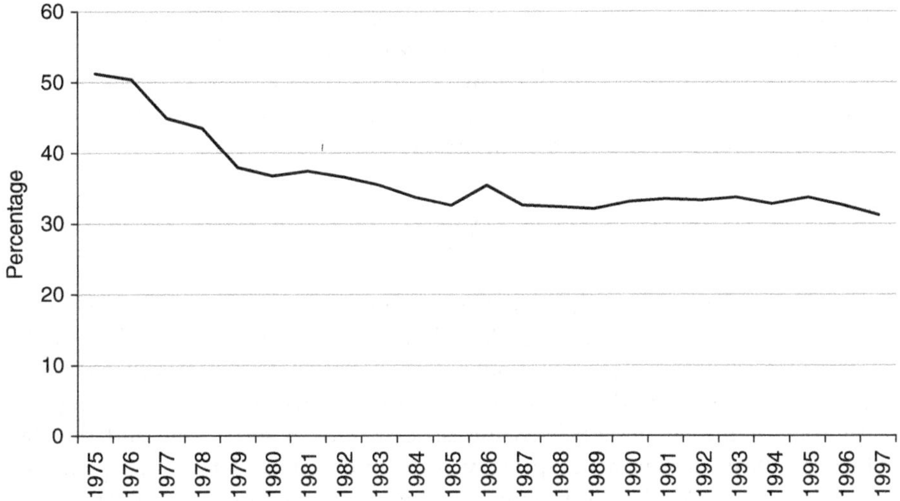

Figure 3.5 Income tax as a share of total tax revenues, 1975–97
Source: HMRC database.

largest and fastest-growing element of this spending, this proved the most difficult area on which to impose cuts. In the 1950s and 1960s the great bulk of the publications of the IEA were focused on criticizing the welfare state and advocating radical market reforms, including the breaking up of the NHS, a move to vouchers for schooling, and major restrictions in the scope of social security.[89] The first two of these were never seriously pursued after 1979. The NHS continued to be a near 'monopoly provider' and apart from a local experiment or two, vouchers for schools have never been taken up seriously in Britain.[90] These proposals made almost no headway; so unpopular were, for example, shifts away from the NHS that Thatcher pretended that she had never seriously entertained the idea, though the evidence suggests that she had.[91]

In the case of social security the pattern has had some parallel with that in health and school education. Expenditure overall has increased, partly because of the demographics of an ageing population driving up spending on pensions, and partly through higher demand for unemployment benefits, though the value of such benefits, unlike pensions, has been consistently eroded. Very importantly, and returned to in this volume's final chapter, we see the beginning of a significant growth in both in-work benefits and housing benefits. In-work benefits began on a very small scale with the Family Income Supplement in 1971, but were significantly expanded with Family Credit from 1988. Housing benefit was linked to the move away from subsidizing houses to subsidizing households, but with abolition of rent controls and the decline of social housing (plus the long-run rise in housing costs), this reform led to escalating expenditure.

[89] Bosanquet, *After*, p. 75. [90] Bosanquet, *After*, pp. 165, 170–1.
[91] Klein, 'Health'; Walsh, 'When?', pp. 500–4.

In the immediate period after 1979 the Conservatives had also to contend with the impact of the 'automatic stabilizer' of increased spending, derived from higher levels of unemployment raising the demand for social security, even while, for the unemployed individual, benefits were squeezed. The recession also created pressure for increased spending on employment programmes (see Chapter 6).

IV

Beyond public expenditure, the Thatcher government's desire to roll back the state led to some clear policy successes. Most dramatic perhaps is the very large-scale privatization programme, selling off publicly owned assets in the years after 1983.[92] This was composed of both previous public corporations and council housing.

The sale of the old nationalized industries helped raise revenue and thereby reduce the PSBR significantly, especially in the mid-and late 1980s, though it was only in one year, 1988/9, that revenues only amounted to more than 3 per cent of public spending.[93] More important in the long run was the attempt to use these sales to create a 'popular capitalism' by greatly extending personal share ownership, to both the general public and employees of specific privatized enterprises. To this end discounts were given and major publicity campaigns mounted. The initial effects were substantial, with enterprises like British Gas and British Telecom finding large markets for their discounted shares. By 1997 approximately 22 per cent of the adult population held shares directly, compared with around 7 per cent in 1979.[94] But the average holding was tiny; for example, British Telecom had 1.4 million shareholders in 2006, but two-thirds of these held fewer than 800 shares.[95] The idea of a major transformation in the number of Britons holding substantial equity largely failed; for the great bulk of the population, escaping the 'tyranny of earned income' remained implausible.[96] The trend towards a rising proportion of shares held by institutions, evident since the 1960s, had continued through and beyond the period of privatization; the proportion in the hands of private owners fell from 28 per cent in 1983 to 10 per cent by 2010.[97]

Probably even more important, certainly politically, was the sale of public (council) housing at discounts to sitting tenants. Under this policy eventually 1.5 million units were sold off, reducing public housing to a largely residual role (though large parts of the previously public stock ended up being owned by not-for-profit housing associations).[98] This privatization progressed successfully because it combined at least three aims in one policy. Housing sales contributed substantially to the reduction in public borrowing, a key target of the 1980s. Like asset sales, housing sales gave financial windfalls to purchasers, consolidating electoral support for the Conservatives. Third, ideologically, they fitted with notions of

[92] Parker, *Privatization, Vol I.* and *Vol II.*
[93] Parker, *Popular Capitalism*, p. 505.
[94] Parker, *Popular Capitalism*, p. 520.
[95] Parker, *Popular Capitalism*, p. 517.
[96] Froud et al., 'Escaping?'
[97] Parker, *Popular Capitalism*, p. 520.
[98] Murie, 'Housing', pp. 150–4.

extending 'property-owning democracy', an important part of Conservative thinking, especially in regard to housing, since the late nineteenth century and Salisbury's 'villa conservatism'.[99] This last objective was crucial to the Thatcher project of sidelining class divisions by making the great majority of the population house-owners—perhaps up to 80 per cent.[100]

Since the 1950s both council housing and private ownership had risen fast at the expense of private renting, with private ownership almost doubling between 1950 and 1980, from 29 to 53 per cent.[101] Thatcher's objective was to reverse the growth of the public sector by further expansion of home ownership, but not to significantly roll back the decline of the private rented sector. Council house sales were concentrated amongst unskilled and semi-skilled workers, whose voting behaviour does seem to have been influenced by the policy.[102]

Also carried through were a wide range of deregulatory measures. The labour market was one area where 'market forces' were given much freer rein. This victory was predicated on a highly successful assault on the trade unions. With the successful construction of an anti-union account of the Winter of Discontent, a combination of cumulative legislative restrictions, defeats for key groups of workers (especially the National Union of Mineworkers in 1984/5), de-industrialization, and ideological 'de-legitimization' of union activity saw membership shrink radically.[103]

The weakening of unions created political space for such measures as the abolition of most wage councils, which historically had set industry-level minimum wages in a number of low-paid sectors.[104]

Very important also was the deregulation of the financial system. As soon as it came to office the Conservative government abolished exchange control, and policies in the mid-1980s culminating in the 'Big Bang' fundamentally changed the banking system.[105] This in turn underpinned a huge expansion of personal credit in the mid-and late 1980s, greatly aiding the consumption-led, inflationary boom in the last half of the decade.[106]

Crucial to the attack on the post-war settlement in the 1980s was the repudiation of Keynesian responses to recession. In 1981 the Thatcher government directly contradicted the idea of using fiscal policy to sustain output and employment by introducing a budget aimed at cutting the deficit in the midst of sharply rising unemployment. This decision evoked a major confrontation with a large number of academic economists, but the government stuck to its fiscal constraint.[107] Politically, this was an important victory for the new government's approach, even if in overall macro-policy terms the rhetoric of 'the lady's not for turning' was belied by the reduction in interest rates already begun in Autumn 1980.[108]

[99] Daunton, *Property-owning?* Property-owning democracy is not an inherently Conservative notion: see Francis, '"Crusade"'; Jackson, 'Property-owning democracy'; Jackson, 'Revisionism'.

[100] Lawrence and Sutcliffe-Braithwaite, 'Thatcher', p. 143.

[101] Dunleavy, 'Urban', p. 411.

[102] Butler and Kavanagh, *British General Election of 1983.*

[103] Pencavel, 'Surprising'.

[104] For an example of the effects of this abolition, Craig et al., *Abolition*.

[105] Offer, 'Narrow'.

[106] Backhouse, 'Macroeconomics', pp. 328–9.

[107] Booth, *Were?*

[108] Needham and Hotson, *Expansionary.*

From a longer-term perspective it is far less clear that this episode represented a decisive defeat for 'Keynesianism'. In the recession of the early 1990s the Conservative government under John Major allowed the automatic stabilizers to work, with the effect of a very sharp rise in public borrowing. Strikingly, the public sector deficit was higher in the early 1990s than it had been in the mid-1970s 'fiscal crisis of the state'.[109]

This reordering of priorities has been sustained. Most of the nostrums of 1970s monetarism about 'controlling the money supply' have been abandoned, with policy based on inflation-targeting by an independent central bank. In pursuing this target an eclectic range of indicators are used to judge the path of inflation, and interest rates are the main instrument of control.[110] The public discussion of economic policy has continued to highlight the importance of employment, whilst policy has subordinated employment goals to the achievement of low inflation.

Public borrowing, too, has varied with the economic cycle, but at levels significantly higher than in the preceding 'Keynesian age'. Of course, much of this has reflected the impact of the automatic stabilizers in a much more unstable macroeconomic environment; but, strikingly, apart from in 1981, these stabilizers have been allowed to operate, or even been reinforced by discretionary fiscal action when recessions have occurred.

Up until 2010 employment in Britain continued to be shaped by the role of the state in the direct provision of jobs. Parallel with the rise in real levels of spending, between 1979 and 1997 there was a growth in tax-funded public employment (leaving aside employment in the privatized, previously publicly owned, industries, which were largely funded by commercial receipts).

This growth was obscured by the problematic way in which public sector employment is defined by the ONS: 'the difference between the public and private sector is determined by where control lies, rather than by ownership or whether or not the entity is publicly financed'.[111] This definition means that not only are all employees in further and higher education treated as part of the private sector, along with all GPs, but so are the much more numerous workers in outsourced activities supplied to the NHS, local authorities, and other public bodies. But fortunately we have the analysis of researchers at the Centre for Research on Socio-Cultural Change (CRESC) in Manchester, who use a much more satisfactory definition whereby, if more than half of an entity's activities are publicly funded, it is deemed a part of the public sector.[112] They estimate what they christen para-state employment, producing figures back to 1978, by adjusting the ONS category published in the Quarterly Public Sector Employee Survey. The adjustment is done by taking the industries in the Standard Industrial Classification and making an informed judgement about how far each of these is reliant on the public purse (Buchanan et al. 2009, p. 18). On this basis they calculate that total

[109] PSNB (unadjusted) peaked in 1993/4 at 7.7 per cent of GDP, compared with 7.0 per cent in 1975/6: ONS database.

[110] Oliver, *Whatever?*

[111] ONS definition quoted in Cribb, Disney, and Sibieta, 'Public'; Tomlinson, 'From'.

[112] Buchanan et al., 'Undisclosed'. These calculations are similar to those in Centre for Cities, 'Cities Outlook 2014'. These figures include employment in universities as 'public sector'.

Table 3.1 State and 'para-state' employment in the UK, 1978–97

1978	5.6 million
1987	6.2 million
1997	6.7 million

Source: Froud et al., *Rebalancing*, p. 18.

state and para-state employment together grew from 5.6 million in 1978 to 8.0 million by 2008—1.7 million more than the official estimate (see Table 3.1).[113]

The majority of these jobs have been in education, health, and social care. The mechanisms of this expansion are complex, but a large part of the explanation is the high income elasticity of demand for health and education observed by Baumol.[114] Fiscal pressures, in combination with neo-liberal ideology, have meant that this expansion of public sector services was increasingly done by cheapening labour in this sector by contracting out. So while there have been lots of well-paid and relatively secure public sector jobs, these have been accompanied by burgeoning numbers of low-paid and insecure posts in the 'para-state' sector.

V

When first in power in 1979 the Conservative government was strongly aware of the political dangers of a 'cuts' narrative. While it was believed that there was strong public support for curtailing benefits for the unemployed, support for economies elsewhere was far less evident. Not only that, but surveys of public opinion conveyed to government ministers also suggested that the electorate believed the Conservatives were much bigger 'cutters' than was actually the case.[115] This evidence also suggested the extent to which expenditure on the NHS had become sacrosanct, reinforcing the commitment to ring-fence this sector.[116]

The government did not, of course, take the state of public opinion as a given: in the language of political science, they aimed to be 'preference-shaping'.[117] Soon after the 1987 election, Ivor Crewe wrote that 'A distinctive feature of Thatcherism is its pedagogic impulse. It has been at pains to educate the electorate about economic realities. Persuading the public to change economic expectations and assumptions is one of the few constructive economic roles it allows the state'.[118] He went on to challenge the idea that the electoral successes of the Conservatives in the 1980s demonstrated the success of this 'educational' project.

113 Froud et al., 'Rebalancing'. These figures tell a quite different story from that based on the official data: Newell, 'Structural', pp. 45–6.

114 Baumol, 'Macroeconomics'.

115 TNA: PRO T371/799, G. Cardona to Chancellor of the Exchequer 'Opinion Poll: Public Expenditure' 22 February 1980.

116 Klein, 'Health', pp. 189–207; Walsh, 'When?', pp. 500–4.

117 Stubager, 'Preference-shaping'.

118 Crewe, 'Has?', p. 35.

After stressing that 'Mrs Thatcher owed victory in 1979 to the Winter of Discontent, not to her radical manifesto', Crewe goes on to criticize the view (popular amongst both critics and opponents of Thatcherism) that she subsequently forged a new supportive consensus. In the 1980s Gallup regularly asked whether the electorate would prefer tax cuts, even at the expense of some reduction in government services such as health, education, and welfare, or for these services to be extended even if this meant tax increases. When Thatcher came to power the electorate were evenly divided; by 1983 there were twice as many service-extenders as tax-cutters; by 1987 six times as many. Whilst the question may be problematic, the trend in the data is striking.[119]

A similar, slightly more nuanced, question has been asked for the period since 1983 by the British Social Attitudes survey. The question asked offers respondents three options, and asks for their preference between:

(a) 'reduce taxes and spend less on health, education and social benefits'
(b) 'keep taxes and spending on these services at the same level as now'
(c) 'increase taxes and spend more on health, education and social benefits'

The first of these has never been a popular option, with a maximum of 9 per cent support. Support for the other two has been cyclical or 'thermostatic', with support for more spending rising when the growth of spending has been reduced, and vice versa. So, for example, support for option (c) rose from 32 per cent in 1983 to 65 per cent in 1991, remained at roughly this level into the early 2000s, then fell to 31 per cent in 2010 in the wake of the financial crisis.[120]

There is clear evidence of a downward trend in the proportion agreeing that more should be spent on social security benefits, from 50–60 per cent in the 1980s down to 30 per cent in early 2000s (with some rise during the recession after 2008). This is dominated by the trends towards a less favourable view of the unemployed, with growing numbers of respondents believing that benefit levels are a disincentive to work, and that benefit fraud is widespread. Where in 1983 46 per cent said unemployment benefits were 'too low', by 2012 the figure was down to 22 per cent.[121]

Those surveyed were also asked questions on public spending priorities: responses show that health and education are consistently by far the highest priorities, with health varying around the 70 per cent-plus level, and education typically in the low 60s.[122] This plainly fits with the revealed priorities of governments since the 1970s, with NHS and school spending expanding most rapidly, and being 'ring-fenced' in the 1980s and after 2010.

One of the most complex issues raised in the survey is that of inequality and the government response. There has been a persistently large proportion, over 70 per cent, who agree that the 'income gap is too large', but the proportion agreeing that

[119] Crewe, 'Has?', p. 37.
[120] Pearce and Taylor, 'Government', pp. 35–6.
[121] Pearce and Taylor, 'Government', pp. 44–6, 37.
[122] Pearce and Taylor, 'Government', p. 39.

Table 3.2 Public opinion on the role of government, 1985–2006

Percentage saying it should be the government's responsibility to...	1985	1996	2006
Reduce income differences between the rich and the poor	69	63	69
Provide a job for everyone who wants one	68	65	52
Provide a decent standard of living for the unemployed	81	73	59
Provide decent housing for those who can't afford it	n/a	84	81
Provide health care for the sick	98	97	98
Provide a decent standard of living for the old	97	95	96
Keep prices under control	91	82	89

Source: Pearce and Taylor, 'Government', p. 38.

'government should redistribute income' is much lower, varying between 30 and 50 per cent.[123]

On the overall view of the role of government—an issue which might be thought to be at the core of neo-liberalism—there is a striking solidity of opinion over the survey period in favour of government continuing to have extensive responsibilities, as shown in Table 3.2.

The evidence suggests that popular opinion has not moved strongly in a neo-liberal direction. This is interesting in the light of the purported importance of think tanks like the IEA in generating support for Thatcherism and rolling back the state. The IEA spent much of its initial efforts, from the early 1960s, producing propaganda attacking 'state monopolies' in health and education on the back of producing public opinion polls which purported to show a strong popular appetite for 'marketization' in welfare.[124] Yet health and education seem to be the areas where there was least movement amongst popular opinion against the 'post-war consensus'.

The IEA's strategy focused on converting *elite* opinion. This drew on a broader agreement amongst neo-liberals in Britain to focus their attention on persuading 'opinion-formers'. Hayek used Keynes's famous claim that in the long run 'the ideas of economists and political philosophers . . . are more powerful than is commonly understood. . . . I am sure that the power of vested interests is vastly exaggerated compared with the gradual encroachment of ideas' to ground a strategy of focusing on 'second-hand dealers in ideas' as the key audience to be persuaded.[125] Following this logic the IEA aimed its pamphlets at journalists, politicians, teachers, and lecturers, and all those deemed likely to embrace simplified expositions of neo-liberal thought to inform their own activities.[126]

This strategy had considerable success, perhaps most obviously amongst journalists. But it greatly helps in understanding the constraints on the success of

[123] Pearce and Taylor, 'Government', p. 40.

[124] Bosanquet, *After*, pp. 75–83; Harris and Seldon, *Choice*, culminating in Harris and Seldon, *Welfare*.

[125] Cockett, *Thinking*, pp. 111–13.

[126] Blundell, 'Introduction'; Cockett, *Thinking*, pp. 122–58; Desai, 'Second-hand'.

neo-liberalism and the politics of rolling back the state if we also note the limitations of such a strategy in shaping *popular* opinion. Popular opinion does show changes, and is affected by the dominant political narratives (most obviously on unemployment), but the effects of broader neo-liberal anti-state ideology is much harder to detect.

If the failure to convert popular opinion to an overall project of rolling back the state has greatly constrained cuts to overall public spending, that project has nonetheless led to a reshaping of the state. This is most obvious in the welfare state, with the use of quasi-market mechanisms in the NHS and education with a 'purchaser/provider' split. One might characterize this as a managerial form of market fundamentalism, aiming to mimic market forces with government-run bodies which still supplied service free at the point of supply. This shift, much of it initiated in 1988–90, can be seen in large part as a reaction to the *failure* to cut these areas of social spending in the preceding decade.[127] Once begun, this policy became entrenched and was deepened and extended under successive governments.

Finally, arguments about the tax system have similarly failed to cut overall taxation levels but led to major reshaping of not only the tax structure (as shown in Figure 3.5), but also what we may call 'tax discourse'. Underpinned by annual budgets in which income tax rates are often given top billing, these rates have assumed a totemic status as indicators of tax policy. Yet these rates are poor indicators—they ignore not only the huge revenue-raising and (largely regressive) distributive role of other taxes, especially National Insurance and VAT, but also the crucial role of definitions of the income tax base in determining incidence. The extraordinarily regressive aspect of pensions contribution exemptions is only the most striking example.

The issue of public spending in the wake of the 2007/8 crisis is returned to in Chapter 5, but a brief summary of events in the six decades prior to that crisis might be that state provision suffered an ideological crisis, linked to both structural change in the economy and ideological assault from the Right.[128] However, in that same period, the project of 'rolling back the state' achieved only very partial success.

[127] Wilding, 'Welfare'. [128] Offer, *Why?*

4
Globalization

From the 1970s, and accelerating in the 1980s, the British economy became significantly more open, its links with the international economy greatly intensified by the rapid growth of trade and capital movements. In the 1990s the word globalization quite suddenly became ubiquitous in public and academic accounts of this trend.[1] In 1998 Anthony Giddens rightly suggested that: 'only about ten years ago the word was hardly used in either academic works or the popular press. From being nowhere, the word is everywhere—no political speech is complete, or business manual acceptable, without reference to it'.[2] But this word was never a simple description of growing international interconnectedness. Rather, it always carried strong (if variable) ideological and political connotations. While the term seems to have originated in academic discussions, in Britain its initial spread into policy and public discussion owed much to the Labour Party, and is best understood as a highly political interpretation of changes in the international economy offered largely by those on the Centre-Left of the political spectrum. For New Labour, initially in opposition in the 1990s, and in office after 1997, globalization was the key defining term which underpinned the economic narrative it offered. Characteristically, Gordon Brown described the financial crisis that engulfed Britain in 2007/8 as the 'first great crisis of globalization'.[3]

This chapter looks first at the trends towards international economic connectedness in the British economy, especially those evident in the post-war years. It analyses the 'how and why' of these trends, and especially the reasons for their acceleration from the 1970s and 1980s. The second section looks at the emergence of the term 'globalization' to describe these trends, and the freighting of this term with great political and ideological significance. In particular, it analyses the relationship between the deployment of this term and the emergence and development of New Labour. The third section looks at some of the limits and problems posed by framing discussion of the British economy in the last few decades in terms of 'globalization'. The chapter concludes with the denouement of this narrative in the Brexit decision of June 2016.

[1] Rapid growth in publications using 'globalization' in their titles dates from the 1990s: Busch, 'Unpacking', pp. 22–4; James and Steger, 'Genealogy'.

[2] Giddens, *Third*. The word seems to have become popular after its use in Levitt, 'Globalization'.

[3] Brown, *Beyond*.

I

The history of Britain's links with the international economy show a cyclical pattern. Between the 1870s and the First World War the country was the key participant in the 'first great globalization'.[4] Driven by the European invasion and settlement of North and South America and Australasia, the levering open of much of Asia and Africa by imperial conquest, and the industrialization and urbanization of Western Europe, and greatly aided by the contemporary falls in transport and communications costs, the scale of movement of goods, capital, and people was unprecedented and extraordinary.[5]

In the interwar years, this process went into reverse. Stimulated by the First World War, the growth of protectionism, flights of 'hot money' between financial centres, and the collapse of the gold standard which had provided so much stability to the system before 1913, meant that by the end of the 1930s international trade was far below its pre-war level, and in many countries didn't surpass that level until many years after 1945; capital movements had shrunk even more.[6] By most measures and in most countries, the 'great reversals' meant that financial integration levels in 1913 were not attained again until the 1980s.[7]

This reversal of economic integration was the background against which the designers of the post-war international economic architecture, largely the Americans and the British, worked during the 1940s. They sought to avoid what they regarded as the 'beggar-my-neighbour' policies of the 1930s by building institutions that would underpin a revival of international trade in a regime of stable exchange rates.[8] They recognized that this new system had to be compatible with participant countries having room to pursue domestic stability and high employment; what they proposed was an 'embedded liberalism', which sought to combine the benefits of active national economic management with the advantages of expanding multilateral trade.[9]

This design was the one which emerged from the Bretton Woods conference of 1944, and survived, at least as an ideal, from the 1940s to the 1970s. It involved an international regime of growing trade liberalization with fixed exchange rates and tight limits on capital movements. Least contentious in this package was trade liberalization, which was largely consensual, as a principle (at least amongst most of the political elite), from the 1940s. Thus, despite its commitment to vague notions of 'planned trade', the Labour leadership in the 1940s endorsed the long-term liberalization project, however much this support was qualified in

[4] Some historians identify a much earlier globalization, in the expansion of European empires from the sixteenth century, but if the emphasis is on the intensity as well as the extent of global economic interconnectedness, the nineteenth century can be seen as being when the process really began: O'Rourke and Williamson, 'When did Globalization Begin?'

[5] O'Rourke, 'Empire'.

[6] Maddison, *Dynamic*, Table F3; Obstfeld and Taylor, *Global*, pp. 129–45.

[7] Rajan and Zingales, 'Great'.

[8] Gardner, *Sterling–Dollar*; James, *End*; Schenk, *International*, pp. 20–38.

[9] Rodrik, *Globalization*; Ruggie, 'International'.

the short run by balance-of-payments considerations.[10] Likewise, on the Right, the Conservative leadership in the mid-1950s won out against those within their ranks with a continuing attachment to imperial preference, and the party embraced non-discrimination. Despite these broad political commitments, the pace of trade liberalization was relatively slow until the 1960s, with the use of quotas and tariffs only gradually reduced as balance-of-payments constraints eased.[11]

By contrast with the trade regime, where practice eventually followed the ideas laid out by the proponents of Bretton Woods, the liberalization of capital movements was a case where there was increasing divergence from that design. Initially, the controls on short-term capital movements were equally uncontroversial. While policy encouraged both the inflow and outflow of long-term, especially direct, investment, controls on short-term flows were seen as crucial to insulating the national economy from disruptive capital movements that would threaten exchange rate stability. As Keynes put it at the time of Bretton Woods, 'the whole management of the domestic economy depends on being free to have the appropriate rate of interest without reference to the rate prevailing elsewhere in the world. Capital control is a corollary to this'.[12] Thus when Britain eventually decided to restore currency convertibility at the end of 1958, this was restricted to the current account, and the purchase of foreign currency for investment abroad continued to be heavily regulated.

Post-war Britain soon re-emerged as a major exporter of long-term capital, especially to the Sterling Area, the 1940s outflows dominated by South Africa and Australia.[13] The control system on non-Sterling Area outflows was loosened in the 1950s, allowing the total volume of overseas investment to rise to an average of 1.3 per cent of GDP per annum between 1950 and 1958; still a low level by historic standards, but a significant increase from the 1930s.[14] The impact of this on the balance of payments caused recurrent concerns to the authorities in London, and exchange control was periodically tightened to control outflows, especially in the 1960s. Even for investment in the Sterling Area there was a governmental call for restraint in 1965.[15] Both British and American governments in these years tended to see exports of goods and services as a *substitute* for foreign investment, rather than the more positive perspective of seeing the investment as encouraging exports.[16] But sceptical views on the national benefits of such investment outflows, and the controls that followed, had only limited effects in slowing the growth of multinational investment activity in both countries, given the profitable opportunities perceived by multinational companies. However, their direct impact on the balance of payments (the issue which so exercised governments) was reduced because these corporations could reduce the immediate foreign exchange impact of their investment by reinvesting profits and using funds raised in the countries where the investment was made, rather than in the home country.[17]

[10] Toye, 'Attlee'. [11] Milward and Brennan, *Britain's*.
[12] Keynes, 'Letter to Harrod', p. 147; Bloomfield, 'Post-war'.
[13] Cairncross, *Years*, p. 158. [14] Ringe, Middleton, and Rollings, *Economic*, p. 87.
[15] Rollings, 'Multinational'. [16] Reddaway, *Effects*. [17] Cairncross, *Control*.

Alongside slowly rebuilding its position as a significant foreign investor, Britain after 1945 saw a big expansion of long-term capital *inflows* in the form of direct investment by multinational companies, mainly from the USA.[18] These influxes were very strongly encouraged by successive British governments, starting with Stafford Cripps, a key figure in economic policy in the Attlee years, who saw not only balance-of-payments benefits, but also the potential for employment creation and for higher productivity by the introduction of US techniques and management.[19]

If the grand design of the Bretton Woods regime was for countries to get the benefits of multilateral trade whilst retaining substantial control over the management of the domestic economy, these aims were largely realized, despite periodic problems in individual countries.[20] In the 1950s and 1960s global trade grew faster than GDP, even whilst the latter grew consistently faster than ever before.[21] Employment also expanded rapidly, and there was no return to the depressed conditions of the 1930s. Governments of the rich countries, whilst using different policies and having different political perspectives, were able to combine participation in this international boom with maintaining powerful capacities to manage their national economies. Long-term investment by multinationals also assisted the growth of this period, especially via American investment in Western Europe, which aided the convergence between these economies. This influx provoked little questioning except in the case of France, where a critical book sold over 600,000 copies when published in 1967.[22]

But this regime was eventually undermined, in part due to policy decisions which can be traced back well into the Bretton Woods period.[23] Very important here was the growth of short-term capital movements, aided initially by British and US support for the emergence of Euromarkets from the late 1950s; this meant especially the growth of London-based trading in dollar-denominated US financial assets, which was accepted by the USA. This was accompanied by a huge influx of foreign, especially US, banks into London. British policy was driven by balance-of-payments concerns which overlapped with the desire to rebuild London as a financial centre not wholly based on sterling. This last condition was seen as crucial for the City's future expansion; freed from the incubus of a troubled sterling, it was envisaged, it could again become a global financial centre.[24]

There was also growing political pressure from those who argued for the economic benefits to Britain of the City's activities, focused on what came to be popularly called its 'invisible earnings'.[25] Especially under the Labour government in the 1960s, these claimed benefits were used to attack policies deemed to be restricting the City's activities. We can see here the effective beginning of the powerful narrative that the City lays golden eggs, and therefore is a goose that needs to be nurtured—especially by Labour governments. This claim is multifaceted, and has

[18] Dunning, *American*. [19] Tiratsoo and Tomlinson, *Industrial*, pp. 131–52.
[20] Rodrik, *Globalization*, pp. 67–76. [21] Maddison, *World*, pp. 131–7.
[22] Servan Schreiber, *American*. [23] Helleiner, 'Explaining'; Thompson, 'Nation-state'.
[24] Burn, *Re-emergence*; Schenk, 'Origins'; Schenk, 'New City'.
[25] Clarke, *City's*; Committee on Invisible Exports, *Britain's*.

shifted over time, but in the 1960s was focused especially on the benefits of these City exports to the balance of payments, fitting with the governmental obsession with that issue which characterized that decade.[26]

The growth of short-term capital flows was in part facilitated by the very success of Bretton Woods in encouraging trade expansion, as 'leads and lags' in settling foreign trade accounts provided a significant avenue for masking capital movement.[27] This growth, however caused, along with diverging inflation rates, contributed to the growing pressure on the fixed exchange rate structure. Along with the mounting instability of a dollar-reserve system in the face of US payments deficits, these pressures eventually caused the demise of the Bretton Woods system in the early 1970s, and the move to a floating exchange rate regime, a transition in which Britain took the lead.[28]

Foreign exchange speculation was a key element in the collapse of Bretton Woods, and in the 1970s transactions expanded as companies sought to hedge against future fluctuations.[29] These fluctuations were much more dramatic and frequent than advocates of floating rates had predicted.[30] Another important moment in the liberalization of capital flows came in the 1970s, when the US resisted calls from Japan and countries in Western Europe for cooperative capital controls as envisaged at Bretton Woods. Helleiner argues that this rejection was seen as helpful for the USA in its desire to manage the dollar and sustain financial hegemony, but was also bolstered by the 'anti-control' notions of a strengthening neo-liberalism in the economic ideas feeding into policymaking in Washington.[31]

Overall, greater turbulence in foreign exchange markets in the 1970s was not the occasion for a reversal of the broad trend towards reducing capital controls. In Britain, where exchange control continued to exist until 1979, significantly tighter controls were part of the 'siege economy' advocated by Labour Party supporters of the Alternative Economic Strategy, but were decisively rejected in the Cabinet discussions which accompanied the crisis surrounding the application for an IMF loan in 1976.[32] In 1979 the incoming Conservative government abolished the remaining elements of exchange controls. While the new government was to be buffeted by shifts in the value of the pound in the 1980s, none of its members suggested that this should be dealt with by a reversion to controls on foreign exchange markets. Ideologically, the now dominant neo-liberal strand in Conservative economic policymaking was committed to the notion that the verdict of these markets was a proper measure of national economic responsibility; something to be accepted rather than fundamentally challenged. Further expansion of the City's role in financial markets was encouraged by the liberalization of the mid-1980s, culminating in the creation of a highly deregulated system at the time of the 'Big Bang' of 1987, which followed up the policies of Competition and Credit Control

26 Tomlinson, 'Labour'. 27 Obstfeld and Taylor, *Global*, pp. 158, 169.

28 Schenk, *International*, pp. 55–75; for a powerful critique of this process, Varoufakis, *Global*, pp. 91–112.

29 Strange, *Casino*, pp. 2–19. 30 Bleaney, 'Comparison'.

31 Helleiner, *States*, pp. 146ff; Helleiner, 'Explaining', pp. 321–4.

32 This episode is returned to in the next section.

of 1972, finally ending the cartels and 'cosy' restrictions which had previously inhibited the City's expansion.[33]

The decade of the 1980s was one of general liberalization of capital movements in the world, with this policy spreading to Japan and most of Western Europe alongside Britain and the USA, the two countries that had taken much of the initiative.[34] This leading role was driven partly by pressure from their domestic financial interests, partly by a growing adherence to neo-liberal economic ideas on both sides of the Atlantic. Other countries found they had to fall into line or face the loss of capacity to sustain a role for their own national financial centre—there was a 'competitive deregulation dynamic'.[35]

Helleiner has asserted that 'by the early 1990s, the restrictive Bretton Woods financial order had been completely overturned and an almost fully liberal pattern of financial relations had emerged between advanced industrial states, giving market operators a degree of freedom unparalleled since the 1920s'.[36] This seems an apt summary, though this pattern was still confined mainly to 'advanced industrial states'; in much of the rest of the world there were considerable institutional barriers to 'globalized' capital markets.

In much contemporary academic literature this process was not presented as reducing national governments' powers. Rather, proponents of deregulation and floating exchange rates argued that this would *enhance* national policymaking capacity, because countries would be able to pursue their own monetary goals without restricting capital flows.[37] But this expected benignity was not realized, as exchange rate fluctuations and destabilizing capital flows characterized the post-Bretton Woods era.[38] Of course, the level of instability was not just a function of the exchange rate regime, the world economy from the 1970s being buffeted by oil and asset price volatility, large fluctuations in inflation, and a variety of political crises. The new 'regime' was aided by continued international economic cooperation in times of crisis, such as the banking crisis of 1974, the 1982 debt crisis, and the 1987 stock market crash. So while highly unstable, the new regime was managed and hence sustained despite its shortcomings.[39]

In principle, in line with neo-liberal views, the Conservatives under Thatcher regarded the balance of payments as a non-problem under floating exchange rates, though ironically their period in office nearly came to a rapid end because of the way exchange rate 'overshooting' in 1979–81 rendered much of British industry uncompetitive and trebled the level of unemployment.[40] Thus a generally positive posture towards liberalization did not rule out practical policy concerns about

33 Moran, *Politics*, pp. 55–87.

34 Goodman and Pauly, 'Obsolescence'; Moran, *Politics*.

35 Helleiner, 'Explaining' p. 334.

36 Helleiner, *States*, p. 146.

37 Thus, it was argued, resolving the 'trilemma' or 'impossible trinity' between fixed exchange rates, freedom of capital flows, and domestic monetary autonomy: see Obstfeld and Taylor, *Global*, pp. 29–41.

38 Helleiner, *States*, pp. 123–4.

39 Helleiner, *States*, pp. 69–191; Toniolo and Clement, *Central*.

40 'Overshooting' means that exchange rates respond in exaggerated fashion to policy announcements, in this case leading to a huge appreciation of the pound when monetary policy was tightened: see Dornbusch, 'Expectations'.

movement in the exchange rate, especially because of the rate's effect on short-term inflation as well as unemployment, though the latter was less of a concern after 1983 (see Chapter 6). Arguments about Britain's attitude to stabilizing the pound's value via the European Exchange Rate Mechanism (ERM) persisted within the Conservative governments in the late 1980s and down to the crisis of 1992.[41] But none of this controversy affected the embrace of liberalization of international economic transactions, symbolized by the 'Big Bang'.

The governments of Thatcher and Major did not use the politicized language of globalization with any frequency: it was a concept 'largely absent from the discourses of the Conservative governments of the 1980s and 1990s'.[42] Rather, they took growing international economic integration as given, and within that talked a lot about the need to improve British *competitiveness*, itself a highly problematic notion when applied to a country.[43] This goal they saw as being simultaneously required, and aided, by the competitive pressures arising from the increasing internationalization of the economy.[44] On one side, in line with past British governments, they thought that British firms could be revitalized by foreign direct investment (FDI), and so enhanced the traditional welcoming stance towards these investors by tax breaks and deregulation of the labour market. Simultaneously, by removing controls over exchange and capital movements, they encouraged British financial institutions to provide financial services, believing this would yield high returns and expand the role of the City. The Conservatives had no painful history of problems with the international credibility of their domestic policies (though the debates on the ERM showed nagging worries on this front). Relative unconcern with this issue was strikingly justified in the crisis of the early 1990s, when public borrowing exceeded that under Labour in the mid-1970s but without any fiscal crisis or 'loss of confidence'. Unlike Labour, the Conservatives had no 1931 or 1976 moments to come to terms with.

While in the 1970s and 1980s we can see in Britain a trend back towards the levels of international economic connectedness reached before the First World War in the fields of trade and foreign investment, this was much less evident in migration. Movement out of the UK, mainly to the traditional destinations in North America, Australasia, and South Africa quickly revived after 1945, and for the next forty years Britain was to be a country of net emigration, though never on the scale of the years before 1914. This net loss was partly a result of the introduction of the first controls on immigration from the Commonwealth in 1962, brought in to reduce the influx from the Caribbean and South Asia.[45] In retrospect it appears clear that the levels of global migration before 1914 were a one-off consequence of European movements to the sparsely populated regions of North America and

[41] Thompson, *British*.

[42] Berry, *Globalization*, p. 69; though some analysts have diagnosed an adherence to 'hyperglobalism' amongst Conservatives: Baker, Gamble, and Seawright, 'Sovereign'.

[43] Krugman, 'Competitiveness' argues that the term 'national competitiveness' suggests that trade is a zero-sum game, whilst obscuring the fact that the key measure of national economic welfare is real wages, underpinned by productivity.

[44] For example, Cm. 2563, p. 6.

[45] Paul, *Whitewashing*.

Figure 4.1 Net immigration into Britain, 1992–2015
Source: ONS—international migration statistics.

Australasia, combined with shifts within the European empires (e.g. the mass movement of South Asians to Africa within the British Empire).[46]

Largely unregulated economic migration was not part of the 'globalized' world of the late twentieth century. But a desire to get the benefits of the international movement of skilled and educated people propelled Britain into a more liberal phase, so that by the 1990s immigration was regularly exceeding emigration for the first time for a century and a half (Figure 4.1).

Measuring the exact degree of openness of an economy is never entirely straightforward, though easier for migration and trade than for capital. However, the broad pattern seems quite clear. In the case of merchandise and commodity trade, Maddison suggests that globally the ratio of exports to GDP rose from 5.5 per cent in 1950 to 17.2 per cent in 1998, the growth being especially rapid before 1973, starting from the low levels of the 1940s.[47] In the British case the shift was much less dramatic, the ratio rising from 36.0 per cent in 1950 to 42.6 per cent in 1994, still below the 44.7 per cent of 1913.[48] This rise was accompanied by less 'globalization' in a geographical sense, with an increasing focus on Western Europe, from 42 per cent in 1975 to 58 per cent in 1998.[49]

Measuring international capital flows and the degree of capital market integration is more complex, and a variety of approaches is possible.[50] Overall, Hirst and Thompson have shown that the data suggest a much more dramatic post-war shift globally than in the British case. Using measures of capital stocks (rather than flows) Obstfeld and Taylor suggest that the foreign investment/world GDP ratio rose from 0.05 per cent in 1945 to 0.92 by 2000, with most of the growth coming after1960, and expansion accelerating after 1985. For Britain the timing of growth

46 Hatton, 'Emigration'. 47 Maddison, *World*, p. 127.
48 Hirst and Thompson, 'Globalization', p. 337.
49 Hirst and Thompson, 'Globalization', p. 349. These figures relate to the EU14.
50 Obstfeld and Taylor, *Global*, pp. 43–122.

was similar, but the pace slower, so that the UK share of the world total fell from 40 per cent in 1945 to 15 per cent by 2000 (it had been over half in 1913).[51] But while growth was slower than for the world as a whole, Britain remained a huge capital exporter, and had a similar high level of capital imports to GDP. As with trade the distribution of these flows was becoming less 'globalized', again the links with Western Europe intensifying: with FDI only 14.7 per cent went to the fourteen members of the European Union in 1984, compared to 36 per cent in 1995, a decade later.[52]

Nevertheless, while many other countries had been opening up over the previous decades, by the end of the twentieth century Britain remained an exceptionally open economy—as it had been for over a century. This degree of exposure was very evident in the level of foreign ownership of domestic manufacturing and service activity, and in the scale of overseas investment, and Hirst and Thompson suggested this pattern makes relocation by international companies (whether based in the UK or elsewhere) easier, and led to a lesser development of a distinctive national manufacturing system than was found in less 'exposed' economies.[53] Without doubt Britain also had an unusually internationalized financial system, measured by foreign exchange turnover. Compared with other European countries, Britain also had an unusually large proportion of household wealth in foreign assets, again potentially exposing the economy to powerful external forces, while also allowing many to benefit from global growth and innovation.[54]

'Globalization' was a less dramatic change in Britain than in many countries in the post-war years because of the level from which it started. Conversely, because it started from such a high base, the further increase in internationalization left it one of the most 'globalized' countries in the world.

Britain's position was partly a consequence of technological changes which affected almost all countries. In trade, containerization was a key shift, an innovation combining the simplest of technologies (metal boxes of uniform size) with a huge impact by cutting out most of the transshipment costs associated with labour-intensive methods.[55] Falling transport costs also encouraged migration, but the impact was much less significant than in the movement of goods. Speed and ease of movement was greatly facilitated by the revolution in information and communications technology (ICT), and such changes were unidirectional, and therefore always encouraged more international movement of goods and services. In parallel, the growth of FDI was driven by the changing strategies of multinational corporations (MNC), whose activities greatly expanded trade in intermediate, as opposed to final, outputs. Increasingly, these corporations constructed an international division of labour in which their component parts traded intensively with each other.[56]

[51] Obstfeld and Taylor, *Global*, pp. 52–3.
[52] Hirst and Thompson, 'Globalization', p. 350.
[53] Hirst and Thompson, 'Globalization'.
[54] Hirst and Thompson, 'Globalization'. [55] Levinson, *Box*.
[56] Around 40 per cent of world trade is now in such intermediate goods: Straw and Glennie, *Third*, p. 23.

But while these technological and business trends mattered, so too did policy, as it had during the interwar reversal of pre-1914 globalization. In Britain, in concert with the USA, post-1945 policymaking was shaped by a broad acceptance of liberal views of the international economy; that international exchange was likely to be beneficial for the goals of full employment and growth. In the early post-war decades the dominant view in Britain was a version of 'embedded liberalism', combining this liberal view of international exchange with a strong commitment to managing the national economy. But when this management, and hence this 'embeddedness', was threatened by the unintended consequences of policies to liberalize short-run capital movements, it was the management of the national economy which became fragile. The politics of globalization in Britain was a particular attempt to deal with that tension.

II

Writing in the early years of the New Labour government, David Coates and Colin Hay argued that 'both in opposition and now in government, Blair's Labour Party has, to an unprecedented extent, emphasized the degree to which international (indeed, global) processes, pressures and tendencies serve as external constraints circumscribing the parameters of political possibility'.[57] This nicely summarizes a key element in the rise of the globalization narrative—its links to the political 'project' which underpinned the emergence of New Labour in the 1990s. There were, as always, complexities to the narrative: were the constraints of globalization to be welcomed as preventing error by national governments, or reluctantly acceded to as simply reflecting hard-headed, realistic perceptions about how the world really is?[58] But that 'globalization' was key to understanding New Labour cannot be doubted.

Those who deployed it argued that 'globalization' was the shorthand term that best summarized the new circumstances that required Labour to renew itself. The leaders of New Labour argued that they retained Labour's old values, but had to interpret and apply these in a world which had changed. The 'globalization' narrative underpinned the necessity for Labour to change. A characteristic statement was in the 1997 election manifesto: 'In economic management, we accept the global economy as a reality and reject the isolationism and "go-it-alone" policies of the extremes of right or left'.[59]

Of course, the idea that governments (and perhaps especially Labour governments) are constrained by international economic forces did not originate in the 1990s. The British Labour Party had been born and grown up in a highly internationalized economy, so Labour had always faced the problem of external credibility.[60] The second Labour government split and collapsed precisely over that

[57] Coates and Hay, 'Internal', p. 448; also Clift, 'Social'; Hay, *Political*; Hay and Rosamond, 'Globalization', pp. 148, 154–6, 158–9.
[58] Hay, 'Negotiating'. [59] Labour Party, *New Labour*, p. 3.
[60] Wickham-Jones, 'New', pp. 4–5.

issue in 1931. The Attlee government had not been much troubled on this front because of the continuation of wartime exchange controls after 1945, except for a brief, quickly reversed period of liberalization in 1947.[61] But the problem had returned for the Wilson government in the 1960s, with strong external pressure to change its fiscal policies in the face of balance-of-payments crises. However, whilst the Bretton Woods structure remained in place, accompanied by exchange controls and fixed exchange rates, the pressures were painful but containable.[62] But after Labour came to power again in 1974 the combination of the collapse of Bretton Woods and increasing difficulties in regulating the growth of international capital flows, along with fiscal problems following OPEC 1 and 'stagflation', eventually exposed Labour to pressure akin to that of 1931 either to change its policy stance or face an insurmountable loss of confidence.

The 1976 crisis is crucial to understanding later Labour views on 'globalization'. As argued in Chapter 3, and contrary to much commentary, the Wilson government began to reverse its macroeconomic policy in 1975, well before the crisis over sterling and recourse to the IMF in 1976. But the *perception* of the events of that summer was crucial in shaping the politics of Labour. To many, across the party, it showed the power of international financial markets to constrain national economic policy. This pushed some on the Left to urge a 'siege economy', but the conclusion drawn by many on the Right of the party was that this crisis showed that future policy would have to focus on maintaining credibility with financial markets, as a precondition for Labour to get elected and stay in power.

This view of the difficulties of pursuing 'social democracy in one country' was reinforced by many interpretations of the French experience in the early 1980s, when an initial reflationary and redistributive strategy under President Mitterand was reversed in the face of the loss of external credibility and pressure on the franc.[63]

These events were used in both France and Britain to support a politics which emphasized the limits 'globalization' place on social democratic governments.[64]

Another long-standing input into Labour's understanding of the international economy can be traced right back to Raymond Vernon's seminal work 'Sovereignty at Bay', which argued that the growth of American multinationals after 1945 had seriously undermined national economic sovereignty.[65] In Labour circles this theme was taken up especially forcefully in the work of Stuart Holland, who in the 1970s was trying to alert the party to the significance of the rise of these corporations, suggesting that their impact was to deprive national governments of much of their previous power. Holland was on the left of the party, and his response to the problem he described was to find ways of limiting the powers of MNCs. His broad arguments about these companies gained considerable endorsement in Party documents.[66] The argument, that the rise of MNCs brought a weakening of national government (and national labour organizations) in the face of changes in levels of international economic connectedness, ran on very similar lines to those

[61] Cairncross, *Years*, pp. 121–64; Obstfeld and Taylor, *Global*, pp. 153–5.
[62] Tomlinson, *Labour.* [63] MacShane, *French.* [64] Clift, 'Social'.
[65] Vernon, *Sovereignty.* [66] Holland, *Socialist*; Labour Party, *International.*

about short-term capital flows and the capacity to manage the economy at macro-economic level.

So the common, retrospective deployment of 'globalization' emerged from a highly politicized *interpretation* of the 1970s and of the trends in world economy. Initially, in Labour's economic policy discussions after 1979, those who saw the response to the problem of external constraints to be a degree of insulation via import controls and reintroduced exchange controls were influential. The 1983 election manifesto said:

> We must therefore be ready to act on imports **directly**: first, in order to safeguard key industries...second, so as to check the growth of imports should they threaten to outstrip our exports and thus our plan for expansion....Our purpose in trade policy is **not** to reduce trade but to make possible an orderly expansion of imports, paid for by our growing export trade. We will thus be able to replace the present policies of deflation, which **restrict** world trade, by policies of expansion, which **increase** world trade. We will also encourage international action for expansion and increased world trade.[67]

But after the election defeat of that year such views were slowly marginalized, and by the late 1980s there was a slowly growing focus not on resisting the expansion of international connectedness, but seeing maintaining credibility within this environment, and especially with international financial markets, as the key issue to be faced. While Labour after 1983 continued to advocate a reflationary policy to combat unemployment, there was much more caution about how quickly this reflation could take place, partly because of the difficulties the Mitterrand government's reflationary policy had faced.[68] However, the big shift in Labour's macro-economic stance came only after the next defeat, in 1987.

A key document registering this shift was 'Looking to the Future' in 1990, which did not focus on the full employment goal, but rather urged that the key objective was 'a monetary framework which will provide long-term exchange rate and interest rate stability'.[69] The perceived greater openness of the economy was one of the key drivers for this shift.[70] The specific policy instrument linked to this new objective was adherence to the ERM, but after the fiasco of Britain's exit from this system in late 1992, coupled to Labour's loss of the election earlier the same year, this policy was abandoned.[71] The immediate aftermath of the election defeat was some movement back in policy pronouncements towards the primacy of full employment. But as the economy recovered after the ERM exit, and after the election of Blair as the new leader in 1994, there was a reassertion of the focus on stability as the central goal, and 'globalization' now emerged as key term in suggesting the constraints and possibilities in aiming at this goal.[72]

In 1996 Blair argued that 'the driving force of economic change today is globalisation...where capital and technology are mobile...[and] people are our key resource'. Labour's aim, he stressed, was 'to accept globalisation and work with it'.[73]

[67] Hill, *Labour*, pp. 125–30. [68] ibid., p. 136. [69] Labour Party, *Looking*, p. 7.
[70] Hill, *Labour*, p. 147. [71] ibid., pp. 179–90. [72] ibid., pp. 155–8.
[73] Blair speech in Tokyo, 5 January 1996, cited in Froud et al., 'Stakeholder Economy?', p. 133.

Labour's general election manifesto for 1997 spelt out this line of thinking. The document began by justifying the creation of New Labour by the need to adapt to the new globalized world: 'The reason for having created New Labour is to meet the challenges of a different world'. This stance was further spelt out, and its politics emphasized, when it was stressed that New Labour saw itself as occupying a middle ground, embracing the global economy and rejecting the isolationism of the extreme right and left. Where did this position lead Labour? The narrative fed directly through into a range of specific policy decisions by New Labour. In the run-up to the 1997 general election, a striking commitment was made to maintain the restrictive public spending and tax trajectory established by the Conservatives, to try and undercut the 'tax-and-spend' polemics which had been used so effectively against Labour in the previous, 1992, election. More strategic was the announcement of the 'golden rules' for fiscal policy. These said that over the cycle current government spending should be balanced, and that the debt: GDP ratio should be contained to a low and sustainable level.[74] If this was seen as the key to credibility in fiscal policy, the crucial innovation in monetary policy with a parallel intent was giving of independence to the Bank of England. This meant that the Bank would decide when to change the monetary stance in order to achieve the mandated target of 2.5 per cent inflation.[75]

Alongside this macroeconomic strategy, the New Labour government made clear it would countenance no reversal of trade or capital liberalization. It would continue to encourage the inflow of FDI.[76] Blair explicitly repudiated the idea of a financial transactions (Tobin) tax to discourage short-term movements, saying it 'is the wrong thing to do, because you actually want people to be able to move money very, very quickly'.[77] Ten years later Brown was equally clear that the appropriate response to the growth of financial flows remained to adopt policy to their existence, not to stem the tide: 'When there are ever more rapid financial flows across the world that are unpredictable and uncertain, the answer is to ensure stability through establishing the right long-term policy objectives and to build credibility in the policy through well understood procedural rules that are followed for monetary and fiscal policy.'[78] Two years later he went further, in stressing the positive benefits of the growth of integrated international capital markets: 'On the other hand, governments which pursue, and are judged by the markets to be delivering, sound monetary and fiscal policies, can attract inflows of investment capital more easily and in greater volume and at a lower cost than even ten years ago.'[79]

But globalization framed not just the issues of credibility, and hence fiscal and monetary policy, and approaches to the free movement of goods and capital; it shaped almost all policy positions taken by New Labour. In a 'globalized world' which had to be accepted and worked with, the issue of competitiveness was

[74] On these fiscal rules, Balls and O'Donnell, *Reforming*, pp. 155–81.

[75] Glyn and Wood, 'New', pp. 2–3.

[76] Labour Party, *New*, p. 15.

[77] Tony Blair interview with John Humphries, cited in Held, 'Globalisation', p. 26.

[78] Chancellor's speech at the Mansion House, 11 June 1998, at http://www.pickinglosers.com/page/bruno/20090125/gordon_brown_mansion_house_speech_11_june_1998.

[79] Brown, 'Conditions', C. 34.

presented as a supply-side issue. 'Progressive competitiveness' meant a focus on education and training to provide the skills for the workforce to fit a new era of international competition; this linked to Blair's famous declaration in favour of 'education, education, education'.[80] It also meant that industrial policy was dominated by financial support for high-technology activities deemed likely to be able to survive global competition, given that more dirigiste approaches were ruled out: 'In a world of ever more rapid globalization and scientific changes we need to create the conditions in which existing businesses can prosper and adapt, and new businesses can be set up and grow.'[81]

How much of an intellectual retreat from positions previously occupied did the acceptance of 'globalization' and its asserted policy implications represent? This question has led to an enormous amount of scholarly and political debate. Some of this debate has focused on specific areas of policy; even more on the broader question of the relationship of globalization as proclaimed by New Labour to the possibilities for social democracy.

One hugely important policy area where the significance of New Labour's globalization narrative has been contested is in the area of Keynesianism. The key figures in shaping the party's economic policy were clear in their own minds that, far from abandoning Keynes, they were maintaining the spirit of his positions, but applying them in new circumstances.[82] In this account, maintaining credibility did not mean abandoning all intent to manage the economy in the face of the potential hostility of financial markets. Rather, it meant the fiscal and monetary rules establishing a credibility within which discretion could be exercised, giving government 'constrained discretion'. This went along with an eschewal of the kind of short-term management of demand associated with the old Keynesianism of the 1950s and 1960s, but a continuing commitment to actively manage the economy in the event of recession.[83]

Ed Balls, a key figure in New Labour's economic thinking, used (the then unpublished) work of Mosley to suggest that participants in these capital markets are interested in only a very narrow range of macroeconomic indicators—above all, current and projected inflation rates and fiscal deficits.[84] The implication Balls draws from this work was highly significant; as long as they retain credibility with respect to these two indicators, national governments are pretty much free to do as they wish in economic policy decisions, such as determining 'the tax/spending share of GDP, the corporate tax rate, the level of the minimum wage or the toughness of competition policy to name but four'. In this account, 'credibility' can

[80] Coates and Hay, 'Internal and External Face'; Glyn and Wood, 'New', pp. 20–1. The 'education, education, education' pledge was made by Blair at the 1996 Labour Party conference.

[81] Tony Blair and Gerhard Schroder, cited in Arestis and Sawyer, 'Economic Analysis', p. 262. Detailed policy statements such as *Our Competitive Future* (1998), with foreword by Blair.

[82] Balls, 'Open'; Brown, 'Conditions'.

[83] For debates about interpreting New Labour's macroeconomic positions, see Arestis and Sawyer, 'Economic'; Clift and Tomlinson, 'Credible?'

[84] Balls, 'Open', p. 123; Mosley, *Global*; Mosley, 'Room'.

coexist with a very substantial room for manoeuvre in a range of policy areas including fiscal policy, and indeed is compatible with 'coarse tuning'.[85]

Arguments about Keynesianism were just one element in debates about how long the components of post-war social democracy could survive for. A key text in these arguments was by Scharpf, who in *Crisis and Choice in Social Democracy* in the late 1980s argued that social democrats had in future to focus on supply-side policies in order to achieve full employment.[86] A much stronger version of the view that globalization had rendered social democracy obsolete was John Gray's *False Dawn* of 1998. In a very powerful critique of this proposition, which eventually developed over a number of years and publications, Paul Hirst argued that while globalization was clearly an issue in Britain, especially because of the 'over-globalized' nature of the economy, the constraints thereby put on domestic policy were being seriously exaggerated by writers such as Gray.[87] Hirst made the basic but hugely important historical point that post-1945 social democracy had not flourished in a closed economy, but in Britain especially had *always* coexisted with a considerable degree of economic openness.[88] This argument paralleled that noted in the previous section, about how historically social spending had *increased* with the level of globalization. Hirst did not argue that nothing had changed in the 1980s and 1990s, nor that globalization did not pose challenges to social democracy, but that much of the deployment of this term had an overt conservative political agenda; it was a way for Labour leaders to try and 'frighten the children'.[89]

The most important theorist of New Labour's political positions was Anthony Giddens, and his proposed 'Third Way'.[90] While for him globalization was only partly about levels of international economic integration, he is clear in his assessment of what had recently happened to those levels. Writing in 1998, he insisted that the world had entered a new, distinct phase in this integration, especially in regard to financial markets. Citing data on the expansion of international capital flows since the 1970s, he insists that 'Economic globalization therefore is a reality, and is not just a continuation of, or a reversion to, the trends of previous years. While much trade remains regionalized, there is a "fully globalized economy" on the level of financial markets'. For him globalization is foundational of the new society he sees developing: 'It is more than just a backdrop to contemporary policies: taken as a whole, globalization is transforming the institutions of the societies in which we live.'[91] It is also clear to him that its political implications are profound; social democracy has to be reinvented to take account of the new realities, and for him those who deny the reality of globalization are those 'who wish to

[85] Compare Arestis and Sawyer, 'Economic', p. 262. [86] Scharpf, *Crisis*.

[87] Hirst, 'Has?'; Hirst and Thompson, 'Globalization'; the most extensive critique was developed in Hirst and Thompson, *Globalization?*

[88] Whereas Gray claimed the 'social democratic regime presupposed a closed economy': *False*, p. 88.

[89] Hirst, 'Has?'

[90] Giddens contributed greatly to the foundational myths of New Labour, gravely distorting as they were of 'Old Labour': Tomlinson, 'History'.

[91] *Third*, pp. 30, 33. For Giddens, a sociologist, globalization is fundamentally about the 'transformation of time and space in our lives': p. 31. For this sociological framework see Finlayson, *Making*, pp. 125–31.

defend aspects of old-style social democracy'.[92] Giddens does not focus much attention directly on economic policy, so it would be erroneous to see New Labour's policies as directly descended from 'Third Way' thinking. In addition, Giddens himself makes the important point that New Labour had drawn substantially on ideas from Scandinavian policies and from the American 'New' Democrats so we cannot see their policies as having a single source.[93] Nevertheless, Giddens did give weight to New Labour's key claims about the 'reality' and significance of globalization, and to the inescapability of adjusting an avowed social democracy to this new reality.

Whatever the ideological context, in terms of standard economic policy outcomes the new fiscal and monetary rules embraced in 1997 were initially a success. Low inflation was maintained more successfully than under the preceding Conservative government, aided by the low import prices brought about by the expansion of cheap imports from China. Unemployment was also significantly lower than in the preceding period, when the official figure had risen to over three million in the mid-1980s, and risen again in the early 1990s.[94] In retrospect, the first decade of New Labour government became the 'age of complacency', with 'non-inflationary continuous expansion' (NICE). Gordon Brown was only reflecting the contemporary consensus when he proclaimed 'the end of boom and bust'. Critics pointed to the continuing process of deindustrialization as a result of a strong exchange rate, but this strength was in New Labour's own terms a sign of how far credibility had been sustained.[95]

Contemporary New Labour supporters were also able to point to the extent to which at the beginning of the new millennium the fiscal rules were compatible with an enormous expansion of public spending, on education but especially health care. In these years we can see New Labour delivering key parts of a classic social democratic agenda of rapidly expanding welfare expenditure financed from the proceeds of economic growth. This was accompanied by policies which stemmed (although did not reverse) the huge increase in inequality of the 1980s, especially by wage subsidies through tax credits for those in work and improvements in pensioner entitlements.[96]

As discussed in Chapter 3, this perceived success of policy in preventing 'boom and bust', along with a reluctance to raise taxes, led to some slackening in adherence to the 'golden rule' on budget balance, with the deficit (public sector net borrowing) rising to a pre-crisis peak of 2.4 per cent of GDP in 2007/8 (compared to 3.4 per cent in 1996/7). As a result, the debt: GDP ratio started to rise, having fallen in the late 1990s as a result of GDP growth combined with budget surpluses. But on the eve of the crisis of 2007/8 the ratio, at 36.5 per cent, was still below that inherited in 1997 (43 per cent).[97]

92 ibid., p. 28. 93 ibid., p. x.
94 Cobham, Adam, and Mayhew, 'Economic'.
95 Arestis and Sawyer, 'Economic', p. 273.
96 Corry, 'Labour', ss. 123–39; Hills, Sefton, and Stewart, *Towards*.
97 Dolphin, *Debts*, pp. 4–5.

III

In 1996 Tony Blair told executives from News Corporation: 'What is called globalization is changing the notion of the nation state as power becomes more diffuse and borders more porous. Technological change is reducing the power and capacity of government to control its domestic economy free from external influence.'[98]

Treating globalization as a consequence of technological change reinforced the New Labour rhetoric of emphasizing the process as inevitable and irreversible, rather than, as it was, largely the product of policy decisions. What was most distinctive about the globalization of the last quarter of the twentieth century was the liberalization of capital flows. This was the product of political decisions, decisions in which Britain played an important role, as free movement of capital spread from the USA and UK to the rest of world. This happened in an atmosphere of the 'low political visibility' of the issue; as suggested above, it was the result of incremental changes going back to the late 1950s.[99]

But simultaneously there was the suggestion that Britain could 'make globalization work for us'. Globalization, in this account, offered the possibility, if responded to appropriately, of raising growth and living standards. How exactly this was to be achieved was surprisingly little emphasized in New Labour pronouncements. Historically the benefits of a key component of globalization, free trade, had been cheap imports of food, an issue which had been decisive in resisting protectionism in the Edwardian period and the 1920s.[100] But in post-1945 Britain this argument had less purchase. The proportion of income spent on food declined rapidly, and food prices no longer had the same political salience. In the EEC referendum debate of 1975, access to cheap Commonwealth food, such as New Zealand butter, was part of the arguments deployed against British membership, but with relatively little effect. By that date food was still around a quarter of household expenditure, but by the end of the century it was less than 15 per cent.[101]

Cheap food imports fitted into a world in which Britain exported industrial goods in exchange for food and raw materials—the classic pre-1914 system. But after 1945 such a pattern no longer characterized Britain's trade. Self-sufficiency in food had increased with agricultural subsidies (first under a British system of 'deficiency payments', later under the Common Agricultural Policy), whilst trade was increasingly dominated by manufactures on both sides of the account.[102] From the 1980s the price of manufactured imports relative to exports began to fall ('the terms of trade improved'), reflecting the flood of cheap products from Asia.[103] While the economic benefits of lower prices for consumers were clear, to argue the case for unrestricted imports when these were competitive with home-produced *industrial* goods was politically much more difficult than when only politically marginal domestic farmers were those whose livelihoods were threatened. Other arguments that persuaded economists of the benefits of free trade, such as the

[98] *Financial Times*, 20 March 1996. [99] Helleiner, *States*, pp. 19, 203–7.
[100] Trentmann, *Free*. [101] Blow, Leicester, and Oldfield, *Consumption*, p. 8.
[102] Rowthorn, *Deindustrialization*. [103] Spange and Young, 'Macroeconomic'.

enhanced competition making domestic producers more efficient, were not readily made congenial to a general audience, some of whom felt this competition in the loss of employment.

Globalization in Britain coincided with deindustrialization. It was not the main cause of deindustrialization, which owed more to a combination of changing consumption habits as incomes grew, and fast-rising productivity in industry, reflected in the lower prices of manufactured goods compared with services, where productivity growth was much slower.[104] Of course, there were obvious examples where 'globalization' could be seen at work in deindustrialization, as cheap imports undermined domestic production, whether it was in textiles or steel. Less obvious but also important has been the process whereby companies continue to manufacture in Britain, but have outsourced some of the less skill-intensive activities to developing countries.[105] Painful as these shifts were of course for those affected, they only accounted for a fraction of the industrial job losses, which began in large numbers well before the surge in globalization, in the 1950s and 1960s. Losses in those decades were notable for embracing not only tradeable sectors, but also those which were largely sheltered from international competition. Coal is a striking example, with no significant imports into Britain before the 1970s, but the loss of almost half a million jobs in the industry between the mid-1950s and early 1970s.[106]

In fact, in terms of the price of imported consumption goods, late twentieth-century globalization did yield substantial benefits to consumers, as the flood of cheap clothing and cheap electrical goods plainly illustrated. This was a particular feature, and major contributor, to the happy consumer times of the late 1990s and early 2000s (the 'NICE' years). But politically, perhaps unsurprisingly the emphasis was much more on the opening up of export markets than the opening up of the British market to cheap imports; Britons may have lived in a 'consumer society', but cheap imports were too problematic in their effects on producers to be a common object of public celebration.

Free movement of capital was likewise a feature of 'globalization' that was harder to link to an obvious celebratory message than in the early post-war decades when influxes of especially US capital were clearly employment-generating. The economists' view that the free movement of capital would enhance economic efficiency was not readily translatable into a popular narrative once this influx was reversed. Again, to many in Britain the background of deindustrialization seemed to suggest 'free movement' of capital meant a free *outflow*, with the loss of productive investment in jobs in Britain. Amongst policymakers, free movement of capital was most commonly defended as part of the underpinnings of the City of London, presented as a major contributor to the economy, a view which was little challenged before 'NICE' turned into crisis in 2007/8.[107]

104 Broadberry and Leunig, *Impact*.

105 Hijzen, Gorg, and Hine, 'International'.

106 Logan Turner, 'Post-war Pit Closures'.

107 Many of these claims were problematic: the growth of employment in 'the City' as opposed to mundane retail banking was limited; the tax revenues were of course offset by the costs of bank rescues after 2008, but even more so by the lost revenues from the recession caused by the City's behaviour; more profoundly, much of the City's revenue is better described as 'rent' rather than as a reward for

For New Labour, free movement of people was not generally emphasized as part of the benefits enjoyed by Britain as a result of 'globalization' (though Britons going as workers to Germany or as pensioners to Spain were a feature of the 1980s and 1990s). The regime governing the movement of labour was two-dimensional. First, for citizens from outside the European Union, the policy pursued was increasingly one which sought to maximize British benefit by allowing entry to those who had been educated at other countries' expense and offered skills in strong demand in the home economy.[108] Ethnicity became a less significant basis of selection of immigrants, with education and skills taking over. Second, for citizens of the EU, the decision was made to agree to free movement, even from newly acceding countries where temporary restrictions were available under the rules of the Union.

Economists have long argued that the pursuit of globalization should be made politically acceptable to a mass electorate by policies which help offset the costs of the transition for those disadvantaged by its immediate effects, and the provision of compensation for the losers by providing a significant safety net. New Labour placed a lot of emphasis, rhetorical and practical, on the first of these. Improved education and skills provision, 'education, education, and education', was a defining feature of New Labour.[109] But the issue of compensation for losers was more complex. New Labour aimed to reduce social security support by its policies of 'welfare to work'. In part this was successful during NICE, as employment expanded and unemployment fell (though much remained hidden in the official statistics). But despite this, overall public spending on social welfare increased, as emphasized in Chapter 3. Partly this was a matter of demographics, an ageing population driving up the demand for pensions (pensioners notably improved their relative position under New Labour), health, and care. With the inclusion of substantially increased expenditure on education, the New Labour period as a whole was characterized not only by a sharp rise in social welfare spending, but also by a very large rise in publicly funded employment (health, care, and education provision are all highly labour-intensive). Although not publicly stated in this way, New Labour partly compensated for the impact of globalization and deindustrialization by providing publicly funded employment. Overall, this pattern meant that, just as in the first great globalization before the First World War, far from globalization driving a 'race to the bottom' in social welfare provision, it was compatible with a large rise in such spending.[110]

This having been said, unlike the pre-1914 era, globalization in the later twentieth century, if it aided growth of GDP, also encouraged greater inequality.

useful activity. Andrew Haldane, Bank of England, Wincott Lecture 2011: http://www.bis.org/review/r111026a.pdf.

[108] Clarke, *Brave*, p. 19. The redistribution of income from poor to rich countries that flows from this migration has long been recognized by development economists and led, for example, to Jagdish Bhagwati's call for a migration tax: Collier, *Exodus*, pp. 149–53.

[109] Thus, for New Labour, education was both a way of offsetting the downside of globalization, and the (only) way of achieving its benefits.

[110] Rodrik, 'Why?'

This contrast is now widely accepted with, for example, O'Rourke arguing that 'Late nineteenth-century globalisation increased both average incomes and equality, but late twentieth-century globalisation probably made Britain richer, but more unequal'.[111] The rise in inequality evident in Britain from the 1980s was certainly not all due to globalization (an issue returned to in the closing chapter), but it played a part via outsourcing and the general impact on reinforcing the declining demand for skilled workers in manufacturing.[112]

This failure of globalization to deliver on the promises of New Labour is now recognized by adherents of those politics.[113] At the time, these effects of globalization meant that under New Labour the government's strong commitment to poverty reduction was always battling 'up a down escalator' as underlying economic forces were generating increased poverty and inequality. The huge sums spent on these policies had some effects in reducing poverty, especially child poverty, but overall inequality was broadly flat, with no reversal of the step increase experienced in the 1980s.

Finally, there is the problem of the way globalization is commonly understood as an all-embracing phenomenon. Standard stories told by economists and historians talk of globalization cycles, but assume that at any one time an economy is uniformly moving in the same direction. So Britain, for example, is either becoming less or more globalized. The problems of this conception can best begin with an example. In 1913, Dundee in Scotland could plausibly have been called the most globalized city in the world, measured as the proportion of its output and employment reliant on international economic factors. This position arose from Dundee being 'Juteopolis'; a city with an almost unparalleled reliance on one industry, jute (a coarse textile fibre, historically much used for sacking and bagging, later for linoleum and carpet-backing). In turn the jute industry relied both on international markets for its raw material (all grown in Bengal) and its markets for the manufactured product (sold all over the world, but especially in North America and other major primary producers). A hundred years later, jute had disappeared, and Dundee had become a classic 'post-industrial' city, its biggest employers in the public sector: the NHS, two universities, and the local authority. This means Dundee's economic fortunes became much more reliant on political decision-making in Edinburgh and London, and much less on global forces; the city had become 'deglobalized'.[114] Dundee is an extreme case; it was exceptionally globalized in 1913, and an exceptionally 'public sector city' a century later. But similar trends may be observed across the UK, and this should counsel us against talking about 'globalization' as if the economy and all its sectors and regions are moving in the same direction.

[111] 'From Empire to Europe', p. 91; note the changing views of this issue by Paul Krugman, as noted by Rodrik, *Globalization*, pp. 84–5.

[112] Haskel and Slaughter, 'Trade'; Hijzen et al., 'International'.

[113] Mandelson, 'Foreword'.

[114] The Dundee story is complicated by the fact that in the 1940s through to the 1970s the city saw a very substantial influx of American MNCs, creating thousands of manufacturing jobs; but most of these were lost in the 1970s and 1980s.

Deglobalization is especially evident in previously heavily industrial areas, dominated by companies exporting the staple products of Victorian Britain and often using imported raw materials; the areas which have suffered major declines in industrial activity and employment. These include the textile areas of Lancashire, Yorkshire, and Scotland; and the shipbuilding areas of Merseyside, Tyneside, Clydeside, and Belfast. Ironically, while New Labour was proclaiming the advent of 'globalization', in many parts of the country where its support traditionally lay, the economy was becoming less reliant on internationally traded goods, with fast growth of employment in private, and especially public sector service, jobs.[115]

So the idea of a uniform tendency (national or international) to globalization is misleading and unhelpful. In 1933, Keynes, foreseeing a more nationally self-sufficient future, wrote 'as wealth increases, both primary and manufacture products play a smaller relative part in the national economy compared with houses, personal services and local amenities which are not the subject of international exchange'.[116] His prophecy was not perfect, and most obviously he did not foresee the extent to which the ICT revolution would make possible international trade in some services, especially financial. Nevertheless, in linking the transition to a 'post-industrial' economy to levels of international economic globalization, he was pointing to an important truth.

IV

With the 2007/8 recession and the demise of New Labour in 2010 globalization was displaced by a debt and deficit narrative, as discussed in Chapter 5. But the Brexit victory of June 2016 brought the term back into prominence, as the decision was widely interpreted as a popular, especially working-class, rejection of globalization. Newspaper headlines and the blogosphere speculated whether globalization could survive this rejection.[117] As usual, the term 'globalization' was being deployed with considerable vagueness and under-specification. But the polling evidence certainly suggested that one component of globalization, large-scale immigration, was very important in deciding the vote.[118]

Ironically, perhaps, it was the 'Europeanization' of the labour market, rather than its 'globalization' which proved politically most problematic. By and large the British public adjusted to the influx of Filipino nurses and Indian doctors, but as Brexit was to show, resentment could be readily stirred against the inflow of much more diversely skilled migrants from the new EU accession states. While the numbers

[115] Buchanan et al., 'Undisclosed'; *Cities Outlook 2014*. [116] Keynes, 'National', p. 238.

[117] 'Brexit is a rejection of globalisation' *The Guardian* 26 June 2016; 'Will "Brexit" mark the end of globalization?' *Los Angeles Times* 24 June 2016; 'Britain's Brexit just killed globalisation as we know it' *Sydney Morning Herald* 26 June 2016; D. Coyle, 'Brexit and Globalisation' Vox http://voxeu.org/article/brexit-and-globalisation.

[118] Lord Ashcroft, 'How the UK voted on Thursday…and why': http://lordashcroftpolls.com/2016/06/how-the-united-kingdom-voted-and-why/; J. Curtice 'How deeply does Britain's Euroscepticism run?' http://www.bsa.natcen.ac.uk/latest-report/british-social-attitudes-33/euroscepticism.aspx.

of these migrants was smaller than from non-EU countries, they undoubtedly had an effect in slightly depressing wages in some low-skill occupations.[119]

The evidence suggests that this anti-immigration feeling was long-standing, and in fact only slightly increased by the surge in numbers entering from the 2004 accession states. The British Social Attitudes survey in 2012 showed that throughout the period of the surge in net immigration from the early 1990s, a clear majority of respondents wanted immigrant numbers cut, the figure rising from 63 per cent in 1995 to 78 in 2008, falling slightly to 75 in 2011.[120]

The context was also one of stagnating wages in the period since the recession, especially in areas outside London and the South East.[121] But only a small proportion of this stagnation can be plausibly ascribed to globalization in any useful sense, rather, most of it reflected the long-standing processes of deindustrialization, and accompanying wage polarization, along with the economic stagnation of the post-crisis period.[122]

Importantly, little of the popular debate leading up to the referendum focused upon the traditional areas where a backlash against globalization might be anticipated. For example, the respected polling organization YouGov posed the following question to its respondents in 2011: 'People sometimes talk about "globalization", with companies investing, trading and employing people around the world. In general, do you think globalization is generally good or bad for the British economy?', and found that only 30 per cent of respondents thought it was good.[123] But the idea that corporate freedom, especially to 'export jobs', was crucial to globalization did not figure much in the Brexit debate, though the contraction of jobs in Tata Steel in the face of Chinese competition was being debated in March and April 2016.

Unlike in the USA, where the issue of job losses from Asian competition seems to have been much more politically significant, in Britain this aspect of globalization was much less emphasized than migration.[124] Strikingly, the 'Remain' campaign focused attention on the size of the EU market, entry to which was allegedly to be curtailed for British producers in the event of an exit vote. By contrast, very little was said about the benefits to consumers of cheap imports, despite this, taken by itself, being perhaps the most unambiguous benefit of globalization for British people.

By so relentlessly proclaiming the recent period as one of globalization, politicians (mainly on the Centre-Left) and other commentators opened the way for those (for whatever reason) discontented with their economic lot to view this

[119] Clarke, *Brave*, pp. 5, 13–18.

[120] Ford, Morrell, and Heath, '"Fewer?"', p. 30.

[121] D. Coyle, 'Brexit and Globalisation' Vox http://voxeu.org/article/brexit-and-globalisation.

[122] Clarke, *Brave*, p. 17.

[123] https://d25d2506sfb94s.cloudfront.net/today_uk_import/YG-Archives-Pol-Prospect-SocialMoralIssues_101026.pdf. The question strikingly sidesteps the substantial role of governments as agents of globalization.

[124] On the USA: Democracy Corps 'Taking on trade, unions and banks in 2016' http://www.democracycorps.com/Rewriting-the-Rules-of-the-Economy/taking-on-trade-unions-and-banks-in-2016/.

process in a negative light. Paradoxically, exaggerations about the inevitability and ubiquity of this process, commonly intended to persuade the public into acceptance of its 'reality', rebounded in the Brexit debate. Those who proclaimed themselves 'anti-globalizers' (especially on the Right of the political spectrum) were emboldened by the June 2016 decision, whilst 'globalizers' found themselves very much on the defensive.

5

Deficits, Debts, and Austerity

'The first crisis of globalization' was how Gordon Brown characteristically described the financial crisis which unfolded from 2007.[1] Yet the narrative which dominated British economic life as that crisis gained momentum was little related to its *global* aspects, but focused on arguments about the *national* economy, above all national finances and the fiscal deficits and increased national debt the crisis produced. Equally, the dominant policy debate through to and beyond the 2015 election was around the desirability and implications of a national policy of 'austerity'.[2]

The shaping of the economic debate was, of course, highly party political. The crisis opened up an opportunity for the Conservatives to attack the incumbent Labour Party, especially as the leading architect of New Labour's economic policy, Gordon Brown, had become the party's new leader and Prime Minister just before the crisis began. (Brown became Labour leader in June 2007, the beginning of the run on the Northern Rock bank coming in mid-September). But in focusing on deficits and debts as the key problem, and austerity as the solution, the Conservatives were drawing upon arguments which had roots well beyond the immediate circumstances. In explaining the success of this narrative we undoubtedly need to look at the politics of the time, but also to go beyond those to analyse why this political posture achieved such a dominance of the debate.

Debt and deficits had not had such prominence in the economic narrative in Britain since the aftermath of the First World War, when radical measures, such as a capital levy, were widely debated in mainstream circles, so serious was the perception of the problem. The debt relative to GDP after the Second World War was almost three times that of the 2000s, but, as pointed out in Chapter 1, it was *not* the focus of contemporary policy debate. Like most economic narratives, that of debts and deficits had a large historical element, but one with strong contemporary political purpose: the Conservatives seeking to blame New Labour for 'reverting to type' and causing the deficit problem. In this story, the Labour government had pursued an inappropriate and irresponsible fiscal policy which had 'failed to mend the roof while the sun was shining'. So this narrative combined an attack on Labour's competence to manage the economy with a strongly moral aspect alleging profligacy and lack of concern for consequences.

[1] Brown, *Beyond*.

[2] Generally Conservatives eschewed the term 'austerity', preferring the more positive, and positively morally charged 'living within our means'.

The narrative offered diagnosis, prognosis, and cure: the accumulation of deficits and debt in the crisis allegedly threatened a profound breakdown of the economy, and this could be avoided only by a radical policy of austerity in public spending. This 'austerity', it should be stressed, was very different in meaning to that pursued after 1945. It was overwhelmingly about cutting public spending, and though there was talk of the irresponsibility of debt accumulation, private as well as public, and the need for 'rebalancing' the economy, nothing like the 1940s programme of constraining consumption to favour investment and exports was seriously proposed or pursued.[3]

This narrative was powerfully propagated in the run-up to, during, and after the 2010 election, and continued to dominate economic arguments through the period of Coalition and into the Conservative government after 2015. This chapter examines the underpinnings of that narrative by looking in turn at the development of Labour's pre-crisis fiscal policy, then at the nature and significance of the 'Keynesian moment' of 2008–9. Following this is an analysis of the Conservatives' economic policy stances up to 2007/8, and then how they used the crisis to construct an effective narrative in opposition to Labour. The next section looks at the two successive budgets of 2010 and how they sought to define the economic policy options; while the general election of that year polarized economic debate, this section explores how far apart the parties' postures really were. The penultimate section looks at the meaning of austerity after 2010 and the significance (or otherwise) of the notion of 'rebalancing' the economy. Finally, a brief summary is given of the way in which the 'Brexit' debate and outcome crowded out the 'debt and deficit' narrative.

I

After the traumas of 'Old Labour' in the 1970s, a key part of New Labour's claim for electoral support was based on its embrace of fiscal prudence, backed up by the announcement of new fiscal rules. Such rules were strongly urged by economists, who believed they were crucial to policy credibility, and had been taken up by the IMF and other bodies. For New Labour they seemed to offer a means of reassuring financial markets about the responsible stance that would be upheld by future Labour governments, in parallel with the credibility on monetary policy to be secured by Central Bank independence.[4]

The first of these fiscal rules was known as the 'golden rule'. It was set out in the March 1998 Budget, and stated that over the economic cycle the government would only borrow to invest rather than to fund current expenditure.[5] This rule was based on notions of fairness as well as credibility, as 'public-sector investment will bring benefits tomorrow as well as today, so it would seem inappropriate that

[3] Froud et al., 'Rebalancing'. [4] IMF, 'Fiscal'; Wysploz, 'Fiscal'.

[5] For the background: Balls, 'Open'; Balls and O'Donnell, *Reforming*, pp. 155–81; Brown, 'Conditions'.

this investment should be financed out of today's taxes. Public consumption, however, will only bring benefits today, so it should be paid for today'.[6] The inclusion of 'over the economic cycle', a standard feature of fiscal rules, was to ensure that the government would have room to accommodate fluctuations in the fiscal balance arising from variations in economic growth, via budget surpluses and deficits (the 'automatic stabilizers').

The second fiscal rule was known as the 'sustainable investment rule'. The Treasury aimed to keep debt at a 'stable and prudent' level, which they defined as less than 40 per cent of GDP.[7] This aimed to run budget deficits only to fund investment, in order to ensure that public debt could not creep up to unsustainable levels. With this rule Labour set a ceiling for its debt levels, rather than trying to reduce the overall level over time, which obviously meant a vulnerability to the rule being broken if there was a shock.

In Labour's first years in power the public finances strengthened further, as the new government stuck to the restrictive public spending plans laid out by the Conservatives before the 1997 election (see Table 5.1).[8] In the first two years of his chancellorship, Brown maintained a tight control on spending, for example in 1998 public finances were in a better position than forecast, yet the Budget announced further tightening of 1 per cent of GDP in 1998/9. Expansion came

Table 5.1 Public finances, 1996/7–2014/15

	Public spending (total managed expenditure as percentage of GDP)	**Public borrowing (PSNB as percentage of GDP, + = *surplus*)**	**Public debt (outstanding debt as percentage of GDP)**
1996/7	38.1	3.3	39.7
1997/8	36.9	0.7	39.1
1998/9	36.2	+0.5	37.3
1999/2000	35.9	+1.5	34.4
2000/1	36.1	+1.6	29.9
2001/2	37.1	0.1	29.3
2002/3	37.9	2.3	30.3
2003/4	38.7	2.6	31.8
2004/05	40.1	3.4	34.3
2005/6	40.1	3.1	35.4
2006/7	39.9	2.6	36.1
2007/8	40.3	2.7	36.9
2008/9	43.8	6.9	51.9
2009/10	46.1	10.3	65.2
2010/11	45.3	8.7	71.7
2011/12	43.9	7.1	75.2
2012/13	43.5	7.2	78.9
2013/14	41.9	5.9	81.0
2014/15	40.8	5.0	83.3

Source: OBR databank.

[6] Wren-Lewis, 'Aggregate', p. 26.
[7] Chote et al., 'Public', p. 4.
[8] Chote et al., 'Public', p. 1.

at the turn of the millennium with the Budget of 2000; again public finances were in a better state than forecast—due to strong growth.[9] However, Wren-Lewis points out that at the time the National Institute of Economic and Social Research criticized the government as they 'were interpreting these errors (beneficial ones) as structural rather than temporary', yet 'there was little criticism of the move to fiscal expansion' from any political party.[10] Britain was still running a budget surplus of between 1 and 2 per cent between 2000 and 2001.[11] In its first term in office, 1997–2001, Labour was able to eliminate an (unadjusted) deficit of 3.3 per cent of GDP, and thus reduce the net debt from 39.7 per cent of GDP to 29.9 per cent.[12]

Labour's second term in office marked the beginning of deterioration in the public finances, with a reduction in tax revenue and a continuation of expansionary fiscal policy. The first budget of the term in 2002 was a 'turning point' as 'for the first time fiscal outturns were less favourable than had been projected – expansion continued, however'. During the second term Brown announced major spending commitments, most significantly a 7 per cent increase in NHS spending per year until 2007. This was partly matched by an increase in National Insurance contributions; however this was a one-off rise, whereas the NHS spending commitment was to maintain a share of 7 per cent of GDP of a continually growing economy.[13] There was also an unexpected fall in tax receipts from the financial sector, especially in the earlier part of the second term, as the sector did not perform as strongly as was anticipated. Tax receipts stabilized in 2004, and rose by 1 per cent of GDP in 2005. However, Brown was reluctant to introduce any new tax increases before the 2005 election to finance the increases in spending. By the time of the 2005 election, the (unadjusted) deficit stood at 3.4 per cent of GDP and the net debt had risen from its lowest level at 29.3 per cent of GDP in 2001/2 to 34.3 per cent in 2004/5.[14]

After the 2005 election, Labour began to move again towards fiscal contraction, albeit in a 'small and slow' manner.[15] To avoid breaking the golden rule, there were tax rises in the 2006 Budget. Between 2005 and 2007 tax receipts grew by 1.5 per cent of GDP, whilst spending only grew by 0.5 per cent.[16] On the eve of the crisis, there was an (unadjusted) deficit of 2.6 per cent of GDP, with an adjusted figure of 0.6 per cent. Over Labour's pre-crisis years (1997/8 to 2007/8) the cyclically adjusted deficit averaged precisely zero.[17] Net public debt in 2007/8 was 36.9 per cent of GDP—less than when Labour came to office in 1997.[18] A balanced summary of the debt position is that 'The UK had a relatively low level of debt in 2007 by international standards but had done less than most other advanced countries

[9] Wren-Lewis, 'Aggregate', pp. 34–5. [10] ibid., p. 35.

[11] Ussher, 'Labour's', S. 112. Note that the more up-to-date numbers cited from Table 5.1 differ very slightly from those used by Ussher, but the pattern described is exactly the same.

[12] Ussher, 'Labour's', S. 112. The figures given in Table 5.1 for the deficit make no allowance for the state of the economic cycle. Policy often focused on the deficit adjusted for the cycle (the 'structural deficit'), but the scale of these adjustments was highly contentious and varied significantly over time.

[13] Wren-Lewis, 'Aggregate', p. 36. [14] Ussher, 'Labour's', S. 112.

[15] Wren-Lewis, 'Aggregate', p. 39. [16] Ussher, 'Labour's', S. 113.

[17] Dolphin, *Debts*, p. 3. [18] Chote et al., 'Public', p. 10.

to reduce debt between 2004 and 2007—in fact, the UK's debt level had grown over this period'.[19]

In the expert literature there is plenty of criticism of Labour's management of public finances in the decade between taking power in 1997 and the crash of 2007. The Institute for Fiscal Studies (IFS) singles out the Treasury's optimistic fiscal projections for the worsening of public finances, which was used as justification for resisting bigger tax increases: 'Between 2002 and 2007, the Treasury's initial forecasts for borrowing were consistently lower than borrowing actually turned out to be'.[20] The IFS also make an international comparison, stating that 'most OECD governments did more to reduce their structural deficit during the period from 1997 to 2007 than Labour did'.[21] Liadze and Weale highlight the complacency of the Labour government, arguing that 'the Government assumed, despite a past history of forecasting errors, that there was no possibility of recession'[22]—Brown subscribed to a theory amongst many economists that they had achieved the end of 'boom and bust' economic cycles.

The golden rule was a problem, as it was to be met over the 'economic cycle', which allowed Brown to be backward-looking in achieving the target in 2007. Wren-Lewis stresses that 'the problem was that these rules were backward-looking, and that early surpluses were being used to justify current deficits which were not sustainable in the long term'.[23] However, there is a broad consensus in the applied economics literature that whilst Labour's fiscal policy was not perfect, it was by no means disastrous. The IFS point out that 'the public finances were in a stronger position than they had been when Labour came to power in 1997'.[24] Wren-Lewis believes that 'the line that the Labour government was responsible for leaving a disastrous fiscal position which requires great national sacrifice to put right is pure spin'.[25] He also states that 'The government cannot be reasonably blamed for failing to foresee the timing and extent of the Great Recession', the implication being that it was the recession that was most at fault for the huge level of public debt. But the domination of particular economic narratives is not usually determined by the assessments of economists, and politically driven 'spin' was to prove more powerful than close analysis of the data for the first decade of New Labour's time in office.

The crisis quickly brought a dramatic change in the public finances. Unadjusted PSNB rose to a peak of 10 per cent of GDP in 2009/10, while cyclically adjusted net borrowing rose from 2.6 per cent in 2007/8 to 6.3 in 2008/9 and 8.7 per cent in 2009/10. The public sector net debt rose by 15 per cent in one year, 2007/8 to 2008/9, and continued to rise thereafter. The first budget after the crisis struck saw the government pursuing modest deliberate fiscal loosening with an acceptance that in combination with the automatic stabilizers this would yield a widening short-run fiscal deficit. The view was clear that 'the increase in borrowing supports economic stability, in line with one of the key purposes of the fiscal framework'.[26]

[19] Emmerson and Tetlow, 'UK', p. 567.
[20] Chote et al., 'Public', p. 6.
[21] ibid., p. 11.
[22] Liadze and Weale, 'Economic', R. 3.
[23] Wren-Lewis, 'Aggregate', p. 38.
[24] Chote et al., 'Public', p. 10.
[25] Wren-Lewis, 'Aggregate', p. 45; also Wren-Lewis, 'Lessons'.
[26] HMT, *Budget 2009*, p. 1.

The UK government claimed this policy stance (with some fiscal tightening from 2009/10) was fully in line with golden and sustainable debt rules.[27] By the time of the spring 2009 budget the environment had worsened sharply. This was the time of the April London G20 summit, which announced a 'global plan for recovery' pledging to 'restore confidence, growth and jobs' by 'undertaking an unprecedented and concerted fiscal expansion' and committing to 'deliver the scale of fiscal effort necessary to restore growth'.[28]

In the UK, GDP was expected to fall by 3.5 per cent in the calendar year, and the fiscal position to deteriorate sharply due to deliberate policy loosening and the effects of the automatic stabilizers, and the costs of bailing out failing financial institutions. The projection was that PSNB would rise sharply to peak at 12.4 per cent of GDP in 2009/10, with debt rising to 79 per cent of GDP[29] (the outcome is in Table 5.1). The expectation was that, with projected fiscal tightening once the recession abated, there would be a return to cyclically adjusted fiscal balance by 2017/8, the same year that the debt ratio would start to fall.

These projections clearly pushed policy outside the existing New Labour fiscal rules, and the government offered a new 'temporary fiscal operating' rule. This pledged 'to set policies to improve the cyclically adjusted current budget each year, once the economy emerges from the downturn, so it reaches balance and debt is falling as a proportion of GDP once the shocks have worked their way through the economy in full'.[30] The challenge to credibility from this shift of 'rules' was responded to by appealing to authoritative international bodies, notably the IMF, as alternative sources of credibility. Thus, the presentation of the fiscal argument was placed in the context of the international agreement made by the G20 countries and the European Council, which included a commitment to coordinated fiscal stimuli endorsed by the IMF, with the British position also being emphasized as in line with the G7 average.[31]

The response by New Labour to the recession led to 'a surprisingly coordinated if short-lived proto-Keynesian counter-offensive to the crisis'.[32] This policy response was certainly important, and undoubtedly prevented an even worse recession. The possibility of such a response drew in large part on the coincidence of Gordon Brown's premiership with the Presidency of Barack Obama, allowing for a degree of ideological agreement on the need for activist government.[33] But most of the fiscal stimulus to the British economy came from the automatic stabilizers; as in the early 1990s (but unlike the early 1980s), these stabilizers were allowed to work, and were assisted by a *small* reflationary package (tax cuts and spending increases).[34] Thus, as always, *deliberate* fiscal policy was only a limited part of the explanation for the scale of deficits and debts that were incurred. In addition, and unlike any

[27] HMT, *Budget 2008*, pp. 4–5, 23–30.

[28] G20, 2009. Communiqué from the London summit. London, 2 April, p. 2. https://www.imf.org/external/np/sec/pr/2009/pdf/g20_040209.pdf.

[29] HMT, *Budget 2009*, p. 29. [30] ibid., pp. 19, 27, 31, 35–8. [31] ibid., pp. 15, 27–9.

[32] Hay, 'Treating'. [33] Brown's account is in *Beyond*, pp. 113–32.

[34] Hodson and Mabbett, 'UK': the Treasury calculated the discretionary stimulus to be worth 1.1 per cent of GDP: HMT, *Pre-Budget Report* November 2008, p. 3.

other modern recession, the government also borrowed and spent heavily to rescue financial institutions. The 'Keynesian moment' was at its strongest between the G20 summits in November 2008 and March 2009, when Gordon Brown, along with Obama and the head of the IMF, Dominique Strauss-Kahn, and others were singing the praises of internationally coordinated countercyclical fiscal policy to stave off global depression.[35]

Signs of a shift in the UK fiscal stance are evident as early as the *Pre-Budget Report* of November 2008. Whilst supporting the international agreement to counteract the recession by countercyclical measures, the *PBR*, along with the budget of the following spring, announced a sharp slowing of the growth of public spending, with substantial cuts in some areas. Borrowing was projected to fall by £56 billion, with one quarter coming from increased taxation, three-quarters from expenditure cuts. The Chancellor estimated that with around 60 per cent of spending ring-fenced, the remaining government programmes would be subject to an average cut of 15 per cent.[36]

The election of a Conservative-led government in June 2010 coincided with an ebbing of the tide that had supported fiscal action during the downturn. The move is captured by contrasting the London April 2009 G20 summit—with its emphasis on Keynesian countercyclical fiscal stimulus, coordinated internationally—with the Toronto June 2010 G20's shift of tone to an emphasis on 'growth-friendly fiscal consolidation'.[37] This shift reflected recognition that recovery had begun in late 2009, in Britain and most other countries. In Britain, the recession had bottomed out in the second quarter of 2009.

In making an overall assessment of the fiscal policy of New Labour prior to 2007/8, Johnson makes an instructive comparison with the late 1980s. As he suggests, in the early 2000s,

> just as happened in the late 1980s, a degree of hubris allowed the government to convince itself that it had achieved what no government had previously achieved—in Nigel Lawson's case that the trend growth of the economy had risen to much higher levels and in Gordon Brown's case that he had abolished the economic cycle, or 'boom and bust' as he put it.[38]

But the shift of Chancellor from Brown to Darling in 2007 sharpened the debate in the Labour Party as the recession took hold. Darling rejected Brown's view that the political argument should be posed as Labour 'investors' versus Tory 'cutters'. Instead, he successfully pursued the line that while using supportive fiscal policy as long as it was needed, Labour should make it clear that the previous expansion of public expenditure needed to be radically slowed, some areas subject to retrenchment, and preparation made for fiscal consolidation once the worst of the crisis

[35] Blyth, *Austerity*, pp. 54–62.

[36] Darling, *Back*, p. 266; HMT, *Pre-Budget Report* November 2008, pp. 1–3; HMT, *Budget 2009*, p. 1.

[37] G20, 2009, Communiqué; G20, 2010, Communiqué from the Toronto summit, 26–27 June. http://www.oecd.org/g20/summits/toronto/g20-declaration.pdf.

[38] Johnson, 'UK', p. 435.

was past. For him, the dividing line with the Tories, from 2009, was simply the appropriate pace of deficit reduction.[39]

This victory for Darling's approach had ambivalent political consequences. While it may have aided Labour's electoral position in 2010, it left a complex legacy for when the party went into opposition. When the Conservatives came forward with their plans after June, Labour opposition to expenditure cuts could be easily contrasted with what had been previously said. Thus when Harriet Harman attacked the cuts proposed by Osborne, a Conservative MP could rightly point to the small differences between the parties on the scale of proposed reductions advocated in the run-up to the election.[40] 'Cutters versus investors' was a political narrative with limited purchase.

II

The Conservative manifesto for the general election of 2005 criticized Labour's fiscal policy, alleging that the 'government is spending too much, wasting too much . . . if we are to secure our future prosperity, government must once again start to live within its means'.[41] But no major cuts were identified, and economies were to come from the perennially appealed to (and perennially vague) 'efficiency savings'.

The failure of the Conservatives to win the 2005 election led to the election of another new leader, and a shift in the *tone* of political argument about the economy, though the underlying ideas did not shift very much.[42] The party's initial stance under the new leadership of Cameron was linked to the fundamental claim for post-Thatcher Tories that Thatcherite policies had solved Britain's basic economic problem, and now the focus should be on the 'social problem', evidenced in a huge 'Breakdown Britain' report in 2006.[43]

On the back of this complacent view of the economy, Conservatives promised to match or even exceed New Labour spending on NHS and education up until November 2008.[44] However, the policy review of 2006/7 and the discussions that followed showed continuing tensions in the party, above all on how far priority should be given to tax cuts. The leadership's line was that the proceeds of growth should be shared between tax cuts and public spending increases, but obviously once growth halted in the crisis this stance had to be revised.[45]

The Conservative responses to the crisis of 2007/8 involved a significant sharpening of the attacks on government policy. Having criticized Labour's excessive

[39] Darling, *Back*, pp. 224–9, 282.

[40] A. Tyrie MP, *Hansard* (Commons) vol. 512, col. 185, 22 June 2010; he cites the work of the IFS, for which see, for example, IFS, *Election Briefing 2010*, pp. 12–13.

[41] *Conservative Manifesto 2005*, http://www.politicsresources.net/area/uk/ge05/man/manifesto-uk-2005.pdf, p. 3.

[42] Hayton, *Reconstructing?* [43] Bale, *Conservative.*

[44] ibid., p. 349; Dorey, Garnett, and Denham, *Crisis*, pp. 92–108.

[45] Speech by Osborne, 23 January 2006, 'stability before tax cuts' http://conservative-speeches.sayit.mysociety.org/speech/600153; Dorey, '"Sharing"'.

regulation of banks as late as 2007, Cameron attacked the rescue of Northern Rock in 2007, and the fiscal stimulus that Labour announced in that year.[46] Initially, as Kavanagh and Cowley note, this negative attitude to the government's initiatives seems to have damaged the Conservatives' polling position, in the face of popular support for the government's emergency measures.[47] But despite this, by the time of the Conservative Party conference of 2008 the narrative was in place and set the agenda for the succeeding period.

David Cameron's conference speech set out this narrative very clearly:

> At the heart of the financial crisis is a simple fact. The tap marked 'borrowing' was turned on—and it was left running for too long. The debts we built up were too high. Far too high. The authorities—on both sides of the Atlantic—thought it could go on for ever. Gordon Brown's second big mistake (after taking away Bank of England's role in financial regulation) was on government borrowing. After a prudent start... he turned into a spendaholic. His spending splurge left the government borrowing money in the good times when it should have been saving money. So now that the bad times have hit, there's no money to help. The cupboard is bare.[48]

This was supported by Osborne:

> The reason why our banking system is under such strain, why thousands of people fear for their jobs, and why all the talk has been of rescue deals and bail outs is this: In Britain, and in America too, we forgot something we should never have forgotten... that an economy built on debt is not an economy built to last. For a decade the whole world enjoyed the good times—and nowhere was the boom greater than here in Britain. We borrowed and borrowed as if the party would never end. Banks did. Businesses did. Families did. And so did this government. And then like any party that goes on too long, things got out of hand. British households borrowed more than any in Europe. British house prices rose faster than in America. Britain's budget deficit grew larger than any in the developed world. And instead of trying to rein in the boom, Gordon Brown led by example. Think you're borrowing too much? Don't worry, Gordon Brown said, your government is borrowing even more....
>
> What we need is a wholly different approach.... It is a plan to end Britain's dependency on debt. We will bring fiscal responsibility to our government. And we will bring financial responsibility in our economy.[49]

Bale has identified the autumn of 2008 as the time when the Conservatives decisively changed tack in economic policy:

> The decision made by Cameron and Osborne in late November 2008 not only to abandon their year-old pledge to match Labour's spending plans until 2010–11 but to go even further than the government in trying to find efficiency savings in order to reduce borrowing, suggested that the global downturn exposed the limits of the Party's rhetorical commitment to the centre ground.[50]

[46] Conservative Party, 'Freeing'; *Daily Telegraph* 16 September 2007.
[47] Kavanagh and Cowley, *British General Election of 2010*, p. 91; Bale, *Conservative*, pp. 351–2.
[48] http://www.theguardian.com/politics/2008/oct/01/davidcameron.toryconference1.
[49] http://www.theguardian.com/politics/2008/sep/29/toryconference.georgeosborne.
[50] Bale, *Conservative*, p. 384.

By the time of the 2009 conference the policy stance had solidified. Osborne argued that, while not opposed to fiscal stimuli in all circumstances, it was inappropriate for a country with Britain's scale of deficit. He also announced a big programme of public expenditure cuts to be pursued by a future Conservative government.[51] In the run-up to the 2010 election Andy Coulson, Conservative Director of Communications and Planning, 'shared Osborne's view that a key to Conservative success was pinning blame for the economic recession on Brown'.[52]

The 2010 Conservative election manifesto carried this strategy through, setting out the Conservative stance thus:

> Our belief in responsibility with public finances is the starting point of our plan for economic recovery and growth. We want your consent for a programme of public spending control that will deal with Labour's debt crisis and stop the Labour jobs tax that would kill our economic recovery.... [T]he real prize for Britain is to create a new economic model, one founded on investment and savings, not borrowing and debt.... *Gordon Brown's debt, waste and taxes have wrecked the economy and threaten to kill the recovery. A Conservative government will take action now to cut the deficit, stop Labour's jobs tax, help keep mortgage rates low and get the economy moving. We will create a new economic model built on investment and savings, not borrowing and debt....* One thing is clear. We can't go on with the old model of an economy built on debt. Irresponsible public spending, an overblown banking sector, and unsustainable consumer borrowing on the back of a housing bubble were the features of an age of irresponsibility that left Britain badly exposed to the economic crisis. Now, with the national debt already doubled and in danger of doubling again, it is this debt—together with the jobs tax that Labour will introduce to help pay for it—that threatens to kill the recovery.[53]

While this strategy was very clear by 2010, and can be seen as emerging from 2008, it was not without tensions. While the Conservatives attacked Labour's policies before the crisis struck, their attitude to Labour's 'Keynesian' response was ambiguous. While criticizing the rescue of Northern Rock and the stimulus package, they certainly did *not* call for the overriding of the automatic stabilizers, crucial to the policy of the Thatcher government in the early 1980s. Equally, in response to the April 2009 G20 agreement they attacked it as a 'mirage', offering no real new money, and emphasized the scepticism of the Germans about the deal, rather than attacking the principle of a coordinated fiscal stimulus. These were George Osborne's words in the House of Commons:

> Finally, the great thing missing from the communiqué is the one thing that the Prime Minister lobbied hardest for—that is, a new commitment to a significant second fiscal stimulus, so that the Chancellor would have cover to announce one in the Budget later this month. That commitment is very obviously not there. Indeed, the $1 trillion

[51] http://www.theguardian.com/politics/2009/sep/15/george-osborne-speech-full-text.

[52] Kavanagh and Cowley, *British General Election of 2010*, p. 83.

[53] Conservative Party, *Invitation*, viii, 3, emphasis added (the 'jobs tax' relates to Labour's proposal to raise National Insurance contributions). The manifesto illustrated its claims with charts of the growth of Britain's national debt from 1997 (absolute numbers, not relative to GDP), international comparisons of budget deficits, and debt interest relative to other elements of public spending.

> being trumpeted today is $1 trillion of loans, credit lines and guarantees. We welcome that, because we, too, have talked about loans and credit guarantees. What it does not contain is a single extra dollar or pound of additional fiscal stimulus. In the communiqué it is explicitly left to individual countries to decide for themselves what their own public finances can support.
>
> The communiqué says that the signatories should put in place 'credible exit strategies' from the fiscal position that they are in. That is exactly as it should be. It is a vindication of the argument made by the Conservative Party in recent months. It must mean that the Chancellor now pays attention to the advice of the Governor of the Bank of England and rules out a significant second fiscal stimulus in the Budget.[54]

III

The March 2010 Budget document argued that the recession had had a twofold effect on the fiscal balance. First, the workings of the automatic stabilizers, and the government's deliberate fiscal loosening to offset the fall in demand, had worsened the position. But in addition, it was argued, the recession

> had a more persistent impact on the public finances, due to its downward impact on the trend level of output in the economy, which is assumed to be just over 5 per cent, a permanent loss of tax receipts from the financial and housing sectors and the projected rebalancing of the economic activity, which will result in less tax-rich growth in the economy.[55]

However, the economy had begun to recover in late 2009, so by the time of Labour's last budget in March 2010 the policies announced in the budget were stated to be 'fiscally neutral', with a further loosening (estimated at £1.4 billion) in 2010/11 followed by a more than offsetting tightening thereafter, reaching £1.6 billion by 2014/15. It also stipulated a requirement that debt be falling in 2015/16, a more conservative stance than envisaged in the 2009 budget. So the budget statement was clear that 'fiscal policy should shift towards consolidation in 2011/12'.[56]

Public spending was still to rise in 2010/11 'to help support the economy through the recovery'. But, as already announced in 2009, the growth of such spending would fall to 0.8 per cent per annum from 2011/12 to 2014/15, while public investment would fall. This was coupled to a forecast that the PSNB would peak at 11.8 per cent of GDP in 2009/10, then fall to 4 per cent by 2014/15.[57] (The data in Table 5.1 suggest this was overly pessimistic about the immediate deficit, but overly optimistic about how quickly the deficit would fall, because of exaggerated hopes about how quickly the economy would recover. This led in turn to an over-optimistic view of the public debt, which it was envisaged would peak at 74.9 per cent in 2014/15.)

[54] *Hansard* (Commons) vol. 490, col. 1140, 2 April 2009; *Independent* 4 April 2009; *The Times* 4 April 2009.
[55] HMT, *Budget March 2010*, p. 21.
[56] ibid., pp. 13, 29.
[57] ibid., pp. 1–4.

While public spending was to continue to grow, as suggested in the *Pre-Budget Report* for 2009, there would be cuts to some areas, mostly arising from 'operational efficiencies'. To slow the pace of expansion the most radical policy was a restriction in public sector pay increases to 1 per cent per annum for 2011/12 and 2012/13. On the tax side, income tax allowances were to be frozen, and there would be an increase in National Insurance contributions.[58]

But the plans of the March budget were soon overtaken by the May general election, which brought the Conservative-led Coalition to power, and they introduced a new budget in June. This proposed an 'accelerated plan' for reducing the deficit, claiming that 'to continue with the existing fiscal plans would put the recovery at risk, given the scale of the challenge'. The new government therefore 'set a forward-looking fiscal mandate to achieve cyclically adjusted current balance by the end of the rolling, five-year forecast period. At this Budget, the end of the forecast period is 2015–16.' By this policy it was hoped that public sector debt would peak at 70.3 per cent of GDP in 2013/14.[59]

At the centre of the new strategy was a plan for spending cuts additional to those announced by the Labour government of £32 billion, of which £11billion would come from 'welfare'. In addition there would be £8 billion raised from higher taxes, mainly from an increase in VAT to 20 per cent. Thus fiscal consolidation was to be dominated by new expenditure cuts in the ratio of 80:20, which, combined with previous measures, would, it was argued, deliver a ratio of 77:23. The document went on to compare this balance of spending cuts and tax increases with that put forward by Labour in March, suggesting that Labour's plans involved a ratio of 71:29.[60] The implications of such ratios are complex, but in the context of 2010 a strategy of emphasizing expenditure cuts fitted with the 'rolling back the state' approach, so that fiscal management also delivered broader ideological goals.

The details of the proposed cuts were not spelt out in the budget, this being postponed until a Comprehensive Spending Review, to report in October. However, it was noted that with only the NHS and international aid being exempted, the cuts were likely to be around 25 per cent across unprotected areas. By contrast, Labour had also proposed 'ring-fencing' schools, 16–19 education Sure Start, and police numbers, implying cuts of perhaps 20 per cent in other areas.[61] The Conservatives were also careful to spell out the distributional impact of the budget, in carefully chosen words suggesting that as a result of its proposals, 'the richest will contribute the most to deficit reduction, and the impact on child poverty *in 2012/13* is statistically insignificant'.[62]

The Conservatives' argument since 2005, and reinforced in this budget, was that Labour's fiscal 'rules' were insufficient to keep policy on track, and so the Conservatives created the OBR with a remit to provide an independent assessment of the government's fiscal stance. This was the Conservatives' way of furthering the movement towards improving policy credibility by introducing an independent

[58] ibid., p. 91.
[59] HMT, *Budget June 2010*, pp. 1–3.
[60] ibid., pp. 2, 15.
[61] ibid., p. 17.
[62] ibid., p. 4 (emphasis added).

element into fiscal policy discussions, though, unlike the Bank of England in monetary policy, the OBR had no operational role.

The Coalition critique of Labour's fiscal policies suggested that the problem was partly the result of the rules employed. The 'key failing' of Labour's framework, it was argued, was that the golden rule was 'too backward-looking, especially at the end of the economic cycle, allowing persistent fiscal deficits when growth was strong, on the basis of past surpluses'.[63] In sum, to achieve fiscal credibility, the June 2010 budget, alongside the already noted cyclically adjusted fiscal balance by 2015/6, set out the aim of a falling ratio of net debt to GDP by the same date. Both targets were to be monitored by the OBR in order to underpin the credibility of the government's stance. The document itself used OBR forecasts as the basis for its critique of where Labour's policies would have led.[64]

When introducing his budget to the Commons, the Chancellor used Labour's (old) fiscal rules as a stick to beat them with, noting that 'We are set to miss the golden rule in this cycle by £485 billion'. Citing the Toronto June 2010 G20 meeting, the Chancellor stressed the need for a new 'fiscal mandate' for fiscal consolidation, hence the targets of a structural balance by 2015/16, and a falling share of debt to GDP by the same year. Credibility for this mandate would be enhanced by the creation of the OBR: 'the judge on whether we are on course will not be the Chancellor but the OBR'.[65]

But the OBR analysis of Labour's policy stance suggested that the March budget's figures for future borrowing were over-cautious, and made clear that 'we expect the economic recovery to strengthen in 2010 and beyond, as private sector demand continues to pick up'. The tone was generally upbeat, with the expectation of average growth of 2.25 per cent per annum over the next three years, based especially on a strong revival of business investment.[66]

Their summary of the fiscal position was as follows:

> [R]eal general government consumption continues to grow in 2010. From 2011 onwards, the fiscal consolidation envisaged by the previous government implies that government consumption falls, with an increasing rate of decline throughout the forecast. General government investment falls sharply in 2011 and continues to decline until 2013, although at a decreasing rate. Government investment returns to growth in 2014.[67]

Conversely, the OBR's analysis of the Conservatives' budget suggested that it would reduce growth slightly in 2010 (from 1.3 to 1.2 per cent in 2010, and from 2.6 to 2.3 in 2011). Growth might be faster by 2013, but the overall result would be a smaller economy in 2014.[68]

But for much of the summer of 2010 arguments about the differences in the parties' budget stances were sidelined by disputes about how far Britain was likely

[63] ibid., pp. 12–13 [64] ibid., pp. 12–14.

[65] *Hansard* (Commons), vol. 512, col. 167, 22 June 2010.

[66] OBR, *Pre-Budget Forecast June 2010*, pp. 3, 10. [67] ibid., p. 10.

[68] OBR, *Budget Forecast*, (June 2010), p. 80; this was cited by Harriet Harman in the House of Commons, vol. 512, col. 182, 22 June 2010.

to succumb to a Greek-style sovereign debt crisis. The crisis began in earnest in late 2009, but became much more serious in March and April as financial markets lost faith in the ability of the Greek government to finance its debts. Fears about a parallel path being followed in Britain were deployed very effectively by the Conservatives to give an urgency to the debate about debts and deficits.

In the budget document itself the dangers of a 'Greek-like' financial crisis are dealt with cautiously:

> While the fiscal position in the UK is very challenging, the financing environment has remained supportive and, among other factors, the new Government's fiscal credibility has already helped to keep interest rates close to record lows. . . . Accelerated fiscal consolidation will help keep market interest rates lower for longer, supporting economic recovery and lowering the proportion of tax revenues devoted to debt service payments. The government has set out a credible deficit-reduction plan that should provide businesses with the confidence they need to plan and invest, supporting the necessary recovery in business investment.[69]

But when the budget was presented to the House of Commons in June 2010 the issue of credibility, and potential sovereign debt risk, was put at the centre of the government's case for their fiscal policy. Osborne, the Chancellor, argued that Britain had the 'largest budget deficit of any economy in Europe, with the single exception of Ireland' and that 'fear about the sustainability of sovereign debt is the greatest risk to the recovery of European economies'. The government, he argued, had already suggested policies that have 'earned us credibility in international markets. . . . But unless we now deliver on that promise of action with concrete measures, that credibility—so hard won in recent weeks—will be lost'.[70]

In responding to the budget, Harriet Harman for Labour explicitly attacked the use by the government of Greece as a warning of what could occur in Britain: 'Greece is in a completely different position from us: it is still in recession; it does not control its interest rates; and its debt is over 115 per cent of its GDP. Greece is no alibi for this Tory budget'. The issue of Greece was returned to later in the debate, when a Labour MP stressed that 'the debt–GDP ratio in Greece is two and a half times that of the UK, and the maturity of the debt is, on average, 13 years, compared with an Organisation for Economic Co-operation and Development (OECD) average of two to three years. In addition, the Greek economy remains in recession.'[71]

But sovereign debt was to continue to be a powerful part of the debt and deficit narrative, aided by the fact that the Greek problem was to be a recurrent one for years after 2010. So for the Conservatives, the fundamental justification for UK fiscal policy settings, and the implied threat of a Greek-style crisis, remained unchanged. In September 2011, Osborne noted 'Greek one-year interest rates are now at a staggering 84 per cent. Our bond yields are just 2.3 per cent. Abandoning

[69] HMT, *Budget 2010*, p. 9.
[70] *Hansard* (Commons) vol. 512, col. 166, 22 June 2010.
[71] *Hansard* (Commons) vol. 512, cols 183, 206–7, 22 June 2010.

the plan we have set out would put Britain back into the firing line, lead to soaring interest rates and cripple any hope of a sustainable recovery.'[72]

Two months later, attacking Labour's plans, Osborne argued that 'if we had pursued that path, we would now be in the centre of the sovereign debt storm'.[73] This and subsequent justifications of the Coalition government's economic stance made much of the need to stave off a Greek-style crisis, which was alleged to be imminent in the UK in mid-2010.

The implication of Conservative statements that Labour's path was leading to a 'sovereign debt storm' was that the Labour government had lost credibility by its fiscal policies. Is this supported by the evidence? A standard of judgement commonly applied here is the behaviour of interest rates on government debt; if these rates are low and/or declining this is taken as evidence of high levels of financial confidence in the government's policies. Unfortunately, things are not so simple. The behaviour of bond rates certainly partly reflects concerns about government financing, and the experiences of Greece and Spain since 2008 show how fears of default can drive rates up very hard. But bond rates also reflect the general pattern of interest rates, which in turn partly respond to growth expectations, so that if expansion is expected to be low, rates, including bond rates, will be low. But markets are often, in the words of Oliver Blanchard of the IMF, 'schizophrenic about fiscal consolidation and growth', celebrating fiscal orthodoxy whilst worrying about its effects on growth.[74] Finally, rates in any one country will reflect what is happening elsewhere in the world. Thus there seems no dispute that both Britain and the US were able to have lower rates in 2011 and 2012 because they were safe havens from the chaos in the eurozone.

Despite these complications, with care we can still use bond rates to make some judgements. The pattern of bond rates since the onset of the crisis in late 2007 is clear. If we take the ten-year rate, it trended downwards from around 5 per cent in 2007 to under 2 per cent by the end of 2012. While the rate fell especially fast from late 2011, until then there was no obvious difference in behaviour between the Labour and Coalition periods in office. Undoubtedly that trend has been underpinned by the two effects noted above—the general fall in rates because of recession, and the 'safe haven' effects. But if the dangers of the policies pursued under Labour had been as stark as depicted by the Conservatives one would have expected to see some evidence of this in the behaviour of these rates—but there was no direct evidence from the market of loss of confidence in the UK, as the IMF subsequently pointed out.[75]

This is not to suggest bond markets were happy with the Labour government's policies. But their responses were measured.[76] Thus, for example, in October 2009

[72] Speech to the Lloyd's of London annual City Dinner, 6 September 2011: https://www.gov.uk/government/speeches/speech-by-the-chancellor-of-the-exchequer-rt-hon-george-osborne-mp-the-lloyds-of-london-annual-city-dinner.

[73] Autumn Forecast Statement by the Chancellor of the Exchequer, 29 November 2011: http://www.hm-treasury.gov.uk/press_136_11.htm.

[74] Cited in Blyth, *Austerity*, p. 3.

[75] IMF, 'United Kingdom: 2011 Article IV Consultation—Staff Report'.

[76] Gillian Tett, 'There are reasons to be cheerful about UK gilts' *Financial Times*, 5 March 2010.

the *Investors Chronicle* ran an article headed 'benign bond markets belie political panic', stressing that worries about borrowing levels were outweighed by factors such as the very high level of global savings relative to government borrowing as well as pessimistic macroeconomic trends.[77] In the run-up to the 2010 election, while it was still unclear who would win, the *Financial Times* surveyed the views of bond market participants, and summarized their views: 'Although every single investor has reduced their holdings in gilts in recent months because of worries over the UK budget, the end of quantitative easing and a hung parliament, they are almost unanimous that a funding crisis for government bonds and a collapse in prices will be avoided.'[78]

The OBR's June 2010 forecast on the basis of the Labour government's policies, 'assumed that short-term and long-term interest rates move in line with market expectations. Rates used in this forecast are the average for the 10 working days ending 25 May. Short-term interest rates are defined as the 3-month sterling interbank rate (LIBOR).'[79]

Whatever the historical judgement on the counterfactual likelihood of a Greek-style crisis in Britain, there seems little doubt that conjuring up that possibility formed an important element in the persuasiveness of the Conservatives' debt and deficit narrative in the electorally crucial months of early 2010. Apart from its general effects on opinion, it may also have contributed to shifting the views of the few Liberal Democrats previously sceptical of Conservative fiscal policy.[80]

IV

The agreement which acted as a foundation stone for the Coalition government formed in May 2010 showed the Liberal Democrats fully supportive of the Conservatives' fiscal policy and the strategy of presenting the fiscal deficit as a product of Labour's profligacy. There was also no dissent from the overall thrust of Conservative policy of securing large cuts in public spending as the route to fiscal consolidation. The planned cuts were largely achieved over the next five years.[81] The government faced much less effective opposition to its policies than did the Thatcher government in the early 1980s.

But the overall fiscal strategy laid out by the new government in 2010 proved far less successful than hoped, as the targets set out in 2010 were not achieved. The government had set itself a fiscal target called a 'fiscal mandate'. This stated that the structural current budget must be forecast to be in balance or surplus by the end of the rolling, five-year forecast horizon. In other words, after taking into account the likely impact of the economic cycle, tax receipts should be projected to be equal to or greater than government current spending.

77 *Investors Chronicle*, 6 October 2009.

78 FT.com 19 April 2010: http://www.ft.com/cms/s/0/bc23a686-4b49-11df-a7ff-00144feab49a.html#axzz4KP7dUaIH.

79 OBR, *Pre-Budget Forecast*, p. 13.

80 Cable, 'Keynes'; Darling, *Back*, p. 304.

81 Emmerson and Tetlow, 'UK', p. 575.

At the time of the June 2010 Budget, the OBR's forecasts suggested that on the basis of the new government's policies the structural current budget would reach a surplus of 0.3 per cent of national income by 2014–15, a year ahead of the end of the forecast horizon at that point. But two successive Autumn Statements in 2011 and 2012, citing changed external circumstances and slower-than-expected growth, pushed back the achievement of balance until 2016–17, and it only occurred then because Osborne had made additional tax increases and spending cuts since June 2010 (amounting to 2.4 per cent of national income).[82] The 2010 target to reduce the national debt from the 2014/15 level was also missed (see Table 5.1).

Unsurprisingly, this retreat was not presented as such. Osborne had always argued that there was no 'Plan B'; 'There Is No Alternative' was a Thatcherite slogan with continuing resonance, and a necessary part of the claim that only the Conservative plan had prevented a Greek-style meltdown. 'Yet gradually the Chancellor, without announcing it, shifted to Plan B, a form of disguised Keynesianism to stimulate the economy. He relaxed the pace of deficit reduction and announced a series of infrastructure projects in the 2012 autumn spending statement.'[83]

By the time of the Conservative Party conference in the Autumn of 2013 the achievement of fiscal targets was being pushed into the next parliament. Osborne told the conference: 'So I can tell you today that when we've dealt with Labour's deficit, we will have a surplus in good times as insurance against difficult times ahead. Provided the recovery is sustained, our goal is to achieve that surplus in the next Parliament.'[84] This revised approach was confirmed in the summer budget of 2015:

> The government will continue to reduce the deficit by around 1.1 per cent of GDP a year on average, the same pace as over the last Parliament. This fiscal path means that the deficit falls smoothly, and that debt falls as a share of GDP in every year of the Parliament.... As a result of this plan, a surplus will be achieved in 2019–20, and debt as a share of GDP in that year is forecast to be lower than expected at the March Budget 2015. New fiscal rules will cement this and ensure that governments run surpluses in normal times.[85]

This failure to achieve fiscal objectives after 2010 reflected the slow growth of the economy and the permanent damage done to the public finances by the recession. It meant that the gap between Labour's fiscal consolidation *plans* in March 2010 (on which the Conservatives poured such scorn), and the *outcomes* under the Coalition was quite small—estimated at a difference between a deficit of 6.5 and 5.0 per cent of national income.[86] This failure, it can be noted, did not lead to a

[82] HMT, *Autumn Statement 2011*, p. 5; HMT, *Autumn Statement 2012*, pp. 5–6.

[83] Cowley and Kavanagh, *British General Election of 2015*, p. 7.

[84] http://www.politics.co.uk/comment-analysis/2013/09/30/george-osborne-s-conference-speech-in-full.

[85] HMT, *Summer Budget 2015*, HC 264, p. 2.

[86] Emmerson, Johnson, and Joyce, *Green Budget 2015*, pp. 26–7. Comparing plans and outcomes means, of course, that this gap makes no allowance for how Labour's plans may have changed had they been in office after 2010.

sovereign debt crisis, which supports the view that fears of such a crisis were always exaggerated.

Alongside the performance of the economy, one of the reasons for the modification of the original 2010 strategy was the weight of critical economic analysis, especially that offered by the IMF. The Labour and Conservative parties had both long sought to use the views of the IMF to give credibility to their policy stance. For much of its history, especially since the 1980s, the IMF had been a reliable supporter of conservative fiscal policies. But in the wake of the crash the Fund had undergone a fundamental rethink concerning its policy stance, leading to a more Keynesian attitude to deficits. Signalling the radically changed context of economic policy for advanced economies, some IMF discussion referred to the conduct of post-crisis macroeconomic policy as 'navigating the new normal'.[87]

This shift was evident in IMF support for the Obama/Brown policies of 2008/9. In November 2008, Strauss-Kahn noted how

> the financial crisis has created a sharp fall in demand, what economists call a Keynesian recession.... To help confidence revive, there is no alternative but to use macroeconomic tools to boost demand and sustain output.... Fiscal policy must, therefore, play a central role. Fiscal expansion is always risky, as it adds to debt and raises dangers later. But, given where we are, the benefits exceed the costs in countries with sustainable debt.[88]

He called for a coordinated global fiscal stimulus in a major speech on 15 November 2008, following the formulation of the G20 action plan at the Washington summit.

As the prospect of global depression receded in late 2009 and early 2010, the tide of explicit enthusiasm for Keynesianism began to ebb in some quarters, such as the G20, the European Central Bank, and the German government.[89] Yet the IMF continued to emphasize the importance of the 'fiscal space' enjoyed by some countries, and the need to use it better, especially to tackle shocks. In May 2010, the IMF still asserted the need to boost aggregate demand as a major priority for fiscal policy, identifying counter cyclical policy as an important tool and highlighting the need to increase fiscal space in good times: 'A timely and simultaneous application of supportive fiscal and monetary policies prevented a far worse outcome.'[90] In April 2012 the IMF's *World Economic Outlook* sustained the same emphasis. While medium-term fiscal consolidation was vital, in the face of a threatened 'double-dip' recession, some countries should ease up on short-term consolidation where market conditions allowed: 'those with room for fiscal policy manoeuvring, in terms of their fiscal accounts and credibility with markets, can reconsider the pace of consolidation'.[91]

[87] El-Erian, 'Navigating the New Normal in Industrial Countries', Per Jacobsson Foundation Lecture, 10 October 2010. http://www.imf.org/external/np/speeches/2010/101010.htm.

[88] Strauss-Kahn, 'Staving off a Global Depression', *The Guardian*, 3 November 2008.

[89] Blyth, *Austerity*, pp. 56–62.

[90] Strauss-Kahn, 'Foreword', p. 4.

[91] IMF, *World Economic Outlook*, p. 21.

All of this was pitched in general terms, but it contains at least an implicit critique of the ramping-up of fiscal retrenchment in the UK after May 2010. While the IMF is always loathe to directly criticize the policies of a member government, there were undoubtedly tensions between the Fund over the pace of Osborne's initial fiscal consolidation.

Britain's IMF membership commits it to annual consultation with the IMF ('Article IV'). The November 2010 Article IV report noted merit on both sides of the argument about fiscal tightening. One important criticism was of fiscal tightening undermining fragile growth, a view that hinged on scepticism about the private sector 'picking up the slack' as the public sector retrenches. Secondly, 'a bleak assessment of the UK's structural deficit could be self-fulfilling: because policy-makers assume a large permanent drop in potential output, they tighten policies too early; this causes capital scrapping and human capital losses that a faster recovery would help prevent'. Finally, the need to placate bond markets is overstated, given the evolution of long-term UK interest rates.[92]

In both 2011and 2012, the IMF downgraded UK growth forecasts, eroding the case supporting current UK fiscal policy settings. As it became clear in these years that this purported return of growth was a mere chimera, the analysis and recommendation changed. The IMF became mildly critical of UK fiscal policy, focusing on the adverse growth effects of the fiscal retrenchment as the UK economy fell back into recession.

By mid-2012, there was no longer any ambiguity, rather a bald recognition of stagnation since late 2010: 'recovery has stalled.... [W]ith current policy settings the pace will be insufficient to absorb significant slack in the economy, raising the risk of a permanent loss of productive capacity'.[93] In this context, the 'priority for UK policymakers', Chopra notes, is 'more expansionary economic policies'; failure to change UK policy risks 'weak demand that leads to persistently slow growth and high unemployment, which in turn will affect decisions made by consumers and investors, and permanently damage the long-run capacity of the UK economy'.[94]

One especially telling point made by the Fund was that a slowdown in UK fiscal consolidation would not provoke an adverse reaction in the bond markets. The IMF analysis is worth quoting in full:

> In particular, fiscal indicators such as deficit and debt levels appear to be weakly related to government bond yields for advanced economies with monetary independence. Though such simple relationships are only suggestive, they indicate that a moderate increase in the UK's debt-to-GDP ratio may have small effects on UK sovereign risk premia (though a slower pace of fiscal tightening may increase yields through expectations of higher near-term growth and tighter monetary policy). This conclusion is further supported by the absence of a market response to the easing of the pace of structural adjustment in the 2011 Autumn Statement. Bond yields in the US and UK

[92] IMF, *United Kingdom: 2010 Article IV Consultation*, p. 28.

[93] IMF, *United Kingdom: 2012 Article IV Consultation Concluding Statement of the Mission*, May 2012: http://www.imf.org/external/np/ms/2012/052212.htm.

[94] A. Chopra 'Transcript of a Conference Call on the 2012 Article IV Consultations with the United Kingdom', July 2012: http://www.imf.org/en/news/articles/2015/09/28/04/54/tr071912.

> during the Great Recession have also correlated positively with equity price movements, indicating that bond yields have been driven more by growth expectations than fears of a sovereign crisis.[95]

Thus not only the Coalition's party political critics but also the IMF suggested that the Coalition government had over-egged the sovereign debt risk for the UK, and overstated the imperative nature of the scale and speed of their fiscal retrenchment. In the crisis, the IMF encouraged the UK government to display more flexibility and nimbleness of response to changing circumstances. The UK government, however reluctantly, did eventually move to exploit the 'fiscal policy space' the IMF identified. So one of the more surprising features of the crisis and its aftermath was an increasingly 'Keynesian' Fund encouraging a UK government to ease a very draconian fiscal consolidation strategy, which was hampering growth.

When recovery did clearly get underway from 2013/14 onwards, the IMF offered an apology for some of its previous criticism, especially the suggestion that in 2013 the policy was 'playing with fire'.[96] But its own previous analysis would clearly suggest that policies since 2010 had slowed the recovery, with the speed-up from 2013 hardly a vindication of the approach of the previous three years.[97]

If the pace of fiscal consolidation was much slower (and without disastrous consequences) in 2010–16, so too was the impact of the government's austerity programme on *absolute* levels of public spending much less than much contemporary rhetoric would suggest. Table 5.2 shows how limited *in aggregate* the cuts were. Having said that, the effects of the cuts on the share of GDP being spent by government was dramatic, falling from around 46 to 40 per cent in the years of Coalition government, and projected to fall further to around 36 per cent by 2018/19, which would take it back to the levels of 1999/2000.[98]

The relatively limited fall in absolute levels of spending was the consequence of the extensive ring-fencing of spending programmes, especially the NHS and pensions. By contrast, in some areas the cuts were enormous, especially in local government, where central government (successfully?) shifted much of the political pain of the squeeze on services. Local authority spending per person fell in real terms by 23.4 per cent between 2009/10 and 2014/15.[99] The burden of these cuts fell especially heavily on poorer areas of England and Wales, as cuts in central government grants did not take into account the greater reliance of such areas on this form of finance (local resources being scarcer), or their level of needs.[100]

A feature of public debate in the 2000s was a revival of concern with inequality, across the political spectrum.[101] In the rhetoric surrounding austerity the Conservatives were sensitive to this issue. For example, in the key budget of June 2010, it

[95] IMF, *United Kingdom: 2011 Article IV Consultation,* p. 38.

[96] http://www.independent.co.uk/news/business/news/christine-lagarde-grilled-over-osborne-apology-9509687.html.

[97] Keegan, *Mr Osborne's*, p. 81.

[98] Crawford and Johnson, 'UK Coalition Government's Record', pp. 276–7.

[99] Innes and Tetlow, 'Delivering', p. 303.

[100] ibid., pp. 322–4.

[101] Including the IMF: see Christine Lagarde, 'Inclusive Capitalism', May 2014: www.imf.org/external/np/speeches/2014/052714.htm.

Table 5.2 Public spending in crisis and recovery, 2007–17

	Total managed expenditure in 2015/16 prices (£ billions)
2007/8	686
2008/9	727
2009/10	754
2010/11	764
2011/12	754
2012/13	755
2013/14	748
2014/15	747
2015/16	754
2016/17 (projected)	765

Source: OBR databank.

was asserted that: 'As a result of the budget measures the richest will contribute the most to deficit reduction, and the impact on child poverty *in 2012/13* is statistically insignificant.'[102] But what were the effects of the Coalition's policies on distribution?

As noted, the cuts to local spending were inegalitarian in their effects, and the cuts to such locally funded items as bus subsidies and libraries are likely to have exacerbated inequality, these services being heavily used by lower income groups. Most analysis of the distributional effects of the Coalition's policies focuses on central government policies on tax and benefits (rather than services in kind). Such analysis suggests that the initial effect of the recession, as usual for an economic downturn, was to slightly equalize incomes, as the work incomes received by the better-off fell, while benefits received by those on lower incomes were less affected.[103] However, the policy response to the recession was largely to counter this initial equalizing impact: 'For those towards the bottom, dependent more on benefit incomes, falls in real income will happen largely as a result of the post-recession fiscal tightening between 2010/11 and 2015/16.'[104] Although the bulk of austerity took the form of spending cuts, most of which fell more heavily on poorer groups, there were some tax rises at the top of the income distribution.[105] In the words of one summary: 'Between 2010 and 2015, cuts in welfare spending were accompanied by some very sharp tax increases for the richest, but also by a package of tax measures that ensured that those in the middle to upper-middle parts of the income distribution were protected'.[106] The plans put forward by the Conservative government for further large cuts in social security for those of working age have been kept by the government of Theresa May, and will further increase inequality.[107]

[102] HMT, *Budget June 2010*, p. 4 (emphasis added). The government later stopped publishing data on child poverty.

[103] Brewer et al., 'Short', pp. 188–9.

[104] ibid., p. 180.

[105] Changes in policy after 2010 tilted the balance even more towards spending cuts, to a ratio of around 85:15: Emmerson, Johnson, and Joyce, *Green*, p. 23.

[106] Crawford and Johnson, 'UK', p. 281.

[107] ibid., p. 280.

How far this pattern would have been different under Labour is unclear. By much more limited ring-fencing, implementing large regressive tax changes (especially the rise in VAT), and focusing much more of the fiscal tightening on social security (for those of working age), the Conservatives delivered a significantly more regressive package than would *probably* have been followed if Labour had won in 2010.[108] But this must be in part a speculative conclusion. The Labour stance in March 2010 focused only slightly more on spending cuts (rather than tax increases) than the Conservatives, and the precise shape of these projected cuts was not spelt out. It is moot whether such a scale of cuts could have been delivered without considerable regressive impact. A similar uncertainty exists on the tax side; Darling had been keen to raise VAT, but had been thwarted by the Prime Minister's opposition.[109]

V

The British recession which began in 2007/8 has rightly been called the worst since the 1930s. Globally it was less severe, above all because the major economies of China, India, and the rest of Asia as a whole, whilst their expansion slowed, continued to grow significantly. In Britain unemployment was less severe than in the 1930s, rising much less than was expected despite the severity of the fall in output. But that fall was large, and what was most striking was the slow pace of output recovery, slower than any other recession since the First World War.

Recessions usually ignite debates over fiscal policy, given the inevitable deterioration in public finances caused by the automatic stabilizers (though the debate was muted in the early 1990s). So the focus on debts and deficits in the wake of 2007/8 is not in itself remarkable; there was a very large deterioration in the fiscal balance. That this focus was so sharp on this occasion was occasioned partly by the scale of the deficit, though Figure 5.1 shows the peak was not very much larger than in previous recessions. That said, in retrospect it is clear that debt accumulation was much larger than in these previous cases, partly because recovery was much slower and partly because this recession led to a bank bailout which had not been required on previous occasions.

The debt and deficit narrative, and its close relative, austerity, were not invented in the 2000s. The narrative was deeply embedded in long-standing debates about the economy. But its prominence in the wake of the 2007/8 crisis has to be linked to immediate political circumstances; it provided an opportunity for the Conservatives to draw much sharper dividing lines in economic policy than seemed attractive or plausible during the 'great complacency'.

[108] It is especially hard to answer the 'what would Labour have done if they had won the election' question because of the divide in senior Labour circles about fiscal strategy, which is a key theme of Darling, *Back*.

[109] Darling, *Back*, p. 269.

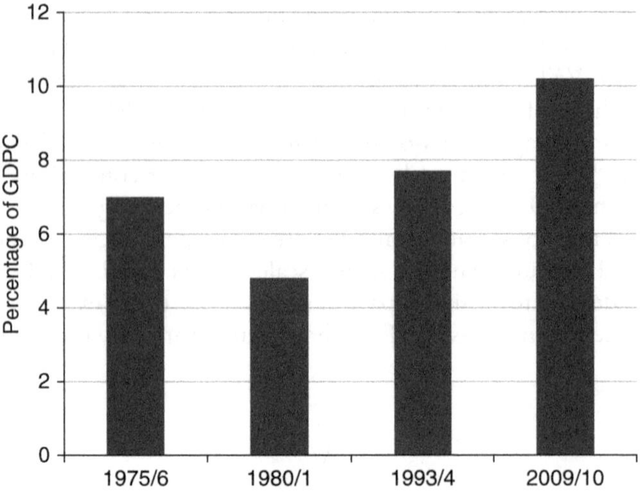

Figure 5.1 Peak PSNB in four recessions
Source: ONS database.

But in many respects the highly politicized debate, especially at the time of the 2010 election, exaggerated the difference between the main parties. As we have seen, the dividing line over the appropriate fiscal response concerned the pace of fiscal consolidation, not its pursuit. The budget of March 2010 and what we may call the 'adjusted Osborne' position (the policy after 2012) were not very much different in terms of macroeconomic outcomes, with Osborne's policies slowing the recovery which began in the second half of 2009.

A historical comparison could be with events in the mid-1970s. As shown in Chapter 3, the turning point in Labour's macroeconomic policy was not with the IMF visit in 1976, as so often stated, but in the budget of 1975. Similarly, the shift in fiscal stance around the more recent financial crisis can best be seen as beginning with the announcements in the *Pre-budget Report* in the Autumn of 2008 (effectively, a budget statement), then consolidated in the budget in Spring 2009.[110]

The sound and fury of the 2010 fiscal debate, which exaggerated the inter-party differences, is in large part to be explained by the investment of these economic arguments with a moral dimension. While there was a pragmatic debate about the appropriate scale of fiscal stimulus, and the necessary speed of fiscal consolidation, this was not the dominant narrative.[111] As we have seen, Conservative proponents of the need to radically cut debts and deficits always imbued these matters with moral imperatives. Alternative, Keynesian-style, arguments about focusing on the growth of GDP as a way of reducing the significance of debt failed to find a moral register. Rather, the debate was dominated by a combination of prudential and moral dimensions.

110 HMT, *Pre-budget Report* (2008).

111 Blanchflower and Skidelsky, 'Vince Cable'; Cable, 'Keynes'.

On the prudential side, the aphorism was that Labour had 'failed to the fix roof when the sun was shining'. Data showing that the Conservatives had left New Labour a larger legacy of debt than Labour had incurred when 'the sun was shining', before the crisis hit, were to little avail. On the debt side there was the immediate power of the Greek case to suggest what could happen if nations got into too much debt. But while the narrative about sovereign debt was central, there was also reference to private sector debt as a problem. 'Debt' was imbued with a moral dimension which seems to have had an electoral resonance which was largely immune to 'rationalist' arguments about the inescapable role of debt in a capitalist economy.

As always, there is a danger of treating the electoral success of a party as clear evidence of support for all aspects of its narrative. But the evidence does suggest that there was public support for the Coalition desire to rebalance the budget, and polling in 2011 showed strong support for the view that the government was clearing up 'Labour's mess'. When asked who was to blame for the cuts, voters blamed the banks, the last Labour government, and the eurozone countries more than the Coalition.[112] Labour's use of deficits to stabilize the economy in 2008/9 does not seem to have been electorally effective.

What might be seen as the political triumph of the debt, deficit, and austerity narrative in the election of a Conservative government in 2015 was followed, astonishingly quickly, by the superseding of this narrative. The commitment to a vote on Britain's membership of the European Union paved the way to a complete shift in the nature of debates about the British economy. The referendum debate largely focused on immigration and globalization (see Chapter 4).

In the wake of the Brexit vote, the new Prime Minister explicitly renounced the previous strategy on 'fiscal consolidation' and further cuts in social security, even while continuing a broad adherence to the need for austerity.[113] In the Autumn Statement of November 2016 this stance was to the fore: 'given the weaker growth outlook, and the period of uncertainty that is likely while the UK negotiates a new relationship with the EU, the government will no longer seek to reach a fiscal surplus in this parliament'.[114] With historically low interest rates and slow-growing output and productivity, 'infrastructure' investment became the watchword. The deficit and debt narrative had delivered the political opportunity for significant economies in parts of the budget, even if, as already suggested, the 'rolling back' of the state was extremely uneven in its impact, and in aggregate much less radical than much of the political rhetoric suggested. But, post-Brexit, this narrative was no longer predominant.

[112] Cowley and Kavanagh, *British General Election of 2015*, p. 8; Hellwig and Coffey, 'Public', pp. 417–26.

[113] http://www.theguardian.com/politics/2016/jun/30/theresa-may-launches-tory-leadership-bid-with-pledge-to-unite-country.

[114] HMT, *Autumn Statement 2016*, p. 11.

PART II

PERSUADING THE PEOPLE?

6
Unemployment

The high priority accorded to full employment is the most distinctive feature of the economic policy regime in the quarter-century after 1945. Indeed, the achievement of such a low (official) unemployment rate, averaging around 2 per cent, is the aspect which most justifies the description of this period as a 'golden age' of popular economic welfare. (The 2 per cent figure notionally covered both men and women, but as many fewer women registered for work, it was misleading about women's labour market position. There was a 'hidden female labour reserve').[1]

The employment issue was also distinct in that, of all post-war policy objectives, it was the one for which popular support was the most important. Other factors mattered, most obviously the growth of belief in the capacity of the state to regulate the economy, itself linked to both new economic doctrines and wartime experience. But the employment goal had an unmatched popular resonance. For post-war governments this resonance was a constraint and eventually a problem. It meant they had to treat sustaining low unemployment as crucial to political survival, and the pursuit of other policy objectives was constrained by what was happening to unemployment. In the golden age the trade-offs involved were relatively small; the achievement of full employment imposed few constraints on the achievement of other economic goals. But from the 1970s there began a sustained attempt to reduce the salience of unemployment and to distance government from responsibility for trying to reduce it.

This chapter examines the underpinnings of full employment policy, and the popular understandings of economic life that went along with it. It then examines how and why the defeat of unemployment achieved such importance, and how the policy was understood and represented from the 1940s onwards. Next it looks at the tensions surrounding this policy aim from the 1970s, and how it unravelled in the 1980s. It suggests that the downgrading of the significance given to full employment was accomplished by a variety of strategies to reshape understanding, from the questioning of the 'reality' behind official enumeration of unemployment in the early 1970s through to the revival of 'scrounger' narratives concerning the unemployed evident especially in the 1980s. It draws on recently released government records to look in detail at how the Conservative government after 1979 reacted to the surge in unemployment; both how they perceived the problem and how they

[1] For example, Taylor, 'Hidden'. Until 1977 women could opt out of paying National Insurance contributions for unemployment pay, thus removing an incentive to register as unemployed: Garside, *Measurement*, p. 84.

tried to establish a new popular understanding of the causes of job losses. The final section looks at the 'career' of employment policy since the 1980s, and the extent to which 'the unemployment problem' has been reconstructed.

I

The 1944 White Paper on *Employment Policy* marks a new political commitment on employment, promising that governments would pursue a 'high and stable' level of employment.[2] Of course, governmental concern with unemployment did not begin in the 1940s. Ever since the term 'unemployment' in its modern sense had come into use in the 1880s, governments had, to varying degrees, recognized the issue as one requiring a response.[3] Before the First World War the policy mainly focused on attempts to reform the labour market, accompanied by the beginnings of National Insurance to relieve the unemployed outside the framework of the Poor Law. In the interwar period, in the face of mass unemployment, argument raged over the appropriate response (though the question of how to relieve the unemployed was even more politically divisive). In the run-up to the 1929 election the Liberals argued that 'We Can Conquer Unemployment', through a programme of public works. But in the slump that followed after 1929, policy largely focused on reviving the economy through restoring prices and profitability by means of tariffs and monetary easing.[4] Thus the 1931 'package' of protectionism and departure from gold, a revolutionary break from Victorian norms, was accompanied (at least on the surface) by continued adherence to fiscal conservatism, in the name of sustaining financial confidence.[5]

The problem of the 1930s was not that some policymakers were indifferent to unemployment, but that there were profound disagreements about its causes and the appropriate policy responses. Many were doubtful about the capacity of government to deal with the problem, so there was a wariness about making any formal commitments to its reduction, though governments in the 1930s did seek to claim credit when the level fell, albeit slowly, in the middle of that decade.[6]

The demands of war resolved the problem by bringing the economy to full employment.[7] The war also saw a revolution in national economic management, with the 'first Keynesian budget' of 1941 establishing the notion that government could and should act to balance overall supply and demand in the economy. Underpinned by a major enhancement of statistical measurement of the economy, policy after 1941 sought to contain wartime inflationary pressures by methods which suggested that the overall level of economic activity (and, by implication, the level of employment) was something that could be effectively controlled.[8]

[2] Cmnd. 6527. [3] Harris, *Unemployment*; Walters, 'Discovery'.

[4] Booth, 'Britain'. [5] Middleton, 'British'.

[6] And, of course, the notionally 'National' government did retain power in the 1935 general election.

[7] This itself underpinned an important rhetorical point—if full employment could be achieved in war, why not in peace? See, for example, Labour Party, *Full Employment*, p. 2.

[8] Booth, *British*, pp. 59–75; Peden, *Treasury*, pp. 303–24.

Parallel to these radical changes in the instruments of economic management there developed a 'war politics' which argued that to sustain popular morale and support for the war effort, a promise of wholesale post-war reconstruction was needed. This became much more deeply embedded than the always superficial 'homes fit for heroes' rhetoric of the Great War.[9] In government this intent was most obviously marked by the establishment, as early as March 1941 of a 'Reconstruction Problems Committee' whose terms of reference were to provide 'practical schemes of reconstruction . . . these plans should have as their general aim the perpetuation of the national unity achieved in this country during the war, through a social and economic structure designed to secure equality of opportunity and service amongst all classes of the community'.[10]

Within government planning for post-war reconstruction followed a complex and tortuous path. Plans developed eventually embraced almost all aspects of British life, including town planning, education, health care, and social security, as well as all aspects of industry and the economy. What united much of this agenda was a focus on reducing insecurity. This was eloquently articulated in the most famous wartime plan, Beveridge's report on social security.[11] His report advocated a radical extension of the social security system to provide income security; to attack Want, alongside the other 'giants on the road of reconstruction'—'Disease, Ignorance, Squalor, and Idleness'.[12]

In a key part of his report, Beveridge argued that social insurance could only work effectively if there was maintenance of a high level of employment. This was not just necessary for the satisfactory administration of social insurance, and crucial to its affordability, but,

> most important, income security which is all that can be given by social insurance is so inadequate a provision for human happiness that to put it forward by itself as a sole or principal measure of reconstruction seems hardly worth doing. It should be accompanied by an announced determination to use the powers of the state to whatever extent may prove necessary to ensure for all, not indeed absolute continuity of work, but a reasonable chance of productive employment.[13]

The *Employment Policy* White Paper was this 'announced determination'. While the Beveridge Report was largely the product on one man's mind, *Employment Policy* was the result of complex negotiations within the state machine over three years.[14] But together these two publications came to symbolize governmental embrace of a new dispensation, to which the promise of popular economic security was central.

How far did these governmental activities reflect popular pressures and opinions? This has been much debated since the pioneering work of Calder and Addison

[9] Middlemas, *Power. vol. 1.*, pp. 46–7.
[10] TNA: PRO CAB 87/1, First Meeting of Reconstruction Problems Committee, 6 March 1941.
[11] Cmd. 6404. For the production of the report, Harris, *Beveridge*, pp. 365–412.
[12] Cmd. 6404, para 8. [13] Cmd. 6404, para 440.
[14] Tomlinson, *Employment*, pp. 45–63.

on the shift in political attitudes leading up to Labour's victory in 1945.[15] Plainly these government statements were not simple emanations of popular sentiment. Indeed, in broad respective they can be seen as elite attempts to shape popular opinion towards continuing support for capitalist parliamentary democracy, by offering economic security to undermine anti-capitalist 'extremism'.[16] Yet this persuasive interpretation itself presupposes that popular sentiment had to be managed in a new, more systematic way.

The evidence we have on popular opinion in the war is much more extensive than for any previous period. It does show a clear and growing interest in how far the post-war world would be characterized by greater economic security. Interest in and support for the Beveridge Report is well attested.[17] While there was no queuing round the block to buy the *Employment Policy* White Paper, the government's regular survey of opinion showed a high level of interest in the question of post-war employment prospects going back to at least 1942—alongside a scepticism about whether talk of the absence of future slumps was to be believed.[18]

It is surely unsurprising that employment was so important for the mass of the population. It is a basic but important point to note about twentieth-century Britain that it was the most proletarianized population in the world, with both town and country dominated by wage earners, following the long-term destruction of the peasantry. For the great bulk of the population, with little in the way of savings, wages and salaries were almost the sole source of economic resources. This broad structural point helps us understand why the experience of mass joblessness in Britain in the 1930s was so significant for subsequent politics and policy, despite national unemployment levels never reaching those recorded in Germany or the USA. Evidence from, for example, Mass Observation, shows how far this experience of unemployment created in the late 1930s a longing for future security.[19]

More immediate wartime factors in making employment so important are suggested by Macleod. As he notes, the disastrous experience after World War One, when rapid decontrol had led to the sharpest slump of the twentieth century in 1920–2 led to the argument that this time there had to be a plan for something different. Second, the rhythm of the war itself gave time and opportunity for focusing on post-war plans. From 1942 it was clear that the tide was running in the direction of victory, and it was between the time of that realization and the Normandy invasions that public interest was focused on post-war improvement, especially employment.[20]

The 1944 White Paper was unambiguous only in stating a broad commitment to 'high and stable' employment; the complex discussions behind its production meant it 'became a palimpsest whose original ink and pigments showed through'.[21] As many have pointed out, its relationship to Keynesian prescriptions was ambivalent.

[15] Addison, *Road*; Calder, *People's*. [16] Cutler, Williams, and Williams, *Keynes*.

[17] Calder, *People's*, p. 528; Harris, *Beveridge*, pp. 406–7, 415–17.

[18] TNA: PRO INF 1/292 Home Intelligence Weekly Reports, for example for 8 April, 15 April, 20 May, 4 June, and 18 June 1942. For Mass Observation material, see Macleod, 'Promise', p. 83.

[19] Gazeley and Langhammer, 'Meanings'. [20] Macleod, 'Promise', p. 96.

[21] Middlemas, *Power, vol. 1*, p. 77.

On one hand, it asserted the basic Keynesian truth: 'A country will not suffer from mass unemployment as long as the total demand for its goods and services is maintained at a high level'; on the other hand, whilst committing governments to pursue policies to maintain demand, it was stressed that: 'none of the main proposals contained in this Paper involves deliberate planning for a deficit in the National Budget in years of sub-normal trade activity'.[22]

Even more important in the context of this book's arguments is the less often noted statement in the Report that hedged the government's commitment around with the following:

> [E]mployment cannot be created by Act of Parliament or by Government action alone. Government policy will be directed to bringing about conditions favourable to the maintenance of a high level of employment.... But the success of the policy outlined in this Paper will ultimately depend on the understanding and support of the community as a whole—and especially on the efforts of employers and workers in industry; for without a rising standard of industrial efficiency we cannot achieve a high level of employment combined with a rising standard of living.[23]

Margaret Roberts (later Thatcher) highlighted the above passage in her copy of the White Paper, along with others that stressed the conditions that needed to be met if high and stable employment was to be sustained.[24] These passages included: 'in an expanding economy workers must be ready and able to move freely between one occupation and another'; 'Stability of wages and stability of prices... is a condition vital to the success of employment policy'; and 'workers must examine their trade practices and customs to ensure that they do not constitute a serious impediment to an expansionist economy and so defeat the object of a full employment programme'.[25]

This 'conditionality' of the White Paper allowed Thatcher and other neo-liberals to later argue that what they aimed at was not a repudiation of the document, but a reassertion of its truths in a world where these conditions had not been met. This was one way of dealing with the political need to state a continuing support for the objective of 1944, whilst distancing government from the responsibility for failing to achieve it.[26]

Keith Middlemas has argued that the 1944 White Paper rested on an unwritten, implicit contract between the government and employers and unions that they would support its objective. How far employers and unions accepted that changing their behaviour would be a condition of success of the policy is unclear. Most discussion of this has focused on the trade union view, and how far unions accepted that attitudes to wage bargaining would need to change in a full-employment environment. Middlemas persuasively suggests why this issue was not directly confronted in the 1940s, despite being commonly discussed in policymaking circles.[27]

[22] Cmd. 6527, foreword and para 74. [23] Cmd. 6527, foreword.

[24] Margaret Roberts's copy of the White Paper, MTFW 110368; Green, *Thatcher*, pp. 76–8.

[25] Margaret Roberts's copy of the White Paper, paras 31, 52–3, 54.

[26] Jewkes, 'Defence'. Thatcher's relationship to the White Paper is returned to in Section III below.

[27] Beveridge's *Full* advocated much more restriction on the rights of labour: Harris, 'Political', p. 248.

Partly it was because the unions were wary of the whole process of policymaking that had produced the White Paper, which had largely excluded any involvement from them. Partly it was because they envisaged a post-war world where, whatever political promises were made, the big threat would be the return of slump and deflation.[28] So whilst some economists pointed out the potential systemic significance of full employment for wage bargaining, no specific policy departure followed.[29]

What *was* envisaged by policymakers was not movement to a system of wages policy or compulsory arbitration, but, as Middlemas stresses, the 'incorporation' of unions 'by continual "education" politically and ideologically into the polity precisely as envisaged in the 1944 White Paper'.[30] This 'education' was, initially, aimed at balancing a continuing commitment to full employment with other economic policy objectives (explored in the following chapters). But from the 1970s this 'education' shifted to explaining why without radical changes in behaviour full employment would not be deliverable by government.

II

Despite the promises made, popular pessimism about employment prospects continued into the post-war years. In 1948 Mark Abrams reported to the government that 'unemployment still dominated people's minds, even those of the younger generation in whom the fear had been implanted by their parents'.[31] But, especially after the American recession of the early 1950s passed without significant impact on Britain, such pessimism was eroded by the evidence of the labour market: from the 1940s until the late 1960s measured unemployment fluctuated at around 1–2 per cent, lower than the most optimistic wartime discussions had assumed. The reasons for this are disputed. In the 1960s there was a triumphalist Keynesian narrative which ascribed post-war full employment to the adoption by government of Keynes's theories; full employment was the happy consequence of a Keynesian revolution flowing from theory into policy.[32] But such a view was challenged even then. Using a simple Keynesian model, Matthews argued that the key to post-war buoyancy was a major upward shift in private investment, largely based on the profitable exploitation of wartime technological breakthroughs.[33] His story was complicated by the fact that while he could show that the post-war policy regime was not one of simple Keynesianism given the norm of budget surpluses in this period, this ignored both the feedback effects of prosperity on the budget and also the importance of even a balanced budget for demand if total public expenditure was increasing, as it was.[34] But Matthews, like most commentators, did accept that the political commitment of the 1944 document may have acted as a

[28] Middlemas, *Power, vol. 1*, pp. 95–6. This scepticism about the credibility of promises on full employment was widely shared. Compare Macleod, 'Promise', p. 93.

[29] Jones, *Wages*, pp. 15–33.

[30] Middlemas, *Power, vol. 1*, p. 95.

[31] TNA: PRO INF 12/245, Economic Information Production Campaign: Briefing and Policy, Meeting 29 September 1948.

[32] Lekachman, *Age*; Stewart, *Keynes*.

[33] Matthews, 'Why?'

[34] Stafford, 'Full'.

reassurance to investors that if deflationary forces were evident government would respond to try and sustain demand.

Beyond this broad political commitment, post-war governments contributed to the achievement of full employment in ways envisaged in the White Paper. First, by pursuing a highly active regional policy of 'taking work to the workers', thereby not requiring all the burden of geographical mobility to fall on labour. This policy was begun under the wartime Coalition with the 1945 Distribution of Industry Act of 1945. It was reined back in the 1950s, only to be expanded again, first under the Conservatives in the early 1960s and much more so under the Wilson government of the late 1960s.[35]

Second, successive British governments contributed to the construction of a more stable and expansionary international economy. This requirement had been highlighted in 1944, though the construction of the new institutions of the IMF, and what became the General Agreement on Tariffs and Trade (GATT), was in its infancy at that time. One persuasive account of these new arrangements highlights their contribution not only to economic expansion, but also to easing the political challenges of managing the fully employed economy. Eichengreen has argued that the major feature of the IMF agreement at Bretton Woods was the commitment to fixed exchange rates.[36] These fixed rates were heavily invested in by politicians, so that pressure was exerted on policymakers to change direction when the rate came under threat. This created part of the context for the chronic balance-of-payments problem of golden age Britain, as, with a fixed rate for the pound, excess demand at home spilled over into payments deficits. This was by no means the whole story of this particular 'problem', whose construction is explored in the next chapter. But there is no doubt that the fixed rate did provide an anchor for policy, and was used to educate popular expectations.

For a long time the Coalition's White Paper effectively bound successor governments.[37] The common perception amongst the political class was, as a senior civil servant put it in 1952, 'my belief is that the British people have an almost pathological fear of unemployment'.[38] But, as noted, this constraint on policy was not acutely felt because of the general benignity of economic conditions. Commitment to full employment may have constrained the government from radical policy departures, as with the discussion of floating the pound in the ROBOT scheme in 1952.[39] But the gradual progress to currency convertibility and international economic liberalization—key aims of government, especially in the 1950s—was not stopped by the commitment.[40]

For all the focus on budgetary policy in mid-century discussions of full employment, it was not until 1959 that there was a budget whose prime purpose was to reflate the economy to achieve a higher level of employment.[41] Throughout the golden age there was a policy of 'stop-go', in which macroeconomic policy (combining

[35] Parsons, *Political*, pp. 96–169. [36] Eichengreen, 'Institutions'.
[37] Middlemas, *Power, vol. 1*, p. 109.
[38] TNA: PRO T229/323, E. Plowden to Chancellor of the Exchequer, 11 April 1952.
[39] Burnham, *Remaking*. [40] Middleton, 'Struggling'.
[41] Budd 'Unemployment', p. 104.

fiscal and monetary measures, but especially the former) was highly active in seeking to maintain the economy at close to full employment without too much disturbance to the balance of payments. This policy regime was much criticized at the time, but in retrospect, given the high trend levels of activity, these debates look somewhat like 'Much Ado about Nothing'.[42]

Despite the relative ease with which full employment was maintained until the late 1960s, the perceived need to educate the public on the conditions for its continuation was emphasized regularly throughout the period. The potential problems were highlighted especially by the Conservative government in the mid-1950s, when they were seeking to move towards full convertibility for sterling, and wanted to contain inflation in order to maintain international financial confidence. From this emerged a major publicity effort aimed at shaping economic expectations.[43] This involved a new White Paper on the *Economic Consequences of Full Employment*, but also efforts aimed at a broader audience, including a popular version of the White Paper called *Must Full Employment mean Ever-rising Prices?*

These publications sought to educate public opinion by spelling out the problems created by full employment for the aim of price stability. The full range of anti-inflation arguments were deployed:

> Unless the upward pressure of rising money incomes on prices is moderated, the economy is likely to be exposed to serious and increasing strains. These strains, if not relieved, will prevent us from realising the full potentialities of economic growth and may lead to unemployment by making it more difficult to secure our imports.[44]

In the more popular language of the *Must* document this became: 'If prices go on rising, and the value of money goes on falling, it leads to social unfairness and all kinds of economic difficulties'.[45]

One of the most striking features of the White Paper's presentation of the issues is the emphasis given to income distribution. Over a quarter of its length (and all three tables) concern this issue, the argument being that wage earners had done well since 1938, profits had been stable, and a much larger proportion of the latter were being devoted to investment than was true before the war. Alongside this attempt to persuade the working class of the gains they had achieved was emphasis on the prospects of future improvement in living standards: new prominence was given to the dangers inflation posed for those prospects: 'Quite apart from the economic and social strains they create, rising prices endanger the full realisation of the possibilities of economic progress'. More starkly in the popular version, inflation 'could easily lead to rising unemployment and falling living standards'.[46]

[42] 'Stop-go' was, of course, one of the alleged culprits for 'decline'. It had most impact on consumer durable industries, where controls on consumer credit ('hire purchase') slowed working-class acquisition of these goods: Dow, *Management*, pp. 275–82.

[43] Booth, 'Inflation'. [44] Cmd. 9725, p. 1.

[45] Cmd. 9725. p. 9; HMT/COI, *Must*, p. 12. On the complex process involved in producing these documents see TNA: PRO T230/300 and 301, 'National wages policy/full employment policy: draft White Paper on economic implications of full employment', 1955–6, and T234/91–94, 'Study by committee on industrial relations of the implications of full employment', 1955.

[46] *Implications*, p. 3: *Must*, p. 117.

The threat to full employment posed by inflation was a hardy perennial of policy seeking to educate the public in the 1950s and 1960s. It was prominent in the early 1960s with the Council on Productivity Prices and Incomes.[47] It was very much part of the rhetoric of the Wilson government in the 1960s.[48]

But it was only after the devaluation of 1967, and the simultaneous rise of both inflation and unemployment, that the 1944 settlement came under serious strain. The budget that followed the devaluation sought to free up resources for redeployment to the export sector, and this licensed the belief that slightly higher unemployment in the short run would be beneficial to the economy. This fitted with the Labour government's previous introduction of income-related unemployment benefits and redundancy payments, both aimed at raising out-of-work incomes to reduce resistance to short-run unemployment, in the name of enhancing labour mobility (the Selective Employment Tax was also aimed at 'shaking-out' labour from services for employment in manufacturing; ironically, we now know that this legislation coincided almost exactly with the historic peak of manufacturing and employment).[49] Registered unemployment rose slowly but steadily from a low of 1.5 per cent in 1965 to 2.7 per cent in 1970. After 1967 inflation also showed a clear trend; having fallen from 4.8 to 2.5 per cent from 1965 to 1967, it then rose year by year to 6.4 in 1970.[50]

Initially the Conservatives, who took office in 1970, did not focus directly on employment, in some respects pursuing a more neo-liberal, microeconomic-focused agenda. This included one innovation with enormous long-run significance, the introduction of Family Income Supplement (FIS). In itself this was a small-scale measure, of limited cost, giving extra financial support to employed households with children. But it marked a turning point towards attempts to increase the margin between in-work and out-of-work incomes by state subsidy of low wages. In this way, it used neo-liberal assumptions about the causes of unemployment to support a policy which, at a minimum, was in tension with neo-liberal views about reducing the role of government in the labour market.[51] The introduction of FIS coincided with the peak in 'generosity' of unemployment benefits; after that date the trend was to widen the gap between wage levels and unemployment pay by supplements to the former and cuts to the latter.[52]

III

Another key moment in shaping the role of unemployment in public policy also came under this Conservative government, with the 'U-turn' of 1972. This reversal of a tight macroeconomic policy came when the rising trend of unemployment persuaded the government to reflate the economy (see Figure 6.1 for changes in

[47] Jones, *Wages*, pp. 54–6. [48] Tomlinson, *Wilson*, pp. 123–51.
[49] 'Employment in Public and Private Sectors', *Economic Trends* 180 (1968), pp. 42–5.
[50] *Economic Trends Annual Supplement*, various issues.
[51] This general theme is returned to in Chapter 10.
[52] TNA: PRO CAB 184/505, 6 August 1981.

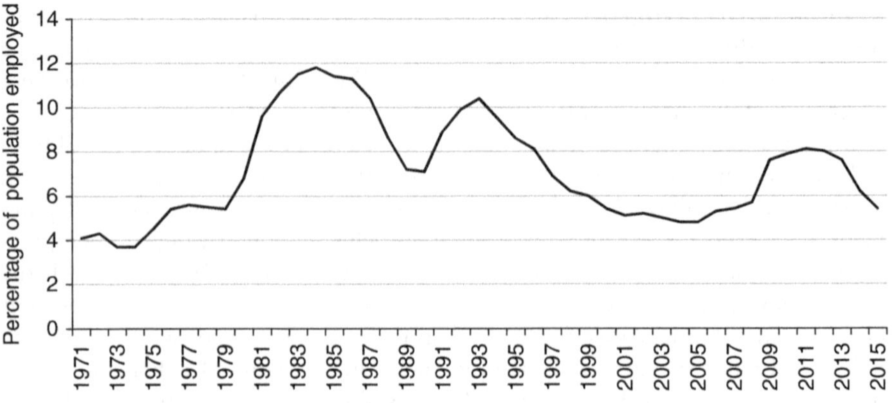

Figure 6.1 Unemployment, 1971–2015
Source: ONS database.

the level of unemployment). For many neo-liberals this about-turn was when the determination to attack the post-war economic policy consensus hardened.[53]

The idea that unemployment should be addressed by policies to alter aggregate demand had already come under attack within economic theory. In the late 1960s Milton Friedman argued that there was no long-run trade-off between inflation and unemployment, but instead a 'natural rate' of unemployment determined by technology and above all the workings of the labour market.[54] In the early 1970s this argument was taken up with enthusiasm by authors writing for the neo-liberal think tank the IEA.[55] As suggested in Chapter 3 this theoretical macroeconomics literature had its effects, especially when taken up by economic commentators in major newspapers. Crucially, it provided an intellectually respectable rationale for downgrading the responsibility of government for unemployment.

But another, neglected, example of the assault on the post-war consensus on employment came in two IEA pamphlets in 1972 and 1975. In these, John Wood (a Deputy Director of the IEA) focused upon the significance of the data on unemployment which had been the key trigger for policy action in the golden age and in the 1972 'U-turn'.[56] In his 1975 pamphlet he argued that:

> it is hardly too much to argue that the most persistent and perhaps the most important explanation for the failure of 'demand management' during the last thirty years is that the British authorities, especially the Treasury, have never fully appreciated how misleading the unemployment figures are as a test of the pressure of demand on the economy.

[53] Denham and Garnett, *Keith Joseph*, pp. 226–76; Joseph, *Reversing*.
[54] Friedman, 'Role'. This is referred to by Budd as 'the most important contribution to the employment debate in the post-war period': Budd, 'Unemployment', p. 128.
[55] For example, Friedman and Laidler, *Unemployment?*; Hayek, *Full?*
[56] Wood, *How Much?*; Wood, *How Little?* These were followed by Miller and Wood, *What Price?*

Or, on similar lines: 'the unimaginative presentation and misleading use of statistics about unemployment must bear a large responsibility for the appalling mismanagement of the British economy since the end of the war'.[57]

He suggested a wholesale recasting of unemployment data with a 'new strategic indicator' of 'the male labour force aged 25 to 55 without work for more than six months, linked to a crucial distinction between "job-changers" and the "long-term unemployed". He also stressed the scale of turnover, and that the unemployment figure was the difference between two large numbers'.[58]

According to Wood's calculations, the 'strategic unemployed' in July 1975 numbered 115,900, compared with the official figure of 1,036,000, of whom 809,700 were male. This lower figure still includes 'unemployables' in the 25–55 age range; if this is taken into account, Wood suggested that strategic unemployment varied from 40,000 to 120,000 between 1970 and 1975. This statistical manipulation was linked directly to the 'U-turn' of the Heath government. For Wood, policy was so bad in 1970–4 crucially because the government used the wrong unemployment figures as well as failing to recognize the lags in policy effectiveness. At the key moment in January 1972, when the official figure hit 928,600, Wood's 'strategic' figure was only around 120,000 ('almost certainly lower than the natural rate') and this meant the reflationary measures of 1971 and 1972 were mistaken, as the economy was starting to expand following the expansion of money supply from spring 1970.[59]

Woods's 'strategic' figure excluded occupational pensioners, students, school-leavers (up to 25), and all women. The latter exclusion was on the basis that women operated in a separate labour market with practically no long-term unemployment. He argued that there was no shortage of jobs for women given the persistent availability of more female vacancies than registered female unemployed. He also argued that there had long existed a large number of unemployables: 'as many as half of all men on the register in times of high employment are unfit for normal work'—he cites official surveys on this and argues for the Department of Health and Social Security to keep a register of unemployables. Finally, he suggested that vacancies were grossly underestimated, with employment exchanges only registering perhaps 20 per cent of vacancies.[60]

Woods's work is worth citing at some length because it brings together many of the key features of the 1970s attacks on treating the figure of registered unemployed as a trigger for changes in macroeconomic policy. His critique is similar to many others. For example, in November 1972, at the time of the 'U-turn', a group of 'economic radicals' had written a memorial to the Prime Minister suggesting that the current official level of unemployment at around 800,00 exceeded the 'real' number by half a million.[61]

The debate about the statistics in the context of the upward shift in the numbers from 1968 led to an official working party on unemployment statistics, which reported in 1972. The working party suggested separating out the temporarily

[57] *How Little?*, pp. 11, 58. [58] *How Little?*, pp. 12–14.
[59] *How Little?*, pp. 36–8, 43–5. [60] *How Little?*, pp. 25–7, 30–4, 40.
[61] Cited in Worswick, 'Introduction', p. 13.

stopped from the main body of the unemployed, but rejected the notion that it was possible to identify those 'not genuinely seeking work' or 'unemployable'.[62] At this time the only official unemployment data were based on registration at labour exchanges (apart from the decennial census), and it was not until 1973 that the Labour Force Survey allowed for a more comprehensive assessment, which showed that many *more* people regarded themselves as unemployed than the previous official statistics measured. Failure to register was particularly high amongst married women (about two-thirds), and this needs to be taken into account when assessing the debates of the 1970s; in particular, this gives a very different sense of the labour market position of women compared with Woods's arguments.[63]

These statistical arguments mattered because of the high profile unemployment numbers had attained in post-war policy decisions. In that sense, the neo-liberal attack on the meaning of these numbers was well-aimed at undermining an important underpinning of the public representation of economic arguments. Such arguments about the figures were to return with renewed intensity with the great surge in unemployment after the election of the Thatcher government in 1979.[64]

In the years before that election, after Margaret Thatcher captured the Conservative leadership in 1975, the Conservatives focused a great deal of attention on criticizing the rising number of unemployed under the Wilson/Callaghan government. Hugely ironically, in view of what was to follow, the party's most famous poster attacking Labour's record in the general election of 1979 concerned unemployment, with the slogan 'Labour isn't working'.[65]

Some have argued that this purported Conservative concern was all a front, and that the rise in unemployment after 1979 was foreseen by the Conservatives, and secretly planned for as a way of weakening Labour's bargaining power and undermining the trade unions. A typical expression of this is by Dennis Skinner in the House of Commons in 1981: 'The truth about this Government is that they deliberately engineered 2½ million people on the dole—the figure is still rising, and will probably rise to well over 3 million—in order to subjugate the trade unions and the workers, through fear. That is the policy of the Government....'[66]

This view has been endorsed by some academic commentators, and undoubtedly there was a shift in attitude to unemployment in Conservative circles in the 1970s. In 1975 Thatcher had argued that 'No government deliberately creates unemployment. But equally, politicians should not be hypnotised by dubious statistics into subsidising the wrong things'.[67] Some increase in unemployment was

[62] Cmnd. 5157. [63] Thatcher, 'Statistics', pp. 88–90.

[64] For an overview of the statistics from 1979, Levitas, 'Fiddling?'

[65] Unemployment did not figure highly in the election, see Butler and Kavanagh, *British General Election of 1979*, pp. 153–8; in its manifesto Labour promised to restore full employment, whilst the Conservatives attacked Labour's record on the issue and called for less emphasis on preserving jobs, and more on creating new ones: Craig, *British General Election Manifestos 1959–1987*, pp. 284, 272, 273.

[66] *Hansard* (Commons), vol. 998, col. 418, 5 February 1981; Thatcher replied, 'That is not the truth. It is just plain rubbish'.

[67] Cited in Green, *Thatcher*, p. 68; Jim Prior, the Employment Minister in 1980/81 summarized her attitude: 'As far as she was concerned, inflation was a much greater social evil than unemployment, and in any case, in her eyes, you could only cure unemployment by curing inflation': Prior, *Balance*, p. 119.

expected to result from tight money policies. But no one expected the scale of increase after 1979, and it is clear that Tory leaders greatly feared the political consequences of this mass unemployment.[68] A common view about the politics was expressed in his own way by Hayek:

> To put it crudely, I would say that it is possible to cause twenty per cent unemployment for six months if you can hold out a hope that things will get better after that. You cannot have ten per cent unemployment for three years. Yet that is what the government's present course asks for and I don't think it can hold out.[69]

Amongst the Tory rank and file, attitudes to unemployment were different, and these attitudes seem to have drawn directly on the kind of statistical critique undertaken by Wood. For example, at a meeting of the party's Finance Committee in 1980, the general tone was that the headline figure exaggerated the problem, with a London MP asserting that 'Much of the talk about unemployment was misjudged. There were 100,000 vacancies in London'. More broadly, Alan Clark, MP for Plymouth, asserted 'the level of unemployment was what was holding the party activists steadfastly together in many constituencies. For better or for worse it was seen as giving the Trades Unions their deserts.'[70]

The much greater than expected rise in unemployment occasioned something approaching panic in government circles in 1981. This surprise is best seen against the background of the years of Opposition. In those years the Conservatives' economic policy discussions were dominated by taxation issues and trade unions.[71] Whilst committing themselves to 'monetarism', the new leadership spent strikingly little time analysing monetary policy in any depth.[72] While there were some largely theoretical discussions on monetary matters, there was little detailed practical work, partly because the party seems to have believed it had little to learn from past British experience, on the assumption that it was going to pursue unprecedented policy departures in seeking to control the money supply. This meant, in particular, that they ignored the experience of the Competition and Credit Control of 1972, when the Bank of England had experimented, unsuccessfully, with quantitative monetary policy. Indeed, the Conservatives had little contact with the Bank of England, which they distrusted as an 'anti-monetarist' body.[73]

This gap between the rhetoric of 'monetarism' and actual policy preparation justifies the view that 'at the heart of Thatcherism was a reckless enthusiasm for ad hoc experimentation in pursuit of libertarian ends'.[74] This recklessness was hugely significant, not least in ignoring the recent experience of Germany and Switzerland, where monetary tightening had led to a sharp appreciation of exchange rates in the mid-1970s. This exchange rate 'over-shooting' was to be the key cause of the rise

[68] Evans, *Thatcher*, p. 17; compare Williamson, *Conservative*, pp. 236–8.

[69] Letter to *The Times*, 12 November 1980.

[70] Report on meeting of Finance Committee, 11 November 1980, MTFW 112645.

[71] Williamson, *Conservative*, pp. 58–88. On trade unions and the 'Stepping Stones' programme, see Hoskyns, *Just*, pp. 39–58.

[72] Needham, *UK*.

[73] Needham, 'Britain's'.

[74] Harling, *Modern*, pp. 192–3; also Tomlinson, 'Mrs Thatcher's'.

in unemployment after 1979, as the nominal rate rose fast at a time when British prices were also rising above those of most competitors, so that the real rate increased by an extraordinary 30 to 50 per cent. As Otmar Emminger, former President of the Bundesbank, told a Commons Committee, it was 'by far the most excessive overvaluation which any currency has experienced in recent monetary history'.[75] Unsurprisingly, this overvaluation had a devastating effect on the traded, especially manufacturing, sector, where, between the second quarter of 1979 and the second quarter of 1981, employment fell by 17 per cent and output by 20 per cent.[76] Later on this slump was added to by a worldwide downturn caused largely by OPEC 2, but Britain's problems began earlier and were much greater because of the exchange rate problem.[77]

The strategic problem for the Conservative leadership was that the centrepiece of their economic policy, the MTFS, was based on the assumption that Sterling M3 was an appropriate measure of monetary tightening. As this aggregate grew faster than the target in 1980 and 1981, it was necessary, at least in public, and for the sake of coherence of policy, to deny that the government's policy was causing the collapse of manufacturing. The problem of sterling's appreciation was apparent to some of the government's advisers as early as the 1979 election. John Hoskyns, first Head of the Number Ten Policy Unit, recorded that on 31 May 1979 he had 'clashed again with Margaret over need for a lower pound'. He found the Prime Minister initially unreceptive: 'Margaret seemed to believe that "the higher the pound, the better for the economy"'.[78] A ministerial meeting of July 1979 found ministers almost wholly uninterested in the external factors which were having such a major impact on the economy.[79] Only slowly did Thatcher and her close colleagues come to recognize the need to respond to the unemployment problem, whilst simultaneously suggesting that the responsibility for the problem lay outside their control.[80]

The public records for the period between late 1979 and the 1983 election show a persistent fear amongst ministers and their advisers that rising unemployment would end their economic experiment prematurely at the next general election. This fear called forth a variety of responses. Monetary policy was eventually relaxed from November 1980, despite the overshooting of the monetary targets. This retreat on the monetary aspect of the MTFS was obscured by the budget of 1981, which symbolically sought to tighten the fiscal stance and override the automatic stabilizers.[81] This stance allowed the famous claim by Thatcher that 'the lady's not for turning', which glossed over not only the preceding change in monetary policy, but also the depth of concern evident in policymaking circles about the rise in unemployment.

[75] Cited in Keegan, *Mrs Thatcher's*, p. 171. [76] Nickell, 'Government's Policy', p. 108.

[77] Dow, *Major*, pp. 273–320; Keegan, *Mrs Thatcher's*, p. 203. [78] Hoskyns, *Just*, p. 107.

[79] TNA: PRO CAB 134/4336, Ministerial Committee on Economic Strategy: CPRS, 'Strategy', 16 July 1979.

[80] Sometimes it was conceded that 'the rapid increase in the exchange rate caused tremendous problems, particularly for industries that are exporting', but the government disclaimed responsibility for this appreciation: Thatcher, *Hansard* (Commons) vol. 998, col. 418, 5 February 1981.

[81] Booth, *Were?*; Needham and Hotson, *Expansionary*.

The 1981 budget was followed in July 1981 by a package of measures designed to reduce the unemployment count. In fact, changes to how the numbers were constructed had already begun the previous year, and such changes were to become a recurrent feature of the next decade. Between 1979 and 1989 thirty such alterations were introduced, twenty-four of them reducing the count, one raising it, and five having an equivocal effect.[82] But in 1981 there were also substantive changes in policy, reflecting the very considerable degree of panic in government circles at this time. The July package was hastily put together, and was preceded by a struggle between the 'Wets' in the Cabinet, led by Jim Prior the Employment Minister and Thatcher and Howe, with the 'Wets' for a while in the ascendant.[83] Prior proposed a large package of ameliorative measures, which Howe criticized in the following terms:

> I fully understand why he comes to make these proposals, but I do not believe they strike the right balance. They involve massive additional expenditure (rising to over £1.5 billion in each of 1983–4 and 1984–5). And quite apart from the difficulty of finding money on that scale, I do not believe that they propose anything like enough of freeing the labour market.[84]

In the event, a more limited set of proposals was agreed, then supplemented at the last moment before the announcement was made during a censure debate in the Commons on 27 July. The measures included more money for more students to stay in further education, subsidies for employing young workers on low wages, encouragement to early retirement, and an expansion of the Youth Opportunities Programme.[85]

The package was a characteristic mix. Part of this was purely cosmetic, as recognized in government circles.[86] The term 'cosmetic' should embrace much of the enhanced training.[87] This merely added to an already existing policy trajectory in which government-funded training became 'associated with programmes for the unemployed rather than with skill enhancement'.[88] This money was mainly channelled via the Manpower Services Commission, whose budget expanded from £727 million at the beginning of the 1980s to £3,232 million in 1987/8—figures which are a good index of the government's determination to keep the unemployment

[82] Royal Statistical Society, *Report*, appendix A1.

[83] Howe, *Conflict*, pp. 222–3; in response Thatcher reshuffled her Cabinet to strengthen her supporters. Prior's account is in Prior, *Balance*, pp. 113–32.

[84] TNA: PRO T 430/22, Ministerial Committee on Economic Strategy Chancellor of the Exchequer 'Measures against unemployment in 1981–82 and beyond', 7 July 1981.

[85] TNA: PRO CAB 184/505, 'Record of Meeting on Friday July 24th at 10 Downing St to discuss measures to deal with unemployment'.

[86] The cosmetic nature of what was being done is unabashedly clear in the comments of the government's advisers, such as Ferdinand Mount (Head of the Number Ten Policy Unit after John Hoskyns), questioning whether it was worth spending so much on 'avowedly cosmetic' measures: TNA: PRO PREM 19/1157, 'Temporary unemployment measures', 3 December 1982.

[87] Another policy, the Enterprise Support Allowance, encouraging self-employment, falls somewhere between the substantive and the cosmetic. Support for 'enterprise' was of course part of the government's ideology, but the evidence suggests that self-employment moves upwards in recessions: Tatomir, 'Self-employment'.

[88] King, *Actively*, p. 133.

figures under control. Another feature of the package was the attempt to reduce wages. Ministers were quite clear that this was a crucial issue, and as the quote from Geoffrey Howe above suggests, it was on this as much as the public spending issue that the 'Wets' and the Thatcherites disagreed.

In summing up the emergency package, Thatcher was conscious of the need to 'present the figures with care in order to avoid an adverse reaction from the financial markets'.[89] This was in line with the determination to maintain the tightness of fiscal policy asserted in the recent budget, and avoid any suggestion that the MTFS had been loosened.

In retrospect ministers suggested the July 1981 measures had been 'an expensive package... rushed through with insufficient time for detailed official or Ministerial consideration'.[90] But at the time such a package was seen as unavoidable because, as Hoskyns summarized, the position of the current strategy was 'failing. The outlook for unemployment and recovery is bad; and for inflation unsatisfactory'.[91] Straight after the July package, Howe reiterated his view that some such small-scale package was acceptable, but that he was opposed to any more such measures: 'valuable though some of these schemes may be on a small scale, they change their character as they expand so that they become a threat to our whole economic strategy.' He wanted future policy to concentrate on downward adjustment of real wages, which would involve a range of options, including further reduction in the power of trade unions and reforms to wage setting by wage councils, both of which became important features of the ensuing policy direction. Another strand, he argued, should be 'measures affecting incentives to work' through changes to the benefit system. Third was a reduction in the costs of employing labour, such as through cuts to employers' National Insurance.[92]

Howe's paper provides a good summary of most of the policy options actively discussed between 1979 and 1983. The focus on real wages is perhaps the most important. In part this derived from the 'economics 101 'position that labour is a commodity like any other, where demand varies inversely with price. Of course, there are all sorts of theoretical issues raised by this, from the fallacy-of-composition problem (what may be true for one employer may not be true for employers taken together because of the impact of lower wages on aggregate demand), through to the efficiency wage argument (paying higher wages may induce higher productivity, so making a higher wage affordable—a venerable argument, going back to Alfred Marshall). But such arguments were in the 1980s somewhat beside the point in terms of the government's political strategy in the face of rapidly rising unemployment. The key aim of this strategy was the denial of any significant role for the government's policies in that unemployment, and to blame it upon excessive wages.[93]

[89] TNA: PRO CAB 184/505, 'Record of Meeting on Friday July 24th'.

[90] TNA: PRO T 461/100, 'Special Employment measures: meeting with the PM and others, 1 July 1982.'

[91] TNA: PRO CAB 184/505, J. Hoskyns, 'Measures to reduce unemployment', 21 July 1981.

[92] TNA: PRO CAB 184/505, G. Howe to PM 'Employment measures', 11 August 1981.

[93] Howe's memoirs are strikingly limited in their discussion of unemployment, and the role of the exchange rate is mentioned only in passing: Howe, *Conflict*, p. 202.

The government recognized this was a 'hard sell', though there doesn't seem to have been any quantitative assessment of the scale of the fall in wages that would have been required to offset the appreciation of the pound, though the figure would surely have had to reach wholly implausible levels given the scale of that appreciation. Although there is some discussion of the interwar unemployment problem in the government debates of the early 1980s, especially regarding the impact of benefit levels on unemployment (see later in this section), the idea of a wage-reducing 'treaty', which was discussed as an offset to the overvaluation of the pound in 1925, seems never to have surfaced.[94]

The government hoped that the slackness of labour demand would do most of the job of reducing wages. Treasury discussion of wages recognized that this was likely to be a slow process, which led to the inevitable conclusion that 'policies which could produce a rapid increase in employment without doing lasting damage to counter-inflation objectives simply do not exist.'[95] Part of the government's strategy to improve the chances of success for the policy was a publicity campaign to 'correct public misapprehensions about the link between pay and employment'.[96] As result, major set piece speeches, such as the budget, foregrounded this linkage. For example, in 1982 Howe asserted:

> And so today we face the huge task of helping to create the conditions in which the unemployed can obtain work, in jobs that will last and, as a vital step in this, encouraging wages to be at a level which will enable these more secure jobs to be created.[97]

Keith Joseph urged that more needed to be done on this front. Stressing the centrality of low labour costs, he argued that:

> while I believe that speeches explaining this thesis are essential and might be useful, I think that we should try to persuade business representatives and leader writers and interviewers of the analysis in the hope that union leaders and politicians who put the responsibility for reducing unemployment only on the government might much more often than now be met by shrewder questioning.[98]

Overall, as far as the exchange rate consequences of their policies were concerned, ministers seem to have largely been in denial. While some advisers, notably Hoskyns, frequently emphasized this point, ministers preferred not to face up to it, as plainly it would have raised questions about the government's whole strategy. When Hoskyns circulated a report by Niehans, the Swiss monetarist economist (sponsored by the CPS), which argued that the growth of Sterling M3, the preferred measure of monetary growth in the government's strategy, was highly misleading

[94] Howe does discuss why wages failed in the 1930s to adjust to mass unemployment, as they had failed to do so far in the 1980s: TNA: PRO T 461/99, Chancellor to PM, 'Unemployment and the labour market', no date, but 1981.

[95] TNA: PRO PREM 19/525, P. Jenkins, Treasury, to R. Dykes, Dept. of Employment, 'Action to combat unemployment and improve the working of the labour market', 25 September 1981.

[96] TNA: PRO T 470/122 CPRS, 'Unemployment: issues for discussion and decision', no date but 1982.

[97] Howe, Budget speech 9 March 1982, MTFW 111447; TNA: PRO T430/116, P. Dixon, 'Budget speech—labour market', 9 February 1982.

[98] TNA: PRO PREM 19/529, Keith Joseph to PM, 13 July 1981.

about the tightness of monetary policy, and that the appreciation of the exchange rate was a clear sign of just how far policy had been tightened, there was consternation at the top of the government.[99] As Alan Walters recorded in his diary, 'MT very defensive: NO-ONE must know about it, especially Bank of England'. The problem was clear; public recognition of what Niehans was saying would not only undermine the logic of targeting M3 in the MTFS, but even more importantly give a potentially crucial victory to the Wet critics of government policy.[100]

In public, the 'too high wages' rhetoric continued, without any attempt to argue how that mechanism had suddenly trebled unemployment in the space of two years.

Alongside the wage argument, and linked with it, was the position that benefit levels were crucial to the unemployment problem. This, of course, was not a new argument in the 1980s. In the interwar period there had been the 'search for the scrounger'.[101] From the early 1970s such arguments came back into fashion in Conservative circles, backed by neo-liberal writings such as those of Wood.[102] But in the atmosphere of the early 1980s this argument took on a whole new prominence, as leading figures in the government sought for an analysis of unemployment consonant with their neo-liberal beliefs.

Like most modern governments, the first Thatcher administration hired advisers sympathetic to its political positions (Hoskyns and Mount as Heads of the Number Ten Policy Unit, Walters as Economic Adviser) or sought outside advice from supporters. On the issue of unemployment, the government, encouraged by Walters, invited a report from Patrick Minford, which was circulated in September 1982.[103] This was matched by a report from the Central Policy Review Staff.[104]

While the tone and style of these reports differed, the major policy thrusts were the same. The immediate agenda they set out was summarized by Mount and Walters, and comprised:

(i) Some reduction in income tax to the lower paid.
(ii) Some improvement in FIS and child benefit to help poor working families.
(iii) Some device-CAP or wage-stop to attack the Why Work syndrome.
(iv) Some kind of no-benefit-without-work-scheme—'Workfare'.
(v) Some further steps to reduce trade union immunities.
(vi) The abolition of Wage Councils and other impediments to the labour market.[105]

[99] J. Niehans, 'The Appreciation of Sterling—Causes, Effects Policy Implications', January 1981, MTFW, Walters Papers WTRS 1/4, p. 14.

[100] Walters's diary, 8 January 1981, MTFW 128824; Hoskyns's diary, 9 January 1981, MTFW 113310; P. Middleton to Chancellor 'Niehans', 16 February 1981, MTFW PO-CH-GH0167, p. 2.

[101] Deacon, *In Search*. [102] King, *Actively*, pp. 179–80.

[103] TNA: PRO PREM 19/1159, 'UK unemployment—analysis and policy proposals. A Report prepared for the PM by Prof Patrick Minford and members of the Liverpool Research Group in Macroeconomics under the overall direction of the Economic Adviser to the PM', September 1982. The substance of this was published as Minford, *Unemployment*.

[104] TNA: PRO PREM 19/1158, 'CPRS report on unemployment', September 1982.

[105] TNA: PRO PREM 19//1157, A. Walters and F. Mount 'Unemployment: the next steps', 27 September 1982.

Neither report focused on the multiplication of unemployment in the previous three years. Rather, they emphasized what they regarded as the trend of deterioration in the labour market, caused by microeconomic forces, whilst describing a significant part of current joblessness as caused by soon-to-be-reversed cyclical factors. Whilst voicing support for the government's macroeconomic policies, they stated: 'In this Report we focus on these "underlying" factors and remedies for them rather than on cyclical or "demand-management" factors and policies'.[106]

None of the policies listed above was novel to the discussion already taking place in government circles. What Minford in particular did was to give a new sharpness to the arguments about cutting unemployment benefit; he argued for a cap at 70 per cent of previous wage levels, where the CPRS argued for a 90 per cent level. Minford's advocacy was particularly focused on this issue because, he argued, the current level of benefits created a national wage floor. In his analysis, workers priced out of the labour market by trade union bargaining were unable to find alternative employment in the non-union sector because of this floor.[107] So although Minford was a strong supporter of those who wanted the government to go faster and further in curbing trade unions, he regarded the benefit issue as even more important; in his analysis, without 'high' benefits, the unemployment effects of union bargaining would be much reduced.[108]

Minford's analysis, and in particular his calculations of the scale of unemployment effects from the level of unemployment pay, were widely disputed both by other academic economists and people inside the government machine.[109] But probably more important than the analytical disagreement was the political calculation about his proposal on benefits. Even his supporters suggested caution for this reason:

> But could we justify introducing a 70% cap in the depth of the world recession, as Professor Minford suggests? We should not only be accused of blaming the unemployed and blaming them for that recession—for which we have previously blamed external actors. It would also be pointed out that social security benefits have *fallen* as a percentage of income-in-work during the period (1965–1982) in which unemployment has risen.

In the light of these points, they argued for a 90 per cent cap.[110] The policies actually pursued were more stealthy: abolition of earnings-related supplement and no indexation of benefit rates, and the taxation of benefits.[111] Alongside these policies

[106] Minford, 'UK Unemployment', p. 2. [107] ibid., pp. 3–4.

[108] This belief explains the use of the singular in the title of Minford, *Unemployment*, which asserts that 'the fundamental cause of unemployment is... the operation of the unemployment benefit system' (pp. 2–3).

[109] Stephen Nickell disputed Minford's key assertion that there were always jobs available at a going rate as based only on 'Liverpudlian anecdotes' (Minford then taught at the University of Liverpool): Nickell, *Review*, p. 2.

[110] Walters and Mount, 'Unemployment', p. 5.

[111] There were thirty-eight significant changes in benefits between 1979 and 1988, almost all involving a worsening of the position of the unemployed: Atkinson and Micklewright, 'Turning', pp. 125–6.

went an even stronger emphasis in Conservative rhetoric on the 'welfare scrounger', a trend evident from the mid-1970s.[112]

Similarly on workfare, the principle was widely accepted in Conservative circles in the early 1980s, but faced considerable practical and political obstacles. The major practical obstacle was that linking benefit payment to acceptance of the offer of work required that there be jobs available to be offered, what Minford called a 'job pool'. But in the labour market circumstances of the early 1980s such a pool was plainly very difficult to construct. In addition, it was recognized that workfare was strongly opposed politically, and this would make constructing the pool even more difficult, as such construction would require extensive cooperation from local authorities and other local bodies.[113] In the event, in the years before the 1983 election, workfare was introduced only on a limited scale, for young people.

Finally, it is important to note that Minford and the CPRS, in line with the general thrust of their neo-liberal analysis, were keen to raise in-work incomes as well as reduce and make more conditional the payment of out-of-work benefit. This led to a number of specific proposals, including raising tax thresholds and more support for working families through measures such as improvement to FIS. The former was politically uncontentious, as there was widespread recognition of how far income tax thresholds had fallen; the impact of employees' National Insurance thresholds—income tax by another name—had much less salience.[114] Much more significant in the long run was the support for wage subsidies through mechanisms like FIS and later family credit. The logic here was clear: if you believed that the wage/benefit gap needed to be widened, but also recognized the political problems of being very radical on benefit levels, wage subsidies were an 'obvious' answer—though, of course, ideologically, they could not be named as such.

While the Conservatives debated the causes and cures for unemployment, and introduced some measures which either substantively or cosmetically reduced the unemployment figures, headline unemployment rose without respite between 1979 and 1983, though the pace of increase was slackening (see Figure 6.1).[115] The prospect of fighting a general election with over three million unemployed made most Conservatives highly apprehensive.[116] But, of course, in the end they had no need to worry. The election result was an increased majority, rising from 70 seats more than Labour in 1979 to 188 seats, albeit the Conservative share of the vote fell from 43.9 to 42.4 per cent.[117]

Political scientists have spent a great deal of effort seeking to explain this result. As Ivor Crewe points out, it was at odds with what many models of electoral behaviour would have forecast. The 'misery index', combining the levels of

[112] Howell, *Why Work?*; King, *Actively*, pp. 179–80.

[113] Walters and Mount, 'Unemployment', pp. 5–6.

[114] For income tax thresholds, see Daunton, *Just*, p. 311.

[115] Though output and incomes bottomed out in late 1981.

[116] The project of redefining and thereby radically reducing the 'strategic' unemployment figure as proposed by the IEA's authors was never taken up. This would have involved a radical reduction in the figures; for July 1981 from an official figure of 2.7 million down to 483,000: Miller and Wood, *What Price?*, p. 62. But the figures were adjusted many times in other ways.

[117] Butler and Kavanagh, *British General Election of 1983*, pp. 299, 300.

unemployment and inflation, was notably higher than in 1981, and while inflation was back down to 5 per cent it had peaked at 22 per cent only three years earlier.[118] In another piece, Crewe sarcastically observed of the misery index: 'the econometric equation produced a Conservative vote of minus 156 per cent! But the electorate re-elected the Conservatives with a handsomely increased majority.'[119]

What explains the Conservative success? The split in the opposition, with the creation of the Alliance, and the Falklands factor were clearly significant. The latter was perhaps especially important symbolically; 'it served as a perfectly timed metaphor for all that the government hitherto had claimed about its domestic strategy. It would not duck tough decisions about the economy; it did not wriggle out of its commitment to the Falkland islanders.'[120]

Why did the level of unemployment seem to have so little impact on voting behaviour? It was not because people expressed themselves unconcerned with the issue. The percentage mentioning unemployment as one of the two most important issues rose from 27 per cent in 1979 to 72 per cent in 1983. In addition, Labour was the preferred party (by 16 per cent) to effectively deal with the issue. But this was not enough. The Conservative lead on its two 'preferred' issues, defence and prices, was much larger (54 and 40 per cent respectively). Furthermore,

> the lengthening of the dole queues made more people put unemployment at the top of the agenda, but no more people than before were convinced that Labour would do better than the Conservatives at shortening the lines. In 1979 Labour's edge over the Conservatives as the party of jobs was 15 per cent; after a tripling of unemployment in four years of Conservative government, its edge was 16 per cent.[121]

While the electorate accepted that Labour cared more about unemployment, they doubted its ability to do much about the problem: for many voters unemployment was, in the language of psephology, a 'valence issue', where the crucial issue was not whether a policy objective was desired, but the perceived competence to achieve that objective. While Labour's manifesto promised a reduction from 3.5 to 1 million within five years, the electorate was profoundly sceptical. A MORI poll showed that a majority of respondents expected the unemployed in two years to number 3.5 million if the Conservatives were re-elected, but at least 3 million if Labour won, with other polls conveying the same message. Unemployment did affect the geographical pattern of voting, with high-unemployment areas more likely to vote Labour—but this often just piled up bigger majorities in Labour-held seats.[122]

In the wake of the election result some Conservative ideologues argued that it was unsurprising that the Conservatives had won, and cited the 1935 election as the appropriate parallel where a government won whilst presiding over a recovering economy but with high unemployment. Mount went on to argue that this result should not induce complacency, and that policy should continue to focus

118 Crewe, 'How', p. 155.
119 Crewe, 'Has?', p. 28.
120 Crewe, 'How', p. 160.
121 ibid., pp. 176–7; quote at p. 177.
122 ibid., p. 179; Butler and Kavanagh, *British General Election of 1983*, pp. 339–42.

attention on reducing jobless numbers: 'I am convinced that unemployment will eventually come to arouse stronger political emotions in this Parliament than it did in the last.'[123]

Most existing policies perceived to reduce unemployment were strengthened after 1983, whether these were reductions of trade union power, cuts to benefits, or expansion of workfare and 'training'. But alongside this the government sought more than ever to persuade the electorate that its policies represented a new, effective combination that provided the only route to low unemployment. This purported radicalism was evident in the presentation of macroeconomic policy in the important Mais lecture given by the Chancellor (now Nigel Lawson) in 1985. This proclaimed a 'reassignment' of policy instruments. In place of using demand management to control unemployment, in the new regime such management would focus on inflation, whilst within that stable macroeconomic environment the level of unemployment would be determined by microeconomic forces, including government policy on the labour market.[124]

Alongside this, the government prepared a new White Paper on employment policy.[125] In the introduction this document cites the words from the 1944 White Paper on the dependence of policy success upon 'the understanding and support of the community as a whole', and this is used to suggest the limits to the role of government in dealing with the problem, above all the need to focus on improving the working of the labour market. So the main purpose of the White Paper was not to announce new policies, but to put forward a particular account of the problem in order to educate the public: 'There must be nationwide understanding of the origin and nature of the problem, and nationwide action, if it is to be solved.'[126]

In line with all the previous public discussion initiated by the government, no responsibility for the increase in unemployment after 1979 reflected policy in those years. Instead, according to the 1985 White Paper, the doubling of employment between 1977 and 1982 can be explained 'in large measure as the disguised unemployment of earlier years, with overmanning rife, was forced into the open.'[127] As Steve Nickell pointed out, as an explanation this was

> somewhat curious...given that most jobs were lost between quarter 2 of 1979 and quarter 2 of 1981 when manufacturing employment fell by 17 per cent and manufacturing output fell by 20 per cent. This is hardly consistent with the overmanning view, for were this correct the loss in output should have been negligible rather than more or less proportional to the loss in employment.[128]

Nickell also noted that another key claim of the document, that Britain was having to respond to 'great shifts in the structure of employment', reflecting 'the biggest economic transformation since the industrial revolution' had no basis in the evidence, which suggested structural change in the early 1980s was around the long-run average.[129]

123 F. Mount to PM, 'Unemployment', 24 June 1983, MTFW 131107.
124 Mais lecture, at MTFW 109504.
125 Cmnd. 9474.
126 Cmnd. 9474, para 1.2.
127 ibid., para 2.7.
128 Nickell, 'Government's', p. 108.
129 ibid., pp. 108–9.

The White Paper went on to itemize the policies the government had pursued to try and free up the labour market, with the intention of reducing the growth in money wages, thereby, according to its overall strategy, maximizing the growth of employment for a given expansion of nominal demand. These policies were: industrial relations legislation, weakening employment protection, reducing the role of wage councils, removing labour market monopolies, tax changes, and bearing down on public sector pay. Analysing each of these in turn, Nickell concluded 'their overall contribution to reducing wage pressure has not been, and is not likely to be, very great'. But more than this, he noted that these policies were aimed overwhelmingly at the lower end of the wage distribution, whereas between 1979 and 1983 the real earnings of non-manual male workers rose by 19 per cent (for manual workers the rise was 11 per cent).[130] In other words, while the government's policies had been notionally aimed at reducing unemployment, what had been the most striking aspect of the period, along with rising unemployment, was a rise in inequality. This is not to suggest the government had a 'hidden agenda' of raising inequality, but that if you focus policy on controlling wages at the bottom end of the distribution, increased inequality is an unsurprising consequence.

Thatcher had never hidden that she believed greater inequality was desirable as a means of reviving incentives and improving economic performance:

> But I don't know of many people who go for equality as far as equality of income and earnings are concerned. Certainly the trade unions don't. One of the problems there is differentials for extra skill and extra effort, so I don't believe many people go for equality, except in equality before the law, equality in voting rights. No, you will get a more thriving society when people can rise to the limit of their talents, and out of the wealth they create, we shall all be better off.[131]

In the event inequality increased by 50 per cent in the Thatcher years (the Gini Coefficient rising from 0.23 in 1978 to 0.34 in 1990), and poverty (proportion of households with below half average income) doubled.[132] But in the current context what is striking is the perhaps less well-documented impact on the specific position of the unemployed; always more prone to poverty than the employed, but this gap increased significantly from the mid-1980s.[133]

The 1985 White Paper invoked its predecessor of 1944, and that Conservative policies were simply returning to the forgotten truths of that document was a common trope of Conservative discussion in the 1970s and 1980s.[134] In Thatcher's copy of the document, as already noted, she highlighted some of the key conditions that had been laid down if 'high and stable' employment was to be achieved. But one of those conditions was the maintenance of external as well as internal demand, and this was where policy in the 1980s, recklessly rather than deliberately, had been so damaging. However, politically this could not be accepted. Instead,

[130] ibid., pp. 113, 114.

[131] Interview with Brian Walden, 6 January 1980, MTFW 104210.

[132] Hills, Sefton, and Stewart, *Towards*, pp. 2–3: this picture is robust for the use of other measures of inequality: Clark and Leicester, 'Inequality', p. 145.

[133] Hauser and Nolan, 'Unemployment'.

[134] Wood, *How Little?*, pp. 61–2.

the focus was on 'educating the public' to accept the government's versions of why unemployment had shot up. This version included 'international conditions', but treated these as a wholly exogenous force. But, much more significantly, the government argued that it was too-high wages at the bottom end of the labour market, abetted by over-generous benefits, over-mighty trade unions, and an overly interventionist state, that were chiefly to blame.

How far the populace was persuaded of this analysis is very difficult to say. Hostility to trade unions was certainly very evident in the early 1980s, though this seems to have owed more to the portrayal of 'over-mighty trade union barons' and 'greedy strikers' as responsible for the 'chaos' of the Winter of Discontent, than to any clear belief that unions were major culprits specifically for unemployment. There is also evidence that the 'scrounger' story was affecting attitudes towards social security for the unemployed.

The British Social Attitudes survey only began in 1983, so can't be used to compare with attitudes prior to Thatcher, though it does show that even at the bottom of the slump in 1982/3 only 33 per cent of respondents thought unemployment pay should be a first or second priority for social security spending, and this figure, with a slight cyclical element, declined to 12 per cent by the end of the century.[135] Other recent data relating to unemployment also suggest a trend towards a 'tough' attitude to the unemployed, so that by 2014 a majority (52 per cent) thought that benefits for the unemployed were too high and discouraged work.[136] This attitude goes along with gross overestimates of the proportion of social security spending going on unemployment benefits: in a 2012 survey on average respondents thought that 41 per cent of Britain's welfare budget goes on benefits to unemployed people, whereas in fact the figure is 3 per cent.[137]

Overall, the evidence from the crucial 1983 election is that whilst post-war sympathetic attitudes had started to shift, many remained very concerned about unemployment; much of the electorate was fatalistic about its existence, and not inclined to believe that any government could make much difference. This attitude was enough to effectively neuter the criticism of the policies which emerged after 1979 that which gave a lower priority to unemployment reduction alongside disguising the level of hardship endured by the unemployed.

[135] Taylor-Gooby and Hastie, 'Support?', p. 79.
[136] Taylor-Gooby and Taylor, 'Benefits?', pp. 9–10.
[137] http://d25d2506sfb94s.cloudfront.net/cumulus_uploads/document/xzmltcdt5i/YG-Archive-results-TUC-121212-welfare-benefits-knowledge.pdf.

7

Productivity

In his diary entry for 25 January 1976 Tony Benn noted that 'Harold [Wilson] said he had invented the concept of output per man shift and even the concept of productivity which had been a theoretical concept before he got it extended all over industry. A terrible thing to have on his conscience.'[1]

Though somewhat exaggerated, Wilson's claim indicated two important truths.[2] First, as Wilson detailed elsewhere, his pioneering role in introducing 'productivity' had happened during the Second World War, when he was responsible for constructing data on coal production.[3] While it had been used before 1939, the term had mainly been restricted to academic debate or in 'broad brush' understandings of economic change, not as a term to be 'operationalized' as part of everyday economic discussion and policy. Second, Wilson's role was indicative of the way 'productivity' was to be a term especially associated with social democratic politics in post-war Britain—whilst Benn's comments suggest the hostility this aroused on other parts of the Left.[4] Governments of the Right did talk about productivity, but none of them placed it at the centre of their agenda as governments of the Left did in the 1940s and 1960s.[5]

Like the commitment to 'high and stable' employment, the initial governmental focus on productivity arose from the exigencies of war. By 1941 the British economy had moved from excess supply to excess demand, and there was a sharply increased focus on getting more output from a workforce now, of course, reduced in size by military mobilization. Alongside efforts to mobilize the previously 'non-working' groups such as housewives and the disabled came an effort to raise productivity, Harold Wilson's pioneering role in coal being a key example where demand for the industry's output ran up against the constraint of a contracting workforce.[6]

Unlike the drive for full employment, that for higher productivity never readily attained universal popular support. But in government circles it was widely believed that such popular support was absolutely essential to achieve this goal. So while

[1] Benn, *Against*, p. 506.

[2] Productivity data were used for example in 1931 in Cmd. 3897, appendix VI, tables 2, 3, and 4, in a quite different context.

[3] Wilson, 'Statistics', pp. 1–2.

[4] The concern with productivity was also opposed by elements of the Conservative Right: '. . . the world in which "standard of living" is the ultimate criterion . . . so that productivity—the extremely important thing—must be kept on the rise, at whatever cost to protesting conservative habit'. F. R. Leavis, 1962, cited in Gwyn, 'Jeremiahs', p. 15.

[5] For a survey of productivity policy up until the 1990s, see Bufton, *Britain's*.

[6] In 1939 the mining workforce was 735,000; by the end of 1946, 690,000: Crofts, *Coercion?*, p. 188.

most of the productivity drive came from the top—from government—it involved, at times, extensive and ambitious publicity campaigning. Hence the theme of productivity improvement is a particularly important element in the overall story of government attempts to shape economic understanding since the 1940s.

When, in both the 1940s and the 1960s, a Labour government placed increasing productivity at the centre of its economic policy agenda, this was accompanied by extensive publicity aimed primarily at the 'shop-floor' worker. But while there were continuities in the stances taken in propagating the importance of productivity, there were also differences in approach and tone, which, along with the differences in the methods of propaganda employed, help us to understand the varying resonances the term had in these two decades. The concluding section of this chapter offers some retrospective judgement on the impact and significance of these campaigns.

I

Like full employment, productivity emerged in wartime both as a question of immediate necessity and something which then became part of plans for post-war reconstruction. In 1941–2 Britain was rocked not only by military reverses but also by a perceived production crisis at home, as deliveries of armaments and munitions fell short of requirements.[7] Part of the response to this crisis was to emphasize productivity as the only way to produce more, now that few reserves of labour remained to be mobilized. This point of emergence of the productivity term explains why, at this time, it was used almost always to mean *labour* productivity, and most often as *physical* output per head, as with Harold Wilson's 'Output per Man Shift' (OMS) in coal, where output was measured in tons. This, it should be emphasized, was a very specific, narrow definition of productivity, but one with profound implications. The standard abstract definition of productivity relates the *value* of output to the *value* of *total* inputs. The focus on physical outputs, whilst explicable in wartime when market pricing was downgraded and, especially in industries like coal, where total physical output needed to be maximized, makes much less sense in a normally functioning market economy where it is the *value* of output which matters (otherwise productivity may encompass the production of goods no one wants to buy). Even more importantly, focusing on *labour* productivity ignores the crucial role of the capital input into the production process, and seems to carry the implication that it is the labour element which is the key variable in explaining changes in productivity. It is a short distance from this assumption to the idea that it is the intensity of labour *effort* that is behind productivity differences. As we shall see, these connotations of productivity fed strongly into the politics which surrounded the attempts to propagandize around the term.

[7] Hinton, *Shop*, pp. 27–52; Mass Observation, *People* argued that the inefficiency of factories was being exaggerated by newspapers uncritically retelling stories from disaffected shop stewards.

Wartime concern to raise productivity led to a large number of governmental initiatives, ranging from, in the most radical case, government taking over the running of a company (Short Brothers) through to the setting-up of a Production Efficiency Board (PEB).[8] These involved a degree of state intervention in the running of industry without precedent, though there were precursors in the First World War. A large part of this intervention was linked to persuading industrial workers of the need for them to prioritize production increase on a day-to-day basis. This led to a great deal of exhortation, but also to institutional initiatives, most importantly Joint Production Committees (JPCs), aimed at involving workers in discussion about production issues.[9] Focusing on the engineering industry, Hinton has argued that these bodies helped to mobilize union activist and some broader worker support for expanding production, partly because they provided a linkage between productivity and enhanced worker power which was congenial to the Left, and whose political position was strengthening.[10] There is evidence in support of this view from the aircraft industry, where a 1943 survey found that 63 per cent of discussion in JPCs concerned production issues (welfare 27 per cent) and 'most items are concerned with constructive suggestions for improvement from the workers rather than with unconstructive complaints'.[11]

Productivity also figured in much more abstract wartime government discussions of post-war reconstruction. General debate about how production efficiency was to be enhanced was an important element on the agendas of wartime committees on post-war planning, but came into sharp focus in discussion about to what extent plans for major reforms of social security could be afforded.[12] In the effort to calculate this affordability by forecasting post-war national income, estimates of productivity trends were crucial but contentious.[13]

In many ways the wartime initiatives laid the ground work for the pursuit of the productivity agenda under the Attlee government. An important element in this continuity was the role of Stafford Cripps, who as Minister for Aircraft Production in 1942–5 played a key role in productivity initiatives in that crucial sector, including the introduction of JPCs to encourage worker involvement. He was to play an even more vital role as President of the Board of Trade (1945–7) and Chancellor of the Exchequer (1947–50), continuing and intensifying this wartime work.[14]

The Attlee government's inheritance from the war was a potentially disastrous balance-of-payments deficit, a hugely run-down capital stock, but excess demand and full employment. In this way macroeconomic conditions, as in the war,

[8] Tiratsoo and Tomlinson, *Industrial Efficiency*, pp. 21–42; the PEB's focus was on production techniques, but it also pressed for improvements in welfare provision: TNA: PRO AVIA 9/37, 'Utilization of manpower in the aircraft industry: Investigation by Sir Charles Bruce Gardner', 4 January 1943.

[9] Croucher, *Engineers*; Inman, *Labour*, pp. 371–92, 434–5.

[10] Hinton, *Shop*.

[11] TNA: PRO AVIA 9/57, M. Locke, 'JPCs in the aircraft industry', 7 January 1943.

[12] Wartime discussions can be followed in TNA: PRO BT64, Board of Trade Reconstruction Committee and TNA: PRO CAB 87/5-18, Reconstruction Priorities Committee.

[13] TNA: PRO CAB87/13, Treasury, 'Factors affecting the level of the National Income', 25 June 1943.

[14] Clarke, *Cripps*, pp. 479–538; Toye, *Labour*, pp. 122–4, 197–9, 201–7.

focused attention on producing more with a limited workforce, which is what was normally meant by 'increasing productivity' in the immediate post-war years. Given the limits on increasing investment, the focus was once again on *labour* productivity. Increased production, especially through higher productivity, was at the heart of Mr Attlee's 'supply-side socialism'.[15]

The very specific focus on productivity developed within the austerity policies of the 1940s, as outlined in Chapter 1. Part of this emphasized raising production as the key to easing the burden of this policy, and a concern with enhancing productivity logically followed; increased productivity was the 'road to prosperity'.[16] Government economic propaganda focused much more explicitly on productivity as the main route to more production from 1948 onwards. Partly this was because, while some additional workers had been attracted into industry (e.g. married women into cotton) and sources such as displaced workers (e.g. Poles) used to supplement the indigenous workforce, the limits on expanding labour supply were being reached. Also important was the broad geopolitics of these years, and the openness of the British government to American pressures to see raising productivity as the basis for a prosperous capitalism which would reduce the attractions of Communism to Western European workers.[17] Partly from this strategic imperative came the AACP, which in the years 1948–52 sent sixty-seven teams from Britain to study the reasons for higher American productivity and the possibility of applying the lessons to Britain.[18] Some have seen this as part of a bigger process of attempted 'Americanization' of the British economy, an important theme in post-war British industrial history.[19] But what needs to be stressed here is the ready embrace of this productivity agenda by Britain's governing social democrats, not least Stafford Cripps. There *was* opposition, especially on the Left, to what some perceived as alien and anti-socialist ideas from across the Atlantic, but the bulk of Labour opinion at least went along with the Crippsian view.

The Attlee government sought to raise productivity through wide-ranging measures, from enhancing technical training through to sponsoring the creation of the British Institute of Management. But this action had a distinctly political character, in two ways. First, it involved significant intervention by the state, through such mechanisms as development councils, which involved unions and government as well as employers overseeing industrial restructuring in the sectors concerned. This dirigiste aspect helps explain why Labour's productivity campaign never found strong support amongst Conservatives. It was not that they opposed the principle of raising output per head, but they saw Labour's agenda as one of using this desirable goal as a basis for wholesale and counterproductive interventions in the private sector.[20] Second, Labour's productivity agenda in the 1940s involved a belief that positive changes in workers' roles and attitudes to industry

[15] Tomlinson, 'Mr Attlee's Supply-Side Socialism'.

[16] TNA: PRO CAB 134/188, 'Official steering committee on economic development Leaflet for "Prosperity Campaign"', 13 June 1946; Crofts, *Coercion?*, pp. 35–47.

[17] Maier, 'Politics'. [18] Tomlinson, 'Failure'. [19] Carew, *Labour*.

[20] Dennison, 'Industrial'.

were crucial ways of raising productivity in a politically acceptable manner. This was to be achieved in a number of ways: by 'industrial democracy' in the form of revived JPCs and joint consultation; by improved industrial welfare for workers; and by management understanding and acting in accordance with the 'human factor' in industry. In addition, workers were to be persuaded that only by raising (their) productivity could the goals of full employment and a rising standard of living be achieved; productivity increase would be part of a 'social contract' between workers and government.

Each of these strands of what may be called a social democratic approach to productivity posed challenges for the Attlee government. JPCs had declined after 1945, and when the Labour government sought to revive them in 1947 it found tensions aroused concerning how far they could and should give workers any effective say in the running of industry. There was a great deal of hostility from employers to the idea of imposition of these committees, but also a danger that they would decline into focus not on production issues but on 'tea and toilets'.[21] Another aspect of their functioning was their relationship to collective bargaining. In principle, wage issues were outside their remit, but, of course, policies to change how production was organized were bound to be interwoven with wage determination. One illustration of the problem relates to work study or time and motion analysis, very much favoured by 'progressive' management opinion in the 1940s. But while some sought to focus on the purely technical, ergonomic aspects of such approaches, it was hard to separate any assessment of the work process from questions of worker effort and payment.[22]

Improved industrial welfare was an important part of the wartime attempt to encourage higher productivity, and this effort continued post-war. But many employers were reluctant to undertake costly new initiatives. As in many other policy areas, Labour sought to ally itself with 'progressive managers' who would lead the drive for treating workers better as a way of raising output, but found these allies unrepresentative of the broad mass of employers who were reluctant to change their practices.[23]

When the government set up its Committee on Industrial Productivity at the end of 1947, this in turn established a 'Human Factors Panel' to investigate the ways in which better human relations could contribute to productivity growth. The panel sponsored a wide range of research, including general work on foremen and joint consultation case studies on 'human engineering' and 'methods of communication in industry'.[24] What is striking is the attention in some of these studies to worker psychology—attention to which, it was believed, could unleash attitudes beneficial to higher productivity. In part this movement reflected the broader rise of psychology as an influential discipline in British society in the middle decades

[21] TNA: PRO CAB 134/640, Production Committee, Ministry of Labour, 'Publicity on economic situation', 4 October 1949; Hinton, *Shop*, pp. 184–97.

[22] TNA: PRO BT 195/19, Report of TUC regional advisory committee, 19 October 1948.

[23] Tiratsoo and Tomlinson, *Industrial*, pp. 111–30.

[24] Ministry of Labour, *Human Relations*, appendix II. Two important case studies were Jacques, *Changing*, and Scott, *Joint*.

of the twentieth century.[25] In its crudest versions this approach amounted to little more that the assertion that the 'happy worker is a productive worker'. But it was based on extensive research by such bodies as the old-established National Institute for Industrial Psychology, and the newly created Tavistock Institute of Human Relations. The latter was grounded in Freudian psychoanalysis, something which many contemporary socialist intellectuals were interested in, not least Cripps.[26]

While some policymakers and politicians had a clear (and quite radical) idea of what improving 'human relations' might mean, it was a term which could cover many approaches to management. In some 'high-level' discussions it was reduced to an anodyne notion of management keeping the workers 'well informed'. Certainly many employers were sceptical of ideas coming from government-supported experts, while unions had to be reassured that it was not all about 'psychoanalysing the workers'.[27]

When the government launched its focused campaign on productivity it was partly driven by feedback on the effects of its previous propaganda efforts, which suggested that what was needed was propaganda that sought specific actions rather than simply providing information.[28] The resulting strategy included material aimed at three audiences: the general public, 'industry in general', and workers.[29] The second of these was politically most fraught, with the government agreeing that the main responsibility for this aspect of the campaign would be left to industry itself. This meant that the government did not directly involve itself in recommending any particular management policies in the technical field.[30]

But a key part of the new campaign was the distribution through managements of 700,000 copies of *Productivity Pays*, aimed at the factory floor, alongside a refocusing of an already existing periodic publication, *Target*, similarly aimed, which was sent to all factories with over fifty workers.[31]

Productivity Pays was a twenty-page pamphlet which offered reasons why productivity was such a key issue, whilst also spelling out what workers would need to do to support this agenda[32] (see Illustration 2). On the first of these there was a reiteration of themes from previous campaigns about production as the basis of economic recovery. But there was also an emphasis on productivity enhancement as the

[25] Miller and Rose, 'Governing'. [26] Miller, 'Psychotherapy'.

[27] TNA: PRO CAB 124/1097, Committee on Industrial Productivity, Schuster to Nicholson, 16 March 1950.

[28] Crofts, *Coercion?*, pp. 70–4.

[29] TNA: PRO CAB 134/591, Productivity (Official) Committee: EIU 'Publicity about higher productivity', 31 August 1949.

[30] TNA: PRO BT 195/19, Committee on Industrial Productivity, G. Blaker to Miss Loebl, 15 June 1949; TNA: PRO CAB 134/642, Production Committee, 'Report of Productivity (Official) Committee', annex IV 'Publicity about productivity'. This reflected employers concerns about the productivity drive providing an excuse for government intervention in 'workshop affairs': BT 195/19', Discussions with FBI and TUC on publicity about productivity', 24 November 1948.

[31] TNA: PRO CAB 134/642, 'Publicity about productivity'.

[32] EIU/COI, *Productivity Pays*.

Illustration 2 A curious pun for the productivity campaign (1949).
Source: Image courtesy of the National Archives.

key to full employment, a theme from the 1944 *Employment Policy* White Paper, as noted in Chapter 6. The rationale for including this section was that 'this theme is necessary because, after a long period of high unemployment and defensive and restrictive policies in many sections of both sides of industry, there is not enough general understanding of the industrial policies and personal attitudes which full employment requires'. This emphasis also reflected the resistance to previous propaganda for higher output driven by the fear that this would only hasten the return of unemployment.[33] The argument made in response to this fear was seen as:

> while the full employment policy is safe from any return of the circumstances that caused it before the war, it is not safe from the consequences of failure in the export drive, and the risks of that failure would be greatly increased by any failure to improve productivity and to lower costs.[34]

[33] TNA: PRO CAB 134/642, 'Publicity about productivity'.
[34] TNA: PRO CAB 134/591, EIU Brief, 'Publicity about higher productivity'.

Despite these attempts at reassurance, survey evidence suggests fears about future employment remained pervasive in the late 1940s; in 1948 31 per cent of respondents thought it likely that heavy unemployment would return in the next few years.[35]

A third major issue identified by the designers of this propaganda was to specify the key factors in raising productivity. In the language of the time, it was stated: 'This is necessary because without such explanation increased productivity would be connected by many people with longer hours and nigger-driving methods.' Three key factors were identified: mechanization, healthy industrial relations, and sound technical management. However, it was pointed out that the first of these was severely constrained by shortages of materials, especially steel.[36]

The specific requirements for workers suggested by the pamphlet focused not on working harder but working efficiently, through the acceptance of time and motion studies, changes to shop layout, machine arrangement and working routines, and the possibility of learning new skills.[37]

The campaign on productivity continued through the lifetime of the Attlee government, though the intensity of the effort slackened in late 1949 when the government cut back on all of its home publicity in the face of political opposition.[38]

Like other economic propaganda of the 1940s, the effects of the productivity campaign were carefully assessed by the government. Mass Observation was asked to do a specific study of the reception of *Productivity Pays*. About half of those who received the booklet claimed to have either read or 'glanced at' it, but only 6 per cent of the whole sample 'gave some objective evidence of having paid attention to the contents of the booklet'.[39]

More sustained and systematic analysis was done by the Government Social Survey. Part of this assessment was framed in terms of gauging public understanding of the word itself. Here the results show little evidence of change in response to the most intense period of propaganda (see Table 7.1). The survey assumed that there was a 'correct' definition in terms of output per man hour (OMH)—a definition which was

Table 7.1 Social Survey evidence on public understanding of 'increasing productivity', 1948–51 (percentage of those surveyed)

	November 1948	July 1949	February 1951
In the main correct	18	18	16
Confused with 'production'	22	23	37
Incorrect/off the point	10	14	14
Don't know/not answered	43	43	43

Source: TNA: PRO RG23/103, 'Survey of knowledge and opinion about the economic situation: production and productivity', November 1948; RG23/115, 'Survey of knowledge and opinion about the economic situation: production and productivity', February 1951.

[35] TNA: PRO RG23/103, 'Survey of knowledge and opinion about the economic situation', November 1948.

[36] TNA: PRO CAB 134/642, 'Publicity about productivity'.

[37] *Productivity Pays*, pp. 11–12.

[38] Crofts, *Coercion?*, pp. 77–9, 218–42.

[39] TNA: PRO RG23/536, '*Productivity Pays* investigation: summary of results' 21 July 1949.

Table 7.2 Beneficiaries of increased production (percentage of those surveyed)

	November 1948	July 1949	February 1951
Workers more	6	8	5
Employers more	13	14	13
Both equally	45	47	43
Don't know or unaware of propaganda	n/a	23	25

Source: as Table 7.1

indeed the one purveyed by the government, and fitted the context and objectives of the time, but one which cannot be seen as 'correct' in a wider framework.

More illuminating in suggesting some of the limits to the effects of the propaganda is the survey response to the question 'who benefits more when production is increased?' (see Table 7.2). This does suggest a persistent, if unchanging, acceptance of the line emphasized in the propaganda aimed at the shop floor, that higher productivity was not just a ruse to extract more from the workers, but could have benefits for everyone.

There are enormous data problems with measuring productivity. These were well recognized in the 1940s, and indeed one reason why the physical OMH measure was focused upon at this time was that it was more readily measured than by using more complex definitions. At the beginning of the prosperity campaign in 1946, ministers were lamenting that, 'As the campaign is concerned so largely with increasing productivity, the Committee is particularly concerned over the lack of facts or statistics bearing upon productivity'.[40] To address this, the Board of Trade appointed the leading expert in the field, Laszlo Rostas, to compile data. His first report stressed the difficulties in doing so (not least that employment and production data were compiled on different bases), and as a result recommended OMH.[41] As Rostas made clear in his published work, this measure was *not* just related to worker effort: 'relative physical output per head is influenced, for example, by differences in the skill and effort of the workers, but is equally influenced by differences in a managerial efficiency, differing technical equipment, rate of operations, and various other factors.'[42]

This point was hugely politically important in the 1940s, when the government in its official pronouncements was always concerned to stress that the higher productivity it sought would not come from 'sweating labour', but would be the result of 'working smarter, not harder.' This was seen as crucial if popular support for productivity was to be gained. But this caution was not shared by many in the 1940s (or later), who were happy to ascribe the 'productivity problem' to lack of effort by the workers.[43] Some academics followed suit, a particularly egregious

[40] TNA: PRO CAB 134/188, Official steering committee on economic development, 'Prosperity campaign material for leaflet', 13 June 1946.

[41] TNA: PRO CAB 134/190, Official steering committee on economic development: Board of Trade, 'Changes in productivity in British industry', 15 January 1947.

[42] Rostas, *Comparative*, p. 2.

[43] Crofts, *Coercion?*, pp. 42, 47.

contemporary example being the economist Peter Wiles, who provided a long history of the decline of the 'British will to work', a will which was apparently lower here than in any other country.[44]

A key feature of the contemporary debate on productivity, which also opened the way to lots of tendentious comment, was international comparison, especially with the USA. Rostas, who emerged as the key expert commentator on this topic in this period, wrote about this in academic journals, but also broadcast on the BBC.[45] In the broadcast Rostas was careful not to rush to judgement on the role of the worker in accounting for differences between US and British productivity levels. As he noted, 'when we realise that productivity can more than double in a generation, it is obvious that it is not the increase in the effort of the worker which has been the prime moving factor, either here or in the United States'. However, he did go on to say that 'Perhaps greater importance should be attached to the worker's attitude to change, the way in which he is prepared to co-operate with management in giving a chance to new methods, new processes, new techniques.'[46] This attitudinal theme was a feature of the rhetoric of many of the AACP reports, though as with Rostas's broadcast, it was backed by no evidence, and seemed to function as a residual explanation when all others had failed.

This approach was effectively satirized in the *New Statesman*:

> The teams, it seems, have found the real secret of high productivity: it lies not in machinery, not in factory layout—in short not primarily in technical improvements, but in the American way of Life. If only the American way (the reports suggest) could be transferred to Britain, how hardworking, how comfortable everyone would be.[47]

The workers' reception of this campaign was partly shaped by the attitude taken up by the trade unions. The official union position was strikingly supportive of the government, with the TUC endorsing the productivity drive and organizing its own conference to encourage union members in their support, sending union officials to the USA to see how American unions helped increase productivity, and supporting union participation in the AACP missions.[48]

But we must be wary of translating this official union support into evidence of general worker support. The belief that the productivity drive was a drive for harder work was widespread, and one that Cripps, for example, went out of his way to try to dispel, stressing to the TUC that 'either we must use more muscle or more brain and I am in favour of more brain' and 'It is only those most bankrupt of ideas who

[44] Wiles, 'Notes'; for a more nuanced version see Dennison, 'Industrial productivity'. Wiles was but the first of many to use productivity in this way. For a powerful critique of some of the most important of the later treatments see Nichols, *British*.

[45] Rostas, 'Productivity'; 'British and American Industry Compared' transcript of broadcast in *The Listener* 11 November 1948, pp. 713, 727.

[46] 'British and American Industry Compared', p. 727. In an assessment published in 1952 Rostas offered an upbeat summary of the productivity performance of 1946–50, suggesting that OMH in industry and manufacturing had increased by 5 and 6 per cent per annum respectively, a rate of increase similar to the USA's: Rostas, 'Changes'.

[47] *New Statesman*, 29 December 1951.

[48] TUC, 'Productivity'; TUC, 'Trade'. On unions and the AACP see Booth, 'Corporate'.

insist that the only way to increase production is to make other people work harder and longer hours'. He went on to say that part of this strategy was the use of more machinery, but had then to accept that macroeconomic priorities limited the increase in machinery possible.[49] This dilemma helps to explain why he and others in the government were so keen on the 'human factors' approach, which seemed to be the answer to the conundrum of extracting more output without either greater worker effort or investment in machinery.

But the productivity drive of the 1940s not only had to operate in the context of the austerity of the period, with its priority for resources going into exports, it also had to deal with the shortages that characterized these years. This was a problem in two distinct ways. First it meant that, whatever government might urge and workers want to do, shortages of fuels and materials often meant production was interrupted.[50] Second, it meant that the claims about productivity being the route to a higher standard of living were undermined by continuing shortages of consumer goods, politically the most problematic consequence of 1940s-style austerity, as emphasized in Chapter 1.

The final issue was the link between productivity and wages. Once governments started having incomes policies they were drawn inevitably into questions about what circumstances justified what level of wage increases. If the government was simultaneously exhorting wage earners to increase production, linking the two aims had a compelling logic, but also obvious dangers in threatening existing patterns of wage determination. The productivity–pay linkage was made in the 1948 incomes policy, but it was not central, and had limited impact in shaping the fortunes of the productivity drive. The story of the 1960s was very different.

II

Productivity did not suddenly disappear from government policy or pronouncements in 1951. The BPC (the AACP reformed) continued to pursue the agenda, though with growing scepticism about its effectiveness. In 1962/3 it sponsored 'National Productivity Year', launched by the Duke of Edinburgh, in which he spoke in appropriately downbeat terms of the Council's aim to 'ginger things up a bit'.[51] At the government level there was evidence of consensual 'Butskellism', with a film featuring Labour's Hugh Gaitskell and the Conservative Rab Butler, made in 1953.[52] But while such limited propaganda was consistent with Conservative politics, the rhetoric of 'set the people free' ruled out the interventionist policies favoured by the Attlee government, and the Conservatives were

[49] TNA: PRO BT195/19, 'Chancellor of the Exchequer's statement to the TUC at Margate', 7 September 1948.

[50] Crofts, *Coercion?*, pp. 43–4.

[51] MRC MSS 20/F3/D3/7/102: BPC, Duke of Edinburgh's broadcast, 14 November 1962.

[52] BPC, 'Raising the Standard': expenditure on government publicity was cut in 1952: TNA: PRO T273/200 HMT, 'Government Information Services', 13 October 1950.

happy to go along with employers' resistance to intervention in industrial issues.[53] The broad trajectory of Conservative policy was to emphasize the term 'competitiveness' in the context of a liberalizing economy, and focus primarily on wage costs as the key to this goal, rather than productivity.[54] Emblematically, when they set up the Cohen Committee in 1957 it was called the COPPI, but its work was focused almost entirely on wage-inflation issues.[55] Finally, productivity figured in the first Conservative incomes policy, introduced in 1961, but with little effect.[56]

Productivity came back to centre stage under the 1964–70 Labour government.[57] As with the Conservatives in their last years in power, this government was committed to a programme of economic 'modernization'. Much of this modernizing agenda drew on ideas from the previous Conservative government, but Labour was able to give a new urgency to this issue, presenting itself as the natural source of radical change that the Conservatives could talk about but could never implement. For both parties the focus on modernization drew on the narratives of 'decline' discussed in Chapter 2.

Productivity was especially closely linked with the version of declinism which focused on its alleged domestic origins. Best known of such narratives is the work of Michael Shanks, especially in his *The Stagnant Society*. In this account, Britain's economic problems arose in large part from the conservatism of attitudes amongst both workers and managers, leading to lack of enthusiasm for change on the part of most companies, and resistance to such change on the part of trade unions and the shop floor. The result was an economic stagnation stemming from lack of direction in industry, low levels of innovation, inadequate investment, restrictive practices, and excessive pay increases relative to productivity.[58]

This 'internal' diagnosis of the causes of 'decline' suggested a series of policies which involved a quite different kind of relationship between the government and the populace to those implied by the 'external' version exemplified by Shonfield's *British Economic Policy since the War*.[59] Whereas, ultimately, questions such as the level of foreign military expenditure or the role of the pound could be made without any direct reference to popular attitudes, quite the opposite was true of policies aimed at the internal dynamics of the economy. Indeed, for policies of the latter type, changing popular attitudes and behaviour were at the core of what the government wanted to do.

At the centre of Labour's modernization ambitions was the desire to plan the economy. National economic planning does not sound like a policy grounded in popular agreement. In some versions, indeed, planning may be seen as precisely

[53] The Conservatives in the early 1950s were reluctant to publicly spurn the American enthusiasm for productivity, and the money which flowed to Britain as a result of this enthusiasm: Tiratsoo and Tomlinson, *Conservatives*, pp. 98–101.

[54] Tiratsoo and Tomlinson, *Conservatives*, pp. 20–34.

[55] The records of the Committee are at TNA: PRO T234/730-3; Denison and Presley, *Robertson*, ch. 7; O'Hara, 'Intractable'.

[56] Jones, *Wages*, pp. 56–62.

[57] Tomlinson. '"Productivity"'.

[58] Shonfield, *Stagnant*.

[59] Shanks, *British*.

concerned to curtail popular input into economic decision-making by directing resources into areas given priority by government, rather than to those areas where the play of individual desires may lead. But Labour's planning in the 1960s had little of such dirigiste intent or capacity. It was 'indicative' planning, whose prime purpose was educational: to demonstrate the benefits of future expansion, and by that very demonstration hope to motivate its achievement. *The National Plan* was based on elaborate negotiations between government, trade union leaders, and employers; a process which was itself intended to educate participants into the possibility and desirability of faster growth. In turn, its publication was supposed to cement those expanded expectations and encourage actions to match.

Some historians have highlighted the difficulties in achieving faster growth in this period because of the 'fragmented polity' and the lack of a centralized executive capacity to overcome the competing networks involved in the policy process.[60] However, while providing useful insights into the policy process at this time, and especially establishing the capacity of those outside the core executive to impact on policymaking in Whitehall, this literature does not focus on the attempts of the period to mobilize popular opinion on economic issues. While in some respects a classic example of elite tripartism, clearly the *Plan* was intended to carry a message to a wider audience. As George Brown wrote in the Foreword:

> The Government is discussing with industry the measures needed to implement the plan. Leaders in management and the trade unions have a special responsibility, but it cannot be left solely to them. The achievement of these aims will depend on the involvement and acceptance of responsibility by individuals at every level in industry.

In pursuit of this wider support the government published a popular version of the *Plan*, entitled *Working for Prosperity*, a key example of the return to a 1940s-style high-profile economic publicity campaign, which, apart from the 1956 White Paper on inflation, and its popular companion, had tended to fade away under the Conservatives.[61]

Even before the *Plan* had been published in September 1965, the government had announced a second strand of policy, which even more than the *Plan* required popular understanding and support for its success. This was incomes policy, to which agreement had been reached in December 1964, and announced in the *Statement of Intent*. This document, too, was the product of complex negotiations by the peak associations, who by signing it seemed to commit themselves at least to a degree to a change of attitudes and behaviour. But more broadly, it was recognized by the government that such a voluntary policy could only succeed if it could be 'sold' to the rank-and-file trade unionist.[62]

[60] Lowe, 'Core'; Lowe and Rollings, 'Modernising'; Pemberton, 'Learning'.

[61] Cmnd. 2764, foreword; Department of Economic Affairs, *Working*. Continuities between the 1940s and 1960s are suggested by the role of S. Leslie, who was the first head of the EIU in the 1940s, and returned as a public relations adviser to the Ministry of Technology in the 1960s.

[62] DEA, *Statement*; TNA: PRO EW8/124, J. Groves, 'Preparation of a Popular Version of the Joint Statement', 18 December 1964. No such popular version was produced.

The title of the December statement had included the word 'productivity', but at this stage the inclusion of that word denoted little in the way of policy initiative. In the same way, productivity had been verbally linked to previous incomes policies under both Labour in the 1940s and the Conservatives in the 1960s, but without much significance. But eventually, under Labour, productivity was to emerge as a major policy issue in its own right. The roots of this are complex. In part it was due to the breakdown of the voluntary incomes policy, and the fact that, when a compulsory version was announced in 1966, productivity increase was put forward as one route to avoiding the policy's restrictions. Second, and quite independently of government, a 'productivity movement' was flowering in industry, especially following the well-publicized (alleged) success of a productivity agreement reached at the Fawley refinery of the Esso oil company.[63] Third, the government was increasingly focusing attention on Britain's 'manpower problem'. This was identified in the *Plan* as the gap in labour supply that would arise from the projected faster growth rate and increase in demand for labour—unless labour productivity increased. In conjunction these elements led to 'productivity' occupying centre stage in much of Labour's economic policy, particularly in 1966–8. Though the word came to connote efficiency in a much broader sense, the focus was primarily on *labour* productivity. From this stemmed the centrality to the productivity drive of changing the attitudes and behaviour of labour, so that eventually the drive became the centre of the government's biggest propaganda effort.[64]

In three key areas of domestic economic policy—planning, wage restraint, and productivity increase—Labour saw moulding the beliefs and behaviour of the population as crucial to success, and in each case sought to achieve its goals by major campaigns of popular education. But in none of these three cases was there simply a centrally directed, government-run campaign to change the minds of the populace. Instead, the government, alongside its own efforts, sought to use a variety of intermediary associations. In the case of planning these were especially the NEDC and the EDCs ('little neddies'). In the case of incomes policy the key body was the National Board for Prices and Incomes (NBPI), and, in the case of productivity, the BPC. So while the focus here is on the direct role of government in seeking to change popular economic understanding, regard must be had to the role of these and other intermediary bodies.

In the 1960s, as at other times, economic persuasion deployed a huge range of channels: ministerial speeches and writings, parliamentary statements, and press briefings, alongside an array of official publications. The focus here is primarily on the last of these, especially because they are the forms where discussion of the assumptions and beliefs lying behind the approach taken are most likely to be preserved, and these discussions are likely in turn to reveal something about the genesis of the other expressions of the government line.

[63] Flanders, *Fawley*; criticized in Ahlstrand, *Quest.*
[64] Tomlinson, 'Productivity', pp. 193–7.

In 1965 the Department of Economic Affairs (DEA) took over responsibility for most economic publicity from the Treasury. The previous 'Bulletin for Industry' became the DEA *Progress Report*, while the previous *Broadsheet* became a series called 'Changing Britain'. In addition, and most radically, the DEA launched *Upswing*, as a wall newspaper explicitly aimed at the shop floor. Thus the DEA saw itself as providing publicity across both the full range of possible audiences and all its major areas of policy concern: 'the Plan, Prices and Incomes Policy, the EDCs, the drive to increase productivity and efficiency in industry, and the regional policy'. The official line was clear: 'Many of the objects of the DEA can be achieved only by persuasion, and it is the task of the Information Division to create a climate of opinion in which the specific changes are more readily acceptable'.[65] While there was a ministerial publicity committee, this does not seem to have been of importance in economic publicity, the DEA being the key department, with some role for the Treasury.[66]

Under the aegis of the DEA, the 1960s saw a scale of official economic propaganda unparalleled since the 1940s. In the 1940s the use of statistics was an important element in the campaign of persuasion, but in the 1960s the statistical aspect was particularly prominent. Partly this flowed from what we may call the technocratic aspect of economic statistics—the more governments seek to increasingly regulate and plan economic life, the more they require elaborated data to achieve this end. From 1956, when Harold Macmillan described managing the economy with the limited data available as 'like planning a train journey with last year's Bradshaw', the inadequacy of economic statistics became a common refrain in economic policy circles. From this technocratic perception improvements were continuously being made in the 1950s and early 1960s, boosted by the Radcliffe Committee and its recommendations on financial and balance-of-payments statistics.[67]

The Labour government's policies were to ratchet up the perceived need for improved statistics. But alongside this technocratic impetus was the related but separable issue of statistics as a means of persuasion. Hence data for the *Plan* were not just about designing the plan and judging its success, but about educating the population in the possibilities of prosperity that planning brought with it. In the case of incomes policy, the need for persuasive statistics was even greater. Here the population in general and the unions in particular had to be weaned off a powerful attachment to free collective bargaining and educated into the desirability of 'planned income growth'. This involved the deployment of data seeking above all to demonstrate the 'fairness' of the incomes policy. Most ambitious was the productivity drive, which sought to demonstrate that the benefits from higher productivity would be 'fairly' distributed. Overall, therefore, encouraged by a prime minister who was an accomplished economic statistician, British economic statistics

[65] TNA: PRO EW 4/66, M. Shanks to F. Catherwood, 'Publicity for the work of the Department', 9 June 1965

[66] TNA: PRO EW4/66, 'The work of the information division', no date but June 1966; TNA: PRO EW4/36, Economic publicity committee papers, June 1966 to December 1967.

[67] Cmnd. 827, chapter 10. *Bradshaw* was a Victorian railway timetable published until the 1960s.

were to be revolutionized in the 1960s, for a combination of 'technocratic' and persuasive reasons.[68]

While pre-dated by the *Statement of Intent*, the *Plan* (September 1965) is the best place to start in seeking to understand how the Labour government set out on its tasks of economic persuasion. At around 500 pages (and £1.50), the 'big' version of the *Plan* was not aimed at a popular audience. It was largely written in the subjunctive: *if* a growth of 25 per cent was achieved between 1964 and 1970, what would be the implications?[69] To deal with the balance-of-payments issue alongside increasing growth, the *Plan* argued, required an acceleration in the growth of labour productivity to bridge the 'manpower gap' and a prices-and-incomes policy to contain the rise in money incomes. However, while the prices-and-incomes policy had a chapter all to itself within the *Plan*, the exhortations to higher productivity were little more than the logical consequences of the *Plan*'s macroeconomic arithmetic, and at this stage did not involve any specific policy proposals.

The *Plan* was aimed at the decision makers in industry, rather than at the mass of industrial workers or the wider population. But the *Plan* also asserts that its success rests on 'the action of individual managers and individual workers. Without their active co-operation, involvement and understanding, the *Plan* cannot succeed.'[70] *Working for Prosperity* (hereinafter, *Working*) was much cheaper and shorter than the *Plan*, its central theme being the scale of resources made available from the 25 per cent growth of GNP, and how this could be distributed. While, like the *Plan*, asserting the need to solve the balance-of-payments problem by diverting resources in that direction, a key point is that, having put aside resources for exports, investment, and public spending, there will be substantial benefits in personal consumption from the rest of the growth dividend, to which approximately £4.5 billion of the extra £8 billion will accrue. By contrast, the *Plan*, while suggesting a similar distribution of resources, puts far less emphasis on the growth of consumption. As in the *Plan*, *Working* includes an argument for prices-and-incomes policy, but unlike the former, this is based on an egalitarian argument—the impact of inflation on the old and the lower paid—as well as the implications for the balance of payments.

A faster increase in productivity is invoked as necessary for the *Plan*'s success, alongside charts showing rates of productivity increase for 1960–74 and a higher one for 1964–70, but with no explanation of the meaning of the chart. Productivity is said to be an issue which must be 'stated bluntly and faced frankly', but quite what this implies for the reader is left unstated. Perhaps this discretion was wise, given the paradox of productivity evident in discussion of the coal industry: 'The share of our energy needs met by coal has been falling and will continue to do so despite the industry's success in increasing output per man-shift.'[71]

68 Wilson, 'Statistics'.
69 Hence the hastily added first few paragraphs on the balance of payments.
70 *Plan*, pp. 17–21, 16; TNA: PRO EW4/29, 'The Plan: Popular Version', 1965.
71 DEA, *Working*, pp. 15, 4, 26.

Working makes clear that the *Plan* has no directive role; 'It isn't a *Plan* to tell us all what to do and when and how. That would not be acceptable to a nation like ours'.[72] On the other hand, as already noted, *Working* assumes that it is the prospect of higher personal consumption which is a key 'selling point' for the *Plan*. The *Plan* itself had carefully pitched the prospects for consumption during its period as 'slightly faster than the average of the past few years' but 'at a somewhat lower rate than that of the national product as a whole'. This careful phrasing reflected a serious dilemma of the framers of the plan in relation to incomes policy. If the projected growth of consumption was too slow it might emphasize the need for such a policy to allow faster growth, while making it harder for union leaderships to persuade their memberships that it was a policy worth supporting.[73]

Working was aimed at trade union officials and the like. For the rank and file there was *Upswing*, the factory wall newspaper intended to be in '*Daily Mirror* style'. Like *Working*, it put emphasis on consumption benefits, with a first edition (February 1966) that was headed 'The Plan and You' and promised that if the prices-and-incomes policy was maintained there would be an 'upswing in living standards—by 1970 it is expected that three households out of five may own a car.... The money spent on television and radio sets and electrical equipment is likely to increase by about 30 per cent'. To achieve this, George Brown asserted in his introduction, 'we do not have to sweat our guts out, or work longer hours, but must use our brains and work more sensibly'.[74] (For one response to this propaganda effort see Illustration 3.)

While the *Plan* had its popular version in *Working*, incomes policy proved less amenable to turning into terms deemed likely to find popular support. The government's initial policy on incomes was entirely voluntary, and rested on some extremely closely negotiated verbal formulations.[75] The idea of a popular version of the *Statement* was mooted, but was rejected as being likely to threaten the fragile agreement. It was pointed out, for example, that management was unlikely to endorse giving the policy a 'social' objective, while this was deemed essential in presenting the proposals to the workers. Similarly, the underlying premise of the policy was that if the workers could be persuaded to lower wage pressure, price rises would be reduced—but the government had no means of controlling 'unjustifiable' price increases, and therefore delivering this promise.[76]

The major form of printed publicity for the *Statement* was in the new DEA *Broadsheet* series. Most of these went to union officials, not the rank and file. One strategy to reach a broader union audience was to get articles into union journals,

[72] DEA, *Working*, Foreword.

[73] Cmnd. 2764, p. 15; TNA: PRO EW 24/7, D. MacDougall to J. Caulcott, 17 November 1964; EW4/18, S. Brittan, 'The Draft White Paper', 8 February 1965.

[74] S. Leslie, 'The Plan: From Talk to Action', *Statist*, 17 September 1965; TNA: PRO EW4/60, 'Publicity for the Plan', December 1965; *Upswing* no. 1, February 1966; EW4/60 'The Plan—Follow-Up Publicity', 1965.

[75] TNA: PRO EW8/6, 'Incomes and prices: general policy papers', 1964.

[76] TNA: PRO EW8/124, 'Preparation of a Popular Version of the Joint Statement', 1964; EW4/19, E. Maude to J. Groves, 3 December 1964.

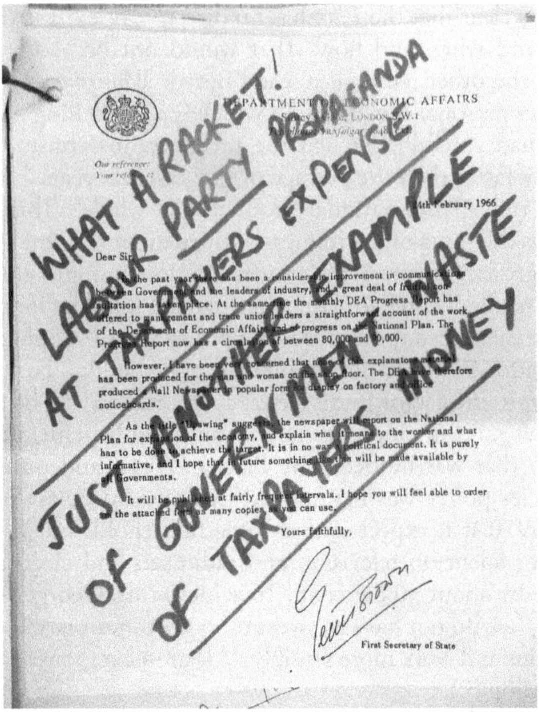

[illegible]PA[illegible]TMENT [illegible] [illegible]NOMIC AFFAIRS

24th February 1966

Dear Sir,

In the past year there has been a considerable improvement in communications between Government and the leaders of industry, and a great deal of fruitful consultation has taken place. At the same time the monthly DEA Progress Report has offered to management and trade union leaders a straightforward account of the work of the Department of Economic Affairs and of progress on the National Plan. The Progress Report now has a circulation of between 80,000 and [illegible],000.

However, I have been very concerned that none of this explanatory material has been produced for the man and woman on the shop floor. The DEA have therefore produced a Wall Newspaper in popular form for display on factory and office noticeboards.

As the title "Upswing" suggests, the newspaper will report on the National Plan for expansion of the economy, and explain what it means to the worker and what has to be done to achieve the target. It is in no way a political document. It is purely informative, and I hope that in future something like this will be made available by all Governments.

It will be published at fairly frequent intervals. I hope you will feel able to order on the attached form as many copies as you can use.

Yours faithfully,

First Secretary of State

Illustration 3 A resistant audience to government propaganda (1966): letter in response to the offer of wall newspapers.
Source: Image courtesy of the National Archives.

but *Upswing* was also used as part of the attempt to link incomes policy and the *Plan* as part of the same grand design for 'planned growth of incomes'.[77]

Upswing no. 1, after asserting that by the end of the *Plan* period 'there will be more to spend all round', went on: 'If the prices and incomes policy is maintained, you will not only be earning more—the increases will go further because prices will not jump as well'. Unfortunately for the government, the preparation of the next *Upswing* coincided with the build-up to the seamen's strike of summer 1966. This led to a proposed lead on exports being scrapped. The strike was followed by the July measures of deflation, which raised worries about whether *Upswing* was still an appropriate title, but no. 2 did eventually appear, with a headline on the compulsory incomes policy introduced as part of these measures: 'The Standstill—What It Means'. This emphasized the failure of the voluntary policy, but still suggested voluntarism was best if it were successful. The subheading of the piece was 'Fair Play For All', stressing that the policy applied to salaries, directors' pay, and dividends, as well as wages. The 'Editorial' to this edition also deployed a classic piece of

[77] TNA: PRO EW4/27, E. Crosfield, 'Broadsheets on Incomes Policy', 23 April 1965; for the full range of publicity envisaged, TNA: PRO EW4/27, M. Foley to Economic Secretary, 17 November 1964.

economic rhetoric: 'The time has come to cry halt. Britain has been overspending her income far too long'. In this account, the incomes policy was about providing a 'breathing space' before expansion could resume.[78]

As the *Plan* faded from view in the wake of deflation, and prices-and-incomes policy became central to the government's domestic economic agenda, the issue of statistics became more complex. The *Plan*, as far as the popular story went, was about how the fruits of higher output could be divided up. In statistical terms the story was straightforward; granted the resources were available, it was not hard to produce numbers to suggest everyone could be better off. This, after all, is always the enticing prospect held out by economic growth. But incomes policy was different. Partly this was a 'technocratic' problem of governmental judgement about the policy in the absence of data about key variables—most obviously movements in earnings, especially at a disaggregated level.[79] But these deficiencies were not just technocratic. Better data were needed, the government argued, not just for assessment of policy effectiveness, but also 'to help those responsible for decisions on incomes and prices apply the criteria of the national interest'; one might add that the key issue was really persuading wage- and price-setters to see 'the national interest' in the same light as the government.[80]

The technocratic problem of the statistics for incomes policy was serious, but persuading wage bargainers of the desirability of the policy raised broader problems. The key word in the selling of the policy was 'fairness', and the idea that the burdens of the policy were being equally shared. But data to demonstrate this were highly problematic and, recognizing this, official statements excluded any detailed discussion of profits and dividends.[81] A final component was productivity, especially because the rhetoric of the incomes policy concerning fairness suggested that those who contributed more in the way of increasing productivity should gain benefit, and this became formalized in the incomes policies of the 1960s where the 'norm' for pay increases was to be breached only in cases where productivity increase justified such increases.[82] The statistics of productivity therefore became an important issue in the 1960s, reflecting the substantial, if temporary, significance of the productivity campaign of these years.

While the word 'productivity' was included in the 1964 *Statement*, and figured in the *Plan* of 1965, it did not move to the centre of the government's agenda until 1966. The central role the term came to play was due to its links to the statutory incomes policy introduced in 1966, and also because higher productivity seemed

[78] *Upswing*, nos. 1 and 2.

[79] TNA: PRO PREM13/1432, B. Trend to PM, 13 April 1967; CAB134/3274, 'Mins of Statistical Policy Committee', 14 April 1967, 20 July 1967; DEA assessment in EW8/567, 'Incomes Policy: Enquiry into Government Statistical Services', 21 April 1966; TNA: PRO EW 8/650, 'Reference to NBPI on productivity agreements 1966/67'.

[80] TNA: PRO CAB 134/3275 DEA, 'Productivity, Prices and Incomes Policy: Earnings Information', 19 July 1967.

[81] Cmnd. 3073.

[82] The problems of productivity as a focus of policy were highlighted by the economists R. Kahn and K. Berrill: TNA: PRO CAB134/3059, 'Prices and incomes policy: an interim memo', December 1966.

the only logical way to increase competitiveness whilst the value of the pound remained sacrosanct. At the same time, it was becoming clear that other components of the *Plan* were slow in taking effect, and therefore too much attention being given to the *Plan* as the key to success seemed less appropriate. In July 1966 a set of papers on productivity went to the Cabinet, setting out a range of government initiatives.[83]

As in the 1940s, the issue of productivity became embroiled in debates about industrial relations and 'governance'. One of the key comments at Cabinet was that 'Management and unions had proved reluctant to link pay, productivity and consultation: and the last of these factors was an essential element in wage settlements.' From such a view, productivity committees were the best way of engaging the mass of workers in the campaign, even though they raised all sorts of classic labour movement issues about worker and union responsibility for management decisions, and the desire of many unions to steer clear of such entanglements. Despite such doubts, *Upswing* no. 1 carried the following question and response: 'What Must I do?: Adopt sensible methods of working and press for productivity committees to be set up in your factory so that sensible production methods can be worked out'.[84] As in the 1940s the extension of productivity committees ran up against substantial obstacles, from both some on the union side and many employers. Many trade unionists thought such committees threatened their bargaining independence. Many employers saw them as a threat to managerial prerogatives. As a result government enthusiasm soon waned.[85]

In their manifesto for the June 1966 general election the Labour Party promised a national conference on productivity. So the productivity publicity effort opened with such a national conference presided over by Harold Wilson in September that year, and he presented this as 'not an isolated occasion, but the beginning of a continuing campaign'. Beyond that, the Prime Minister hoped that 'it might well be from this conference there could grow something like a Parliament of industry'.[86] The deflationary measures introduced by the government in July 1966 made the conference an especially inauspicious time to seek such a level of agreement, and the language of the productivity campaign that followed the conference was generally much less high-flown. The conference was also notable for the absence of shop stewards, supervisors, and works managers; it was a meeting of the 'peak associations'.[87] Much of the rest of the campaign was aimed at less elevated groups, especially shop-floor workers.

Alongside the publicity work of the DEA was the BPC, which pursued a range of tactics to try and raise productivity, especially aiming at the education of management through local productivity associations. The evidence suggests that the national organization had been losing its way in the early 1960s, despite the designation of 1962/3 as 'National Productivity Year'. The Labour government's renewed

[83] TNA: PRO CAB 128/41, Cabinet conclusions, 12 July 1966.

[84] Fielding, *Labour*, ch. 8; *Upswing*, no. 1.

[85] Tomlinson, *Labour*, pp. 180–1.

[86] TNA: PRO CAB 130/296, 'National productivity conference meeting', 23 September 1966; P. Jenkins, 'Limits of Exhortation', *New Society* 208, 22 September 1966.

[87] Jenkins, *Harold Wilson's*.

enthusiasm on this issue is reflected in the BPC's publication, *Target*, which the Council had taken over from the government in 1960 (the latter having published it since 1940), and figured highly in the propaganda of the mid-1960s.[88] The close links between the DEA and the BPC are shown not least by the fact that Michael Shanks, author of *The Stagnant Society* and now industrial adviser to the department, was a frequent contributor to *Target*.

Strategic discussions about publicity for the productivity drive emphasized the potentially 'positive' message that productivity involved, contrasted with the inherently restrictive aspects of incomes policy. But the content of the productivity 'message' had to be handled carefully. The use of productivity as an exception to incomes policy norms brought out the personal incentive aspect: produce more and you will get more pay. But the government's rhetoric about the *Plan* and incomes policy placed a deal of emphasis on *national* goals. This tension between individual incentives and collective aims is evident in much economic propaganda, but is perhaps most evident in the productivity area in the 1960s, where precise data about nationally acceptable rises in wages were set alongside explicit exceptionality for those who claim to do better than the norm.[89]

Concern with popular understanding of economic issues led to a particular focus on the content of the Labour-supporting *Daily Mirror*, at this time by far the most popular tabloid.[90] Close contact was maintained with the paper, and the surprisingly abundant commentary of the paper on economic issues usually kept close to the government line. The *Plan* was enthusiastically supported (though with calls for more direction on the part of government), as were the productivity campaign and incomes policy.[91] The 1960s was also marked by a much greater use of and sensitivity to the impact of television on the part of politicians. The 1964 general election saw great efforts by both parties to use this medium, whose reach was fast expanding.[92] This concern is illustrated in terms of government economic publicity by the Treasury's decision in 1966 to use an outside agency to monitor TV and radio output on economic issues. The documents also suggest a high degree of collaboration with the broadcasters, extending to the vetting of programme material prior to broadcast.[93]

While the Wilson government saw shaping public opinion on the economic issues as crucial, it did very little to directly measure that opinion or the impact of its propaganda (unlike the Labour government of the 1940s). The most that was directly done was to keep a check on the circulation figures of the various publications issued, which on the surface was quite impressive. In the mid-1960s 200,000 *Broadsheets* and 90,000 copies of the *Progress Report* were distributed, plus

88 On *Target*, see TNA: PRO EW4/60, 'The Plan—Follow-Up Publicity', 1965–6.

89 TNA: PRO EW8/949, 'Steering Group on the Development of Productivity, Prices and Incomes Policy' (no date).

90 TNA: PRO EW4/105, 'Follow up to PM's Productivity Conference', September 1966.

91 *Daily Mirror* 17 and 22 September 1965; 14 June and 27 September 1966; 14 June 1968.

92 Blumler and McQuail, *Television*, pp. 168–82, Appendix E.

93 TNA: PRO T245/52, 'Monitoring of TV and radio programmes', 1966–72.

220,000 versions of *Working* and 108,000 copies of the first issue of *Upswing*.[94] But little was known about the impact of all this. DEA analysis of 'public opinion' on the issues turns out to be a survey of *press* coverage. In similar vein, the Ministry of Labour's investigation of 'Workers' Attitudes to Efficiency' was based wholly on official rumination and consultation with experts, but nothing in the way of actually asking the workers.[95]

The Labour government was sensitive to the importance of public consent on a broad range of policy questions, and felt itself to be under pressure to take this more into account.[96] But how exactly this was to be done was unclear. For example, it was agreed 'in principle' that it would be a good idea to survey public opinion on National Insurance, and its relations to taxation, but, precisely because this was such a controversial issue, there was no agreement on what questions should be asked, and the survey was never carried out.[97] Surveys were carried out by the government's Social Survey, on a variety of economic issues, but, while they yielded interesting information about aspects of popular attitudes to economic issues, they only bore indirectly on the matters of concern here.[98]

Some evidence on the more specific policy areas of planning, prices and incomes, and productivity is available from non-government sources. On planning, Mark Abrams conducted a survey four days after the publication of the *Plan*. Of those surveyed, 36 per cent had heard or read about it, and of these a third thought it was about production or productivity. Only a third thought it would affect them or their family, and, perhaps unsurprisingly in the light of this figure, only 7 per cent thought the chances of the plan succeeding were 'very good', while 49 per cent thought them 'poor or bad'. The most that can be said from this is perhaps that the government was wise to attempt to produce a popular version of the *Plan* in order to get its message across.[99]

Incomes policy produced more material on popular opinion than either planning or productivity. Hilde Behrend produced a number of pieces of work based on survey material. Some of this concerned the general issue of inflation, and this, unsurprisingly, produced a picture of a lack of clarity about what this term meant alongside a view that it is a 'bad thing'. On the more specific issue of incomes policy, Behrend found that there was quite wide support for incomes policy, but only as a crisis measure. In addition, this support was conditional upon strict control of prices and exceptional treatment for the low-paid. One interpretation of this might be that where government gives a strong lead, as in the imposition of the 'freeze' of 1966, popular support may be forthcoming in the short run. But

[94] TNA: PRO EW 4/60, J. Groves to S. Leslie, 29 September 1965; TNA: PRO EW 4/29, no author, memo, 22 September 1965.

[95] TNA: PRO EW4/35, Economic Publicity Committee, 1965/6; Ministry of Labour, 'Workers'.

[96] Fielding *Labour*, ch. 8; in the 1940s Leslie had called unsuccessfully for systematic surveys of public opinion on economic issues: TNA: PRO T245/2, S. Leslie to Lord President, 'Economic information and opinion surveys', 30 June 1947.

[97] TNA: PRO T227/2592, 'Survey of public attitudes to social security contributions and benefits', 1968.

[98] Government Social Survey, *Redundancy*; *Women*; *Aid*.

[99] TNA: PRO EW4/60, 'Survey on the National Plan', 1965.

deeply entrenched attitudes and practices are likely to reassert themselves if the policy is prolonged.[100] More broadly, this material may suggest that the government's focus on 'fairness' chimed with popular understanding, however problematic such a term may be. Certainly it was a term widely deployed in popular assessment of economic policy, for example in the key Gallup poll question asked about the budget: 'Do you think the budget is a fair one or not?'[101]

There is less evidence on popular attitudes to productivity. It was taken for granted in most government circles that the British worker was deficient in enthusiasm for higher efficiency, but the evidence is thin. As already noted, the study on 'Workers' Attitudes to Efficiency' was based on official ruminations and the consultation of experts, but there was no popular input.[102] Contrary evidence on this assumption might be found amongst Luton's affluent workers, who showed support for the ideological underpinnings of the productivity drive; a cooperative attitude to management efforts to improve company performance, and an enthusiasm for higher incomes from work.[103] There was certainly plenty of support for productivity deals in the 1960s, despite the hostility of many on the Left. But how far this support was a genuine willingness to change work practices in return for higher rewards, and how far a way of securing incomes policy-busting pay increases in collusion with management, remains obscure.[104] A sign that some of the propaganda may have had the desired effect is perhaps shown by the 'I'm Backing Britain' campaign of 1968, which does seem to have been a genuine example of spontaneous enthusiasm for increasing output, albeit by means of the donation of work time without pay. How widespread such enthusiasm might have been is impossible to gauge, in part because of a parallel 'Buy British' campaign launched by the Labour MP Robert Maxwell which muddied the waters considerably.[105]

But if we are to infer beliefs from behaviour, there is evidence that support for productivity deals waned as the industrial relations climate deteriorated from 1968 onwards. Employers and government had taken the initiative on the productivity front, with agreement from some unions, but there is evidence that union support was declining from 1968. McKersie and Hunter, for example, refer to the 'death of productivity bargaining' in 1968/9 despite continuing official support.[106]

III

It is natural to ask about the success of these campaigns, but difficult to give a useful answer. Economic historians, with good reason, rarely link productivity performance

[100] Behrend, Lynch, and Davies, *National*; Behrend et al., *Incomes*, pp. 51–3.

[101] King, *British*, p. 236. Barbara Wootton, after noting the ubiquity of appeals to fairness in incomes policy, observes the difficulty of the term: 'After all Socrates was put to death for making a fuss about the very question'; Wootton, *Incomes*, p. 85.

[102] Ministry of Labour, 'Workers'.

[103] Goldthorpe, *Affluent Worker*, pp. 73–4, 80.

[104] Fels, *National*.

[105] TNA: PRO EW4/103, 'Back Britain Campaign', 1968; TNA: PRO EW4/97, Ministerial Committee on Home Publicity, 1968.

[106] McKersie and Hunter, *Pay*, pp. 314–15.

directly to specific governments' years in office, given the complex and usually long-term nature of many forces at work, and also the cyclical character of productivity change.[107] The data in Table 7.3 suggest a broad long-run stability in the rate of growth of manufacturing productivity, with the exception of the striking slowdown in the 1970s.[108]

For the 1940s, contemporary estimates by Rostas suggested that industrial output per head and manufacturing output per head rose by respectively 5 per cent and 6 per cent per annum between 1946 and 1950.[109] Estimates for a longer overlapping period yield similar results.[110] One of the first estimates of total factor productivity (allowing for the capital as well as labour inputs) suggested a rate of increase of 3.3 per cent in 1948–51.[111] These favourable trends might be just down to a revival of industry after wartime disruption, but Rostas felt this was not the whole story, suggesting something was owed to enhanced productivity consciousness: 'This meant that the large potentialities for an immediate improvement of productivity were realised, that ways and means to improve productivity were adopted in many factories and workshops for this purpose.'[112]

Productivity performance in manufacturing in the later 1960s was also healthy (see Table 7.4), though the 1968–73 figure is inflated by the effects of output growth in the unsustainable expansion of 1972/3.

Table 7.3 Manufacturing labour productivity in Britain and West Germany, 1951–89 (percentage per annum per person engaged)

	Britain	West Germany
1951–64	4.50	5.32
1964–73	4.18	4.52
1973–9	0.68	3.47
1979–89	4.14	1.92

Source: Broadberry and Crafts, 'UK', p. 723.

Table 7.4 Changes in labour productivity in Britain, 1951–73

	Labour productivity in manufacturing (average annual percentage increase between cyclical peaks)
1951–5	3.6
1955–60	4.6
1960–4	4.7
1964–8	4.0
1968–73	5.7

Source: Tomlinson, 'Not "Decline and Revival"', p. 163.

107 Broadberry, *Productivity*; Feinstein and Matthews, 'Growth'.
108 Cameron, 'Why?', p. 134; Tomlinson, 'Not "Decline and Revival"'.
109 Rostas, 'Changes', p. 20.
110 Nicholson and Gupta, 'Output'.
111 Reddaway and Smith, 'Progress'.
112 Rostas, 'Changes', pp. 24–5.

The productivity campaigns of the 1940s and 1960s stand out amongst all the efforts to shape public attitudes on the economy for the intensity of effort deployed. No other government propaganda was pushed so hard through so many media. This intensity of effort reflected both the importance given to the objective and the perceived obstacles to its popular absorption. The latter was seen to require what one civil servant called 'something very like mass education in elementary mid-twentieth century economics' given that 'even the relatively well-informed are inadequately equipped on the subject, while the mass of the nation suffers from a mixture of economic illiteracy and a litter of half-truths'.[113] Outside these two periods productivity was always a component of public debate on the economy, but never with anything like the same prominence; no other governments matched the kind of campaigns pursued in the 1940s and 1960s.

One reason why it was under 'old' Labour governments that such campaigns were launched is because they had none of the qualms either about interventionism or propaganda that shaped Conservative or New Labour thinking. But this interventionist enthusiasm was not usually reciprocated; these campaigns were constrained by opposition from private industry. But they were also constrained by issues within the Labour movement about how far workers and unions should positively engage with the productivity agenda. Central to the productivity message was something at odds with much of the movement's oppositional views about the private sector and the legitimacy of profit-making. Hence the attempts on one hand to undercut oppositional attitudes by focusing on 'democratizing' the enterprise, and on the other to stress the mutual benefits from output growth.

At its most general, the appeal to produce more with the same inputs is a 'motherhood and apple pie' style of propaganda; who could be opposed? But productivity increase *always* requires change: 'individual productivity measures, such as labour productivity, have little direct significance unless we can relate them to the complex processes of change of which they are a product'.[114]

In the propaganda of the 1940s and 1960s social democratic governments sought to persuade the electorate that the changes they advocated involved people working smarter, not harder.[115] That was one way of trying to garner popular support. But mixed in with that 'more brain-power, not more muscle-power' rhetoric was a strongly *moral* claim that those who contributed to higher productivity would receive a commensurate reward in their wages. Such claims, while understandable

[113] TNA: PRO CAB 134/188, Official steering committee on economic development.

[114] Salter, *Productivity*, p. 3.

[115] There was always an element of bad faith in such claims. In a market economy, profit-seeking companies are interested in prices, costs, and profits, and increasing productivity is simply one way of reducing labour costs; how this is done depends on the circumstances of the case. In post-war Britain 'working harder' was certainly part of the reason for increased productivity, whether it be in such core manufacturing sectors as cars (see e.g. Beynon, *Working*) or in services: Broadberry ascribes the slow growth of the 'modern office' in Britain compared with the USA to poorer educational standards and 'stronger labour force resistance to the intensification of the labour process': Broadberry, *Market*, pp. 5–6. For evidence that such intensification is normal across the British economy in recent years: Green, *Demanding*, pp. 44–93.

as a means of persuasion, were inherently flawed, both as a guide to workable policy and as underlying principle.

As the economists Richard Kahn and Kenneth Berrill pointed out in advice to ministers in the 1960s, such a linkage ignored the fact that in a competitive market most productivity increase would manifest itself in falling prices, not rising revenues. In addition, given the variability in the possibility of realizing productivity gains across different sectors, policy had to find ways of *sharing* the productivity gains in one sector *across* the economy, whether it be by lower prices or broad similarities in the rates of wage increase.[116] So, despite propaganda implying otherwise, the benefits could not be allowed to accrue to those notionally responsible for increased output.

The idea that effort and reward be commensurate is one of the most widespread notions of 'fairness' which no government seeking to persuade the populace can readily eschew, and was always used in support of linking wages and productivity, especially in the 1960s. Against this, it could easily be pointed out that productivity change might have little to do with individual effort.[117] But more broadly we may see this particular notion of fairness as a 'foundational myth' of a capitalist economy. If there is one argument made by Friedrich Hayek that is surely irrefutable, it is that such a notion of fairness (or 'justice') cannot be delivered by a market economy, where rewards simply reflect what sells well; hard-working producers of undesired goods will go to the wall.[118] In one telling example from the 1960s, coal miners whose efforts helped raise coal-mining productivity to new heights simply speeded up their own redundancy as the market for coal contracted.

Such foundational myths necessarily pose a problem for the construction of effective policy narratives. Because they are foundational they have to be deployed; because they are myths the narrative necessarily has a degree of incoherence. In this light it is unsurprising that productivity has featured so often in economic propaganda, nor that it has had such a chequered history.

[116] TNA: PRO CAB 134/3059, R. Kahn and K. Berrill, 'Prices and Incomes policy: an interim memo', 11 January 1967.

[117] ibid.

[118] 'The values which their services will have to their fellows will often have no relation to their individual merits or needs', Hayek, *Law*, p. 72.

8

Inflation

Inflation was a constant feature of the post-war managed economy. Diagnoses and responses fluctuated, but, until the coming to power of the Thatcher government in 1979, the belief that wage bargaining was central to the inflationary process was predominant, even if there were always dissenters. What periodically followed from this belief was the pursuit of incomes policies. These policies in turn became a particularly important stimulus to government attempts to shape popular understanding, as they sought to gain acceptance for the limitation of 'normal' wage bargaining. In the late 1940s, twice in the 1960s, and again in the 1970s successive administrations, of different political persuasions, tried to impress upon the electorate that wage restraint was the key to reducing inflation.[1]

This chapter analyses this inflation problem, assessing how its portrayal changed over time, and how these accounts of inflation in turn shaped the approach to incomes policies and the publicity that accompanied them. The focus is especially on the 1970s, when peacetime inflation reached its numerical peak and the policy focus on its reduction was at its height. In that decade an especially significant effort was made both to persuade the population of the harms done by inflation, and to get them to change their behaviour in order to reduce it.

The discussion is divided into four sections. The first provides some detail on the problems of constructing a narrative about inflation, both before and during the 1970s. The second looks at the Counter-Inflation Publicity Unit (CIPU), created by the government in 1975.[2] Though, as its name suggests, the Unit's purpose was to shape opinion, its activities are especially significant because its remit included sponsoring a substantial number of surveys of public understanding of inflation, so that from its records we can gain insight into not only what government said on the issue, but how that related to what the people thought. This is crucial, because so often when we look at attempts to shape popular opinion, whether it be by mass media or official propaganda, we know the message being propagated, but have much less information about how the message was received. The third section focuses on the relationship between the CIPU's framing of the problem of inflation and popular understanding. The fourth and concluding section seeks to suggest some implications of the analysis.

[1] Jones, *Wages*.

[2] For the high politics background to this see Goodman, *From*, pp. 173–82, 198–9; Pimlott, *Harold Wilson*, pp. 589–606.

I

Political and policy concern with inflation peaked in the 1970s, but such concern was not new in that decade; what changed was not just the rate of inflation, but also how inflation was understood in government. The post-war managed economy had been accompanied by low but persistent inflation, and containing this trend was a recurrent objective of post-war economic policy, but one never given the highest priority during the 1950s and 1960s. When the Attlee government had brought in the first-ever incomes policy to combat the problem, the main stimulus to this policy was the balance of payments, and the impact of inflation on export competitiveness, given a fixed exchange rate. Alongside the general exhortations about the significance of curbing price rises for helping export expansion, the specific message about inflation was that it damaged equity: 'experience has shown that, when it comes to a race between rising prices and personal incomes, prices will always win in the long run, so that conditions become progressively worse for the holders of all personal incomes but particularly for wage earners'.[3] This was a message clearly aimed at the Labour government's working-class supporters.

The Conservative government of the 1950s confronted inflation within a different context, most importantly the return to sterling convertibility (see Chapter 9). This return led to a high priority being accorded to sustaining confidence in the pound by restraining inflationary pressure.[4] The policies pursued in trying to achieve this restraint ranged from restrictive monetary policy to fiscal tightening through to confrontation with trade unions, though each of these proved politically problematic. By the early 1960s the Conservatives, like Labour before them, were attempting to contain inflation by means of incomes policy.[5]

The Conservatives had been extremely hostile to much of the Attlee government's activity in economic propaganda, characterizing it as not only money-wasting but as part of an undesirable extension of the state's role.[6] But in the mid-1950s the inflation issue, in combination with the pursuit of sterling convertibility, led to the government's parallel publication of both a White Paper and a popular tract on the dangers of inflation.[7] The latter was clearly aimed at a wage-earning audience, its central claim (repeated in the White Paper) being that wage inflation was squeezing profits, and in doing so was threatening investment and hence economic growth. This was coupled to an 'equity' argument which noted the decline in share of profits being paid out as dividends, leading to a slower rise in distributed profits than in wages.[8]

There was some strong rhetoric surrounding inflation in the 1950s, especially amongst Conservatives, and the view that the problem should be taken more seriously was very evident in 1957 and 1958 especially. Macmillan's famous 'never had it so good' speech was in fact a warning about how inflation threatened

3 Cmd. 7321, p. 2. 4 Booth, 'Inflation'. 5 Jones, *Wages*, pp. 54–8.
6 TNA: PRO T273/200, 'Treasury Information Unit' 1951/2.
7 Cmd. 9725; HMT/COI, *Must?*.
8 This distributional argument ignored the impact of dividend limitation on capital gains.

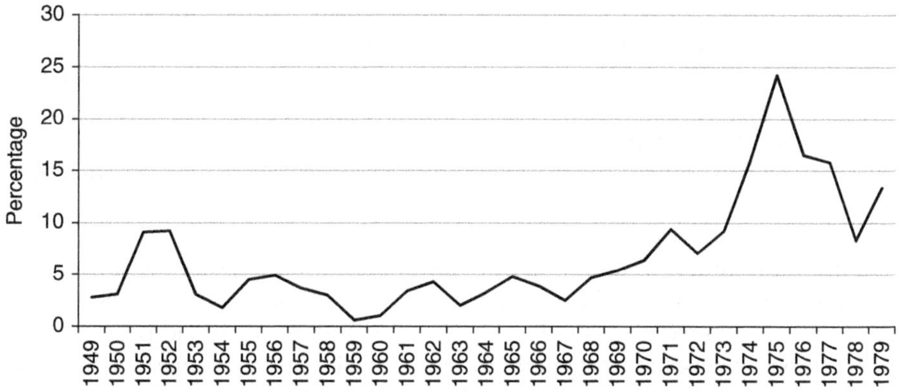

Figure 8.1 Inflation, 1949–79
Source: ONS database.

prosperity. The following year the issue of how to address inflationary pressures lay behind the resignation of the Chancellor of the Exchequer and two allies.[9] But despite these flurries, the predominant view in official and political circles was that it was a regrettable but not wholly unacceptable price to pay for full employment.[10] Inflation was a problem, it was argued, largely because of its consequences for the balance of payments and the exchange rate, and also because of its perceived redistributive consequences. But none of these effects was seen as significant enough for restraining inflation to be at the centre of economic policymaking. This relative quiescence was, unsurprisingly, in the context of fluctuating but low levels of inflation, with no trend in the data between the end-of-the-Korean-War boom in 1952, and the aftermath of the 1967 devaluation (see Figure 8.1).

However, the significance accorded to inflation by the political class rose as price rises accelerated in the late 1960s. For the Labour Party the emphasis on inflation in formal policy statements tended to be more muted than for the Conservatives, so while the issue was mentioned in the 1970 and February 1974 election manifestos, it was only in October 1974 (when the annual rate was approaching 20 per cent) that inflation was focused upon: 'the first priority must be a determined attack on inflation and the appalling overseas deficit which we inherited'. However, there was no elaboration of why inflation reduction should be the 'first priority'.[11]

The emphasis and language of Conservative pronouncements was notably different. In their 1970 election manifesto, the Conservative Party, while not giving inflation the highest priority, stressed it as a problem: 'soaring prices and increasing taxes are an evil and disastrous combination. Inflation is not only damaging to the economy; it is a major cause of social injustice, always hitting hardest at the weakest and poorest members of the community.'[12] This theme of social injustice was much

[9] Green, 'Treasury resignations'.

[10] 'So long as inflation was thought to be no more than the consequence of excess demand it could be dismissed as an error on the right side': Cairncross, *Inflation,* p.71.

[11] Craig, *General Election Manifestos 1959–1987*, p. 119. [12] ibid., p. 243.

in evidence in the early 1970s debates about publicity on inflation just as it had been in the governmental narratives of the 1940s and 1950s.[13]

In the early 1970s the Conservative government also pursued the incomes policy route to trying to control inflation after the 'U-turn' in macroeconomic policy of 1972, and the switch to a stance of fiscal and monetary stimulus to growth. Initially, the government sought a voluntary agreement with the Confederation of British Industry (CBI) and TUC on prices and wages, but when this failed it introduced a statutory policy in November 1972.[14]

During the course of these tripartite negotiations the Treasury considered the possibility of a major publicity campaign because: 'one major weakness in the presentation of Government policy in the prices and incomes field is the general lack of public understanding about the causes of inflation and the connection between wage increases and price increases'.[15] The background to this was both a general concern at the highest levels in the government that it wasn't 'getting its message across', and a more specific recognition that a successful voluntary incomes policy was something which a Conservative government would have especial difficulties in 'selling' to trade unions.[16] Most of the work on this issue was done within the COI, which sought out precedents for such publicity, produced draft booklets, and summarized the state of knowledge on public understanding of inflation, the latter consisting of work by Hilde Behrend and the IEA.[17] The documents suggest a perceived lack of clarity, both in the message the government wished to convey and the audience who were to be the target of persuasion. On the latter point, one COI civil servant suggested that they were looking 'for a text to appeal to a reader of, say, *The Times* or *Telegraph*', while others recognized it would need to have a broader appeal.[18]

In the event this concern with the state of public understanding did not produce a major publicity campaign on inflation, beyond the usual diet of ministerial speeches and consultative documents. The inhibition does *not* seem to have been official doubts about the underlying belief in the responsibility of wage bargaining for inflation. Whilst memoranda, for example from Alan Walters, were in circulation in Whitehall at this time suggesting that it was the money supply not wage increases which accounted for inflation levels, such views do not seem to have been found

[13] For example, TNA: PRO INF12/1194, 'Inflation publicity', no date, but July 1972.

[14] Blackaby, 'Narrative', pp. 62–76.

[15] TNA: PRO INF12/1194, D.Wass, Treasury, to F. Bickerton, COI, 'Inflation Publicity', 12 July 1972.

[16] TNA: PRO INF12/1198, 'Public presentation of government policy. Memorandum by the Prime Minister', 29 June 1972; TNA: PRO CAB184/38 M. Schreiber, 'Inflation', 26 July 1972.

[17] TNA: PRO INF12/1194, E. Kelly to Director General of COI, 'Inflation publicity campaign', 25 July 1972, and TNA: PRO INF12/1194, 'Inflation campaign—booklet texts', 4 August 1972; TNA: PRO INF12/1194, D. Derx to F. Bickerton, 'Inflation publicity', 8 August 1972. For the importance of Behrend's work, see Section II.

[18] TNA: PRO INF12/1194, E. Kelly to Mr Payton-Smith, 27 July 1972; TNA: PRO CAB 184/38, 'Inflation Publicity', 26 July 1972.

persuasive.[19] Rather, the introduction of a statutory basis for policy reduced the incentive to put substantial resources into changing popular opinion.

However, in the two elections of 1974 the stakes were seen as much higher. In their manifesto for February the Conservatives argued that 'Events from overseas have held us back. They will not destroy us. What could destroy, not just our present standard of living, but all our hopes for the future, would be inflation we brought upon ourselves.'[20] By the time of the October election the language was very much starker:

> For inflation at its present pace threatens not only the standard of living of everybody in the country, but also the survival of free and democratic institutions. No major democracy has ever survived such a catastrophic rise in prices.... [I]nflation and rising prices tear society apart. They destroy the confidence of people in one another and in the future; they distort the existing relationships within our country; they poison the social environment; they wipe out people's savings; they imperil our economic system; they lead in the end to high unemployment and to widespread, if not national, bankruptcy; and they bring particular hardship and misery to the most vulnerable people in the land.[21]

This quotation is given at length to emphasize the magnitude of the crisis the Conservatives claimed was to be the likely consequence of the inflation of the 1970s. We can view this emphasis from a number of angles. First, these were not new arguments in the 1970s; rather they drew upon long-standing interpretations of the effects of the inflationary aftermath of the Great War, expressed most vividly by Keynes when he claimed (inaccurately) that Lenin had seen rapid inflation as the quickest way to destroy a capitalist economy.[22] Such arguments enjoyed renewed currency in the early 1970s, for example in the publications of the IEA, but also in 'mainstream' financial and business commentary.[23] Some idea of the tone of this commentary is given by the *Banker*'s claim in March 1974 that unless inflation were dealt with the last opportunity would have been lost 'for the parliamentary system to cope with Britain's economic problems', or by the *Economist*'s suggestion the following year that because of inflation 'Britannia's dream of apocalypse is horribly close to coming true'.[24]

These arguments about the mortal effects of inflation were popular in Conservative circles in the 1970s, and were at the core of what some have seen as the 'grand peur' among sections of the population in these years.[25] More broadly, we may note that such analyses of inflation were a central underpinning of the radicalization of Conservative Party thinking in these years, associated with the rise of Margaret

[19] TNA: PRO CAB 184/38, A. Walters, 'Inflation and more inflation and then... devaluation', 14 June 1972; B. Reading to Lord Rothschild (Central Policy Review Staff), 'Meeting with Professor A. A. Walters', 6 June 1972.

[20] Craig, *General Election Manifestos 1959–1987*, p. 162.

[21] ibid., p. 213.

[22] White and Schuler, 'Who said?'

[23] Hayek, *Tiger*; Robbins, *Against*, pp. 75–92; Robbins, *Inflation*.

[24] *Banker*, March 1974, p. 205; *Economist*, 17 May 1975, p. 9. Conversely, rapid inflation was also used to justify the overthrow of democracy, as in *The Times*'s support for the coup d'etat in Chile in 1972: Beckett, *Pinochet*, pp. 192–202.

[25] Johnson, *Politics*.

Thatcher to leadership of the party. Thatcher claimed in her memoirs that, in the years between 1975 and 1979, 'the foremost issue was how to deal with inflation.'[26] The way it was dealt with under her leadership was to characterize it as the key contemporary symptom of much longer-term and deeper-seated problems of economic failure or 'decline'.[27] Thus the framing of inflation was central to the politics of the 1970s; it was both the most pressing issue for immediate policy debate and action, and the issue around which the crucial battle was fought between the insurgent neo-liberalism of the 'New Right' in the Conservative Party and the ideas of 'Old Labour'—with long-term consequences.

The early 1970s flurry of discussion on inflation publicity came at a time when retail price increases, having accelerated in the wake of the 1967 devaluation, rose further to an average of 7.6 per cent between 1970 and 1972. From 1973 to 1975 there was a further major acceleration, with the average rising to 16.4 per cent per annum.[28] By 1975, with inflation at its all-time high of 27 per cent, counter-inflation policy entered a dramatic new phase, and it is this period which is focused upon here. While there were precedents for governments seeking to shape public opinion on inflation, the campaign of the mid-1970s is distinguished not only by the urgency of its concerns, but also the scale of resources committed to the effort, coupled with a serious attempt both to gauge opinion on inflation and understand how that opinion was formed.[29]

Trying to manage opinion on inflation was especially important because the Labour government of the 1974–9 period aimed to contain that inflation by combining macroeconomic restraint with a 'Social Contract' that sought popular support for limiting pay increases; an incomes policy by another name. This strategy required a major effort of propaganda and persuasion.[30] Shaping opinion also mattered to policymakers because of the role of 'expectations' in the 'Phillips curve'—the predominant (though increasingly challenged) framework used in most contemporary discussions of inflation.[31] Existing literature on the 1970s tends to see economic policy shaped by a conflict between 'Keynesianism' and 'monetarism': but whatever the value of this division for understanding elite policy decisions, it is far from clear that it was these terms that shaped popular understanding.[32]

Labour's key response to the rapid inflation of the early 1970s was a return to the incomes-policies approach of the 1940s and 1960s, but embodied in a voluntary

[26] Thatcher, *Path*, p. 298. [27] Cannadine, 'Apocalypse?; Tomlinson, 'Thatcher'.

[28] Jones, *Wages*, p. 4.

[29] The Retail Price Index (RPI) peaked at an annual rate of 26.9 per cent in August 1975: Britton, *Macroeconomic*, p. 27.

[30] The budget of 1975 heralded the beginning of a relative shift in policy priorities from unemployment to inflation, accompanied by a tightening of the fiscal stance: Britton, *Macroeconomic*, p. 25.

[31] For the doctrinal disputes on the Phillips curve, Middleton, *Charlatans*, pp. 288–95; the curve still played a large role in standard economics textbooks in the mid-1970s; for example, Trevithick and Mulvay, *Economics*, pp. 4–7, 40–61, 106–25. As in the early 1970s, the CPRS in the mid-1970s acted as one channel into Whitehall for monetarist critiques of the focus on wage bargaining, but argued that 'the monetarist solution would involve a permanent and unacceptable level of unemployment': TNA: PRO CAB184/300, 'The case for a permanent incomes policy', covering M. Beenstock and S. Bell, 'UK Inflation: An Alternative Analysis', 21 November 1975.

[32] For a nuanced account of policy in these terms see Middleton, *Charlatans*, pp. 279–306.

Social Contract with the trade union movement. This contract was at the centre of Labour's key strategic claim; that only Labour could 'do a deal' with the trade unions which could both improve the economy, especially reducing inflation, whilst not increasing unemployment, and avoiding the confrontations between government and organized labour that had characterized the years of the Heath government, 1970–4.

The CIPU derived directly from the Social Contract, whose first phase involved a flat-rate voluntary pay limit of £6 per week for those earning up to £8,500 per annum.[33] The Unit was established in parallel with the publication of the White Paper announcing that policy.[34] Its purpose, according to its first director, was 'to explain to the nation just how critical the situation was and, especially, forge links with employers and trade unions to secure their combined support for this campaign'.[35] This director (Geoffrey Goodman) had previously been Industrial Editor of the *Daily Mirror*, at that time by far the leading working-class newspaper in Britain, and it was clear that, as the Prime Minister told him, his task was to explain the Social Contract 'in *Mirror* language' to a predominantly working-class audience.[36]

The Unit lasted just over a year, though after July 1976, when Goodman left, its activities were residual and it was dissolved in November of that year.[37] Its major activities were twofold. First, it oversaw the writing and distribution to every household in Britain of a popular version of the White Paper called *Attack on Inflation: A Policy for Survival* (see Illustration 4). Second, it organized two major press campaigns, one summarizing the Social Contract policy, the other featuring leading trade unionists and employers explaining why they supported the policy. The Unit was also involved in advising the Prime Minister on his national TV broadcast on the policy in August 1975.[38]

How was the problem presented in '*Mirror* language'? In the case of the popular version of *The Attack on Inflation*, the addition of the subtitle *A Policy for Survival* indicates how high the rhetorical stakes were raised. The popular version quoted the argument from the White Paper that present rates of inflation would 'greatly increase unemployment, threaten us with external bankruptcy, and gravely damage the social and economic fabric of the nation'. But, in Harold Wilson's preface, the key question which he says needs to be answered is 'Are the Government's measures fair?'[39] The answer to this question was of course positive, and was justified in two ways: the first being that inflation itself was very 'unfair' because 'it hits hardest at

[33] Goodman, *From*, pp. 171–4; TNA: PRO BA 9/1, 'Work of the CIPU', 1977.

[34] Cmnd. 6151. The COI was involved in the setting-up of the CIPU and worked alongside the Unit: TNA: PRO INF12/1376 deals with this setting-up.

[35] Goodman, *From*, p. 173.

[36] ibid., p. 175; the focus on this audience led to the Prime Minister insisting that the Communist *Morning Star* be included in the newspapers carrying the government's publicity, despite doubts about this in civil service circles: TNA: PRO BA 9/3, CIPU advisory group meeting, 29 July 1975. This was sometimes referred to as 'the shop-floor approach', e.g. TNA: PRO BA 9/4 CIPU, advisory group meeting, 14 July 1975.

[37] TNA: PRO PREM16/1334 covers the period when the CIPU was closed down. Goodman was succeeded by Hugh Cudlipp, but by then the significant activity of the Unit had ceased.

[38] TNA: PRO BA 9/1, 'Work of the CIPU'. [39] Cmnd. 6151, p. 2, preface.

Illustration 4 High stakes in the anti-inflation campaign (1976).
Source: Image courtesy of the National Archives.

the housewives and the pensioners'; the second because at heart the policy was about restoring full employment, seen as a self-evidently 'fair' priority.[40]

This central role for the language of 'fairness' is worth emphasizing. It was a feature of almost all post-war government economic propaganda.[41] The commitment to notions of distributive justice might be seen as central to the post-war settlement, with no politician daring to embrace the Hayekian view that in a market society social justice was an illusion to be attacked as dangerously mistaken.[42] Rather, politicians addressed the public on the assumption spelled out by Barbara Wootton that 'the public is always better at ethics, which are warm and real, than at economics, which are cold and abstract'.[43] The language of counter-inflation publicity did of course use the words of economics, but the key appeals to the audience were indeed ethical, linking inflation to distributive justice, but also treating inflation as the result of human agency, and that agency as the object of ethical judgement.

[40] Cmnd. 6151, pp. 12, 3. [41] Tomlinson, 'Re-inventing', pp. 356–73.

[42] Hayek, *Law*, p. 97. Of course Hayek did believe a market society could and should be just, but only in a procedural, not substantive, sense.

[43] Wootton, *Social*, p. 100.

Another issue for the designers of government publicity was how serious the situation should be presented as being. This problem came to the fore in discussion of the Prime Minister's key broadcast in the summer of 1975. The first draft of this was strongly pitched, opening with the words:

> I want to speak to you tonight about our country's crisis. And I want to begin with a few words about the nature of that word—CRISIS.... In the 30 years since the end of the last war the word CRISIS has never been more valid as a description of our country's condition than it is at this moment.

But in the event the language of the actual broadcast was toned down considerably, beginning 'For hundreds of thousands of British homes this autumn the shadow—for so many of them the reality—of unemployment is threatening standards each family has taken for granted for years past.'[44] This focus on unemployment rather than the generic notion of 'crisis' is not clearly explained in the archives, but it was in line with other discussion within the CIPU suggesting that the audience to be addressed was predominantly working class, amongst whom issues of employment were believed to be pre-eminent.[45]

This focus on the working class was accompanied by a concern with the 'housewife', seen as the person most immediately affected by inflation.[46] This gave the publicity campaign a very clearly gendered aspect, especially evident in the newspaper material. Most of the newspaper publicity featured a double image of a 'boss' and a 'worker' expressing their support for the policy; all of the bosses and workers are men. The only woman to feature is the housewife who appears under the heading, 'I'm not a boss and I don't belong to a union, but inflation affects me as much as anyone'. This gender stereotyping seems to have been regarded as unproblematic in the CIPU, indeed the advertisement (which juxtaposed the housewife with a coal miner) was regarded as one of the very best pieces of publicity.[47]

II

How did this governmental narrative relate to popular understanding of inflation? As noted, perhaps the CIPU is ultimately of most interest because as part of its

[44] TNA: PRO BA 9/5, CIPU 'Draft of the PM's "Speak to the nation" broadcast', no date, but August 1975; 'Text of a Ministerial broadcast by the PM, 20 August 1975'.

[45] The household distribution of the pamphlet was designed to prevent hostile trade unions suppressing its distribution to members via union channels: TNA: PRO INF12/1376, PM's Personal Private Secretary to H. James, COI, 'Counter inflation publicity programme', 6 August 1975.

[46] A very revealing section of the brief given to advertising companies hoping to work on the campaign justified the inclusion of women 'as mothers of future generations, as managers of the household budget, as the voice of common sense in the home': TNA: PRO INF12/1376, 'Briefing to advertisers on campaign', 18 July 1975.

[47] TNA: PRO BA 9/4, 'Summary of research conducted in December 1975', 12 January 1976, p. 3. The focus on the housewife was a key feature of economic propaganda in the 1940s, as it was in the 1960s, albeit in combination with encouragement to married women to enter or remain in the workforce: Fielding, *Labour*, ch. 5; Zweiniger-Bargielowska, *Austerity*.

activities it provided a large amount of empirical material on this understanding, about which otherwise we know rather little.

Prior to the mid-1970s, empirical investigation into popular understanding of inflation in Britain was dominated by the work of Hilde Behrend and her associates, published from the mid-1960s on.[48] Behrend, whose background was in occupational psychology, originally did a lot of work on how the population understood prices, arguing that knowledge of prices was very poor except for 'everyday' commodities subject to frequent purchase. Linked to this, she argued, was a 'slow-learning' problem, whereby memories of past prices lingered on, generating a gloomier picture than was justified by current patterns of prices relative to income.[49]

A problem in analysing popular understanding of economic phenomena is whether one frames the issue in terms of 'degrees of ignorance'; the temptation when dealing with relatively technical economic terms is to measure how far popular understanding falls short of expert views. This approach has been employed by some economists, and yields the unsurprising conclusion that only a small proportion of the population thinks about economic terms the same way as economists.[50] But this is unhelpful. Rather than measuring public 'ignorance' it is better, in line with work in the field of public understanding of science, to recognize that most people *do* have some positive kind of understanding, however far this may depart from received expert knowledge, and it this understanding which can effect their behaviour, so talk of 'ignorance' is not very useful.[51]

In Behrend's survey of comprehension of the term 'inflation' in the 1960s, she found just over 30 per cent of her respondents had no clear view of what the word meant, though we should not equate that with simple 'ignorance'; after all, it would be possible to be a sophisticated (if modest) economist and say you 'don't understand' inflation, given the complex and controversial nature of the term (see Table 8.1).

Behrend is rather inclined to perceive these statistics as showing popular ignorance, concluding on the need for governments to do more explaining in language accessible to ordinary people, and she was critical of the 1960s Labour government for not doing this.[52] Yet her results show one clear bit of 'understanding'; that, however poorly specified, inflation is a 'bad thing'. This, it is worth emphasizing, is far from self-evident. On one hand, it was a well-established view amongst some economists at this time that a mild inflation (at the 2–3 per cent level Britain was experiencing for most of the 1950s and 1960s) was economically *advantageous*, in encouraging an expansionary spirit amongst investors.[53] On the other hand, if

[48] Behrend, *Attitudes*; Behrend, 'Price Images'; Behrend, 'Price and Income Images'; Behrend, 'Public'; Behrend et al., *Incomes*; Behrend, Lynch, and Davies, *National*. Her account of this work can be found in Behrend, *Problems*, pp. 178–223.

[49] 'Price Images'; 'Price and Income Images'.

[50] For example, MacDowall, *Public*.

[51] Knight, *Public*.

[52] Behrend, 'National survey', pp. 25–6; Behrend, *Problems*, pp. 196–7.

[53] Whilst not endorsing this view, John Hicks stressed that 'to the ordinary man it is obvious that inflation matters; but the economist is unwise to take it for granted', Hicks, *Crisis*, p. 2.

Table 8.1 What inflation means

Meaning of 'inflation'	Percentage of respondents
'Don't know or don't understand'	32.9
'Rising prices'	21.9
'Something to do with value of money'	9.6
'Something to do with money or prices'	9.0
'Not paying our way as a country'	8.3
'Money losing value'	7.1
'Something bad'	6.0
'Something getting bigger'	2.6
'Too much money chasing too few goods'	2.0

Source: Behrend, Lynch, and Davies, *National Survey*, (adapted from Table I, p. 3, eliminating answers given by less than 2 per cent of respondents).

inflation redistributes income, as contemporary economic theory suggested, this would necessarily involve winners as well as losers; so it was good for some, albeit at the expense of others. These points get rather lost in Behrend's account, as a key aim of her work was to examine popular understanding in order to find better ways for governments to persuade the population on the need for incomes policy; so she implicitly accepted that inflation was a bad thing, and should be reduced.[54] This assumption seemed to be there despite the fact that her 1960s respondents, whilst viewing inflation unfavourably, did not believe it had adversely affected them *individually*.[55] This links to a further point about the interpretation of Behrend's data. She offers a lament about the level of popular understanding, saying 'this phenomenon is something very abstract and remote and much less real than their own day-to-day problems'.[56] But it is plausible that, precisely because of this 'remoteness', many respondents were not highly engaged with the inflation argument; they lacked any incentive to be so.

In 1972 the NEDO sponsored Behrend to survey popular attitudes to price increases and pay, with field work done in January 1973. This found a much higher degree of concern with inflation than surveys of the mid-1960s, and, perhaps causally linked to that, a higher proportion (70 per cent) who believed their household income had not kept pace with price increases.[57]

As in her work in the 1960s, Behrend's analysis in the early 1970s took it as given that respondents 'should' link inflation to wage increases, with the clear implication that the latter caused the former.[58] With perhaps the exception of the 2 per cent in the 1966 survey who saw inflation in terms of 'too much money chasing too few goods', both the questions and the answers in Behrend's empirical work assumed a 'wage–price spiral' account of inflation. Her project was to find out how a workable incomes policy could gain popular support, and her questions

[54] This aim is most obvious in the title of her *Public Acceptability and a Workable Incomes Policy*.
[55] Behrend, 'National', p. 26. [56] ibid. [57] Behrend, 'Attitudes', pp. 6–7.
[58] ibid., p. 31, where the issue is whether it is possible 'to stabilise prices without limiting pay claims'.

were framed with that in mind.[59] Her work is valuable because there is little other systematic analysis of popular understanding of inflation for the years before the mid-1970s, but those using its conclusions need to bear in mind the very particular mindset which framed her enquiries, and hence the answers she reported.[60]

Another important analysis of popular understandings of inflation is Alt's work, using surveys done at the time of the two 1974 general elections. This is probably the most methodologically sophisticated as well as empirically rich study of the inflation issue in the 1970s, though it only deals with the period up to the end of 1974 in any detail.[61] One important general conclusion of Alt's investigations is that inflation did not lead to the kind of radical questioning of the viability of the economic system amongst 'ordinary' people as it did amongst some journalists and members of the political class. He finds evidence of a loss of enthusiasm for both main political parties because of their perceived failure to deal with the inflation problem, but no threat of a breakdown in the political order. He summarizes his findings in the following terms: 'the reaction to the rapid inflation of 1974 and 1975 was very calm, and far indeed from the doom-laden predictions some journalists made in 1974 of chaos and the breakdown of democracy in Britain' (see Table 8.2).[62]

What is perhaps most important about this data is their suggestion that peaks in popular belief in the responsibility of unions for inflation coincide with the peaks

Table 8.2 Causes of inflation, 1966–75 (percentage of respondents)

Main cause of inflation	Feb. 1966	End 1967	1971/2	Oct. 1973	June 1974	Feb. 1975	Mid-1975
Trade unions/workers' wage claims	39	34	29	14	20	19	51
Management/profits	30	10	15				6
World situation		9	17	31	32	24	28
Present government	31	30	15	6	1	2	15
Last government		17	4				
Joining the EEC				28	24	12	
Decimalization			20	21	23	13	
Price of oil						30	

Source: Alt, *Politics*, p. 162.

[59] Behrend's work on inflation seems to have been stimulated by the COPPI, *Fourth Report* (1961), which said: 'At the heart of the problem of inflation under full employment is a frame of mind': Behrend, 'Reaching', p. 5.

[60] Of course, this mindset was by no means unusual; a number of social scientists as well as politicians in the 'golden age' were searching for ways to make incomes policy more palatable; for example, Barbara Wootton's important work had precisely that aim in mind: Wootton, *Social*; also Fogarty, *Just*. The question whether the public had a notion of a 'just wage' seems to have underlain research by the Ministry of Labour on 'pay perception' in 1974 to 1977 which seemed to find a pattern of general satisfaction with existing relativities: TNA: PRO LAB112/104, 'Pay perception research: progress report', 14 January 1977.

[61] Alt, *Politics*. For a broader assessment of this book, Tomlinson, 'Politics'.

[62] Alt, *Politics*, p. 266.

of government attempts to gain support for incomes policy. The Labour government introduced the 'early warning system' for pay increases after extensive negotiations with the TUC and CBI in November 1965.[63] As noted, the £6 limit phase of the Social Contract and the creation of the CIPU date from mid-1975. This pattern, as argued in this chapter's conclusion, was not a coincidence.

Another feature of this table is the relatively small proportion of the respondents blaming government for the inflation problem, especially in the first half of the 1970s. This is significant in the light of Conservative arguments, particularly after the accession of Thatcher to the leadership of the Conservative Party, which sought to persuade the electorate that state profligacy and excessive monetary expansion was at the heart of the inflationary problem. Against the background of the opinions enumerated in Table 8.2, this was clearly going to be a difficult argument to win.

Alt argues that the 1970s saw popular concern with inflation rising at the expense of unemployment, and he in turn sees this as a result of the differing distribution of effects of the two problems. While unemployment largely harms only those directly affected, inflation affects everyone. In times of crisis, he argues, an altruistic concern with the fate of a minority was displaced by a more 'selfish' concern with the impact of price rises on one's own welfare.[64] In 1974 at least, this was coupled with seriously exaggerated expectations about inflation, with, in both February and October of that year, over half of respondents believing inflation was running at over 50 per cent per annum, when the RPI was actually increasing at between 10 and 20 per cent, depending upon the precise time period chosen.[65]

Thus the evidence suggests that by the time Labour launched its Social Contract in 1975, popular concern with inflation was already substantial, following the acceleration of the inflation rate from 1972 onwards, and the emphasis put upon it in the two elections of 1974.

III

In looking at the evidence provided by the CIPU, it is clear that the authorities were mindful of the need to assess this popular understanding in its own terms, rather than using a 'knowledge versus ignorance' framework. As was said of the public, in a report to the Prime Minister in 1976: 'while they could not juggle and interrelate economic and social concepts as well as an economist, they showed a down to earth grasp of what was happening, and were acutely aware of how economic policies worked out in theory often came to grief when put into practice.'[66]

The first piece of opinion research sponsored by the CIPU was in July 1975 (just after the White Paper was published, but prior to the CIPU doing any publicity) with a sample of 2,431 adults. They were asked about the seriousness of the economic position, and 40 per cent said 'extremely serious', 35 per cent 'very serious', 17 per cent

63 Tomlinson, *Labour*, pp. 136–7.

64 Alt, *Politics*, pp. 183–201.

65 ibid., pp. 69, 66–7.

66 TNA: PRO PREM 16/951, 'Counter inflation III: report on six group discussions', April 1976.

Table 8.3 Seriousness of economic position (percentage of those surveyed)

Main reasons for serious position	Percentage
Large pay rises	27
Inflation	21
Strikes	20
Government	19
Unions	14
World prices	13
Price of oil	6
Management	5
Other	33

Source: TNA: PRO BA 9/5 CIPU, 'Economic attitude surveys—advance results', 4 August 1975, p. 1.

'fairly serious', and 5 per cent 'not particularly serious'. Asked about the reasons for this situation, they answered as shown in Table 8.3.

While 90 per cent of the sample knew about the £6 policy, only 11 per cent thought the policy 'very adequate' to the situation. Eighteen per cent thought the policy 'very fair', 50 per cent 'fairly fair', and 18 per cent 'not very fair'. Seventy-two per cent felt they had enough information on the economic situation, and 75 per cent thought the government should *not* spend money on advertising to give more information.[67] This suggests that a high proportion of the populace felt that, at least to their own satisfaction, they understood the economic situation.

A second survey held a few days later focused on respondents' beliefs about their personal economic situation. Forty-two per cent said that inflation had made them worse off than a year previously, but almost three quarters were 'not at all worried' that they would lose their job 'because of runaway inflation'. Eighty per cent said they would prefer 'lower wage rises and more security' to 'bigger wage rises and take a risk'.[68]

Following its publicity activities in the summer and autumn, the CIPU sponsored a survey of responses to *The Attack on Inflation: A Policy for Survival.* Nearly three quarters of respondents recalled a booklet on inflation, and 32 per cent said they had read it or at least 'flipped through it'. 'The points communicated by the booklet on the effects of inflation related to jobs and the decline in the value of money; and on the Government's programme, to the £6 per week increase limit. The other main message received from the booklet was that it was necessary to pull together/make sacrifices in order to survive.'[69]

More investigations into public opinion followed in December 1975, when a national survey of a thousand respondents was combined with two small qualitative

[67] TNA: PRO BA 9/5 CIPU, 'Economic attitude surveys-advance results', 4 August 1975, pp. 1–2.
[68] ibid., pp. 3–4.
[69] TNA: PRO PREM 16/512, 'Evaluation of household drop of counter-inflation booklet', October 1975.

surveys focusing on trade unionists. Some of the questions in the national survey related directly to recognition of the government's campaign, and 43 per cent said they had seen the advertising. Asked what they understood by the word 'inflation', most focused on price inflation and believed such price increases were causing a fall in their living standards. Thus, respondents readily assumed that inflation was unambiguously a 'bad thing' with uniformly adverse consequences.[70]

Asked about the causes of inflation, most respondents in the national survey saw it in terms of wages, and associated with a clear moral message:

> While only a small number of respondents spoke of inflation as an abstract economic phenomenon, they did see a relationship between attitudes at the work place and price inflation. Inflation was seen as caused by greed. This state of mind manifested itself in a number of things; respondents particularly mentioned strikes, lower standards of workmanship and what they saw as bad management in industry and Government. They were concerned at what they saw as a loss of values in the wage structure.[71]

An evaluation of first months of the CIPU's activities saw this popular focus on wages as the cause of inflation as a success for the publicity campaign: 'In August members of stronger unions felt that their wage demands were a reaction to increased prices and not a cause of them. Today, such a relationship is accepted almost universally.'[72] Thus, the CIPU explicitly saw itself as conveying the message that 'excessive' wage increases cause inflation; the Social Contract would not have made sense as a strategy otherwise. This is not to say that Labour leaders were not aware of the dangers posed by concentrating too much on this linkage. Harold Wilson himself, taking a close interest in the activities of the CIPU, noted in February 1976 that,

> Last spring and summer this attack [on inflation] was directly related to excessive pay settlements, whose impact on prices was direct, if delayed.... However necessary that approach was in mid-1975, we must recognise that it is to some extent offensive to the TUC and that it is only part of a much wider problem of... industrial costs in relation to prices, and about wage levels, productivity, investment and management in relation to industrial costs.[73]

So the political leadership of the Labour government did not want to convey a simple message of blaming the trade unions for inflation. But the linking of the CIPU's propaganda message to the Social Contract inevitably meant that the central idea conveyed by the Unit's activities was that the unions *were* the main agency at work in the inflationary process. The success of the Social Contract required that this message be conveyed and accepted, above all by union members themselves. Focus group studies undertaken in early 1976 suggested that this message had indeed been successfully conveyed, with not only 'housewife' groups

[70] TNA: PRO BA 9/4, 'Summary of research conducted in December 1975', p. 2. [71] ibid.

[72] TNA: PRO PREM 16/950, 'A review of the first six months of the counter-inflation publicity programme and an assessment of its likely development', January 1976.

[73] TNA: PRO: PREM 16/950, H. Wilson, 'Counter-inflation publicity programme', February 1976.

(including the wives of coal miners) but also trade unionists readily blaming unions for inflation.[74]

According to those who answered the CIPU's surveys, the government's £6 wage policy was seen as having had some success by early 1976. At that time, respondents had 'an air of restrained optimism. We were not in a severe crisis, and the situation was better than last spring.'[75] This seems to have led to some slackening off in the focus on inflation, with an National Opinion Polls (NOP) survey, commissioned by the CIPU, partly following the long-standing Gallup survey by asking what respondents thought were 'the most urgent problems facing the country'. The NOP and Gallup results were consistent in showing both that inflation was regarded as the most serious problem, and that since mid-1975 unemployment had been catching up in popular concern. This was despite a majority believing that prices were rising faster than a year previously.[76]

CIPU activity was very limited after the spring of 1976, and it was disbanded later that year. This disbandment was controversial, but a key argument in favour was that its work in support of the £6 per week policy was seen to have been effective 'because the issues involved were simple, urgent and dramatic', whereas in the second phase a 'shock pamphlet' was inappropriate.[77] The disbandment was also linked to the foreign exchange crisis which began in earnest in March 1976 and was given priority in ministerial circles. There was talk of a popular accompaniment to the June 1976 White Paper, *The Attack on Inflation: the Second Year*, but this was abandoned, 'particularly in the light of events then taking place in the foreign exchange markets'.[78]

IV

The aim of the CIPU was to enhance support for the Social Contract, but it is very difficult to assess whether it succeeded.[79] But the material produced by the Unit does help us to grasp popular understanding of inflation in the 1970s, and how this in turn related to the forces shaping economic policy in that decade.

Those, most obviously Thatcherite radicals, who were presented with an opportunity to discredit the existing economic policy regime by the rapid inflation of the 1970s faced two tasks. One was to put inflation at the centre of the political

[74] TNA: PRO PREM 16/951, 'Counter inflation III report of six group discussions', April 1976.

[75] TNA: PRO BA 9/4, 'Summary of research conducted in December 1975', p. 2.

[76] TNA: PRO PREM 16/950, 'Counter inflation campaign: stage 3 evaluation', March 1976.

[77] TNA: PRO PREM16/1334, Hugh Cudlipp to PM, 'Counter-inflation publicity', 12 October 1976. Michael Foot, the Lord President of the Council, was also highly critical of the 'mock Churchillian rhetoric' that the CIPU seemed to favour: ibid., R. Saville to H. Cudlipp, covering Michael Foot's comments on proposed pamphlet, 29 September 1976. The TUC was also worried that further government publicity might be seen as appealing over their heads to union members: TNA: PRO INF12/1377, 'Presentation of Counter-inflation policy', 15 June 1976.

[78] Cmnd. 6507; TNA: PRO BA9/1, 'Work of the counter-inflation publicity unit', p. 4.

[79] Unsurprisingly the Conservative Party view was that the Unit was a woeful waste of money. They persistently asked questions about its cost, for example *Hansard* (Commons), 17 July 1975, vol. 895, cols 544–5; 24 July 1975, vol. 896, cols 276–7; see also 16 May 1989, vol. 153, col. 206.

agenda. As noted above, this attempt was couched in apocalyptic terms; terms which do not seem to have found wide resonance—none of the empirical work on popular understanding of inflation suggests that this apocalyptic view gained broad agreement. The work of Alt and that sponsored by the CIPU shows that the populace did become increasingly concerned with inflation, but this was not accompanied by a general loss of faith in capitalism or democracy. Cynicism about the political system was boosted by the perceived failure of politicians to deal with the problem, but there was never a serious threat to the continuation of existing institutions.[80] Nevertheless, inflation did advance up the political agenda, though it battled with unemployment as the number-one priority of the population.

We may perhaps link this 'don't panic' attitude to the fact that, in retrospect, the effects of the inflation of the 1970s seem to have been only mildly disruptive of the distribution of economic rewards—a disruption seen as crucial to those with an apocalyptic vision of inflation's consequences. The main redistribution was through the failure of building society interest rates in the middle of the decade to keep pace with inflation, thus bringing about a shift of resources from savers in those societies to mortgagees. This was a redistribution from old to young, though particularly the better-off old, with poorer elderly people having fewer deposits, and being protected by the uprating of pensions in line with inflation.[81]

Among the great bulk of wage and salary earners, the real impact of the 1970s inflation was limited, with some small narrowing of the vertical pay differentials during the flat-rate phase of the Social Contract reversed later in the decade. The biggest shift was the decline in public, relative to private sector, pay, as a result of the greatest effectiveness of incomes policy being on the wages of the low-paid in the public sector.[82] This effect was to turn out to be the most politically significant, underlying as it did the 'Winter of Discontent' of 1978/9, an issue returned to shortly.

The second task of those wishing to fundamentally shift the terms of economic debate was to make monetarism the predominant approach to economic policy. But monetarism is, of course, a complex term, with many varieties. Most fundamentally, there is the issue of whether we see it as essentially an economic argument about the relationship between monetary growth and the price level, or in a broader, more political economy sense. In one of the most influential analyses of the 'Thatcher revolution', Bulpitt argued that we should see monetarism primarily in the latter way, as a form of 'statecraft'.[83] By this he means that monetarism, by suggesting that inflation could be controlled simply by regulating the growth of the money supply, would take governments out of the quagmire of a direct role of intervening in price- and wage-setting. Governments would no longer have to bargain with, and make concessions to, unions and employers, but would enjoy considerable 'relative autonomy' from interest groups.

[80] TNA: PRO PREM 16/951, 'Counter inflation III: report on six group discussions', April 1976.
[81] Foster, 'Redistributive'; Piachaud, 'Inflation', pp. 88–116; Smith, *Inflation*.
[82] Fallick and Elliott, 'Incomes'. [83] Bulpitt, 'Discipline'.

This approach has much to commend it, especially because of the way it allows us to escape the idea of a simple binary of 'monetarism versus Keynesianism' as the defining issue of the 1970s; as Bulpitt suggests, Keynesianism promised a similar 'relative autonomy' for state action.[84] But monetarism was also problematic for the Thatcher radicals, because it suggested that monetary growth *not* trade union activity was responsible for inflation. This contradicted a long-standing feature of conservative 'common sense' to the effect that unions were damaging not least because of the inflationary effects of their monopolistic wage bargaining.[85] To give up this argument at a time when rapid inflation could be so readily linked to an attack on trade unions was a politically uncongenial consequence of monetarist doctrine. The doctrine could be reformulated to sustain an anti-union stance by suggesting that, with inflation constrained by tight money, the *level of employment* would be affected by union willingness to constrain their activities. But this was a rather more complex argument than the long-entrenched 'obviousness' of the 'wage–price spiral'.[86]

The evidence on popular understanding of inflation in the 1970s suggests the public retained a stout commitment to the causative role of unions in inflation, and this linkage was much enhanced by the role of the CIPU in framing the inflation issue at the time of the introduction of the Social Contract. The unambiguous message from the focus on incomes policies as an anti-inflationary policy was that it was wage bargainers who were responsible for price rises.

There has been much debate about if, when, and to what extent the Labour government after 1974 was converted to 'monetarism'.[87] If the criterion is the displacement of a focus on reducing unemployment by one on reducing inflation, there is evidence of such a shift from the budget of 1975 (though, equally, some movement in the other direction is evident from 1977). But while key figures in the Labour government may have been, at least for pragmatic reasons, shifting to a macroeconomic policy affected by 'monetarism' at the time of the 1975/6 crisis, this is nowhere evident in the way they sought to shape understanding of inflation through the CIPU.[88] One would seek in vain for any mention of 'money supply', 'excess demand', or any other monetarist terminology in the Unit's work. One reason has already been stressed; the immediate task in 1975 was to gain support for wage restraint, and, for that message to make sense, unions, not the money supply, had to be the 'cause' of inflation. Another factor at play here was the language of economic propaganda. As suggested above, the Wilson government continued a long-standing stance that the British public needed an ethical narrative if they were to be persuaded. While not impossible, it is much harder to put monetary growth in such a normative context than it is the actions of trade unions.

Colin Hay has persuasively argued that the key to the electoral success of the Conservatives in May 1979 was the construction of a compelling narrative about the 'Winter of Discontent', when public sector workers revolted against a 5 per cent

[84] ibid., pp. 33, 37–8. [85] Green, *Thatcher*, pp. 102–6; more broadly, Dorey, *Conservative*.
[86] Tomlinson, 'Thatcher', pp. 69–71. [87] Allsopp, 'Macroeconomic'.
[88] Healey, *Time*, pp. 372–87.

wage limit at a time when inflation was running at around 8–10 per cent. It was the capacity of the Conservatives to portray this crisis as the fault of the trade unions that underlay their victory in 1979.[89] What the current chapter adds to that argument is a sense of how the popular understanding of inflation, and its alleged links to union activity, was shaped in part by deliberate actions of the preceding Labour government. Of course, the CIPU did not invent the idea of a wage–price spiral, but it undoubtedly conveyed that message very strongly, and, the evidence suggests, with some success. It seems clearly to have entrenched an anti-union perspective. In that sense, the attempt to secure support for the Social Contract by constructing a particular narrative about the significance and causes of inflation unintentionally laid some major groundwork for the triumph of a quite different political economy.

[89] Hay, 'Chronicles'; Saunders, 'Thatcherism', p. 39.

9

The Balance of Payments

'Export or die' was only one of the dramatic slogans deployed by the Attlee government to attempt to persuade the population of the need to sacrifice themselves to improve the balance of payments. Down to the end of the golden age such dramatic language was normal in discussions of the payments issue, and successive governments, Conservative and Labour, constructed overlapping but distinguishable narratives about this 'problem' and its allegedly necessary solutions. But from the 1970s, with the floating of the pound, and the rise of neo-liberal accounts of the economy, the balance of payments slowly disappeared from view as far as most public economic discussion was concerned—despite the fact that, by conventional measures of the current balance, the situation was far worse *after* that decade than before. The balance of payments is therefore an especially striking case of both the malleability and partiality of narratives deployed to seek to persuade the public of its importance. It also shows the possibility of long-standing economic 'problems', once deemed vital, disappearing from view as new ways of looking at economic issues, linked to changing institutional arrangements and doctrines, come to the fore. This chapter traces the changing representation of this 'problem', and the reasons for its virtual disappearance as an important narrative about the economy in the last quarter of the twentieth century.

I

British economic policy during the Second World War was characterized by 'throwing caution to wind' in order to achieve military victory. This approach left the balance of payments in a parlous state by the war's end, as exports plummeted while imports fell by much less (see Table 9.1).[1] The inevitable wartime payments gap was financed by a combination of foreign asset sales, accumulation of overseas sterling debts, and Lend-Lease from the USA. The end of the war led to an immediate cessation of Lend-Lease, and left Britain with what Keynes famously characterized as a 'financial Dunkirk'.[2] But as Keynes clearly spelt out, this 'Dunkirk' was not simply about Britain struggling to pay for crucial imports with much diminished export revenues, it was also about the attempt to 'cut a dash in the world considerably above our means'—to pay for the military and diplomatic expenditures overseas

[1] Howlett,'War-time', pp. 15–17. [2] Keynes, 'Our'.

Table 9.1 British balance of payments, 1938–50 (£ millions)

	1938	1946	1947	1948	1949	1950
Exports	564	960	1,180	1,639	1,863	2,261
Imports	849	1,063	1,541	1,790	2,000	2,312
Visible trade	-285	-103	-361	-151	-137	-51
Current account	-55	-230	-381	+26	-1	+307
Government current transactions	-19	-363	-230	-87	-140	-125
Capital exports	+5	-643	-432	-447	+1	*

Source: Tomlinson, *Democratic Socialism*, p. 48.
* no data available.

targeted at sustaining Britain's world role.[3] Thus, while no one can doubt the severity of the war's legacy for the balance of payments, calculation of the depths of this severity depend upon prior policy decisions concerning what overseas expenditures Britain had to undertake. This important point, now well established in the literature on the 1940s, gives a very different perspective to that advanced by contemporary economic propaganda.[4]

The conflict over how much 'great power' expenditure Britain could afford was one fought out within the Attlee government, with some curtailment eventually imposed on initial 'extravagance'. But the question of how much foreign investment could be afforded—a drain of foreign exchange amounting to £1,500 million in 1947–9 (a sum greater than the American loan)—seems never to have surfaced in contemporary debate.[5] Whatever the precise causes of the deficit in this period, and the debates in policymaking circles, the government felt compelled to try and rally the population by a major publicity campaign to improve the situation. In this campaign the complexities of defining a 'deficit' were forgotten, and the picture was clearly presented as one largely concerning the balance of *trade*. The key document in the popular representation of this issue was the 1946 pamphlet *We Live by Exports*. This started with the need to import, then looked at the sources of finance for these imports. It noted how invisible sources of earnings had been hard hit by the war, and went on to show how increased exports were the answer. In setting out the targets for exports, the clear message was that it is exports of *goods* that were at issue: 'the quicker we reach every target we set ourselves, the easier it will be to reach our next target. The markets are crying out for our goods now'.[6]

This message of (visible) exports as a precondition for vital imports was also central to the government's general 'Work or Want' campaign (see Chapter 1), and the particularly extensive publicity in the cotton industry under the heading 'England's

[3] Keynes, 'Political', pp. 465–6.

[4] Cairncross, *Years*, ch. 4; Tomlinson, *Democratic*, ch. 3. Of course, these overseas investments yielded returns directly in interest, profits, and dividends and indirectly in exports, but no calculation of these effects seems to have been undertaken until the 1960s.

[5] Cairncross, *Years*, ch. 6; Conan, *Sterling*; Tomlinson, *Democratic Socialism*, pp. 49–64. Most of this investment went to Australia and South Africa.

[6] Board of Trade, *We Live*, especially p. 16.

Table 9.2 Public support for increasing exports, 1947–50

	Percentage of those surveyed agreeing that 'we should increase our exports'
May 1949	38
September 1949	46
March 1950	42
July 1950	37
November 1950	34
March 1951	31

Source: TNA: PRO RG23/116, 'Survey of knowledge and opinion about the economic situation', March 1951, p. 10.

Bread Hangs by Lancashire's Thread'.[7] What all this propaganda neglected entirely was the use of foreign exchange both for government expenditure overseas and for foreign investment. One can understand, perhaps, why the government did not say 'we must export more so we can help the Dutch reimpose colonial rule in Indonesia' or even 'we must export more so that more can be invested in South African gold mines', but the arguments that were presented in consequence of such partiality can hardly perhaps be called a 'balanced account' of the British payments problem in this period. This simplistic, indeed misleading, representation of the balance-of-payments issue was to be long continued in post-war Britain.

To cast a critical eye on the balance of payments propaganda of the time is not to suggest that the public were necessarily persuaded by what the government was telling them. Table 9.2 shows that only a minority ever clearly supported the call for higher exports, (the Autumn 1949 peak presumably reflecting the intensity of debate in the lead-up to the devaluation crisis), and further analysis of the sample showed that this support was significantly weaker amongst shop-floor workers than amongst managers and professionals.[8]

An earlier survey, shown in Table 9.3, looks at the early months of balance-of-payments propaganda. It suggests not only a misperception of the actual position (the answer being under a quarter), but also, as the survey report suggested: 'It appears that one of the effects of publicity on the export drive, and other statements about exports, during the eighteen months between the two surveys has been greatly to increase the number of people with wrong ideas on this aspect of the subject'.[9]

Usually economic propaganda is almost entirely focused on domestic audiences, but, particularly in the 1940s, the British government had to represent the balance-of-payments problem not only internally, but also externally, especially in the USA. This audience required a rather different approach to that of domestic propaganda. This necessity to speak to Americans flowed, of course, from the need to acquire dollars from the American government—first with the 1946 loan, and

[7] Another slogan of the time was, 'We fill the ships to fill the shops': Crofts, *Coercion?*, p. 36.

[8] TNA: PRO RG23/112, 'Survey of knowledge and opinion about the economic situation', July 1950, Table 3.

[9] TNA: PRO RG23/95, 'Survey of knowledge and opinion about the economic situation', March 1948, p. 17.

Table 9.3 Perception of share of goods exported, 1946 and 1948 (percentage of those surveyed)

	October 1946	March 1948
Three-quarters or more	33	49
About a half	22	25
About a quarter or less	3	5
Don't know	42	21

Source: TNA: PRO RG23/95, 'Survey of knowledge and opinion about the economic situation', March 1948, Table 16.

then through Marshall Aid from 1948. The negotiations about Marshall Aid are especially striking in this regard, because they led to an extended discussion between British and US authorities about what exactly the British problems were, and how they should be addressed. The core of the British claim was of course a shortage of dollars, but in making this claim a story had to be told about the overall balance of payments. This story, like that told to the home audience, concentrated on the current balance as the key issue, but, unlike most domestic propaganda, also made explicit reference to sterling's role as an international currency: 'The economic story of the post-war years has centred therefore upon these two factors: the rebuilding and expansion of Britain's industrial might; and the restoration of confidence in sterling'.[10] The defence of the Sterling Area at this time and to this American audience focused upon the argument that it would encourage international trade in a—for the time being—bilateral world.[11] The government's *Economic Survey for 1947* was written partly with this American audience in mind, defending the Sterling Area for its trade creation possibilities, rather than as some overhang from Britain's imperial past.[12]

The focus of government propaganda and policy in the Attlee period on expanding the export of manufactured goods may be construed in part as an inescapable consequence of the immediate opportunities available to Britain. There was pent-up demand for such goods in many parts of the world, whereas the huge decline in British invisible receipts (categorized as interest profits and dividends, insurance and other financial services, and shipping) could not be reversed so readily in the highly controlled international economy of the late 1940s. So the broad picture of these years is of a successful campaign to bring about a striking expansion of *manufacturing* exports, offsetting the sharp decline in other foreign earnings, especially interest profits and dividends, and the sharp rise in the price of food and raw materials. In the short run this export growth was aided by the war damage to Germany and Japan, but it is important to emphasize that it was part of a longer-run post-war upward shift in the importance of manufacturing to Britain's foreign earnings. The manufacturing surplus was over 8 per cent of GDP in the late 1940s

10 HMT, *Recovery*, p. 5; HMT, *Statistical Material.*
11 Newton, 'Sterling'; Tomlinson, 'Correlli Barnett's History'.
12 Crofts, *Coercion?*, p. 249.

and through the 1950s—significantly higher than any other country (including West Germany, which in this respect did not overtake Britain until the mid 1960s).[13] This new dominance of manufacturing may help to account for the urgency with which the City of London sought to restore its capacity to earn foreign exchange—a capacity seriously diminished in the war years.[14] Overall, as Cairncross emphasizes, the Attlee government was highly successful in diverting resources into exports, and by 1950 the (non-dollar) current account was looking extremely healthy. The dollar position also began to improve rapidly after devaluation in 1949 and before the coming of the Korean War.[15]

Before this recovery, the lack of confidence in sterling's exchange rate was cruelly demonstrated in the summer of 1947, when the freeing of exchange control promised under the 1946 Loan Agreement with the Americans had to be reversed within six weeks because of the downward pressure on the currency.[16] Problems of confidence were also, of course, crucial to the 1949 devaluation.[17] But the Attlee government, however haltingly and reluctantly, was on a path of greater liberalization in international transactions, and such liberalization would be very difficult if confidence remained fragile. From London's point of view, the restoration of currency convertibility relied upon the restoration of confidence, which in turn relied upon not only an improvement in the current account, but crucially upon dealing with the sterling debts (or sterling balances, as they were commonly called)—above all the result of the accumulation of sterling by India, Egypt, and other countries during the war. These debts were seen as a huge threat to the stability of sterling because they were far in excess of the Sterling Area's gold and foreign currency reserves. These balances were run down rapidly by India in the early years of independence, but, very fortunately for Britain, other countries, especially beneficiaries of the Korean boom, offset India's spending of pounds by their own accumulations.[18]

The debates about how to achieve this aim of currency convertibility have been extensively analysed.[19] A crisis point in this area was reached in February 1952, when the Cabinet debated, and then rejected, 'Operation Robot', which would have combined an immediate move to convertibility with the blocking of conversion of most of the sterling balances, combined with a floating of the pound.[20] The rejection of this plan, largely because of its likely consequences in raising both inflation and unemployment, meant a much more gradual policy of movement to convertibility, achieved de facto in 1954, and de jure in 1958. This was combined with almost continual worrying over the sterling balances, with their potential rundown seen as a threat to the value of the pound, until holdings were underpinned by a dollar guarantee under the Basel Agreement of 1968.[21]

13 Rowthorn and Wells, *De-Industrialization*, pp. 96–8, 66–7.
14 Cairncross, *Years*, pp. 499–500.
15 Hence, in part, the suspension of Marshall Aid at the end of 1950.
16 Cairncross, *Years*, ch. 6.
17 Cairncross and Eichengreen, *Sterling*, ch. 4.
18 Schenk, *Britain*, pp. 50–3.
19 Schenk, *Britain*.
20 Burnham, *Remaking*; Middleton, 'Struggling', pp. 120–2; Schenk, *Britain*, pp. 114–19.
21 Tew, 'Policies, pp. 351–2.

The Conservative government elected in 1951 was in principle more enthusiastic about liberalization than its Labour predecessor, but its framing of the international economic dilemma was essentially the same. If the desirability of maintaining the Sterling Area was taken as given, and likewise the expenditure of large sums overseas in pursuit of great power status, then how could the payments position be strengthened to make this possible? This dilemma was all the more intractable because it was taken as read that large-scale foreign investment was not only good for the balance of payments in the long run, but, within the Sterling Area, a key part of the attractiveness of that Area to its overseas members. A final constraint in confronting this issue was the perceived need to build up the reserves in order to improve the international asset:liability ratio.[22] The formal policy response to this conundrum was to lay down targets for surpluses on the current account sufficient to finance government spending, foreign investment, and reserve accumulation. In the early 1950s this target was £200–300 million per annum, and after the disruption of the Korean War, and aided by improved terms of trade, this target was all but reached. As a Bank of England paper pointed out in 1956:

> It has been commonly held since the war that the UK needs a current account surplus on international payments of £200–300 m per annum to keep herself afloat. Few realize how close in fact the UK has come to achieving that surplus. Apart from the exceptional year of 1951 . . . the UK has been is surplus every year since 1947. For 1950–54, [there has been] an average surplus of £229 m if we exclude 1951, £103 m if we include it.[23]

But these seemingly large surpluses were never enough to secure all the desired policy outcomes. Thus in the 1952–5 period, when the current account surplus was calculated at £526 million, a capital outflow of £391 million combined with a rundown of sterling holdings led to a *fall* in the reserves.[24]

The perennial crises which accompanied this pattern of current account surpluses, never quite large enough to avert lack of confidence in the pound, posed both policy and presentational problems for the government. On the policy side the recurrent losses of confidence led to the famous 'stop-go' cycle, with frequent changes in demand management as governments careered between worries about the pound and worries about the level of unemployment.[25] Presentationally, the problem was the need to persuade the country of the importance of 'defending the pound' when the arguments for so doing lacked the compelling 'common-sensical' and moralistic appeal of 1940s-style 'we export to live'. The most sustained attempt to shape public understanding of this issue came in 1957, especially with the publication of the 'popular' pamphlet *The Pound and Our Future* (see Illustration 5).[26]

The publication of this document arose against the background of the economic difficulties that faced the Conservative government from 1955 onwards, involving

[22] TNA: PRO T236/3935, 'Problems of the Sterling Area', 25 June 1956.
[23] TNA: PRO T236/3932, 'The Technical Position of the Pound as it affects the Sterling Area', 24 November 1955.
[24] TNA: PRO T236/3934, 'Sterling Area working party draft Report', 5 June 1956.
[25] Hirsch, *Pound*, pp. 47–9.
[26] Copy in TNA: PRO PREM 11/2047, 'Defence of the Pound and Public Awareness', 1957.

Illustration 5 The moral high ground of a fixed value for the currency (1957).
Source: Image courtesy of the National Archives.

speculative attacks on the pound in the summer of 1955, repeated after the Suez invasion in late 1956 and again in the summer of 1957. These recurrent crises, plus the political debacle of Suez, led to a wide-ranging review of policy.[27] On the domestic front the focus was on the need to slow the rate of inflation—Macmillan's famous 'never had it so good' speech was in fact about the threat to prosperity posed by inflation.[28] But inflation at this point was not accelerating or causing any major domestic discontent; the compelling reason for the government to focus on inflation was its impact on the stability of the pound.[29] This reasoning is nicely exemplified by the Chancellor's memorandum of April 1957, entitled 'Wages, Prices and the Pound Sterling' and which began with the words: 'Under existing policies the question is not whether the pound sterling will be devalued but when'.

[27] Hopkins, 'Macmillan's Audit'; TNA: PRO CAB 129/87, Chancellor of the Exchequer 'Wages, Prices and the Pound Sterling', 27 April 1957; TNA: PRO CAB 129/89, Chancellor of the Exchequer 'The Economic Situation', 14 October 1957.

[28] Horne, *Macmillan, vol. 2*, pp. 64–5.

[29] Green, 'Treasury Resignations', p. 411.

The ensuing argument is that the threat to the pound necessitates a wage policy, although how this is to be framed is left for further discussion.[30]

Both in relation to inflation and to the pound the Conservative government perceived a major problem of 'public awareness'.[31] On the inflation side this led to the 1956 White Paper *Economic Implications of Full Employment*, and its popular version *Must Full Employment Mean Ever-rising Prices?*[32] In the case of the pound it led to *The Pound and Our Future*, with the linking subtitle 'Why We must Protect the Value of Our Money at Home and Abroad'. This pamphlet begins with a general discussion of post-war inflation and the problems it posed. Like most discussions of inflation, the precise harms caused are somewhat vague—as is their severity, described at one point as a 'niggling worry' at another as 'unsettling and dangerous'.[33] But the meat of the paper is an account of the international consequences of inflation leading to devaluation. These are summarized as 'the earning power of our exports suffers in relation to what we have to pay for imports; our food and raw materials cost more and our prices go up; another twist is given to the inflationary spiral at home; and the sterling system is put in jeopardy'.[34] The last of these is the most intriguing, being the most abstract of the alleged consequences. The role of sterling as an international currency is defended as, first, necessary to sustain the volume of world, and hence British, trade. Second, it is argued, the sterling balances are a moral debt we owe to those countries who own this debt. Hence, the resounding finale: 'to keep the pound sterling a reliable piece of money, which we and the world can count on, is our interest and duty'.[35]

II

In the mid-1950s the public face of government policy was a robust defence of the international role of the pound, allied to a focus on the dangers of inflation. The balance of payments issue was not at this stage publicly linked to notions of general economic 'decline', but it was linked to one perceived measure of failing economic performance—Britain's declining share of world trade in manufactures. As discussed in Chapter 2, based on data from the OEEC, this decline and its significance became a source of contention in government advisory circles in the mid-1950s. The propaganda aspect of focusing on this declining share was made clear by the Board of Trade: 'The arguments and comparisons... were those which the Board of Trade must use in its efforts to influence exporters, and the value of export share comparisons must be assessed in that light'.[36] The focus on poor performance in

[30] TNA: PRO CAB 129/87, Chancellor of the Exchequer, 'Wages, Prices and the Pound Sterling', 27 April 1957; TNA: PRO CAB 129/89, Chancellor of the Exchequer, 'The Economic Situation', 14 October 1957.

[31] TNA: PRO PREM11/2047, 'Defence of the Pound and Public Awareness'.

[32] Tomlinson, 'Managing', pp. 563–4. [33] HMT, *Pound*, pp. 3–6.

[34] ibid., p. 10. [35] ibid., p. 16.

[36] TNA: PRO CAB 134/2555, Working Party on Export Trends Economic Section, 'Export Performance and Prospects', 26 March 1957; Board of Trade Export Performance and Prospects', 27 May 1957; Minutes of Working Party, 28 May 1957.

manufactures in the 1950s might in retrospect be thought paradoxical. As already noted, a striking feature of the post-war years was the rapid expansion of manufactured exports to fill the war-induced damage to the invisibles position. Coupled with improvements in agricultural trade following the post-war subsidy regime, the visible account was so strong in the 1950s that 1956 and 1958 saw the first visible surpluses for 140 years, at odds with the 'classic' late nineteenth-century British pattern of a visible deficit being funded by an invisible surplus.[37]

Such evident success was reconcilable with the beginnings of 'declinist' accounts of the balance of payments, partly because of the use of the gloomy 'share of world trade' criteria, and partly because of the emphasis on the need for a large current account surplus to fund government overseas spending and foreign investment. By 1958 the Treasury was raising its target for this surplus from *c.*£300 million to £450 million for the early 1960s.[38] As before, this position was based on a continuation of the policies of encouraging foreign investment, high levels of government overseas spending, and maintaining the pound as an international currency. The wide-ranging Radcliffe report on the workings of the monetary system strongly endorsed this latter objective.[39]

By the end of the 1950s the declinist tide was starting to flow. A key text here was Shonfield's *British Economic Policy since the War* (first published in 1958), which gave a powerful public expression to the view that Britain's slow growth was due to low investment, in turn largely due to excessive overseas ambition by the government, leading to excessive official current spending, excessive investment, and commitment to the Sterling Area with the pernicious consequences of inducing 'stop-go'.[40] Shonfield is commonly regarded as a pioneer in questioning 'official attitudes' to economic policy, including the balance of payments, in the post-war years.[41] As always, precursors can be found, especially the work of Alan Day.[42] More importantly in the current context is the fact that 'official attitudes' were far more questioning of policy than outside critics such as Shonfield alleged. For example, in 1957 Macmillan had expressed scepticism about adherence to the Sterling Area at the time that he was raising broad questions about the benefits of the Empire. He minuted that the future of the Area 'haunts us at every point and makes Foreign policy, Defence policy and Home trade policy very difficult to carry on'; and there were questioning voices in other parts of the government.[43] Similar internal questioning may be found on the related issue of allowing such large-scale foreign investment.[44]

37 Manser, *Britain*, p. 7.

38 Cmnd. 827. There is a complete list of post-war balance-of-payments targets in TNA: PRO T318/457, Appended to 'Publication of Balance of Payments Objectives', 2 February 1971.

39 Cmnd. 827, pp. 240–2.

40 Shonfield, *British*.

41 Hirsch, *Pound*, p. 10.

42 Day, *Future*.

43 TNA: PRO PREM 11/2307, H. Macmillan to Chancellor, 28 October 1957; TNA: PRO PREM 11/3291, T. Bligh to Prime Minister, 25 July 1960. Strange is clearly wrong to suggest 'official questioning of the pound's role only began in 1967', *Sterling*, pp. 75, 303.

44 TNA: PRO CAB 134/1675, Economic Policy Committee, 'Studies on Sterling: capital account', 14 May 1957.

But, despite such questioning, there was little change in policy. Partly this reflected the 'confidence' problem; any *public* questioning of the commitment to the future of sterling would lead to a loss of confidence, with wholly unpredictable consequences for the exchange rate of the pound.[45] Second, in circumstances where its role had been radically reduced, the City was keen to re-establish itself as a major player in the international economy, and, at this time, that role was perceived as closely linked to the value of the pound. Thus the issue of invisible earnings became highly politicized from the late 1950s, as City figures responded to what they saw as the denigration of its contribution to the national economy by radical critics, including Shonfield.[46] Third, in the late 1950s support for sterling was bipartisan; while the emergent critics of 'over-commitment' were predominantly on the Centre-Left, their criticisms were not yet taken up officially by the Labour Party, which remained wedded to defending the international role of the pound.[47] Politically, there were strong pressures to expand overseas expenditure; despite the critics, the Conservatives committed themselves to big increases in foreign aid in the context of accelerating decolonization.[48] Echoing these critics, worries over such commitments were a common theme in the Treasury, but the politics of the situation for the time being outweighed any action on such concerns.[49]

III

From 1960 began the 'great reappraisal' of British policy.[50] Official analysis of the balance of payments around this time spelt out the dilemma which formed a context for that reappraisal. Overseas aid and investment were rising sharply in 1958 and 1959, exceeding the current deficit. On a pragmatic quantitative assessment it was clear that 'The overall deficit thus is, and is likely to remain, too great to cure by practicable reductions in the flow of private investment or Government aid.... *[T]he implication is that domestic measures working on the current account must remain the chief means of keeping the balance of payments in order*'.[51] This analysis was accurate in the sense that attempts to slow the expansion of government spending in the early 1960s were unsuccessful. The ceiling of £400 million for total overseas government expenditure was never effective, and by 1962/3 the figure stood at £475 million.[52]

45 Tomlinson, 'Labour', p. 189.

46 Clarke, *City's*; Committee on Invisible Exports, *Britain's*.

47 Labour Party Archives Re299, 'The Labour Party and the Future of Sterling', 1958; Jenkins, *Labour's Case*.

48 TNA: PRO T236/4066, 'Working Group on Commonwealth Economic Development'; Tomlinson, 'Commonwealth', pp. 417–22.

49 TNA: PRO CAB 134/1687, 'The Balance of Payments and Overseas Commitments', 18 July 1960; CAB 129/101, Chancellor of Exchequer, 'Balance of Payments Prospects and External Investment', 28 March 1960; idem., 'Development Policy', 28 March 1960; discussion in CAB 128/34, Cabinet Conclusions, 13 April 1960.

50 Lowe and Rollings, 'Modernising'.

51 TNA: PRO CAB 134/1407, 'UK External Investment and aid', 12 January 1961, emphasis added.

52 TNA: PRO T277/1320, Treasury Balance of Payments Group, 'Government Expenditure Overseas', 1964.

The inability of the Conservative government to curtail overseas expenditure, or to countenance cuts to foreign investment, led to striking but also unproductive agonizing on the public presentation on the balance of payments. A memo to the Prime Minister in 1960 lamented the 'presentational and psychological damage' done by the focus on the visible account and the reserves, whilst ignoring invisibles and especially the *benefits* of overseas investment: 'during the year we shall increase our net private investment abroad by £275 million. This is nothing to be ashamed of.' The memo concluded, 'There might be a case for a study... of how we could improve the presentation, including overseas, of our economic position. It would be no good leaving it to economists; it should be done by psychologists and publicity experts as well.'[53] But no such study seems to have been undertaken, and the balance-of-payments issue continued to defy being turned into a positive, popular message.

To dilemma of how to finance these continuing external commitments without deflating the domestic economy was to be resolved by policies to promote faster growth, and the increased exports this would hopefully create, and to this end the Macmillan government created the NEDC, as a tripartite forum where this growth could be encouraged.[54] A much amended document was submitted to the new Council in 1962, spelling out the contemporary Treasury perception of the balance of payments to a non-governmental but well-informed audience.[55] This paper is especially informative on official representations of the payments position, partly because it sets out the problem of 'measures of performance' in relation to that position. After noting that the current balance is 'often used' as a measure, it points out that this figure didn't tell policymakers whether they were running into 'exchange difficulties', and advises instead that they should focus on the balance of short-term assets and liabilities. This latter defines a 'balanced monetary position', which, if substantial net foreign investment is to take place, requires a corresponding surplus on the current account. In this framework, the post-war payments problem is defined by the following factors:

(a) Net Government expenditure abroad, both current and capital rose substantially;
(b) There was also a fall in net receipts from private invisible transactions;
(c) With more favourable terms of trade the balance of visibles improved, but this improvement was not sufficient to compensate for the deterioration in (a) and (b).[56]

This is very much the traditional official story, though not how the issue was usually presented to the public. What is also interesting about this document is its studied neutrality on key issues. First, on foreign investment, where it asserts: 'Economists and others are not united in their assessment of the wider effects of overseas investment'. Similar fence-sitting is evident in the discussion of the Sterling Area, for which no defence is offered, and it is merely noted that curtailment of foreign

[53] TNA: PRO PREM 11/3291, PPS to Prime Minister, 'The Balance of Payments and Overseas Commitments', 25 July 1960.
[54] Ringe and Rollings, 'Responding'.
[55] TNA: PRO T308/12, Paper to NEDC, 'The UK Balance of Payments', April 1962.
[56] ibid., pp. 6–7.

investment across the board would undermine one of the main pillars of the Area.[57] There is no such equivocation in the opposition to devaluation, though it is notable that the primary argument made here is the damaging implications for the whole international monetary system, and hence world trade. While harm to the Sterling Area is also noted as a consequence of devaluation, this no longer had the priority it had enjoyed in public pronouncements in the mid-1950s as a reason for defending the value of the currency.[58]

When this paper was discussed at the NEDC there was questioning about the 'fence-sitting' on foreign investment, and, most radically, the suggestion that non-sterling securities owned by British residents should be sold off to finance a 'once-and-for-all' improvement in the reserve position. There was also questioning about why, if the invisible position had weakened in the 1950s, all the government policy focus had been on manufacturing. Above all, the tone was defined by the stated undesirability of sacrificing domestic expansion for balance-of-payments reasons. But while this led to scepticism about the conduct of economic policy, it did not lead on to questions about the key issues of the scale of government spending overseas or the impact of the commitment to the Sterling Area.[59]

The response of the government to such pressures for domestic expansion, alongside the government's own political calculations, was, of course, the Maudling boom of 1962–4.[60] But throughout this boom there was official consciousness of a sharp deterioration in the balance of payments. Analysis made in the run-up to the 1964 election focused attention on both short- and long-term issues. The long-term analysis is important for its problematic combination of argument and data. The argument is one of a straightforward linking of the balance-of-payments position to issues of efficiency:

> Our analysis suggests that our industries, in spite of the very great advances that have been made, still have not shown themselves efficient enough, dynamic enough or competitive enough to accomplish the double task of surmounting all the unfavourable changes that have occurred and are still occurring in our trading position, and at the same time meeting the growing demands we have placed upon them.

This pessimism is linked to the argument that, 'while over the last decade there has been a rough cumulative balance in our external accounts... nevertheless within the last decade or so the trend has been adverse'. But the data reproduced to support this conclusion show a £50 million per annum *improvement* in the balance on visible trade (annual average of 1958–63 compared with 1952–7), and over the same period an improvement in the balance on *private* invisibles of £90 million. The figures make it absolutely clear that the deterioration had come entirely on the official invisibles and official capital accounts, but the discussion of this in the document is cursory in the extreme.[61] Again, the only serious concession is to draw

[57] ibid., p. 35. [58] ibid., pp. 31–2.
[59] TNA: PRO FG2/29 NEDC, 'The UK Balance of Payments', July 1962.
[60] Blackaby, 'Narrative', pp. 23–8.
[61] TNA: PRO T230/639, W. Armstrong, 'Economic Policy: the Balance of Payments', 18 September 1964, covering 'Report on balance of Payments Prospects and Policies', September 1964.

on a separate report of overseas investment which gives some ground to the 'overstretch' critics, it being conceded that some control of foreign investment might be justified on balance-of-payments grounds.[62] However, the issue of government expenditure was seriously examined in official circles at this time, but the diagnosis was gloomy, and no realistic prospects were held out of reducing the upward trend.[63]

IV

The 1964 Labour government came to power amidst a serious balance-of-payments crisis. Analysis of that crisis points up the tensions in governmental characterizations of the nature of the payments problem. On one hand the crisis could be deployed to underpin Labour's message about how the Conservatives had allowed Britain's economic decline to accelerate; in this account, the problem was fundamentally one of inefficiency and lack of competitiveness, for which Labour's policies were the only corrective. Another perspective was that the problem was largely one of 'confidence' in which various malevolent financial interests, the City at home and the 'Gnomes of Zurich' abroad, sought to undermine a Labour government.[64]

The headline problem of 1964 was a balance-of-payments deficit alleged to be £800 million. This figure was never replicated in the published data, and the best starting point for unpicking the balance-of-payments position in 1964 is the (published) visible deficit of £519 million. This was only partly offset by a surplus on invisibles of £143 million. But the government net outflow was £432 million, and there was an outflow of long-term capital of £159 million.[65] It is easy to see from these figures why there was a sterling crisis, but equally evident that the problem was not in any simple sense due to inefficiencies in the British economy. Of course, in the short run the visible balance tends to be the focus of attention as the place where immediately effective action can take place—as it was in 1964, with the introduction of a surcharge on imports. But plainly the roots of the problem lay in an accentuation of the long-term problem of the commercial trading sector of the economy not generating a big enough surplus to pay for all the burdens being placed by investors and above all government on the foreign exchange position.[66] As Thirlwall and Gibson suggest: 'The difficulties of 1964 were cyclical and were on the capital account: they were not the result of forces to be rectified by exchange-rate depreciation.'[67]

62 TNA: PRO T230/639, 'Report on Working Party on Overseas Investment', 1964.

63 TNA: PRO T277/1320, Treasury Balance of Payments Group, 'Balance of Payments Overseas', 1964.

64 Tomlinson, *Labour*, pp. 12–48.

65 *UK Balance of Payments 1971 Pink Book* (London, 1972), tables 1, 2, and 5. The current account deficit was subsequently progressively revised downwards, reaching £327 million in 2005: *Economic Trends 2005*.

66 Manser, *Britain* gives this point a particular ideological edge by contrasting the private sector surplus with the government sector deficit.

67 Thirlwall and Gibson, *Balance*, p. 235.

Despite such analysis, most accounts of the Labour government's response to this crisis in the three years after their election focus on what was *not* done; the failure to devalue.[68] In the current context what is important is the way that decision was linked to particular accounts of the nature of the payments problem. Overwhelmingly, the argument was conducted around the current account, and usually, if sometimes implicitly, the visible account. Wilson's pithy 'it's time exporters got off their backsides and worked for Britain' fitted with more extended narratives which posed devaluation as an inferior way of improving competitiveness compared with measures to enhance efficiency—a 'third way' between currency change and deflation. This is set out in the foreword to the 1965 *National Plan* in the following terms: 'The most serious economic problem facing us at the present time is the balance of payments. We have to eliminate the deficit and repay the debts incurred in financing past deficits.... [W]e shall only get the exports we need to do this by becoming more efficient and competitive.'[69] In the body of the *Plan* the story is rather different. Four recent trends in accounting for current problems are listed. First, a 'heavy and growing deficit on the Government's net expenditure abroad'. Second, 'a persistent net outflow of long-term capital'. Third, slow-growing exports. Slowness is measured both by inadequacy 'to sustain the rate of growth of which we are physically capable', and by a falling share of world trade in manufactures. Finally, a problem of rapidly growing imports of manufactures is stressed.[70] The first two of these are straightforward recognition of the features of policy noted above. The third sets up highly contentious measures of export 'failure'. The notion of a physical capacity for growth assumes it is exports which are the limiting factor, but it might well be the case that the limiting factor is the supply of skilled labour, and exports the dependent variable. Simply asserting that if exports had expanded faster the whole economy would have benefitted begs all the important questions. And as noted above, it is not clear what sense there is in making the share of world exports a measure of performance if the current account is in surplus. The final measure, the rising share of manufactured goods in imports could again be thought odd. As total trade was shifting towards a greater element of manufactures, accompanied by a falling share of primary products in imports, rising imports of manufactures are not good evidence of 'failure'.[71]

Other government publications showed a similar mixture of comprehensive representation of the problem at some points, but a tendency to accentuate the visibles problem at others. For example, *Working for Prosperity*, the popular version of the *Plan*, also had a foreword from George Brown which began: 'Britain has one overriding economic necessity. We must pay our way in the world and to do this we must increase our production. We must sell a greater amount overseas and hold

[68] Bale, 'Dynamics'.

[69] Cmnd. 2764, foreword by George Brown, p. iii.

[70] Cmnd. 2764, p. 70.

[71] The balance on primary products fell from a deficit of 12.4 per cent of GDP in 1951–5 to 7.1 per cent in 1961–5, and 5.7 per cent in 1966–70; Rowthorn and Wells, *De-industrialization*, p. 98. Partly this was the consequence of agricultural protection, which, alongside North Sea oil, had by the early 1980s helped Britain become self-sufficient in primary products for the first time since the industrial revolution.

steady and even reduce the prices at which we can profitably do this.' While the issues of overseas government spending and investment are covered, the discussion comes after a long section saying the key issue is to raise exports.[72] Similarly, the DEA's *Progress Report* in its first number in 1965, while making the case for an incomes policy, highlighted the export issue, and included the perennial representational favourite of a graph showing Britain's declining share of world trade in manufactures.[73] At a more popular level, the government-produced factory wall newspaper *Upswing*, after asserting 'Nearly all our exports are manufactured goods—particularly machinery', went on to argue that, 'Although our exports are big they are not big enough. Last year we had to borrow large sums from other countries because we were not earning enough to pay for our spending overseas' (see Illustration 6).[74]

As the summary of the *Plan*'s detailed diagnosis of the payments makes clear, the government in its policymaking was by no means ignoring the non-visibles aspects. In the discussion of the policies that flowed from this diagnosis the government committed itself to cutting overseas defence expenditure, to scrutinizing the aid programme with 'particular care', and to reducing overseas investment.[75] This was path-breaking; these intentions had never been spelt out so clearly in public before. But, as under the Conservatives, turning intentions into outcomes proved very difficult, certainly in the short run. The Treasury had been opposed to writing quantitative targets into the *National Plan* on these kinds of points precisely because it didn't believe they were likely to be delivered—and they were right.[76] Aid was cut back briefly in 1967 to 1969, but then began to grow again.[77] A decision to cut planned overseas military expenditure was made in 1966, but did not progress far until after devaluation, and foreign investment continued to fluctuate but with a clear upward trend despite increased restrictions, and exhortation.[78]

These short-run failures to deliver economies may be linked to particular circumstances. For example, the continuation of high overseas military spending followed from the crisis with Indonesia, the growth of economic aid reflected the strongly pro-Commonwealth enthusiasm of many in the Labour Party, an enthusiasm commonly grounded in the belief in that body as the channel through which Britain should commit itself to helping development.[79] Also in play in the early years after 1964 was an ambiguity about the Sterling Area. While opinion in the party was divided on this issue, the Commonwealth enthusiasm made itself felt in encouraging the view that the Area (almost coterminous with the Commonwealth) was a 'burden' that a progressive Britain should bear in the name of international

72 DEA, *Working*, pp. 2, 9.

73 HMT, *Progress Report* no. 1, January 1965, p. 3; no. 10, October 1965, p. 1.

74 DEA, *Upswing*, no. 1, February 1966, p. 1.

75 Cmnd. 2764, pp. 71–2.

76 TNA: PRO T230/740, P. Vinter to O. Clarke, 'The National Plan', 2 August 1965.

77 *Annual Abstract of Statistics* 110 (1973) showed a peak of £215.2 million in 1966/7, falling to £207.3 in 1968/9, with 1969/70 at £218 million.

78 *Pink Book*, 1971.

79 Morgan, 'Imperialism', p. 242. On Labour and the Commonwealth more generally, see Alexander, 'Tale'.

UPSWING

25% MORE OUTPUT BY 1970

NO. 2 1966

PREPARED BY THE DEPARTMENT OF ECONOMIC AFFAIRS

SPEEDING THE EXPORTS

DELAYS to export cargoes can mess up the hard work put in on the shop floor to meet delivery dates for export orders. Britain sells over £5 million of exports a day to Europe and it is vital that British trade to the Continent moves swiftly and easily.

The *Little Neddy* on the movement of exports has backed a number of ways of speeding exports. One way is greater use of special ships to take loaded lorries overseas. The lorries roll on at British ports and off at the other end.

SINGLE LOADS

Finding and getting rid of the bottlenecks which delay our exports is the task of the ***Little Neddy*** for the movement of exports. After a year's work, it places greatest emphasis on new ways of transporting export cargoes in single loads by packing them on pallets or in containers which are lifted on and off the ships—or by the "roll on roll off" method. Containers can be passed quickly through the customs and distributed. This saves time and labour at Britain's ports and also reduces the cost.

Port information centres, already in action at London and Liverpool, can tell exporters about the best moment to ship their cargoes and so save jams at the docks.

Export orders are being carried more and more by air and the ***Little Neddy*** thinks that provincial airports will have to be developed in key industrial centres.

IMPROVEMENTS

The ***Little Neddy*** is looking at the need to improve roads and to ensure that ports have the right sort of cranes and other equipment to deal with new techniques of cargo carrying. The modernisation of a number of Britain's ports is already under way.

MEN AND JOBS

The main brake on the increase in our prosperity between now and 1970 is likely to be shortage of manpower. So it does not make sense that in parts of the country like North East and South West England, Scotland and Wales, less than full use is being made of people who are fit for work while in places like London and the Midlands there are more jobs than people to fill them.

What can we do about it?

We can steer more industry into areas where jobs are scarce. Results can already be seen, for example, in the new motor factories in Scotland and on Merseyside.

We can make it easier for people to move to find work and if necessary retrain them. Firms must now make cash payments to workers made redundant. The Ministry of Labour has a Resettlement Transfer Scheme to help some of those who are unemployed or who may become redundant. It has a Key Workers Scheme to help workers to move with their employers to a factory being set up in a Development District with Board of Trade help. It has a Nucleus Labour Force scheme to help unemployed workers from areas of high unemployment, who are given a spell of training at their new employers' parent factory.

Management and unions must work together to ensure efficient use of men and machines.

Upswinging

Copies of the first issue of UPSWING were sent to 26,000 firms, to the nationalised industries and to the trade unions. As a result regular orders for 150,000 copies have been placed from all over Britain and from all types of industry. The response was much bigger than was expected and two reprints have been necessary. UPSWING will be published approximately every two months and the background colour will be changed each time so that you can easily spot a new issue. Additional copies can be ordered from Publications Division, Central Office of Information, Hercules Road, London, S.E.1.

ACTION on the Plan

In each issue UPSWING reports progress on an item from the National Plan's check list. This time the subject is prospects of quick progress in achieving standardisation, variety reduction and longer production runs.

Making goods to approved standards of performance, quality and size means that the customer benefits by getting a better-designed product. The factory can gain great advantage by concentrating men and machines on long runs of a few products.

WHAT IS BEING DONE?

The "Little Neddies" are now studying the manufacturing standards needed in particular industries and the Government are helping the British Standards Institution to make a major revision of British industrial standards.

Government Departments, as industry's biggest customers, are trying to standardise many of their requirements over a wide field. The Ministry of Technology is encouraging industry to change over to the metric system of measurement in Britain.

The Nationalised industries have standardised many of their stores items. The Electricity Boards and the electricity supply industry have agreed to reduce the types of transmission cables up to 22,000 volts from 250 to under 50.

Private firms are becoming more "standardisation conscious".

THE BIGGER THE BETTER

Britain's electricity supply industry has been leading Europe in using very large generating sets, which produce electricity at high efficiency. British manufacturers have developed single shaft generators of 500 M.W. and over (more than two-thirds of a million horse power each). The picture shows blades for steam turbines for generators up to 500 M.W. Sets of large generators have been supplied to the U.S.A. and ordered by Australia, Canada and South Africa. Britain exported generating machinery and switchgear last year worth nearly £87 million.

Prepared by the Department of Economic Affairs and the Central Office of Information

Illustration 6 A 1960s innovation, the wall newspaper (1966).
Source: Image courtesy of the National Archives.

responsibility.[80] By 1966 enthusiasm for the Commonwealth was waning, the end of the Malaysian emergency facilitated a fundamental rethink of East-of-Suez policy, and the question of a reorientation of policy towards membership of the EEC was becoming paramount. But it was not until devaluation that these issues were decisively addressed.[81]

[80] Balogh, *Unequal*. [81] Jones, 'Decision'.

In the interval between the National Plan and devaluation on November 1967 the government actively pursued the theme of enhancing efficiency, even if the *Plan* itself was quickly derailed by the deflation of summer 1966 in response to yet another sterling crisis. Much of the rhetoric and policy in this area placed central focus on productivity, which became a key term in policy debates in these years. This focus was grounded in a range of converging conditions, but it fitted well with the arguments that the payments problem was essentially one of Britain's lagging productivity. There are many examples of this in, for example, *Target*, the paper of the BPC. The January 1965 edition was headlined 'first task is to stimulate progress' and began with the sentence: 'The vital need to increase productivity is receiving a spate of publicity stimulated by Britain's economic position—by which is meant our industrial ability and social affluence relative to our competitors in the world's markets.' The May 1966 edition under the heading 'Why we must produce more' directly linked the target of a current account surplus of £250 million to the productivity campaign.[82] Editorially very much aligned with the government, the *Daily Mirror* bluntly made the same link in a headline in September 1966: 'First of all—productivity is the new catchword. But there's no catch. Failure to increase productivity is what has put this country on the rocks'.[83]

But whatever their other, longer-term effects, the attempts to defend the pound by increased efficiency and productivity failed, and in November 1967 the pound was devalued. This is the only episode in the saga of the post-war balance of payments whose popular representation has been seriously researched. Blaazer shows how the government was drawn into propagating the position that the value of the pound equated to the 'strength of Britain', and that the defence of the existing parity was like a military battle.[84] However, he makes the crucial point that this representation may have had little impact on popular understanding, which saw the value of the pound largely in terms of its impact on the standard of living.[85] But it is nevertheless important to note that the 'battle' metaphor functioned to suggest that the issue was one of competitiveness, and reinforced the linkage between balance-of-payments difficulties and national 'decline'.[86]

After devaluation there was no immediate improvement in the balance of payments, and indeed a serious problem lasted well into 1969.[87] Only slowly did the increase in competitiveness brought about by devaluation, coupled to the deflation and diversion of resources that followed, underpin an export expansion.[88] The devaluation and deflation, and the crisis which occurred before these policies

[82] *Target* 18, 1 January 1965, p. 1; *Target* 19, 5 May 1966, p. 4.
[83] *Daily Mirror*, 27 September 1966, p. 2.
[84] Blaazer, '"Devalued"'. [85] Bale, 'Dynamics', pp. 201–11.
[86] On the linking of the balance of payments to metaphors of decline (especially medical) see Blaazer, '"Devalued"', pp. 129–31.
[87] Talk of a target of current account surplus of £500 million for 1969 was abandoned in April of that year. TNA: PRO T318/275, H. Copeman to A. Figgures, 11 April 1969; 'Oh, what a lovely surplus' *Economist*, 13 September 1969.
[88] By late 1969 there was hubristic talk of the 'largest surplus ever': T318/282, 'Review of the UK's Balance of Payments, Past and Present 1969/70', 10 March 1970.

were effective, led to major changes in Britain's international policy. The withdrawal from East of Suez was speeded up, the external role of sterling sustained only by the guaranteeing of the sterling balances by the 1968 Basel agreement.[89] In this way some key elements of the 'overstretch' problem were addressed, although foreign aid, overseas military expenditure, and foreign investment continued to expand until the end of the 'golden age' in 1973.[90]

With the balance-of-payments problem 'solved', the early 1970s saw a focus of government economic propaganda elsewhere, not least on inflation, which was on a rising trend from 1968 (see Chapter 8). But the rapid expansion of the economy from 1972 brought a deterioration in the payments position which, in the context of the American decision to cut away from fixed exchange rates, led to the floating of the pound in June 1972. This opened up a whole new debate about the balance of payments, and its links to economic 'decline'. On one hand it was argued that with floating rates the 'artificial' problem of the balance of payments driven by the attempt to fix a market price for the currency would be wholly removed.[91] On the other, there was a view that the focus on the current account would be particularly inappropriate in a world of much expanded capital flows, especially in the wake of the oil crisis.[92] In the short run the authorities stuck with current account targets. But much debate ensued on how these were to be interpreted.[93] Whether there existed a balance-of-payments problem in Britain was to remain a hardy perennial of economic policy arguments in the 1980s, especially as a purported measure of the success or failure of the Thatcher government's policies.[94]

V

Such arguments underpinned a change in the policy paradigm surrounding the balance of payments in the mid to late 1980s. The political economy of the Thatcher governments held as an article of faith that, 'provided that the overall fiscal, monetary and exchange rate framework is sound, and markets are working effectively, the results of the private sector's economic activity should not normally be something in which it is sensible for the government to interfere'.[95]

Significantly for our purposes, Lawson as Chancellor sought to apply this principle to balance-of-payments policy in a novel manner. This hinged upon the distinction between public and private activity. Lawson argued at the time of the UK current account deficit in 1988 that 'the government's own finances are very sound indeed.

[89] The guarantee offered to sterling holders by the Basel agreement led to a growth in these balances from 1968 to 1972: Burk and Cairncross, *Goodbye*, pp. 11–12.

[90] Tew, 'Policies', pp. 319–37.

[91] Brittan, *Price*; Zis, 'Elusive Case'.

[92] TNA: PRO T318/458, M. Beenstock, 'Oil Price Increases and the UK Balance of Payments', 18 December 1973.

[93] TNA: PRO T338/102, 'Suggested Method of Full Employment Balance of Payments Surplus', 1971; T318/407, 'Medium-Term Balance of Payments Objectives: 1972 Review', 13 April 1972; T318/457, 'Publication of Balance of Payments Objectives', 2 February 1972; T318/420, A. Budd, 'Balance of Payments Contribution to the Medium Term Assessment', 14 February 1972.

[94] Lawson, *State*; Coutts and Godley, 'Does?', pp. 60–7.

[95] Lawson, *State*, p. 16.

The public sector finances are more or less in balance... so the current account deficit is clearly not associated with excessive spending or borrowing by government.' Lawson continued:

> some see a current account deficit... as a sign of economic weakness—'Britain in the red', as the newspaper headlines are wont to put it. But of course a current account deficit is manifestly not at all like a company running at a loss. A better analogy is with a profitable company raising funds overseas—either borrowing, or reducing its holdings of overseas assets, or attracting new equity. A company with greater investment opportunities than it could finance from retained profits would look for additional funds from outside. A country in a similar position will draw on the savings of the world, which is particularly easy in today's global markets.[96]

Thus in 1988, a year described by one commentator as 'the *annus terribilis* of Britain's external accounts', Lawson took the view that the current account deficit was

> entirely the result of private individuals and businesses making choices about their own financial affairs.... [P]rovided the firm financial framework is in place, a period of private sector induced current account deficit should give no cause for concern, particularly given this country's exceptionally high levels of net overseas assets.[97]

Lawson's 'studied indifference to the balance of payments'[98] effectively meant that he simply did not recognize there to be any balance-of-payments constraints on his stewardship of the UK economy, despite assertions by many economic studies at the time that the government *should* have been alive to the possibility of these.[99] Lawson's characterization of the current account deficit as 'benign and self-correcting' shows how subject to change 'the determination that a particular country is running a chronic payments deficit or surplus' can be, and that changing approaches to this process of determination can effect the 'very serious international political implications' which are deemed to follow from payments imbalance.[100]

The sizeable current account deficits registered continuously after 1987, Snowden and Milner noted in 1992, were, 'in marked contrast to earlier epochs' being 'financed without drama by an increasingly integrated global capital market'. Indeed, given the availability of capital market financing, 'the question arises when, if at all, current account deficits should be a matter of policy concern'. Their conclusion was that 'international creditworthiness, rather than a country's underlying wealth, is the operative constraint'.[101] Paradoxically, it was the temporary return to fixed exchange rates in the ERM in 1990–2 which helped to bring about a major improvement in the current account, by causing a major recession in the economy.

A rather different gloss on the policies of this period was given by the Permanent Secretary to the Treasury in 1996. In a broad survey of economic policy, he argued that 'since the late 1970s' macroeconomic policy had become much less ambitious, and one of the lost ambitions was the attempt to treat reducing

96 ibid., pp. 16, 17. 97 Johnson, *Economy*, p. 210; Lawson, *State*, p. 18.
98 Johnson, *Economy*, p. 208.
99 Coutts and Godley, 'Does?'; McCombie and Thirlwall, 'Comment', pp. 68–74.
100 Block, *Origins*, p. 140. 101 Snowden and Milner, 'External', pp. 1, 2.

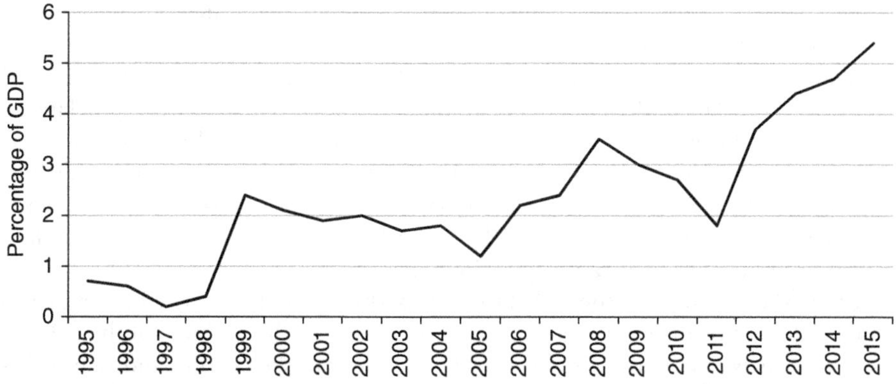

Figure 9.1 Current account deficit as a percentage of GDP, 1995–2015
Source: ONS *Balance of Payments Pink Book*, 2016.

the balance-of-payments deficit as a policy goal.[102] This account, and its implication that the payments position will be self-correcting if the monetary and fiscal framework is got right, aligned comfortably with the prevailing neo-liberal political economic orthodoxy of the 1980s and 1990s.

After the accession of New Labour in 1997, the current account showed almost continuous deterioration as the economy experienced uninterrupted growth (see Figure 9.1). This deterioration evoked little publicly expressed anxiety. Some commentators argued that this deficit reflected continuing weaknesses in underlying performance, but these views received little prominence or support.[103] The government's position, unsurprisingly, emphasized the 'fiscal theory of the deficit', because the Keynesian policies of budget deficit financing pursued under Gordon Brown were pursued rather defensively, and the argument that they had consequences for the payments position has not found favour.[104] Instead, the government emphasized the ease of financing of the deficit because their policies made Britain such an attractive destination for foreign investment. For example, in the years before the financial crisis, the *Financial Statement and Budget Report* for 2007 noted the trade deficit of 4.5 per cent of GDP in 2006, and then simply stated that 'Significant income surpluses continued to offset the deficit on trade in goods and services', leading to a current account deficit of 3 per cent.[105] There follows a detailed discussion of how Britain continues to have a substantial surplus on foreign investment income, despite having substantially more international investment liabilities than assets.[106] Implicit in this story was that squaring the payments circle relied upon Britain combining high levels of attractiveness to foreign investment with lower levels of return on those investments than British companies are earning on their

[102] Burns, 'Managing', pp. 3–4. [103] McCombie and Thirlwall, *Essays*.
[104] Clift and Tomlinson, 'Credible Keynesianism?'
[105] HMT, *Financial Statement* 2007, p. 260.
[106] ibid., pp. 261–2. For the complexities of the capital account in recent years, see Key et al., 'Property Income'.

foreign assets. There is no discussion of the sustainability of this investment position, nor of the current account.

Under the Coalition government after 2010 the need to raise exports and improve the balance-of-payments position was one gloss put on the proclaimed intention of this government to 'rebalance' the economy.[107] However, insofar as 'rebalancing' had more than rhetorical significance, it lay in relation to the shrinking of the public sector, as discussed in Chapter 5. Talk of 'the balance-of-payments problem' was not a feature of the 2015 general election campaign, any more than it had been of other such campaigns since the 1970s.

From Manser's work at the end of the 1960s, through to Lawson's Chancellorship in the 1980s, a recurrent neo-liberal argument was that the problem of the balance of payments is essentially a problem of government misbehaviour, and that if this is reformed, and free markets sustained, the virtues of the private sector will effectively abolish the payments problem. This position seems in turn to have been adopted by New Labour. Talk of 'rebalancing' after the financial crisis notwithstanding, we have, it can be argued, a continuation as regards the balance of payments, of 'the economics of Dr Pangloss'.[108]

VI

The preceding narrative suggests we should be highly sceptical about arguments that golden age balance-of-payments problems can readily be interpreted as signs of economic inefficiency and 'decline', and equally that the lack of attention to the balance of payments since the 1970s is evidence that 'decline' has been halted. In the golden age Britain normally ran a current account surplus, using this position to rebuild an enormous portfolio of foreign assets (see Figure 9.2). Throughout the period the surplus on manufacturing trade was substantial, and much larger than in 1938 relative to GDP. Private sector services were weaker than before the war, but relative to GDP recovered by the late 1960s.[109] Overall, Britain's trade showed a great ability to restructure itself in terms of both commodities and markets, offsetting the huge damage from the war; a point worth emphasizing against the weight of declinist myth-making.

The problem then was not internationally competing goods and services sectors but government spending, coupled to net overseas investment. The issue here is not whether the policy objectives that caused the payments problem were desirable or not. Rather, the point is that the problem was of a different kind to that commonly represented by government at the time, and commonly presented by subsequent commentators. On contemporary representations, the argument is not that governments were dishonest in how they told the story of the balance of payments, but rather that most of the time they found it much easier in their propaganda to link payments issues to domestic economic efficiency and competitiveness than

[107] Froud et al., 'Rebalancing'. [108] Buiter, 'Economics'.
[109] Rowthorn and Wells, *De-industrialization*, p. 98.

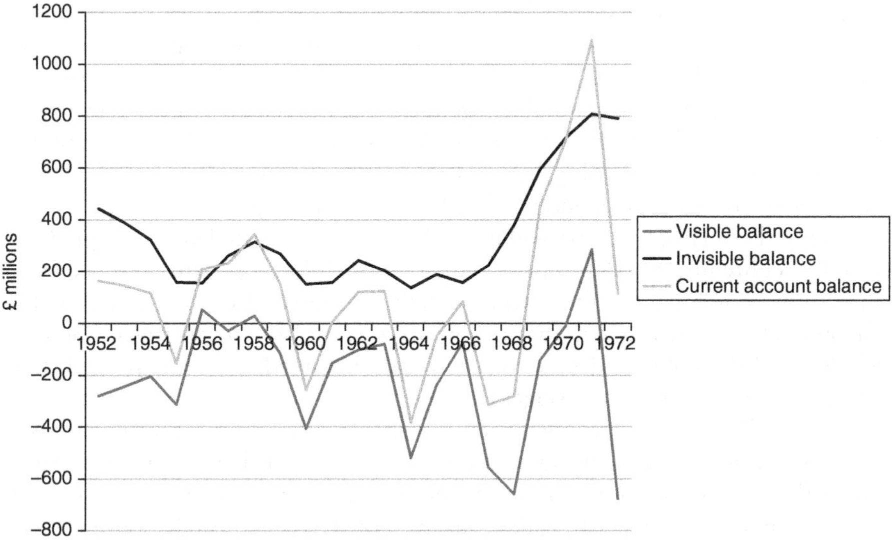

Figure 9.2 The current account in the 'golden age' (1952–72)
Source: ONS *Balance of Payments Pink Book*, 1974.

to expound to the public the case for continuing with foreign-exchange-using policies. In turn, this linkage appealed because it fitted with pre-existing discourses about the economy, which became embedded in the post-war policy debate. Representations of the payments position were also constrained by the need to placate capital markets.[110] These debates focused upon the desirability of faster growth to be delivered by higher efficiency allied to wage restraint. From the late 1950s this took a new turn as 'decline' was diagnosed and rapidly became accepted as an underpinning assumption of most economic argument. In this environment it was only too easy to link the payments problems to this notion of 'decline', and few resisted the temptation.[111] Most subsequent commentators have simply followed suit, testimony to the power of the declinist mindset that has dominated so much economic debate.

If the recurrent problem of the balance of payments in the 1950s and 1960s was not mainly due to a lack of competitiveness, it can certainly be said to have been a consequence of 'overstretch'; of Britain trying to do too much with too few resources. Recognition of this problem came not only from critics of policy; policymakers saw it too. Hence the persistent attempts to build current account surpluses, surpluses which in the event were never big enough to fulfill governmental ambitions for reserve accumulation, overseas spending, and investment. The overstretch thesis was publicly well established from the late 1950s, but like so much argument of the time it tied

[110] For example, TNA: PRO PREM 18/852, 'Economic Strategy', 15 April 1966.
[111] Caves, *Britain's*, pp. 317–18.

its diagnosis to the highly problematic notion of 'decline'. Thus in Shonfield's foundation text on overstretch, the excessive ambitions of government cause the low investment which in his view is the key explanation of decline.[112] The problem here is that (a) decline on the scale suggested never happened; and (b) some of the alleged links from decline to 'overstretch' didn't occur. In particular, as Schenk has persuasively argued, the Sterling Area had a much less damaging impact upon British economic performance than Shonfield and many others alleged.[113]

In sum, the very partial representation of the payments problem which predominated in contemporary debate, and which has so influenced what has been said since, built upon but also in turn reinforced the 'culture of decline'. As suggested in Chapter 2, this is the problem that all narratives about Britain's post-war economic policies, and the political debates that have accompanied and underpinned these narratives, need to put centre stage.

Since the Thatcher government the payments position has been little discussed in policy circles. This is usually rationalized as reflecting the floating of the exchange rate in the early 1970s. Yet there seems more to the story than this. As suggested, there was never a single, self-evident 'balance-of-payments problem' even in the years of the fixed exchange rate. And since the move to floating there has been a switch to policy discourses which in principle believe that 'market forces' in foreign exchange as elsewhere are the solvent of economic problems; in that universe the balance of payments has to be regarded as a 'non-problem': 'the balance of payments always balances'.

Because of these doctrinal alignments, concern with the payments position has come to be almost entirely confined to sceptics of the efficacy of market forces. In academic discussion of economic policy, it is usually seen as a significant issue only by those who see payments deficits as one of the signs of the damage done by deindustrialization.[114] This term, and its significance for narratives of post-war Britain, is discussed in Chapter 10.

[112] Shonfield, *British*. [113] Schenk, *Britain*.
[114] Kitson and Michie, 'De-industrial'.

10

Conclusions

Old and New Narratives

The dominance of the narratives discussed in this volume was contingent. The prominence of each narrative relied on complex combinations of changing economic structures and events, political and ideological changes, and shifts in economic understanding. All of them spread and mutated as their conditions of existence waxed and waned, and other narratives (sometimes overlapping) came into play.

They are not the only narratives that have existed. This chapter examines two others that, whilst never predominant, have recently developed a role in understandings of post-war Britain. In different ways they offer alternative, overarching accounts of British economic life that deserve to be examined seriously. This examination will also allow us to draw together many of the themes from this book.

The two narratives operate in rather different registers. First, the 'rise of neo-liberalism'. Neo-liberalism is a term almost always used only by *critics* of how Britain has developed over the last forty or so years. It has become a hugely influential narrative in academic circles, but, unlike those discussed in the preceding chapters has had little resonance with governments or a wider public. It offers a story locating a fundamental turning point in economic life in the 1970s, when Britain is said to have moved from a broadly social-democratic to a neo-liberal policy regime, characterized above all by the erosion of the role of the state and the unleashing of market forces.[1]

The second narrative, of deindustrialization, identifies not a revolution in political ideas about the economy but a structural shift; a shift that is said to have underpinned many of the other changes in economic life. In the 1970s deindustrialization briefly became a prominent topic of debate, but this quickly faded.[2] It has been less widely used as an overarching framework by academics than neo-liberalism, but there is a growing body of work that sees it as having major significance in understanding post-war Britain.

I

'Neo-liberalism' is a term rooted in economics. As suggested in Chapter 3, as a doctrine it can be seen as combining elements of a number of strands of thought,

[1] Crouch, *Strange*; Prasad, *Politics*.

[2] Bacon and Eltis, *Britain's*; this book first appeared as series of articles in the *Sunday Times*. For a critique: Hadjimatheou and Skouras, 'Britain's'; alternative 1970s views are in Blackaby, *De-industrialisation*; Singh, 'UK'.

most importantly neoclassical economics, ordoLiberalism, and Austrian economics. The addition of public choice theory added an extra, powerful, component. But as also suggested in that chapter, the spread of the doctrine was aided from the early post-war years by its allies in business and politics. It did not suddenly come from nowhere to capture the policymaking agenda in the 1970s. Furthermore, its capture of that agenda cannot be understood except in the context of the circumstances of that decade, and how the experience of rapid inflation and ballooning public deficits was constructed as an indictment of the 'Keynesian welfare state'. In these circumstances, a reinvigorated, right-wing, declinist narrative opened the space for the new pro-market doctrines to flourish.[3]

But to what extent did this doctrinal flourishing turn into policy success? While policy did change in the 1970s, how far was that change deep enough to justify the view that neo-liberalism 'triumphed'? Chapter 3 on rolling back the state has suggested some limits to that triumph. There has been no fiscal 'race to the bottom': public spending did *not* fall after the 1970s. Keynesianism was not permanently defeated, as the expansionary fiscal responses to the crises of the early 1990s and 2008–10 demonstrate; despite globalization, the room for manoeuvre of national economic policy has remained substantial.

This is not to dispute that neo-liberal ideas have been significant underpinnings to some hugely important changes in post-1970s Britain. As Avner Offer has persuasively argued, one of the most striking economic (and social) changes in Britain since the 1970s has been the multiplication of private debt. He argues that this is linked to a switch away from a broadly social-democratic notion of collective risk-bearing, to one of individuals having to provide as best they can for life's contingencies, which has commonly meant debt accumulation, an important aspect of the wider phenomenon of 'financialization', a key shift in corporate structure and behaviour.[4]

Alongside the multiplication of debt, the outstanding effect of the change in policy at the end of the 1970s was the profound increase in inequality in the following decade.[5] The scale of this shift seems to have resulted from a conjunction of forces: as Hills notes, 'most of the factors determining income distribution were pushing in the same direction'.[6] But while the shift was not all policy-driven, there is no doubt that neo-liberal policies made a substantial contribution, and this was consonant with the ideological assault on the pursuit of greater equality by social democracy.

The biggest problem in making the 'triumph of neo-liberalism' the defining narrative about post-war Britain is that its triumph has been constrained by changes in circumstances, especially changes in industrial structure almost entirely beyond its control. In other words, the second narrative to be discussed, deindustrialization, in part derives its explanatory strength from the understanding it can offer about a key change which has cut across and constrained the pursuit of neo-liberal policies.

[3] The term 'market fundamentalism' is in many ways more helpful than 'neo-liberalism', as it emphasizes the visceral, ideological anti-statism which animated much of this shift, rather than the 'rational' and doctrinal underpinnings.

[4] Froud et al., *Financialization*; Offer, 'Market turn'; Offer, 'Narrow'.

[5] Gazeley, 'Income', pp. 154–63.

[6] Hills, 'Introduction', p. 11.

II

Deindustrialization can be used in different senses, but the one which seems most useful is that which defines it in terms of a radical decline in the proportion of the workforce in industrial employment.[7]

Why should we focus on these changing patterns of employment? Primarily because of their links to economic welfare. The post-war period, despite the hopes of some, has not seen the demise of the reliance of the great bulk of the population on wage income. There has been a clear failure to move to 'asset-based' welfare, and with recent postponements in state pensions, the ending of final salary occupational schemes, and the extension of working lives, this situation is likely to continue.[8] In a different register, the project of a 'property-owning democracy', long espoused by Conservatives and some elements of the Centre-Left, has turned out in practice to have results almost entirely in housing.[9] While this has given economic security to some, it has distributed that security unevenly, and may have contributed to macroeconomic instability.[10] So the traditional understanding that under capitalism most people continue to rely on waged work for economic welfare remains fundamentally right.

For the purposes of the current argument we are concerned with economic sectors which, historically, have offered large amounts of regular, relatively well-paid employment to working-class people with limited formal educational qualifications. Or, to put it another way, the sectors of employment which historically underpinned the existence of a distinctive industrial working class. In other words, deindustrialization is defined here to try and capture the belief that as a process it had both major economic welfare *and* broader political economy consequences.

With this logic in mind, we here treat deindustrialization as concerned with decline in employment in industry, which as officially defined equals manufacturing plus mining plus construction. This is the figure which is most widely available and on a comparative basis. But while the same kind of systematic data are not available if we extend the definition, we might also want to include in our narrative some recognition of employment in railways and utilities, which fall outside that definition of industry, but could be included on the basis outlined in the previous paragraph.[11] Even this extended category does not, of course, include all manual workers, excluding as it does those in the service sector and agriculture. Equally obviously, it does not equate with the whole of the working class in the broadest

[7] Blackaby, *De-industrialisation*; Rowthorn and Wells, *De-industrialization*; Singh, 'UK industry'; for an updated analysis, Coutts and Rowthorn, 'UK Balance of Payments'; Rowthorn and Ramaswamy, 'Growth'.

[8] Froud et al., 'Escaping'. [9] Jackson, 'Revisionism'.

[10] On the distribution, Hood and Joyce, 'Economic'; Wadsworth, 'Eyes'. On the destabilizing effects of the housing market: Offer, 'Narrow'.

[11] Broadberry, *Market*, p. 34 calculates that employment in transport and communications fell from 7.9 per cent of the labour force in 1950 to 5.5 per cent in 1990.

sense of all those largely reliant on wage labour, which would amount to over 80 per cent of the population.[12]

Individual industries have, of course, declined from the beginning of industrial capitalism; here the focus is on overall sectoral contraction. Saul talked about deindustrialization before the First World War, but while the service sector was growing at this time, this was primarily at the expense of agriculture.[13] Numbers in industry declined after 1921 with the collapse of the old staples, but overall services growth was constrained by the rapid decline of domestic service. Industrial employment surged during the Second World War to levels only matched in Germany, and initially this level was sustained by protective devices needed to offset the balance-of-payments consequences of wartime losses of foreign assets. Peak employment in industry came in the 1950s, when declines in textiles, coal, and railways began to be significant (see Table 10.1).[14] Manufacturing employment peaked in the following decade.[15]

What has replaced these industrial jobs is a much more polarized structure of jobs in the service sector; 'lovely and lousy' jobs.[16] Lousy jobs are defined by being very poorly paid, as well as often being subject to highly variable hours and insecurity of tenure, and subject to overweening managerial authority.

What is the significance if this for neo-liberalism? A core belief of British neo-liberals in the 1970s and 1980s was that unemployment was in large part the consequence of unemployment pay being too high relative to wages, so incentivizing the unemployed not to seek work.[17] From this premise followed the policy of reducing unemployment pay (pursued from 1981). The other side of this coin was

Table 10.1 Western European industrial employment

	Peak year	Percentage in industry in peak year	Percentage in industry in 1998	Percentage fall, peak to 1998
UK	1955	47.9	26.6	44.5
Belgium	1957	47.0	26.1	44.5
Switzerland	1964	48.8	26.3	46.1
Netherlands	1965	41.1	22.2	46.0
Sweden	1965	42.8	25.7	40.0
(West) Germany	1970	49.3	35.0	29.0
Italy	1971	39.7	31.9	19.6
France	1973	39.5	25.2	36.2

Source: Feinstein, 'Structural change', p. 39.

[12] Hobsbawm's famous article uses non-agricultural manual workers, and on that basis says figures show a fall from about 75 per cent in 1911, to 70 per cent in 1931, 64 per cent in 1961, and a little over half in 1976: Hobsbawm, 'Forward?' There has been an upward trend in levels of self-employment (as well as sharp cycles), but much of this seems to be a reflection of the weakness of the labour market.

[13] Saul, *Industrialisation*.

[14] Rowthorn and Wells, *De-industrialization*, p. 10.

[15] Outside textiles, much early deindustrialization in Britain was in the nationalized sector; it was the unintended fate of this sector to manage a policy of 'humane decline': Tomlinson, '"Failed?"'.

[16] Goos and Manning, 'Lousy'.

[17] Minford, *Unemployment*; Wood, *How Much?*

policies to raise the incomes of low-paid workers. Some of these were straightforward and unproblematic, like cutting income tax thresholds. But alongside this was the beginning of a policy with much more significance for the trajectory of neo-liberalism—in-work benefits or what could equally be called wage subsidies.

The beginnings of this second policy can be traced back to before the 'neo-liberal era', when in 1971 the Conservative government introduced FIS. This was a very modest proposal, but the principle involved, of state supplementation of the market-determined wage, was sufficient to arouse the ideologically acute sensors of Enoch Powell. 'I do not think it can be denied that we are taking a decisive new step now by the overt and direct payment—if I may use old-fashioned but significant and appropriate language—of "relief in supplementation of wages".' He went on to compare FIS with the Speenhamland 'system' of 1795, introduced to supplement the wages of agricultural workers from local rates during the period of high prices caused by the Napoleonic wars. FIS, he argued, was in contradiction with a key (liberal) principle:

> It is the principle that it is an act of fateful consequence to pay relief—cash supplementation of income—to persons in full-time employment; that it is something which is bound profoundly to distort the wage system and to frustrate the ambition—which seems to me to be almost indissociable from the idea of a free society—that a man should receive as near as may be the full value of his work in cash.[18]

The scale of FIS and its successor, Family Credit, expanded rapidly in the 1980s. 'In just the past three years, the Government has tripled spending in cash terms on family credit. Since 1979, spending on benefits for families dependent on low-paid work has increased by 10 times in real terms. Today the average family credit payment is more than £30 a week.'[19] But despite this expansion, there was a continuing ideological commitment to the idea of the market determination of wages, shown in the early 1990s when the Conservatives made ferocious attacks on Labour's proposals for a statutory minimum wage (the Conservatives had abolished most of the sector-specific wages councils in the 1980s). The title of a Conservative Research Department document of 1991 summarized the argument: *The Minimum Wage. Labour's Axe on Jobs*. In a House of Commons debate in 1992 the Conservatives amended a critical Opposition motion to deplore 'the commitment of Her Majesty's Opposition to a National Minimum Wage which would destroy jobs, thereby reducing opportunities and living standards for up to two million people.'[20]

But after Labour introduced a statutory national minimum wage in 1998 against strong Conservative opposition, the party rowed back on its hostility. By 2014 this backtracking had turned to enthusiastic support, when Chancellor Osborne announced a statutory 'New Living Wage', despite the criticism of free-market think tanks.[21]

[18] *Hansard* (Commons) vol. 806, cols 262 and 264–265, 10 November 1970.
[19] *Hansard* (Commons) vol. 194, col. 794, 9 July 1992.
[20] *Hansard* (Commons) vol. 194, col. 791, 9 July 1992.
[21] Bourne and Shackleton, *And?*

The Conservative-led government of 2010 inherited a wage subsidy system which, in part because of New Labour's strong desire to reduce poverty levels as well as encourage people into work, had grown rapidly. Working family tax credits and child tax credits provided much more generous support for low-wage households, so that by 2014 this provision cost £27 billion per annum despite cuts made to this provision after 2010.[22] For Conservatives there was a fundamental dilemma; given the prevalence of wages deemed intolerably low, were Conservatives willing to plunge large numbers into greater poverty by radical pruning of these benefits (which would also reduce incentives to work)? The answer was in the negative, so the maintenance of high (if reduced) spending on these subsidies was combined by using wage regulation to shift some of the burden onto employers. The long-run effects of this policy are as yet unclear, but one obvious problem it has raised is the reliance of many low-wage employers of government contracts (most obviously in the care sector) so firms in that sector can easily be ground between the costs of the living wage and reduced spending by publicly funded purchasers.

In broad terms, a free market in labour in deindustrialized Britain meant politically unacceptable levels of wages. A parallel issue arose in housing, where freeing the rental market (and subsidizing house purchase) have made rent levels unacceptably high, and, coupled with more people relying on the private rented sector, this has led to an explosion in housing benefit, much of it, around £20 billion per annum, paid to those in employment.[23] It is a profound irony of neo-liberal rule that there has been a desperation to cut public spending, a significant part of which arises from the politically unacceptable consequences of market prices for labour and housing.

Much has recently been written on the extent to which the 2008 financial crisis will lead to the reversal of the British neo-liberal experiment.[24] But it may be that a bigger challenge to that experiment will continue to flow from a longer-term and more deep-seated trend towards a labour market polarized by deindustrialization.

The significance of this polarization is profound. The classic mid-twentieth-century Beveridge analysis of the sources of poverty suggested the problem fundamentally lay in 'interruption to earnings' (by unemployment, sickness, or old age) along with large numbers of children, the latter to be addressed by 'family allowances' (later, child benefit).[25] While this analysis always misrepresented the labour market, not least in its barely qualified notion of the 'male-breadwinner household', its fundamental idea that normally paid work would provide a route out of poverty has underpinned most modern understandings of how society works down to the present day. What has changed in the period of deindustrialization has been the numbers earning very low wages and being supported by in-work benefits.

So far the problems for neo-liberalism caused by deindustrialization have been emphasized. But this process is a problem for all political forces, including the enemy of neo-liberalism, social democracy. As a political force, social democracy was historically grounded in a prosperous, employed, industrial working class. But

[22] OBR, *Welfare*, p. 12. [23] OBR, *Welfare*, p. 12.

[24] Bowman et al., *End*; Crouch, *Strange*. [25] Cutler, Williams, and Williams, *Keynes*.

that class has greatly diminished. Social democracy's concern to reduce inequality is also now working against the grain of the labour market. Plainly the labour market is not the only source of increased inequality.[26] But the polarization of jobs obviously increases inequality: 'wage inequality is significantly higher now than it was some thirty years ago. This is true for men and women, and is the case in both the upper and lower halves of the distribution.'[27] Machin calculates the ratio between the 90th and 10th percentiles for the period 1970 to 2009, and suggests that in those forty years this dispersion rose by approximately 50 per cent.[28] This polarization maps on to the pattern of job growth, with growth at each end of the distribution defined by the median occupational wage.[29]

The focus here is on the *employment* aspects of deindustrialization: this is based on the claim that the radical decline in industrial employment has been a major force shaping post-war Britain. (It also needs to be emphasized that such significance might be attached to deindustrialization in other rich countries, given that the process, in broad outline at least, is common to them all, as shown in Table 10.1.) The reasons for this international trend are changes in the composition of demand, relatively rapid growth in productivity in manufactures, and, more contentiously, international competition from poor countries, as discussed in Chapter 4.

Listing the causes of deindustrialization in this way brings out the crucial point that globalization (in the sense of enhanced international competition in industrial goods) is only a part, and probably quite a small part, of the explanation for the fall in the number of industrial jobs. As argued in Chapter 4, exaggerated notions of the impact of globalization in this respect have fuelled an 'anti-globalization' backlash in recent years.

The other link between deindustrialization and globalization was suggested by Keynes in the 1930s. Foreseeing a more nationally self-sufficient future, Keynes wrote 'as wealth increases, both primary and manufacture products play a smaller relative part in the national economy compared with houses, personal services and local amenities, which are not the subject of international exchange'.[30] Keynes's prediction about the future was written at a time when globalization was clearly in retreat. Plainly the globalization evident in the world since the 1970s has exposed more of the economy to international competition than he could possibly have anticipated. Most importantly, significant parts of the outputs of the service sector, especially in the wake of the ICT 'revolution', are internationally traded. But, having said that, the demand for services which are sheltered has also grown immensely, whether these be private sector services such as retailing and distribution; entertainment and personal services such as hairdressing; or public sector services, notably education, health, and social care. These are the activities where the 'personal touch' is very difficult to displace, and where therefore increasing demand translates

[26] Atkinson, *Inequality*; Piketty, *Capital*.

[27] Machin, 'Changes', p. 157. Alongside this trend has been growing wealth inequality, linked in part to the rent-seeking activities of the 'working rich': Savage and Williams, 'Elites', p. 11.

[28] Machin, 'Changes', pp. 157–8.

[29] Goos and Manning, 'Lousy'.

[30] 'National', p. 238.

into approximately equal increases in employment. Hence the point made in Chapter 4 that we should be wary of over-aggregated stories of the 'advance' or 'retreat' of globalization.

But if framing our understanding of recent trends in terms of deindustrialization is fruitful, it also carries dangers. First, there is the danger of seeing the process as involving a normative argument about the effects of that deindustrialization; if one were aiming at a 'balance sheet' of the consequences of that process then there would clearly be substantial elements on both the debit and credit sides. For example, on the credit side, average non-industrial work is safer, cleaner, and less disease-inducing than industrial work.[31] Some effects would not fit easily on either side: the reduction of employment in industry hit hardest in predominantly male sectors of the economy, and conversely facilitated the expansion of women's paid employment. But the aim of focusing on deindustrialization should not be to draw up a balance sheet, but to emphasize the scale and speed of the process in Britain, and the consequently radical impacts, for good or ill. It is a historical argument about the *transition* from an industry- to a service-dominated economy, rather than a comparison of the two in a 'steady state'.

A further danger is an over-politicized view of deindustrialization, which sees it as suddenly happening in the early 1980s, and caused by the policies of the Thatcher government.[32] As outlined in Chapter 6, deindustrialization did indeed reach a crescendo in 1979–82, when a grossly overvalued exchange rate rendered large swathes of British industry uncompetitive, and industrial output fell by 20 per cent. As the Prime Ministerial adviser John Hoskyns noted in his memoirs, the Thatcher government had 'accidentally engineered' a major recession by its misguided adherence to monetary targets and had 'done the economy a great deal of damage by mistake'.[33]

But against this, it is important to emphasize the long-term nature of this change. The 1979–82 episode was extraordinary in its speed and extent, but the process began much earlier, as shown in Table 10.1. While the stress in the literature on the radical effects of the Thatcher period is understandable, it gives a very misleading picture of the chronology and, by implication, the processes at work. It also ignores the very different contexts in which the process took place, and the extent to which its effects were offset.[34]

Much of the literature on deindustrialization has focused on industrial closures and their effects, reflecting an understandable anger and despair at the fate of communities hit by the decline of particular firms or sectors.[35] Much of this literature does not adequately contextualize the long-term nature of the processes at work; nevertheless, the sense of the profundity of effects of the rapid loss of industrial

[31] For changes in the quality of work in all dimensions, see Green, *Demanding*.
[32] Jones, *Chavs*.
[33] Cited in Needham, 'Britain's', p. 89; also Tomlinson, 'Mrs Thatcher's'.
[34] Phillips, 'Moral'; also Phillips, 'Class'.
[35] Examples: Foster and Woolfson, *Politics*; Levie, Gregory, and Lorentzen, *Fighting*; Massey and Meegan, *Anatomy*; Martin and Rowthorn, *Geography*.

employment conveys a hugely important truth about post-war Britain which needs to be retained and developed.

Until the 1970s 'the UK stood out with Germany as "workshop economies" with an unusually high share of manufacturing employment. While this share has declined everywhere, the UK has now joined the pack with an average share of manufacturing employment considerably below Germany's.'[36] But the speed of this change has been very fast. Britain's proportion of industrial workers has fallen further than almost any other country because of the high level from which it began, and the speed of contraction was especially fast in 1979–82.

As a result of the changes in the labour market brought about by deindustrialization, in-work poverty has been a central feature of the post-industrial period. While in the industrial period employment did not guarantee an above-poverty income, most poverty was amongst non-workers (the sick and disabled, pensioners, single mothers), or those with unusually large families. Abel-Smith and Townsend showed that in 1960 about 40 per cent of households in poverty (those below 140 per cent of the then National Assistance level) had a working member. But overwhelmingly they also had a large number of children (four or more).[37] Recent work suggests that a majority of the poor are now members of households with at least one member in work: 'As pensioner poverty is now at low levels, the rate of in-work poverty is the most distinctive characteristic of poverty today'.[38] A different calculation suggests that whereas in the 1970s 3–4 per cent of employed households were in poverty, the figure by 2000/1 was 14 per cent. Between 1975 and the mid 1990s, the incidence of low pay for men in the labour market doubled.[39] In-work benefits have since mitigated, but by no means eliminated this poverty.

III

The four key economic problems of the post-war period discussed in Part II of this volume were all grounded in an industrial economy. Unemployment, from its origins in the late Victorian period, was largely about the malfunctioning of urban, industrial (and male) labour markets. Deindustrialization, accompanied by the proliferation of precarious work, including much classified as 'self-employment', radically challenges our understanding of this problem, however much it remains the case that for the great bulk of the population selling their labour is key to their economic prosperity. Unemployment remains a serious problem, not least because of the long-run squeeze on the incomes of the unemployed, but for many, moving from unemployment into work no longer provides a ready route to significant economic improvement.[40]

The concern with productivity was likewise grounded in the industrial sector; in Steve Broadberry's account of the service sector, he sees the issue as how far different

[36] Coutts, Glyn, and Rowthorn, 'Structural'. [37] Abel-Smith and Townsend, *Poor*, p. 49.
[38] Joseph Rowntree Foundation, *Monitoring*, pp. 1–2; Lawton, *Nice*.
[39] Stewart, 'Low Pay'. [40] Nickell, 'Poverty'.

services have been 'industrialized' as central to their productivity performance.[41] But many services cannot be mass produced so are not subject to 'industrialisztion'. Outside the marketed services that Broadberry focuses upon, in non-marketed provision like education, health, and care, the problems of conceptualizing, let alone measuring, productivity are immense.[42] In a world where personal services of various kinds are becoming ever more important, traditional notions of productivity need a radical rethink.

Perhaps less obviously, the notion of a national rate of inflation, such as the Cost of Living Index and later the RPI, was grounded in attempts to measure the real wages of the industrial working class. With the rise to prominence of the value of housing as a key underpinning for consumption, and the 'financialization' of the economy, this traditional notion of inflation—measuring the cost of a basket of consumables against nominal wages—has been undermined. Asset, especially housing, prices matter much more to many wage earners, whilst the value of financial assets is also important to increasing numbers of people as the population ages (leaving aside the impact of fluctuating asset prices on the macroeconomy).

Finally, the decline of concern with the balance of payments is linked in part to the rise in the relative importance of financial flows, which means that the traditional focus on the manufacturing balance or the current account seems less pertinent. For many years now Britain's external payments have relied on the rates of return on overseas assets exceeding those on domestic assets held by foreigners.[43] We are a very long way indeed from 'England's bread hangs by Lancashire's thread'.

Deindustrialization has not only undercut the coherence and relevance of the four standard economic policy problems of the post-war years, but has also destroyed the primary audience that most post-war economic propaganda was aimed at: the industrial working class. Not only were these problems grounded in the industrial economy, but it was above all the industrial workers in that economy who needed to be persuaded about how the economy could be made to function better. While other audiences were not entirely neglected, it was the worker (usually the male worker), who was the prime target of the narratives and whose understandings and behaviour were seen as the key to the projected solutions.

A recurrent anxiety of this propaganda was the receptivity of those workers to its messages. This anxiety helps to explain much of the 'simplified' language of the propaganda, as well as its patterns of distribution. More fundamentally, this anxiety rested upon uncertainties about what kind of arguments a working-class audience would find congenial; there was perennial debate about the efficacy of appeals to individual as opposed to the 'national' interest.[44] Above all, there was a moral message of distributive justice which infused much of the propaganda, ultimately grounded in the belief that working-class culture had within it ingrained notions of solidarity and 'fairness' that had to be appealed to.[45]

[41] Broadberry, *Market*, p. 2. [42] *Atkinson Review*. [43] Key et al., 'Property'.

[44] For example: 'We should be sacrificing an important part of the publicity, if we chose to treat people as wholly absorbed in their own material problems': TNA: PRO EW8/949, 'Incomes policy: steering group', p. 3, 1968.

[45] Tomlinson, 'Re-inventing'.

But while ethical appeals continued to inform economic propaganda into the twenty-first century, the fragmentation of the old audience accelerated. In addition, given the upward lurch in inequality in the 1980s, and the following period of continuing growth of incomes right at the top of the distribution ('the top 0.01 per cent'), appeals to 'fairness' have become much more difficult to make credible. Strikingly, concerns about inequality emerged across the political spectrum after the 2007/8 financial crisis, at the same time as the narrative of debts, deficits, and austerity had driven post-crisis policies that *increased* that inequality. Widespread talk of 'reducing inequality', whilst having obvious political appeal, especially after Brexit (and the election of Trump in the USA), would seem to be largely rhetorical, in the sense of being poorly related to the realities of the policies being pursued. As discusssed in Chapter 5, the austerity agenda of 2010 onwards has left an underlying framework of fiscal squeeze extending onwards to 2020.[46]

[46] Corlett and Clarke, 'Living Standards'.

Bibliography

1. ARCHIVAL SOURCES

The National Archives: Public Record Office
Board of Trade papers (BT)
Cabinet and War Cabinet papers (CAB)
Counter-Inflation Publicity Unit papers (BA)
Department of Economic Affairs papers (EW)
Government Social Survey (RG)
Ministry of Information/Central Office of Information papers (INF)
Ministry of Labour papers (LAB)
Ministry of Production papers (AVIA)
National Economic Development office papers (FG)
Prime Minister's Office papers (PREM)
Treasury papers (T)

Thatcher Foundation website (http://www.margaretthatcher.org)

2. PUBLISHED SOURCES

Abel-Smith, Brian and Peter Townsend *The Poor and the Poorest* (1963).

Abramowitz, Moses 'Catching Up, Forging Ahead, and Falling Behind', *Journal of Economic History* 46, no. 2 (1986), pp. 385–406.

Abrams, Mark *Must Labour Lose?* (1960).

Abrams, Mark 'Public Opinion Polls and Political Parties', *Public Opinion Quarterly* 27, no. 1 (1963), pp. 9–18.

Addison, Paul *The Road to 1945* (2nd edn, 1994).

Ahlstrand, Bruce *The Quest for Productivity: A Case Study of Fawley after Flanders* (1990).

Alexander, Philip 'A Tale of Two Smiths: The Transformation of Commonwealth Policy, 1964–1970', *Contemporary British History (CBH)* 20, no. 3 (2007): pp. 303–22.

Allen, Roy 'Official Papers: Statistics and the Balance of Payments', *Economic Journal (EJ)* 61, no. 1 (1951), pp. 179–96.

Allen, William *Monetary Policy and Financial Repression in Britain, 1951–59* (2014).

Allsopp, Christopher 'Macroeconomic Policy: Design and Performance'. In *Labour's Economic Policies 1974–79*, edited by Michael Artis and David Cobham (1991), pp. 19–37.

Alt, James *The Politics of Economic Decline: Economic Management and Political Behaviour in Britain since 1964* (1979).

Arestis, Philip and Malcolm Sawyer 'The Economic Analysis Underlying the "Third Way"', *New Political Economy (NPE)* 6, no. 2 (2001), pp. 255–78.

Arndt, Heinz *The Rise and Fall of Economic Growth* (1978).

Artis, Michael and David Cobham 'Summary and Appraisal'. In *Labour's Economic Policies 1974–79*, edited by Michael Artis and David Cobham (1991), pp. 266–77.

Artis, Michael and David Cobham 'The Background'. In *Labour's Economic Policies 1974–79*, edited by Michael Artis and David Cobham (1991), pp. 1–18.

Atkinsion, Anthony *Atkinson Review, Final Report: Measurement of Government Output and Productivity for the National Accounts* (2005).

Atkinsion, Anthony *Inequality: What Can Be Done?* (2015).

Atkinson, Anthony and John Micklewright 'Turning the Screw: Benefits for the Unemployed, 1979–1988'. In *Poverty and Social Security*, edited by Anthony Atkinson (1989), pp. 125–57.

Backhouse, Roger 'The Macroeconomics of Margaret Thatcher', *Journal of the History of Economic Thought* 24, no. 3 (2002), pp. 313–34.

Bacon, Robert and Walter Eltis *Britain's Economic Problem: Too Few Producers* (1976).

Badiou, Alain *Number and Numbers* (2008).

Baker, David, Andrew Gamble, and David Seawright 'Sovereign Nations and Global Markets: Modern British Conservatism and Hyperglobalism', *British Journal of Politics and International Relations (BJPIR)* 4, no. 3 (2002), pp. 399–428.

Bale, Timothy 'Dynamics of a Non-Decision: The "Failure" to Devalue the Pound, 1964–7', *Twentieth Century British History (TCBH)* 10, no. 2 (1999), pp. 192–217.

Bale, Timothy *The Conservative Party. From Thatcher to Cameron* (2011).

Balls, Edward 'Open Macroeconomics in an Open Economy', *Scottish Journal of Political Economy (SJPE)* 45, no. 2 (1998), pp. 113–32.

Balls, Edward and Gus O'Donnell *Reforming Britain's Economic and Financial Policy. Towards Greater Economic Stability* (2002).

Balogh, Thomas *Unequal Partners vol. II* (1963).

Barnett, Corelli *The Audit of War* (1986).

Barnett, Corelli *The Lost Victory* (1995).

Bartle, John, Sebastian Dellepiane, and James Simpson 'Post-war British Public Opinion: Is there a Political Centre?', *BSA 27th Report* (2007), pp. 203–23.

Beatty, Christina and Steve Fothergill *Jobs, Welfare and Austerity* (2016).

Beatty, Christina, Steve Fothergill, Tony Gore, and Ryan Powell *The Real Level of Unemployment 2007* (2007).

Beckett, Andrew *Pinochet in Piccadilly: Britain and Chile's Secret History* (2002).

Beers, Laura 'Whose Opinion? Changing Attitudes Towards Opinion Polling in British Politics, 1937–1964', *TCBH* 17, no. 2 (2006), pp. 177–205.

Beers, Laura 'Labour's Britain, Fight For It Now', *HJ* 52, no. 3 (2009), pp. 667–95.

Beers, Laura *Your Britain. Media and the Making of the Labour Party* (2010).

Behrend, Hilde 'Price and Income Images and Inflation', *SJPE* 9, no. 2 (1962), pp. 85–103.

Behrend, Hilde 'Price Images and National Incomes Policy', *SJPE* 13, no. 3 (1966), pp. 273–96.

Behrend, Hilde 'Public Acceptability and a Workable Incomes Policy'. In *An Incomes Policy for Britain*, edited by Frank Blackaby (1972), pp. 187–214.

Behrend, Hilde *Attitudes to Price Increases and Pay Claims* (1974).

Behrend, Hilde *Problems of Labour and Inflation* (1984).

Behrend, Hilde 'Reaching Policy Makers: An Autobiographical Account', Dept. of Business Studies, University of Edinburgh (1986).

Behrend, Hilde, Harriet Lynch, and Jean Davies *A National Survey of Attitudes to Inflation and Incomes Policy* (1966).

Behrend, Hilde, Harriet Lynch, Howard Thomas, and Jean Davies *Incomes Policy and the Individual* (1967).

Benn, Tony *Against the Tide: Diaries 1973–76* (1989).

Berry, Christopher *Globalization and Ideology in Britain* (2011).

Beveridge, William *Full Employment in a Free Society* (1944).

Beynon, Huw *Working for Ford* (1973).

Blaazer, David '"Devalued and Dejected Britons": The Pound in Public Discourse in the 1960s', *History Workshop* no. 47 (1999), pp. 121–40.

Black, Amy and Stephen Brooke 'The Labour Party, Women, and the Problem of Gender, 1951–1966', *Journal of British Studies* 36, no. 4 (1997), pp. 419–52.

Black, Lawrence *The Political Culture of the Left in Affluent Britain, 1951–64* (2003).

Blackaby, Frank (editor) *De-industrialisation* (1976).

Blackaby, Frank 'Narrative, 1960–74'. In *British Economic Policy 1960–74,* edited by Frank Blackaby (1978), pp. 62–76.

Blackburn, David 'Penguin Specials and the Centre-Left, 1937–1988', (unpublished PhD dissertation, University of Bristol, 2012).

Blanchflower, David and Robert Skidelsky 'Vince Cable is Working, the Coalition isn't', *New Statesman* 24 January 2011, pp. 37–8.

Bleaney, Michael 'Comparison of Real Exchange Rate Stability Across Exchange Rate Systems', *Bulletin of Oxford University Institute of Economics and Statistics (BOUIES)* 54, no. 4 (1992), pp. 557–65.

Block, Fred *The Origins of International Economic Disorder* (1977).

Bloomfield, Arthur 'Post-war Control of International Capital Movements', *American Economic Review* 36, no. 2 (1946), pp. 687–709.

Blow, Laura, Andrew Leicester, and Zoe Oldfield *Consumption Trends in the UK, 1975–1999* (2004).

Blumler, Jay and Denis McQuail *Television in Politics: Its Uses and Influences* (1968).

Blundell, John 'Introduction. Hayek and the Second-Hand Dealers in Ideas'. In F. Hayek, *The Intellectuals and Socialism* (1998), pp. 1–12.

Blyth, Mark *Austerity: The History of a Dangerous Idea* (2013).

Board of Trade *We Live by Exports* (1946).

Booth, Alan 'Britain in the 1930s: A Managed Economy?', *EcHR* 40, no. 4 (1987), pp. 499–522.

Booth, Alan *British Macroeconomic Policy 1931–49. Was There a Keynesian Revolution?* (1989).

Booth, Alan 'Corporate Politics and the Quest for Productivity: The British TUC and the Politics of Industrial Productivity'. In *Management, Labour and Industrial Politics in Modern Europe,* edited by Jo Melling and Alan McKinlay (1996), pp. 44–65.

Booth, Alan 'Inflation, Expectations, and the Political Economy of Conservative Britain, 1951–1964', *HJ* 34, no. 3 (2000), pp. 827–47.

Booth, Philip (editor) *Were 364 Economists all Wrong?* (2006).

Boothby, Robert, John Loder, Harold Macmillan, and Oliver Stanley *Industry and the State: A Conservative View* (1927).

Bosanquet, Nicholas *After the New Right* (1983).

Bourne, Ryan and John Shackleton *And How Much do You Earn? Public Pressure for Government Regulation of Pay* (2016).

Bowman, Andrew, Ismail Erturk, Julie Froud, Sukhdev Johal, John Law, Adam Leaver, Michael Moran, and Karel Williams *The End of the Experiment? From Competition to the Foundational Economy* (2014).

Boyce, Robert *British Capitalism at the Crossroads* (1987).

BPC *Policy and Programme* (1953).

BPC 'Raising the Standard'. A film made in association with the British Film Institute (1953).

Brewer, Anthony 'The Concept of Growth in Eighteenth-Century Economics', *History of Political Economy* 27, no. 4 (1995), pp. 609–38.

Brewer, Mike, James Browne, Andrew Hood, Robert Joyce, and Luke Sibieta 'The Short- and Medium-Term Impacts of the Recession on the UK Income Distribution', *Fiscal Studies (FS)* 34, no. 2 (2013), pp. 179–201.

Brittan, Samuel *The Treasury under the Tories 1951–64* (1964).
Brittan, Samuel *The Price of Economic Freedom* (1970).
Brittan, Samuel 'A Time for Confession'. In *Reassessing 1970s Britain*, edited by Lawrence Black, Hugh Pemberton, and Pat Thane (2013), pp. 61–8.
Britton, Andrew *Macroeconomic Policy in Britain 1974–1987* (1991).
Broadberry, Stephen and Nicholas Crafts 'Explaining Anglo-American Productivity Differences in the Mid-Twentieth Century', *BOUIES* 52, no. 4 (1990), pp. 375–402.
Broadberry, Stephen and Rainer Fremdling 'Comparative Productivity in British and German Industry, 1907–37', *BOUIES* 52, no. 4 (1990), pp. 403–29.
Broadberry, Stephen *The Productivity Race: British Manufacturing in International Perspective, 1850–1990* (1997).
Broadberry, Stephen *Market Services and the Productivity Race 1850–2000: British Performance in International Perspective* (2006).
Broadberry, Stephen and Timothy Leunig *The Impact of Government Policies on UK Manufacturing since 1945* (2013).
Brooke, Stephen 'Problems of "Socialist Planning": Evan Durbin and the Labour Government of 1945', *HJ* 34, no. 3 (1991), pp. 687–702.
Brown, Gordon 'The Conditions for High and Stable Growth and Employment', *EJ* 111 (2001), cc. 30–44.
Brown, Gordon *Beyond the Crash. Overcoming the First Crisis of Globalization* (2010).
Brown, William 'Industrial Relations'. In *Labour's Economic Policies*, edited by Michael Artis and David Cobham (1991), pp. 213–28.
Buchanan, John, Julie Froud, Sukhdev Johal, Adam Leaver, and Karel Williams 'Undisclosed and Unsustainable: Problems of the UK National Business Model' (2009).
Budd, Alan 'Unemployment Policy Since the War'. In *Unemployment and the Economists*, edited by Bernard Corry (1996), pp. 89–135.
Budge, Ian 'Relative Decline as a Political Issue: Ideological Motivations of the Politico-economic Debate in Post-war Britain', *Contemporary Record* 7, no. 1 (1993), pp. 1–23.
Bufton, Mark *Britain's Productivity Problem, 1948–1990* (2004).
Buiter, William 'The Macroeconomics of Dr Pangloss: A Critical Study of the New Classical Macroeconomics', *EJ* 90, no. 1 (1980), pp. 34–50.
Bullock, Alan *The Life and Times of Ernest Bevin: vol 2, Minister of Labour 1940–45* (1967).
Bulpitt, Jim 'The Discipline of the New Democracy: Mrs Thatcher's Domestic Statecraft', *Political Studies (PS)* 34, no. 1 (1989), pp. 19–39.
Burk, Kathleen and Alec Cairncross *'Goodbye Great Britain': The 1976 IMF Crisis* (1992).
Burn, Duncan *The Structure of British Industry* (1958).
Burn, Gary *The Re-emergence of Global Finance* (2006).
Burnham, Peter *Remaking the Post-war World Economy. Robot and British Policy in the 1950s* (2003).
Burns, Terry 'Managing the National Economy', HMT occasional paper no. 5 (1996).
Busch, Andreas 'Unpacking the Globalization Debate: Approaches, Evidence and Data'. In *Demystifying Globalization*, edited by Colin Hay and David Marsh (2001), pp. 21–48.
Butler, David *The British General Election of 1951* (1952).
Butler, David and Richard Rose *The British General Election of 1959* (1960).
Butler, David and Dennis Kavanagh *The British General Election of 1979* (1980).
Butler, David and Dennis Kavanagh *The British General Election of 1983* (1984).
Cable, Vince 'Keynes Would be on Our Side', *New Statesman* 17 January 2011, pp. 31–3.
Cairncross, Alec 'World Trade in Manufactures Since 1900', *Economia Internazionale* 8, no. 4 (1955), pp. 715–41.

Cairncross, Alec *Control of Long-term International Capital Movements* (1973).

Cairncross, Alec *Inflation, Growth and International Finance* (1975).

Cairncross, Alec and Barry Eichengreen *Sterling in Decline* (1983).

Cairncross, Alec *Years of Recovery: British Economic Policy 1945–51* (1985).

Cairncross, Alec 'The Development of Economic Statistics as an Influence on Theory and Policy'. In *National Income and Economic Progress: Essays in Honour of Colin Clark*, edited by Duncan Ironmonger, John Perkins, and Tran Van Hoa (1988), pp. 11–20.

Cairncross, Alec (editor) *The Robert Hall diaries 1947–1953* (1989).

Calder, Angus *The People's War* (1969).

Cameron, Gavin 'Why did UK Manufacturing Productivity Growth Slow Down in the 1970s and Speed Up in the 1980s?', *Economica* 70, no. 277 (2003), pp. 121–41.

Campbell, John *Edward Heath: A Biography* (1993).

Cannadine, David 'Apocalpyse When? British Politicians and British "Decline" in the Twentieth Century'. In *Understanding Decline*, edited by Peter Clarke and Clive Trebilcock (1997), pp. 261–84.

Capie, Forrest *Depression and Protectionism* (1983).

Carew, Anthony *Labour under the Marshall Plan: the Politics of Productivity and the Marketing of Management Science* (1993).

Carruthers, Susan 'Manning the Factories': Propaganda and Policy on the Employment of Women, 1939–1947', *History* 75, no. 244 (1990), pp. 232–56.

Carter, Charles and Andrew Roy *British Economic Statistics* (1954).

Carter, Charles and Brian Williams *Industry and Technical Progress* (1957).

Caves, Richard (editor) *Britain's Economic Prospects* (1968).

Centre for Cities *Cities Outlook 2014* (2014).

Chick, Martin *Industrial Policy in Britain 1945–1951* (1998).

Chote, Robert, Rowena Crawford, Carl Emmerson, and Gemma Tetlow 'Public Spending under Labour', IFS Briefing Note 92 (2010).

Clark, Colin *The Conditions of Economic Progress* (2nd edn 1951).

Clark, Tom, Mike Elsby, and Sarah Love *Twenty-Five Years of Falling Investment? Trends in Capital Spending on Public Services* (2001).

Clark, Tom and Andrew Leicester 'Inequality and Two Decades of British Tax and Benefit Reforms', *FS* 25, no. 2 (2004), pp. 129–58.

Clarke, Peter 'The Treasury's Analytical Model of the British Economy between the Wars'. In *The State and Economic Knowledge* edited by Mary Furner and Barry Supple (1990), pp. 171–207.

Clarke, Peter 'The Rise and Fall of Thatcherism', *Historical Research* 72, no. 179 (1999), pp. 301–22.

Clarke, Peter *The Cripps Version: The Life of Sir Stafford Cripps* (2002).

Clarke, Stephen *A Brave New World: How Reduced Migration Could Affect Earnings, Employment and the Labour Market* (2016).

Clarke, William *The City's Invisible Earnings* (1958).

Clift, Ben 'Social Democracy and Globalization: The Cases of France and the UK', *Government and Opposition* 37, no. 4 (2002), pp. 466–500.

Clift, Ben and Jim Tomlinson 'Credible Keynesianism? New Labour Macroeconomic Policy and the Political Economy of Coarse Tuning', *British Journal of Political Science* 37, no. 1 (2007), pp. 47–69.

Cmd. 3897 (Macmillan) *Report on Finance and Industry* (1931).

Cmd. 6404 *Social Insurance and Allied Services* (1942).

Cmd. 6527 *Employment Policy* (1944).

Cmd. 7046 *Economic Survey for 1947* (1947).
Cmd. 7321 *Statement on Personal Incomes, Costs and Prices* (1947).
Cmd. 9108 *Economic Survey for 1954* (1954).
Cmd. 9703 *Technical Education* (1956).
Cmd. 9725 *Economic Implications of Full Employment* (1956).
Cmd. 9728 *Economic Survey for 1956* (1956).
Cmnd. 124 *Defence: Outline of a Future Policy* (1957).
Cmnd. 827 (Radcliffe) *Report of the Committee on the Working of the Monetary System* (1959).
Cmnd. 2764 *The National Plan* (1965).
Cmnd. 3073 *Prices and Incomes Standstill* (1966).
Cmnd. 5157 *Unemployment Statistics: Report of an Inter-departmental Working Party* (1972).
Cmnd. 6151 *The Attack on Inflation* (1975).
Cmnd. 6507 *The Attack on Inflation: the Second Year* (1976).
Cmnd. 7746 *The Government's Expenditure Plans, 1980–81* (1980).
Cmnd. 9474 *Employment. The Challenge for the Nation* (1985).
Cm. 2563 *Competitiveness. Helping Britain Win* (1994).
Coates, David and Colin Hay 'The Internal and External Face of New Labour's Political Economy', *Government and Opposition* 36, no. 4 (2001), pp. 447–71.
Cobham, David, Christopher Adam, and Ken Mayhew 'The Economic Record of the Labour Government 1997–2010: An Assessment', *OREP* 29, no. 1 (2013), pp. 1–24.
Cockett, Richard 'The Party, Publicity, and the Media'. In *Conservative Century: The Conservative Party since 1900*, edited by Anthony Seldon and Stuart Ball (1994), pp. 547–77.
Cockett, Richard *Thinking the Unthinkable. Think-Tanks and the Economic Counter-Revolution, 1931–1983* (1995).
COI *Fifty Facts about the British Economy* (1957).
Collier, Paul *Exodus. Immigration and Multiculturalism in the Twenty-first Century* (2013).
Committee on Invisible Exports *Britain's Invisible Earnings* (1967).
Conan, Arthur *The Sterling Area* (1952).
Conservative Party *Report of the Policy Committee on Economic Growth* (1962).
Conservative Party *Right Road for the Economy* (1977).
Conservative Party *Freeing Britain to Compete* (2007).
Conservative Party *Invitation to Join the Government of Britain: the Conservative Manifesto 2010* (2010).
Constantine, Stephen 'Bringing the Empire Alive: The Empire Marketing Board and Imperial Propaganda'. In *Imperialism and Popular Culture*, edited by John Mackenzie (1986), pp. 192–231.
Constantine, Stephen 'The Buy British Campaign of 1931', *European Journal of Marketing* 21, no. 4 (1987), pp. 44–59.
COPPI *Fourth Report* (1961).
Corlett, Adam and Stephen Clarke *Living Standards 2017* (2017).
Corry, Daniel 'Labour and the Economy, 1997–2010: More than a Faustian Pact?', *Political Quarterly (PQ)* 81, no. s1 (2011), ss. 123–39.
Coutts, Kenneth and Wynne Godley 'Does Britain's Balance of Payments Matter any More?' In *The Economic Legacy 1979–1992*, edited by Jonathan Michie (1992), pp. 60–7.
Coutts, Kenneth, Andrew Glyn, and Robert Rowthorn 'Structural Change under New Labour', *Cambridge Journal of Economics* 31, no. 6 (2007), pp. 845–61.
Coutts, Kenneth and Robert Rowthorn 'The UK Balance of Payments: Structure and Prospects', *OREP* 29, no. 2 (2013), pp. 307–25.

Cowley, Philip and Dennis Kavanagh *The British General Election of 2015* (2016).
Crafts, Nicholas 'The Golden Age of Economic Growth in Western Europe. 1950–1973', *EcHR* 48, no. 3 (1995), pp. 429–47.
Craig, Christine, Roger Tarling, Jill Rubery, and Frank Wilkinson *Abolition and After: the Jute Wages Council* (1980).
Craig, Frederick *British General Election Manifestos 1918–1966* (1970).
Craig, Frederick *British General Election Manifestos 1959–1987* (1990).
Crawford, Rowena and Paul Johnson 'The UK Coalition Government's Record, and Challenges for the Future', *FS* 36, no. 3 (2015), pp. 275–82.
Crewe, Ivor 'How to Win a Landslide without Really Trying: Why the Conservatives Won in 1983'. In *Britain at the Polls 1983. A Study of the General Election*, edited by Austin Ranney (1985), pp. 155–96.
Crewe, Ivor 'Has the Electorate become Thatcherite?' In *Thatcherism*, edited by Robert Skidelsky (1988), pp. 25–49.
Cribb, Jonathan, Richard Disney, and Luke Sibieta 'The Public Sector Workforce: Past, Present and Future', IFS Briefing Note 145, February 2014.
Crofts, William 'The Attlee Government's Economic Information Propaganda', *Journal of Contemporary History* 21, no. 3 (1986), pp. 453–71.
Crofts, William *Coercion or Persuasion? Propaganda in Britain after 1945* (1989).
Crook, Tom and Glen O'Hara (editors) *Statistics and the Public Sphere* (2011).
Crosland, Anthony *The Future of Socialism* (1956).
Crosland, Anthony 'On the Left Again', *Encounter*, no. 84 (1960), pp. 3–12.
Crosland, Anthony 'On Economic Growth', *Encounter*, no. 91 (1961), pp. 65–8.
Crosland, Anthony *Socialism Now* (1974).
Crouch, Colin 'The Place of Public Expenditure in Socialist Thought'. In *The Socialist Agenda: Crosland's Legacy*, edited by David Lipsey and Dick Leonard (1981), pp. 156–85.
Crouch, Colin *The Strange Non-death of Neo-liberalism* (2013).
Croucher, Richard *Engineers at War* (1982).
Cutler, Tony, Karel Williams, and John Williams *Keynes, Beveridge and Beyond* (1986).
Darling, Alistair *Back from the Brink: 1,000 Days at Number 11* (2011).
Daunton, Martin *A Property-owning Democracy? Housing in Britain* (1987).
Daunton, Martin *Trusting Leviathan: the Politics of Taxation in Britain, 1799–1914* (2001).
Daunton, Martin *Just Taxes: The Politics of Taxation in Britain, 1914–1979* (2002).
Davidson, Roger *Whitehall and the Labour Problem in Late-Victorian and Edwardian Britain* (1985).
Day, Alan *The Future of Sterling* (1954).
DEA *Statement of Intent on Productivity, Prices and Incomes* (1964).
DEA *Working for Prosperity* (1965).
Deacon, Alan *In Search of the Scrounger* (1976).
Deacon, Alan 'An End to the Means Test? Social Security and the Attlee Government', *Journal of Social Policy (JPS)* 11, no. 3 (1982), pp. 289–306.
Denham, Andrew and Mark Garnett *Keith Joseph* (2001).
Dennison, Stanley 'Industrial Productivity', *Lloyds Bank Review*, no. 11 (1949), pp. 37–54.
Dennison, Stanley and John Presley (editors) *Robertson on Economic Policy* (1992).
Desai, Radhika 'Second-Hand Dealers in Ideas: Think-Tanks and Thatcherite Hegemony', *New Left Review*, no. 203 (1994), pp. 27–64.
Devons, Ely *An Introduction to British Economic Statistics* (1958).
Dolphin, Tony *Debts and Deficits. How much is Labour to Blame?* (2011).
Dorey, Peter *The Conservative Party and the Trade Unions* (1995).

Dorey, Peter '"Sharing the Proceeds of Growth": Conservative Economic Policy under David Cameron', *PQ* 80, no. 2 (2009), pp. 259–69.

Dorey, Peter, Mark Garnett, and Andrew Denham *From Crisis to Coalition: The Conservative Party, 1997–2010* (2011).

Dornbusch, Rudiger 'Expectations and Exchange Rate Dynamics', *Journal of Political Economy* 84, no. 6 (1976), pp. 1161–76.

Dow, Christopher *The Management of the British Economy 1945–60* (1965).

Dow, Christopher *Major Recessions: Britain and the World, 1920–1995* (1998).

Dunleavy, Patrick 'The Urban Bases of Political Alignment', *British Journal of Political Science* 9, no. 4 (1979), pp. 409–43.

Dunning, John *American Investment in British Manufacturing Industry* (2nd edn, 1998).

Edgerton, David *Warfare State: Britain 1920–1970* (2006).

Eichengreen, Barry (editor) *The Gold Standard in Theory and History* (1985).

Eichengreen, Barry 'Institutions and Economic Growth: Europe after World War II'. In *Economic Growth in Europe since 1945*, edited by Nicholas Crafts and Gianni Toniolo (1996), pp. 38–71.

EIU/COI *Productivity Pays... and How* (1949).

Emmerson, Carl, Paul Johnson, and Robert Joyce *Green Budget 2015* IFS (2015).

Emmerson, Carl and Gemma Tetlow 'UK Public Finances: From Crisis to Recovery', *FS* 36, no. 4 (2015), pp. 555–77.

Evans, Brendan and Andrew Taylor *From Salisbury to Major* (1996).

Evans, Eric *Thatcher and Thatcherism* (2nd edn, 2007).

Faccini, Roberto and Chris Hackworth 'Changes in Output, Employment and Wages during Recessions in the UK', *Bank of England Quarterly Bulletin (BEQB)* 50, no. 1 (2010), pp. 43–50.

Fairlie, Henry 'On the Comforts of Anger'. In *Suicide of a Nation?* edited by Arthur Koestler, (1963), pp. 19–28.

Fallick, Les and Robert Elliott 'Incomes Policy, Inflation and Relative Pay: An Overview'. In *Incomes Policy, Inflation and Relative Pay* edited by Fallick and Elliott (1981), pp. 246–63.

Favretto, Ilaria '"Wilsonism" Reconsidered: Labour Party Revisionism 1952–64', *CBH* 14, no. 4 (2000), pp. 54–80.

Feinstein, Charles and Robin Matthews 'The Growth of Output and Productivity in the UK: The 1980s as a Phase of the Post-war Period', *National Institute Economic Review (NIER)* no. 133 (1980), pp. 78–90.

Fels, Allan *The British Prices and Incomes Board* (1972).

Fielding, Steven 'What did "the People" Want? The Meaning of the 1945 General Election', *HJ* 35, no. 3 (1992), pp. 623–39.

Fielding, Steven, Peter Thompson, and Nick Tiratsoo *England Arise! The Labour Party and Popular Politics in 1940s Britain* (1995).

Finlayson, Alan, *Making Sense of New Labour* (2003).

Flanders, Allan 'Wages Policy and Full Employment in Britain', *BOUIES* 12, no. 2 (1950), pp. 225–42.

Flanders, Allan *The Fawley Productivity Agreements* (1964).

Flux, Alfred 'The Measurement of Price Changes', *Journal of the Royal Statistical Society (JRSS)* 84, no. 2 (1921), pp. 167–215.

Fogarty, Michael *The Just Wage* (1961).

Ford, Robert, Gareth Morrell, and Anthony Heath '"Fewer but Better?" Public Views about Immigration', in *BSA 31st Report* (2012), pp. 26–44.

Foreman-Peck, James, Andrew Hughes-Hallett, and Yue Ma 'The End of Free Trade'. In *Free Trade and its Reception,* edited by Andrew Marrison (1998), pp. 262–77.

Foster, John 'The Redistributive Effects of Inflation on Building Society Shares and Deposits, 1961–74', *Bulletin of Economic Research* 28, no. 2 (1976), pp. 68–75.

Foster, John and Charles Woolfson *The Politics of the UCS Work-in: Class Alliances and the Right to Work* (1986).

Francis, Martin 'Set the People Free? Conservatives and the State'. In *The Conservatives and British Society 1880–1990,* edited by Martin Francis and Ina Zweiniger-Bargielowska, (1996), pp. 58–77.

Francis, Martin '"A Crusade to Enfranchise the Many": Thatcherism and the "Property-Owning Democracy"', *TCBH* 23, no. 2 (2012), pp. 275–97.

Frankel, Marvin *British and American Manufacturing Productivity* (1957).

Friedberg, Aaron *The Weary Titan* (1988).

Friedman, Milton 'The Role of Monetary Policy', *American Economic Review* 58, no. 1 (1967), pp. 1–17.

Friedman, Milton and David Laidler *Unemployment versus Inflation?* (1975).

Friedman, Milton 'The Line We Dare not Cross', *Encounter* no. 47, Nov. (1976), pp. 8–14.

Friedman, Milton 'Memorandum on Monetary Policy', *Treasury and Civil Service Committee,* HC 720 (1980).

Froud, Julie, Colin Haslam, Sukhdev Johal, Jean Shaoul, and Karel Williams 'Stakeholder Economy? From Utility Privatisation to New Labour', *Capital and Class* no. 60 (1996), pp. 119–34.

Froud, Julie, Sukhdev Johal, Adam Leaver, and Karel Williams *Financialization and Strategy. Narratives and Numbers* (2006).

Froud, Julie, Sukhdev Johal, Johnna Montgomerie, and Karel Williams 'Escaping the Tyranny of Earned Income? The Failure of Finance as Social Innovation', *NPE* 15, no. 1 (2010), pp. 147–64.

Froud, Julie, Sukdhev Johal, John Law, Adam Leaver, and Karel Williams 'Rebalancing the Economy (or Buyer's Remorse)', CRESC Working Paper No. 87 (2011).

Gallup, George (editor) *The International Public Opinion Polls: Great Britain 1937–1975, vol. 1, 1937–1964* (1976).

Gamble, Andrew *The Free Economy and the Strong State* (1988).

Gardner, Richard *Sterling–Dollar Diplomacy* (1969).

Garside, William *The Measurement of Unemployment* (1980).

Garside, William *British Unemployment 1919–1939* (1990).

Gazeley, Ian and Claire Langhammer 'The Meanings of Happiness in Mass Observation's Bolton', *History Workshop Journal,* no. 75 (2013), pp. 159–89.

Gazeley, Ian 'Income and Living Standards, 1870–2010'. In *Cambridge Economic History of Modern Britain, vol. II: 1870 to the Present,* edited by Roderick Floud, Jane Hunphries, and Paul Johnson (2014), pp. 151–80.

Giddens, Anthony *The Third Way: The Renewal of Social Democracy* (1998).

Giffen, Robert 'The Use of Import and Export Statistics', *JRSS* 45, no. 2 (1882), pp. 181–284.

Gilbert, Martin and Irving Kravis *An International Comparison of National Products and the Purchasing Power of Currencies* (1954).

Girvin, Brian 'Affluence, Conservatism and Political Competition in Britain and the United States, 1945–1964'. In *An Affluent Society? Britain's Post-War 'Golden Age' Revisited,* edited by Lawrence Black and Hugh Pemberton (2004), pp. 15–34.

Glennerster, Howard *British Social Policy* (1995).

Glyn, Andrew and Robert Sutcliffe *British Capitalism, Workers and the Profits Squeeze* (1972).

Glyn, Andrew and Stewart Wood 'New Labour's Economic Policy'. In *Social Democracy in Neo-Liberal Times: The Left and Economic Policy since 1979,* edited by Andrew Glyn (2001), pp. 200–22.

Goldthorpe, John *The Affluent Worker: Industrial Attitudes* (1970).

Goodman, Geoffrey *From Bevan to Blair: 50 Years Reporting from the Political Front Line* (2003).

Goodman, John and Louis Pauly 'The Obsolescence of Capital Controls: Economic Management in an Age of Global Markets', *World Politics* 46, no. 1 (1993), pp. 50–82.

Goos, Maarten and Alan Manning 'Lousy and Lovely Jobs: The Rising Polarization of Work in Britain', *Review of Economics and Statistics* 89, no. 1 (2007), pp. 118–33.

Government Social Survey *Redundancy Payments Act* (1967).

Government Social Survey *Women at Work* (1968).

Government Social Survey *Aid and Overseas Development* (1971).

Grant, Mariel *Propaganda and the Role of the State in Inter-war Britain* (1994).

Grant, Mariel 'Historians, the Penguin Specials, and the "State-of-the-Nation" Literature, 1958–1964', *CBH* 17, no. 3 (2003): pp. 29–54.

Gray, John *False Dawn: The Delusions of Global Capitalism* (1998).

Green, Ewen 'Rentiers versus Producers? The Political Economy of The Bimetallic Controversy, 1890–98', *English Historical Review (EHR)* 102, no. 408 (1988), pp. 588–612.

Green, Ewen *The Crisis of Conservatism* (1995).

Green, Ewen 'The Treasury Resignations of 1958: A Reconsideration', *TCBH* 20, no. 4 (2001), pp. 409–30.

Green, Ewen *Ideologies of Conservatism* (2002).

Green, Ewen *Thatcher* (2006).

Green, Francis *Demanding Work: The Paradox of Job Quality in the Affluent Society* (2007).

Gregory, Mary, Ben Zissimos, and Christine Greenhalgh 'Jobs for the skilled: How Technology, Trade and Domestic Demand Changed the Structure of UK Employment, 1979–90', *OREP* 53, no. 1 (2001), pp. 20–46.

Gwyn, William 'Jeremiahs and Pragmatists: Perceptions of British Decline'. In *Britain: Progress and Decline*, edited by William Gwyn and Richard Rose (1980), pp. 1–25.

Hadjimatheou, George and Thanos Skouras 'Britain's Economic Problem: The Growth of the Non-Market Sector?', *EJ* 89, no. 354 (1979), pp. 402–15.

Hall, Margaret 'The Consumer Sector'. In *The British Economy in the Nineteen-fifties*, edited by David Worswick and Peter Ady (1962), pp. 429–60.

Hall, Robert 'Reflections on the Practical Applications of Economics', *EJ* 69, no. 4 (1959), pp. 639–52.

Hancock, William and Margaret Gowing *British War Economy* (1949).

Harling, Peter *The Modern British State* (2001).

Harris, Jose *Unemployment and Politics: A Study in English Social Policy, 1886–1914* (1972).

Harris, Jose 'The Transition to High Politics in English Social Policy, 1880–1914'. In *High and Low Politics in Modern Britain*, edited by Michael Bentley and John Stevenson (1983), pp. 58–79.

Harris, Jose 'Political Ideas and the Debate on State Welfare, 1940–45'. In *War and Social Change*, edited by Harold Smith (1986), pp. 233–63.

Harris, Jose 'Enterprise and the Welfare State in Historical Perspective'. In *Britain since 1945*, edited by Alan O'Day and Terry Gourvish (1992), pp. 39–58.

Harris, Jose *William Beveridge, a Biography* (2nd edn 1997).

Harris, Nigel *Competition and the Corporate Society* (1972).

Harris, Ralph and Arthur Seldon *Choice in Welfare* (1963).

Harris, Ralph and Arthur Seldon *Welfare Without the State. A Quarter-Century of Suppressed Public Choice* (1987).

Harvie, Christopher 'Liturgies of National Decadence: Wiener, Dahrendorf and the British Crisis', *Cencrastus* 21 (1985), pp. 17–25.

Haskel, Jonathan and Matthew Slaughter 'Trade, Technology, and UK Wage Inequality', *EJ* 111, no. 468 (2001), pp. 163–87.
Hatton, Timothy 'Emigration from the UK, 1970–1913 and 1950–1998', *European Review of Economic History* 8, no. 2 (2004), pp. 149–71.
Hauser, Richard, and Brian Nolan 'Unemployment and Poverty: Change Over Time'. In *Welfare Regimes and the Experience of Unemployment in Europe*, edited by Duncan Gallie and Serge Paugam (2000), pp. 25–46.
Hay, Colin 'Narrating Crisis: The Discursive Construction of the "Winter of Discontent"', *Sociology* 30, no. 2 (1996), pp. 253–77.
Hay, Colin *The Political Economy of New Labour* (1999).
Hay, Colin 'Negotiating International Constraints: The Antinomies of Credibility and Competitiveness in the Political Economy of New Labour', *Competition and Change* 5, no. 3 (2001), pp. 269–89.
Hay, Colin, and Ben Rosamond 'Globalization, European Integration and the Discursive Construction of Economic Imperatives', *Journal of European Public Policy* 9, no. 2 (2002), pp. 147–67.
Hay, Colin 'Chronicles of a Death Foretold: The Winter of Discontent and the Construction of a Crisis of British Keynesianism', *Parliamentary Affairs* 63, no. 3 (2010), pp. 446–70.
Hay, Colin 'Treating the Symptom not the Condition: Crisis Definition, Deficit Reduction and the Search for a new British Growth Model', *BJPIR* 15, no. 1 (2013), pp. 23–37.
Hayek, Friedrich *A Tiger by the Tail: The Keynesian Legacy of Inflation* (1972).
Hayek, Friedrich *Full Employment at any Price?* (1975).
Hayek, Friedrich *Law, Legislation and Liberty vol. II* (1976).
Hayton, Richard *Reconstructing Conservatism? The Conservative Party in Opposition, 1997–2010* (2014).
Healey, Denis *The Time of My Life* (1989).
Held, David 'Globalisation: The Timid Tendency', *Marxism Today* special issue, Nov/Dec (1998), pp. 24–7.
Helleiner, Eric 'Explaining the Globalization of Financial Markets: Bringing the States Back In', *Review of International Political Economy* 2, no. 2 (1995), pp. 315–41.
Helleiner, Eric *States and the Re-emergence of Global Finance: From Bretton Woods to the 1990s* (1996).
Hellwig, Timothy and Eva Coffey 'Public Opinion, Party Messages, and Responsibility for the Financial Crisis in Britain', *Electoral Studies* 30, no. 3 (2011), pp. 417–26.
Hicks, John *The Crisis of Keynesian Economics* (1974).
Hickson, Kevin 'Conservatism and the Poor: Conservative Party Attitudes to Poverty and Inequality since the 1970s', *British Politics* 4, no. 3 (2009), pp. 341–62.
Hijzen, Alexander, Holger Gorg, and Robert Hine 'International Outsourcing and the Skill Structure of Labour Demand in the United Kingdom', *EJ* 115, no. 506 (2005), pp. 860–78.
Hill, Richard *The Labour Party and Economic and Economic Strategy: The Long Road Back* (2001).
Hills, John 'Introduction'. In *New Inequalities*, edited by John Hills (1996), pp. 1–16.
Hills, John Tom Sefton, and Kitty Stewart (editors) *Towards a More Equal Society? Poverty, Inequality and Policy since 1997* (2009).
Hilton, Matthew *Consumerism in Twentieth-century Britain* (2003).
Hine, Robert and Peter Wright 'Trade with Low Wage Economies: Employment and Productivity in UK Manufacturing', *EJ* 108, no. 450 (1998), pp. 1500–10.
Hinton, James *Shop Floor Citizens: Engineering Democracy in 1940s Britain* (1994).

Hinton, James *The Mass Observers* (2013).

Hirsch, Fred *The Pound Sterling: a Polemic* (1965).

Hirst, Paul and Grahame Thompson *Globalization in Question?* (1996).

Hirst, Paul 'Has Globalisation Killed Social Democracy?', *PQ* 70, no. 1 (1999), pp. 84–96.

Hirst, Paul and Grahame Thompson 'Globalization in One Country? The Peculiarities of the British', *Economy and Society* 29, no. 3 (2000), pp. 335–56.

HMT *Statistical Material Presented During the Washington Negotiations*, Cmnd. 6707 (1945).

HMT *Recovery Record: the Story of Marshall Aid* (1951).

HMT *The Pound and Our Future* (1956).

HMT *Financial Statement and Budget Report*, HCP 342 (2007).

HMT *Budget 2008: Stability and Opportunity*, HCP 388 (2008).

HMT *Pre-Budget Report* November 2008, Cm. 7484 (2008).

HMT *Budget 2009: Building Britain's Future*, HCP 407 (2009).

HMT *Budget June 2010*, HC 61 (2010).

HMT *Budget March 2010: Securing the Recovery*, HC 451 (2010).

HMT *Autumn Statement 2011*, Cm. 8231 (2011).

HMT *Autumn Statement 2012*, Cm. 8480 (2012).

HMT *Autumn Statement 2016*, Cm. 9362 (2016).

HMT/COI *Must Full Employment mean Ever-rising Prices?* (1956).

Hobsbawm, Eric 'The Forward March of Labour Halted?', *Marxism Today*, September (1978), pp. 279–86.

Hodson, Dermot and Deborah Mabbett 'UK Economic Policy and the Global Financial Crisis: Paradigm Lost?', *Journal of Common Market Studies* 47, no. 5 (2009), pp. 1041–61.

Holland, Stuart *The Socialist Challenge* (1976).

Hood, Andrew and Robert Joyce *The Economic Circumstances of Cohorts born between the 1940s and 1970s*, IFS, Report R89 (2013).

Hood, Christopher and Rozana Himaz 'The UK Geddes Axe of the 1920s in Perspective'. In *When the Party's Over: The Politics of Fiscal Squeeze in Perspective*, edited by Christopher Hood, David Heald, and Rozana Himaz (2014), pp. 73–92.

Hopkins, Tony 'Macmillan's Audit of Empire'. In *Understanding Decline*, edited by Peter Clarke and Clive Trebilcock (1997), pp. 234–60.

Hornby, Richard 'Conservative Principles', *PQ* 32, no. 3 (1961), pp. 229–37.

Horne, Alistair *Harold Macmillan, 1957–86: vol. II of the Official Biography* (1989).

Hoskyns, John *Just in Time: Inside the Thatcher Revolution* (2000).

Howe, Anthony *Free Trade and Liberal England, 1846–1946* (1997).

Howe, Geoffrey *Conflict of Loyalty* (2008).

Howell, Ralph *Why Work?* Conservative Political Centre (1981).

Howlett, Peter 'New Light Through Old Windows: A New Perspective on the British Economy in the Second World War', *Journal of Contemporary History* 28, no. 2 (1993), pp. 361–78.

Howlett, Peter 'The War-time Economy, 1939–1945'. In *The Cambridge Economic History of Britain, vol. 3: Structural Change and Growth, 1939–2000*, edited by Roderick Floud and Paul Johnson (2004), pp. 1–26.

Howson, Susan *Domestic Monetary Management in Britain, 1919–38* (1975).

Howson, Susan *Sterling's Managed Float* (1980).

Hutton, Graham *Politics and Economic Growth* (1968).

IFS *Election Briefing 2010 Summary* (2010).

IMF 'Fiscal Rules—Anchoring Expectations for Sustainable Public Finance', IMF Fiscal Affairs Department (2009).

IMF *United Kingdom: 2010 Article IV Consultation—Staff Report. IMF Country Report 10/338*. (2010).

IMF *World Economic Outlook: Growth Resuming, Danger Remains* (2010).

IMF *United Kingdom: 2011 Article IV Consultation - Staff Report. IMF Country Report 11/220* (2011).

Inman, Peggy *Labour in the Munitions Industries* (1957).

Innes, David and Gemma Tetlow 'Delivering Fiscal Squeeze by Cutting Local Government Expenditure', *FS* 36, no. 3 (2015), pp. 303–25.

Jackson, Ben 'Revisionism Reconsidered: "Property-Owning Democracy" in Post-War Britain', *TCBH* 16, no. 4 (2005), pp. 416–40.

Jackson, Ben 'At the Origins of Neo-Liberalism: The Free Economy and the Strong State, 1930–1947', *HJ* 53, no. 1 (2010), pp. 129–51.

Jackson, Ben 'An Ideology of Class: Neo-Liberalism and the Trade Unions, *c.*1930–1979'. In *Classes, Cultures and Politics: Essays on British History for Ross McKibbin*, edited by Clare Griffiths, James Nott, and William Whyte (2011), pp. 263–81.

Jackson, Ben 'Property-Owning Democracy: A Short History'. In *Property-owning Democracy: Rawls and Beyond*, edited by Martin O'Neill and Thad Williamson (2012), pp. 33–52.

Jackson, Ben 'The Think-Tank Archipelago'. In *Making Thatcher's Britain*, edited by Ben Jackson and Robert Saunders (2012), pp. 43–61.

Jackson, Peter 'Perspectives on Practical Monetarism'. In *Implementing Government Policy Initiatives: The Thatcher Administration 1979–1983*, edited by Peter Jackson (1985), pp. 33–67.

Jacques, Elliott *The Changing Culture of a Factory* (1951).

James, Howard *The End of Globalization. Lessons from the Great Depression* (2001).

James, Paul and Manfred Steger 'A Genealogy of "Globalization": The Career of a Concept'. In *Globalization: the Career of a Concept*, edited by Manfred Steger and Paul James (2015), pp. 1–18.

Jarvis, Martin *Conservative Governments, Morality and Social Change in Affluent Britain, 1957–64* (2005).

Jeffreys, Kevin *Anthony Crosland* (2000).

Jenkins, Peter *Harold Wilson's Productivity Conference* (1967).

Jenkins, Peter *Anatomy of Decline* (1996).

Jenkins, Roy *Labour's Case* (1959).

Jewkes, John 'A Defence of the White Paper on Employment Policy 1944'. In *A Return to Free Market Economics?*, edited by John Jewkes (1978), pp. 39–52.

Johnson, Christopher *The Economy Under Mrs Thatcher* (1991).

Johnson, Paul 'UK Fiscal Policy before the Crisis'. In *The UK Economy in the Long Expansion and its Aftermath*, edited by Jagjit Chadha, Alec Chrystal, Joe Pearlmann, Peter Smith, and Stephen Wright (2016), pp. 409–36.

Johnson, Richard *The Politics of Recession* (1982).

Jones, Matthew 'A Decision Delayed: Britain's Withdrawal from South East Asia Reconsidered, 1961–68', *EHR* 117, no. 472 (2002), pp. 569–95.

Jones, Owen *Chavs: The Demonization of the Working Class* (2nd edn, 2012).

Jones, Russell *Wages and Employment Policy 1936–1985* (1987).

Joseph, Keith *Reversing the Trend* (1975).

Joseph, Keith and Jonathan Sumption *Equality* (1979).

Joseph Rowntree Foundation *Monitoring Poverty and Social Exclusion* (2012).

Kavanagh, Dennis and Philip Cowley *The British General Election of 2010* (2010).

Keegan, William and Rupert Pennant-Rea *Who Runs the Economy? Control and Influence in British Economic Policy* (1979).

Keegan, William *Mrs Thatcher's Economic Experiment* (1984).

Keegan, William *Mr Osborne's Economic Experiment: Austerity 1945–51 and 2010–* (2014).

Key, Tomas Varun Paul, Martin Weale, and Tomasz Wieladek 'Property Income and the Balance of Payments'. In *The UK Economy in the Long Expansion and its Aftermath*, edited by Jagjit Chadha, Alec Chrystal, Joe Pearlmann, Peter Smith, and Stephen Wright (2016), pp. 111–30.

Keynes, John Maynard 'Letter to Roy Harrod', 19 April 1942, in *Collected Writings* vol. 25 (1971), pp. 147–9.

Keynes, John Maynard 'National Self-Sufficiency', 15 July 1933, in *Collected Writings* vol. 21 (1971), pp. 233–46.

Keynes, John Maynard 'Our Overseas Financial Prospects', 13 August 1945, in *Collected Writings* vol. 24 (1979), pp. 398–411.

Keynes, John Maynard 'Political and Military Expenditure Overseas', 11 February 1946, in *Collected Writings* vol. 27 (1980), pp. 465–81.

King, Anthony (editor) *British Public Opinion 1937–2000* (2001).

King, Desmond *Actively Seeking Work* (1995).

Kitson, Michael and Jonathan Michie 'The De-Industrial Revolution: The Rise and Fall of UK Manufacturing, 1870–2010'. In *The Cambridge Economic History of Modern Britain, vol. II: 1870 to the Present Day*, edited by Roderick Floud, Jane Humphries, and Paul Johnson (2014), pp. 302–29.

Klein, Rudolph 'Health Policy, 1979–1983: The Retreat from Ideology?' In *Implementing Government Policy Initiatives: The Thatcher Administration 1979–1983*, edited by Peter Jackson (1985), pp. 189–207.

Knight, David *Public Understanding of Science: A History of Communicating Science Ideas* (2006).

Kravis, Irving 'A Survey of International Comparisons of Productivity', *EJ* 86, no. 341 (1976), pp. 1–44.

Krugman, Paul 'Competitiveness: A Dangerous Obsession', *Foreign Affairs*, no. 73 (1994), pp. 28–44.

Krugman, Paul and Robert Lawrence 'Trade, Jobs and Wages', *Scientific American*, no. 270 (1994), pp. 44–9.

Kynaston, David 'The Bank and the Government'. In *The Bank of England: Money, Power and Influence 1694–1994*, edited by Richard Roberts and David Kynaston (1995), pp. 19–55.

Kynaston, David *Austerity Britain 1945–51* (2007).

Kynaston, David *Family Britain 1951–57* (2009).

Labour Party *Full Employment and Financial Policy* (1944).

Labour Party *Production the Bridge to Socialism* (1948).

Labour Party *Industry and Society* (1958).

Labour Party *Signposts for the Sixties* (1961).

Labour Party *Twelve Wasted Years* (1963).

Labour Party *International Big Business* (1977).

Labour Party *Looking to the Future* (1990).

Labour Party *New Labour: Because Britain Deserves Better* (1997).

Laidler, David *Fabricating the Keynesian Revolution* (1999).

Lawrence, Jon *Electing Our Masters: The Hustings in British Politics from Hogarth to Blair* (2009).

Lawrence, Jon and Florence Sutcliffe-Braithwaite 'Thatcher and the Decline of Class Politics'. In *Making Thatcher's Britain*, edited by Ben Jackson and Robert Saunders (2012), pp. 132–47.
Lawson, Nigel *The State of the Market*, IEA Occasional Paper no. 80 (1988).
Lawton, Kayte *Nice Work If You Can Get It*, Institute for Public Policy Research (IPPR) (2009).
League of Nations *Industrialisation and Foreign Trade* (1945).
League of Nations *Growth and Stagnation in the European Economy* (1954).
Leak, Hector 'Censuses of Production and Distribution'. In *The Sources and Nature of the Statistics of the UK*, edited by Maurice Kendall (1952), pp. 1–16.
Lee, Dwight (editor) *Public Choice, Past and Present: The Legacy of Gordon Tulloch and James Buchanan* (2013).
Le Grand, Julian *The Strategy of Equality: Redistribution and the Social Services* (1982).
Lekachman, Robert *The Age of Keynes: A Biographical Study* (1967).
Leruez, Jacques *Economic Planning and Politics* in *Britain* (1975).
Letwin, William (editor) *Against Equality* (1983).
Levie, Hugo, Denis Gregory, and Nick Lorentzen (editors) *Fighting Closures: De-industrialization and the Trade Unions* (1984).
Levinson, Marc *The Box: How the Shipping Container Made the World Smaller and the World Economy Bigger* (2006).
Levitas, Ruth 'Fiddling while Britain Burns? The "Measurement" of Unemployment'. In *Interpreting Official Statistics*, edited by Ruth Levitas and Will Guy (1996), pp. 45–65.
Levitt, Theodore 'The Globalization of Markets', *Harvard Business Review* 61 (May/June 1983), pp. 92–102.
Lewis-Beck, Michael, Richard Nadeau, and Eric Belanger 'General Election Forecasts in the United Kingdom: A Political Economy Model', *Electoral Studies* 23, no. 2 (2004), pp. 279–90.
Liadze, Iana and Martin Weale 'Economic Performance Under Labour', *NIER* no. 212 (2010), RR. 2–14.
Lindsay, Thomas and Michael Harrington *The Conservative Party 1918–1979* (2nd edn, 1979).
Lipsey, Richard *An Introduction to Positive Economics* (2nd edn, 1966).
Little, Ian 'Fiscal Policy'. In *The British Economy in the Nineteen-fifties*, edited by George Worswick and Peter Ady (1962), pp. 159–87.
Logan Turner Royce 'Post-War Pit Closures: The Politics of De-Industrialisation', *PQ* 56, no. 2 (1985), pp. 167–74.
Lowe, Rodney *Adjusting to Democracy: The Role of the Ministry of Labour in British Politics 1916–1939* (1986).
Lowe, Rodney 'The Core Executive, Modernisation and the Creation of PESC, 1960–1964', *Public Administration* 75, no. 4 (1997), pp. 601–15.
Lowe, Rodney and Neil Rollings 'Modernising Britain, 1957–64: A Classic Case of Centralisation and Fragmentation?' In *Transforming British Government, vol. 1*, edited by Rod Rhodes (2000), pp. 99–118.
Lowe, Rodney 'Modernizing Britain's Welfare State'. In *An Affluent Society? Britain's Post-War 'Golden Age' Revisited*, edited by Lawrence Black and Hugh Pemberton (2004), pp. 32–51.
Ludlam, Steven 'The Gnomes of Washington: Four Myths of the 1976 IMF Crisis', *PS* 40, no. 4 (1992), pp. 713–27.
McCombie, John and Anthony Thirlwall 'Comment: The Re-emergence of Balance of Payments Constrained Growth'. In *The Economic Legacy 1979–1992*, edited by Jonathan Michie (1992), pp. 68–74.

McCombie, John and Anthony Thirlwall *Essays on Balance of Payments Constrained Growth* (2004).
MacDowall, Michael *Public Understanding of Economic Policy: The Tax Cuts of 1962 and 1964* (1978).
Machin, Stephen 'Changes in UK Wage Inequality over the Last Forty Years'. In *The Labour Market in Winter*, edited by Paul Gregg and Jonathan Wadsworth (2011), pp. 157–68.
McKersie, Robert and Lawrence Hunter *Pay, Productivity and Collective Bargaining* (1973).
McLaine, Ian *Ministry of Morale* (1979).
Macleod, Rory 'The Promise of Full Employment'. In *War and Social Change: British Society in the Second World War*, edited by Harold Smith (1986), pp. 78–100.
Macmillan, Harold *Riding the Storm, 1956–59* (1971).
Macrae, Norman *Sunshades in October* (1963).
MacShane, Dennis *French Lessons for Labour*, Fabian Society No. 512 (1986).
Maddison, Angus *Dynamic Forces in Capitalist Development* (1991).
Maddison, Angus *The World Economy: A Millennial Perspective* (2001).
Maier, Charles 'The Politics of Productivity: Foundations of American International Economic Policy after World War II'. In Charles Maier *In Search of Stability: Explorations in Historical Political Economy* (1987), pp. 121–52.
Maizels, Alfred 'Overseas Trade'. In *Sources*, edited by Maurice Kendall (1952), pp. 17–33.
Mandelson, Peter 'Foreword'. In *The Third Wave of Globalisation*, edited by Will Straw and Alex Glennie (2012), pp. 9–15.
Manser, William *Britain in the Balance?* (1971).
Marquand, David 'The Twilight of the British State? Henry Dubb versus Sceptred Awe'. In *The Boundaries of the State in Modern Britain*, edited by Simon Green and Richard Whiting (1996), pp. 57–69.
Marrison, Andrew *British Business and Protection, 1903–1932* (1996).
Martin, Ron and Robert Rowthorn (editors) *The Geography of Deindustrialization* (1986).
Mass Observation *People in Production: An Enquiry into British War Production* (1942).
Massey, Doreen and Richard Meegan *The Anatomy of Job Loss: the How, Where and Why of Employment Decline* (1982).
Matthews, Robin 'Why has Britain had Full Employment since the War?', *EJ* 78, no. 3 (1968), pp. 555–69.
Mercer, Helen 'The Monopolies and Restrictive Practices Commission from 1949–56: A Study in Regulatory Failure'. In *Competitiveness and the State in Twentieth Century Britain*, edited by Geoffrey Jones and Maurice Kirby (1991), pp. 78–99.
Mercer, Helen *Constructing a Competitive Order: The Hidden History of British Antitrust Policies* (1995).
Michael, Mike 'Ignoring Science: Discourses of Ignorance in the Public Understanding of Science'. In *Misunderstanding Science? The Public Reconstruction of Science and Technology*, edited by Alan Irwin and Brian Wynne (1996), pp. 107–25.
Middlemas, Keith *Power, Competition and the State, vol. 1: Britain in Search of Balance 1940–61* (1986).
Middleton, Roger *Government versus the Market* (1996).
Middleton, Roger *Charlatans or Saviours? Economists and the British Economy from Marshall to Meade* (1998).
Middleton, Roger 'Struggling with the Impossible: Sterling, the Balance of Payments and British Economic Policy, 1949–72'. In *The Open Economy Macro-Model: Past, Present and Future*, edited by Arie Arnon and William Young (2002), pp. 103–54.

Middleton, Roger 'Economists and Economic Growth in Britain, *c.*1955–65'. In *An Affluent Society: Britain's Post-War 'Golden Age' Revisited*, edited by Lawrence Black and High Pemberton (2004), pp. 129–48.

Middleton, Roger 'British Monetary and Fiscal Policy in the 1930s', *OREP* 26, no. 3 (2010), pp. 414–41.

Middleton, Roger 'Brittan on Britain: Decline, Declinism and the "Traumas of the 1970s"'. In *Reassessing 1970s Britain*, edited by Lawrence Black, Hugh Pemberton, and Pat Thane (2013), pp. 69–95.

Miller, Peter 'Psychotherapy of Work and Unemployment'. In *The Power of Psychiatry*, edited by Peter Miller and Nikolas Rose (1986), pp. 143–76.

Miller, Peter, and Nikolas Rose 'Governing Economic Life', *Economy and Society* 19, no. 1 (1990), pp. 1–31.

Miller, Robert and John Wood *What Price Unemployment?* (1982).

Milward, Alan *The European Rescue of the Nation State* (1992).

Milward, Alan and Gregory Brennan *Britain's Place in the World: A Historical Enquiry into Import Controls 1945–60* (1996).

Minford, Patrick *Unemployment: Cause and Cure* (2nd edn, 1985).

Ministry of Labour *Human Relations in Industry* (1952).

Ministry of Labour *Workers' Attitudes to Industrial Efficiency* (1966).

Moggridge, Donald *British Monetary Policy 1924–1931: The Norman Conquest of $4.86* (1972).

Moore, Charles *Margaret Thatcher: The Authorized Biography. Vol. One: Not for Turning* (2014).

Moore, Martin *The Origins of Modern Spin: Democratic Government and the Media in Britain, 1945–51* (2006).

Moran, Michael *Politics of the Financial Services Revolution: The USA, UK and Japan* (1991).

Morgan, Kenneth 'Imperialism at Bay: British Labour and Decolonization', *Journal of Imperial and Commonwealth History* 27, no. 2 (1990), pp. 233–54.

Mosley, Layna 'Room to Move: International Financial Markets and National Welfare States', *International Organization* 54, no. 4 (2001), pp. 737–73.

Mosley, Layna *Global Capital and National Governments* (2003).

Mosley, Paul *The Making of Economic Policy* (1984).

Murie, Alan 'The housing legacy of Thatcherism'. In *The Legacy of Thatcherism*, edited by Stephen Farrall and Colin Hay (2014), pp. 143–66.

Murray, Bruce *The People's Budget 1909/10* (1980).

Needham, Duncan *UK Monetary Policy from Devaluation to Thatcher, 1967–1982* (2014).

Needham, Duncan and Anthony Hotson (editors) *Expansionary Fiscal Contraction: The Thatcher Government's 1981 Budget in Perspective* (2014).

Needham, Duncan 'Britain's Money Supply Experiment, 1971–73', *EHR* 130, no. 542 (2015), pp. 1079–101.

Needham, Duncan '"Goodbye Great Britain"? The Press, the Treasury, and the 1976 IMF Crisis'. In *The Media and Financial Crises: Comparative and Historical Perspectives*, edited by Steven Schifferes and Richard Roberts (2015), pp. 261–76.

Newell, Andrew 'Structural Change'. In *Work and Pay in Twentieth-Century Britain*, edited by Nicholas Crafts, Ian Gazeley, and Andrew Newell (2007), pp. 35–54.

Newton, Christopher 'The Sterling Crisis of 1947 and the British Response to the Marshall Plan', *EcHR* 37, no. 3 (1984), pp. 391–408.

Nicholas, Herbert *The British General Election of 1950* (1951).

Nichols, Theo *The British Worker Question: A New Look at Workers and Productivity in Manufacturing* (1986).

Nicholson, Roydon and Sanjeev Gupta 'Output and Productivity Changes in Manufacturing 1948–52', *JRSS* 23, no. 4 (1960), pp. 427–59.

Nickell, Stephen *Review of Minford*, LSE, Centre for Labour Economics (1984).

Nickell, Stephen 'The Government's Policy for Jobs: An Analysis', *OREP* 1, no. 2 (1986), pp. 98–115.

Nickell, Stephen 'Poverty and Worklessness in Britain', *EJ* 114, no. 494 (2004), Conference Papers, cc. 1–25.

NUCUA Conference Report, 1954 (1954).

Nuttall, Jeremy 'Labour Revisionism and Qualities of Character, 1931–79', *EHR* 120, no. 487 (2005), pp. 667–94.

Obelkovich, Jim 'Consumption'. In *Understanding Post-War British Society*, edited by Jim Obelkovich and Peter Catterall (1994), pp. 141–54.

OBR *Pre-Budget Forecast* (June 2010).

OBR *Budget Forecast* (June 2010).

OBR *Welfare Trends Report* (2014).

Obstfeld, Maurice and Alan Taylor *Global Capital Markets: Integration, Crisis and Growth* (2004).

OEEC *The Terminology of Productivity* (1950).

OEEC *A Standardised System of National Accounts* (1952).

OEEC *Statistics of National Product and Expenditure, 1938, 1947 to 1952* (1954).

Offer, Avner 'Why has the Public Sector Grown so Large in Market Societies? The Political Economy of Prudence in the UK *c.*1870–2000', Oxford University Inaugural Lecture, 13th November 2001 (2003).

Offer, Avner 'British Manual Workers: From Producers to Consumers, *c.*1950–2000', *CBH* 22, no. 4 (2008), pp. 537–71.

Offer, Avner 'Narrow Banking, Real Estate, and Financial Stability in the UK *c.*1870–2019'. In *British Financial Crises since 1825*, edited by Nicholas Dimsdale and Anthony Hotson (2014), pp. 158–73.

Offer, Avner and Gabriel Soberberg *The Nobel Factor: The Prize in Economics, Social Democracy, and the Market Turn* (2016).

Offer, Avner 'The Market Turn: From Social Democracy to Market Liberalism', University of Oxford Discussion papers in Economic and Social History, no. 149 (2016).

O'Hara, Glen 'Intractable, Obscure and Baffling: The Incomes Policy of the Conservative Government, 1957–64', *CBH* 18, no. 1 (2004), pp. 25–53.

O'Hara, Glen 'Towards a New Bradshaw? Economic Statistics and the British State in the 1950s and 1960s', *EcHR* 60, no. 1 (2007), pp. 1–34.

O'Hara, Glen 'The Use and Abuse of Foreign Archetypes in British Economic Policy', in *Governing Post-War Britain* (2012), pp. 11–27.

Oliver, Michael *Whatever Happened to Monetarism?* (1997).

Oppenheimer, Peter 'Muddling Through'. In *The Age of Affluence 1951–1964,* edited by Vernon Bogdanor and Robert Skidelsky (1970), pp. 117–67.

O'Rourke, Kevin and Jeffrey Williamson 'When did Globalization Begin?', *European Review of Economic History* 6, no. 1 (2002), pp. 23–50.

Ormerod, Paul 'Incomes Policy'. In *Labour's Economic Policies 1974–79*, edited by Michael Artis and David Cobham (1991), pp. 56–72.

O'Rourke, Kevin 'From Empire to Europe: Britain in the World Economy'. In *The Cambridge Economic History of Britain, vol. II: 1870 to the Present*, edited by Roderick Floud, Paul Johnson, and Jane Humphries (2014), pp. 60–94.

Paige, Deborah and Gottfried Bombach *A Comparison of National Output and Productivity of the UK and US* (1959).

Parker, David *The Official History of Privatization, Vol. I: The Formative Years, 1970–87* (2009).

Parker, David *The Official History of Privatization, Vol. II: Popular Capitalism, 1987–1997* (2012).

Parsons, Wayne *The Political Economy of British Regional Policy* (1986).

Parsons, Wayne *The Power of the Financial Press* (1989).

Paul, Katherine *Whitewashing Britain: Race and Citizenry in the Post-War Era* (1997).

Pearce, Nick and Eleanor Taylor 'Government Spending and Welfare'. In *BSA 30th Report* (2013), pp. 33–61.

Peden George 'Old Dogs and New Tricks'. In *The State and Economic Knowledge*, edited by Mary Furner and Barry Supple (1990), pp. 208–38.

Peden, George *The Treasury and British Public Policy 1906–1959* (2000).

Peden, George *Keynes and his Critics: Treasury Responses to the Keynesian Revolution, 1925–1946* (2012).

Pemberton, Hugh 'Learning, Governance and Economic Policy', *BJPIR* 5, no. 4 (2003), pp. 500–24.

Pemberton, Hugh *Policy Learning and British Governance in the 1960s* (2004).

Pencavel, John 'The Surprising Retreat of Union Britain'. In *Seeking a Premier Economy: The Effects of British Economic Reforms, 1980–2000*, edited by David Card, Richard Blundell, and Richard Freeman (2004), pp. 181–232.

Phillips, Jim 'Class and Industrial Relations in Britain: The "long" Mid-Century and the Case of Port Transport *c.*1920–70', *TCBH* 16, no. 1 (2005), pp. 52–73.

Phillips, Jim 'De-Industrialization and the Moral Economy of the Scottish Coalfields, 1947–1991', *International Labor and Working Class History*, 84, no. 1 (2013), pp. 99–115.

Piachaud, David 'Inflation and Income Distribution'. In *The Political Economy of Inflation*, edited by Fred Hirsch and John Goldthorpe (1978), pp. 88–116.

Piketty, Thomas *Capital in the Twenty-first Century* (2014).

Pilat, Dirk, Agnes Cimper, Karsten Olsen, and Colin Webb *The Changing Nature of Manufacturing in OECD Countries*, OECD (2006).

Pimlott, Ben *Harold Wilson* (1993).

Plehwe, Dieter 'Introduction'. In *The Road from Mont Pelerin: The Making of the Neoliberal Thought Collective*, edited by Philip Mirowski and Dieter Plehwe (2009), pp. 1–42.

Pliatzky, Leo *Getting and Spending: Public Expenditure, Employment and Inflation* (1982).

Pollard, Sidney *The Wasting of the British Economy* (1982).

Porter, Dilwyn 'Downhill All the Way'. In *The Wilson Governments, 1964–1970*, edited by Richard Coopey, Steven Fielding, and Nick Tiratsoo (1993), pp. 10–28.

Prasad, Monica *The Politics of Free Markets: The Rise of Neo-liberal Economic Policies in Britain, France, Germany and the United States* (2006).

Prior, Jim *A Balance of Power* (1986).

Przeworski, Adam *Capitalism and Social Democracy* (1985).

Rajan, Raghuram and Luigi Zingales 'The Great Reversals: The Politics of Financial Development in the Twentieth Century', *Journal of Financial Economics* 69, no. 1 (2003), pp. 5–50.

Ramsden, John 'From Churchill to Heath'. In *The Conservatives*, edited by Rab Butler (1977), pp. 407–78.

Ramsden, John *The Making of Conservative Party Policy: The Conservative Research Department since 1929* (1980).

Reddaway, William and Alan Smith 'Progress in British Manufacturing Industries 1948–54', *EJ* 70, no. 1 (1960), pp. 17–31.

Reddaway, William *Effects of UK Direct Investment Overseas* (1968).

Ringe, Astrid and Neil Rollings 'Responding to Relative Decline: The Creation of the NEDC', *EcHR* 53, no. 2 (2000), pp. 331–53.

Ringe, Astrid, Roger Middleton, and Neil Rollings *Economic Policy under the Conservatives, 1951–64: A Guide to Documents in the National Archives of the UK* (2004).

Robbins, Lionel *The Theory of Economic Policy in English Classical Political Economy* (1952).

Robbins, Lionel (editor) *Inflation: Economy and Society* (1972).

Robbins, Lionel *Against Inflation: Speeches in the Second Chamber 1965–1977* (1979).

Roberts, Ben *National Wages Policy in War and Peace* (1958).

Roberts, Richard 'The Administrative Origins of Industrial Diplomacy: An Aspect of Government Industry Relations 1929–1935'. In *Businessmen and Politics: Studies of Business Activity in British Politics, 1900–1945*, edited by John Turner (1986), pp. 93–104.

Rodrik, Dani 'Why Do More Open Economies Have Bigger Governments?', *Journal of Political Economy* 106, no. 5 (1998), pp. 997–1032.

Rodrik, Dani *The Globalization Paradox: Why Global Markets, States and Democracy Can't Co-exist* (2011).

Rogers, Edmund 'A "Naked Strength and Beauty": Statistics in the British Tariff Debate, 1880–1914'. In *Statistics and the Public Sphere*, edited by Tom Crook and Glen O'Hara (2011), pp. 224–43.

Rollings, Neil 'British Budgetary Policy 1945–54: A "Keynesian Revolution"?', *EcHR* 41, no. 2 (1988), pp. 283–98.

Rollings, Neil 'The Reichstag Method of Governing? The Attlee Government and Permanent Economic Controls'. In *Labour Governments and Private Industry: The Experience of 1945–1951*, edited by Helen Mercer, Neil Rollings, and Jim Tomlinson (1992), pp. 15–36.

Rollings, Neil 'Multinational Enterprise and Government Controls on FDI in the US and the UK in the 1960s', *Enterprise and Society* 12, no. 2 (2011), pp. 398–434.

Rollings, Neil 'Cracks in the Post-War Keynesian Settlement? The Role of Organised Business in Britain in the Rise of Neo-liberalism Before Margaret Thatcher', *TCBH* 24 no. 4 (2013), pp. 637–59.

Rollings, Neil 'Between Business and Academia in Post-War Britain'. In *Liberalism and the Welfare State: Economists and Arguments for the Welfare State*, edited by Roger Backhouse, Bradley Bateman, Tamotsu Nishizawa, and Dieter Plehwe (2017), pp. 101–17.

Roodhouse, Mark *Black Market Britain, 1939–1955* (2013).

Rose, Nikolas 'Governing by Numbers: Figuring Out Democracy', *Accounting, Organization and Society* 16, no. 7 (1991), pp. 673–92.

Rostas, Lazlo 'Productivity of Labour in the Cotton Industry', *EJ* 55, no. 3 (1945), pp. 192–205.

Rostas, Lazlo *Comparative Productivity in British and American Industry* (1948).

Rostas, Lazlo *Productivity, Prices and Distribution in Selected British Industries* (1948).

Rostas, Lazlo 'Changes in the Productivity of British Industry, 1945–50', *EJ* 62, no. 1 (1952), pp. 15–24.

Rowthorn, Robert *De-Industrialization and Foreign Trade* (1987).

Rowthorn, Robert and Ramana Ramaswamy 'Growth, Trade and De-Industrialization', IMF Research Department WP/98/60 (1998).

Royal Statistical Society *Report of the Working Party on the Measure of Unemployment in the UK* (1994).

Ruggie, John 'International Regimes, Transactions, and Change: Embedded Liberalism in the Post-War Economic Order', *International Organization* 36 (1982), pp. 379–415.

Salter, William *Productivity and Technical Change* (1962).

Sampson, Anthony *Macmillan: A Study in Ambiguity* (1967).

Sandbrook, Dominic *Never Had it so Good: A History of Britain from Suez to the Beatles* (2006).

Sanders, David 'The Real Economy and the Perceived Economy in Popularity Functions: How Much do Voters Need to Know?', *Electoral Studies* 19, no. 2/3 (2000), pp. 275–94.

Sassoon, Donald *One Hundred Years of Socialism: The West European Left in the Twentieth Century* (1996).

Saul, Berrick *Industrialisation and De-Industrialisation: The Interaction of the German and British Economies before the First World War* (1979).

Saunders, Robert 'Crisis? What Crisis? Thatcherism and the Seventies'. In *Making Thatcher's Britain*, edited by Ben Jackson and Robert Saunders (2012), pp. 25–42.

Savage, Mike and Karel Williams 'Elites: Remembered in Capitalism and Forgotten by Social Sciences'. In *Remembering Elites*, edited by Mike Savage and Karel Williams (2008), pp. 1–24.

Sayers, Richard 'The Return to Gold, 1925'. In *The Gold Standard and Employment Policies between the Wars*, edited by Sidney Pollard (1970), pp. 85–98.

Scharpf, Fritz *Crisis and Choice in Social Democracy* (1991).

Schenk, Catherine *Britain and the Sterling Area: From Devaluation to Convertibility in the 1950s* (1994).

Schenk, Catherine 'The Origins of the Eurodollar Market in London: 1955–1963', *Explorations in Economic History* 35, no. 2 (1998), pp. 221–38.

Schenk, Catherine 'The New City and the State in the 1960s'. In *The British Government and the City of London in the Twentieth Century*, edited by Ranald Michie and Philip Williamson (2004), pp. 322–39.

Schenk, Catherine *International Economic Relations Since 1945* (2011).

Scott, William *Joint Consultation in a Liverpool Manufacturing Firm* (1950).

Searle, Rebecca 'Is there Anything Real about Real Wages? A History of the Official Cost of Living Index, 1914–62', *EcHR* 68, no. 1 (2015), pp. 145–66.

Servan-Schreiber, Jean-Jacques *The American Challenge* (1968).

Shanks, Michael *The Stagnant Society* (1961).

Shonfield, Andrew *British Economic Policy since the War* (1958).

Singh, Ajit 'UK Industry and the World Economy: A Case of Deindustrialisation?', *Cambridge Journal of Economics* 1, no. 2 (1977), pp. 113–36.

Skidelsky, Robert 'Thinking about the State and the Economy'. In *The Boundaries of the State in Modern Britain*, edited by Simon Green and Richard Whiting (1996), pp. 70–86.

Smith, William *Inflation and Elderly People* (1983).

Snowden, Nick and Chris Milner 'External Imbalance and Policy Constraints in the 1990s'. In *External Imbalance and Policy Constraint in the 1990s*, edited by Chris Milner and Nick Snowden (1992), pp. 1–11.

Snowden, Philip *Labour and National Finance* (1920).

Spange, Morten and Chris Young 'The Macroeconomic Impact of Globalisation: Theory and Evidence', *BEQB* 47, no. 1 (2007), pp. 40–7.

Stafford, George 'Full Employment since the War—Comment', *EJ* 80, no. 1 (1970), pp. 165–72.

Stedman-Jones, Gareth *Outcast London* (1971).

Stewart, Mark 'Low Pay in Britain'. In *The State of Working Britain*, edited by Paul Gregg and Jonathan Wadsworth (1999), pp. 225–48.

Stewart, Michael *Keynes and After* (1972).

Stone, Richard 'The Use and Development of National Income and Expenditure Estimates'. In *Lessons of the British War Economy*, edited by Norman Chester (1951), pp. 83–101.

Strange, Susan *Sterling and British Policy* (1971).

Strange, Susan *The Casino Economy* (1986).

Strauss-Kahn, Dominic 'Foreword' to IMF, *Fiscal Monitor: Navigating the Fiscal Challenges Ahead*, May (2010), pp. 1–10.

Straw, Will and Alex Glennie *The Third Wave of Globalisation* (2012).

Stubager, Rune 'Preference-Shaping: An Empirical Test', *PS* 51, no. 2 (2003), pp. 241–61.

Studenski, John *The Income of Nations*, 2 vols. (1958).

Supple, Barry 'Official Economic Enquiry and Britain's Industrial Decline: The First Fifty Years'. In *The State and Economic Knowledge*, edited by Mary Furner and Barry Supple (1990), pp. 325–53.

Supple, Barry 'British Economic Decline Since 1945'. In *The Economic History of Britain since 1700, vol 3: 1939–1992*, edited by Roderick Floud and Donald McCloskey (2nd edn, 1994), pp. 318–46.

Supple, Barry 'Fear of Failing: Economic History and the Decline of Britain', *EcHR* 47, no. 3 (1994), pp. 441–58.

Sutcliffe-Braithwaite, Florence 'Neoliberalism and Morality in the Making of Thatcherite Social Policy', *HJ* 55, no.2 (2012), pp. 497–520.

Tatomir, Srdan 'Self-Employment: What Can We Learn from Recent Developments?', *BEQB 45,* no. 1 (2015), pp. 56–66.

Taylor, Andrew '"The Record of the 1950s is Irrelevant": The Conservative Party, Electoral Strategy and Opinion Research, 1945–64', *CBH* 17, no. 1 (2003), pp. 81–110.

Taylor, Jim 'Hidden Female Labour Reserves', *Regional Studies* 2, no. 2 (1968), pp. 221–31.

Taylor, Robert 'Scapegoats for National Decline: The Trade Unions since 1945'. In *Trends in British Politics since 1945*, edited by Chris Cook and John Ramsden (1978), pp. 88–108.

Taylor-Gooby, Peter and Charlotte Hastie 'Support for State Spending: Has New Labour Got It Right?', *BSA* 19th Report (2002), pp. 79–96.

Taylor-Gooby, Peter and Eleanor Taylor 'Benefits and Welfare: Long-Term Trends or Short-Term Reactions?', *BSA* 32nd Report (2015), pp. 74–101.

Tew, Brian 'Policies Aimed at Improving the Balance Of Payments'. In *British Economic Policy 1960–74*, edited by Frank Blackaby (1978), pp. 304–59.

Thane, Pat 'The Working Class and State Welfare in Britain, 1880–1914', *HJ* 27, no. 4 (1984), pp. 877–90.

Thane, Pat 'Labour and Local Politics: Radicalism, Democracy and Social Reform, 1880–1914'. In *Currents of Radicalism*, edited by Eugenio Biagini and Alastair Reid (1991), pp. 244–70.

Thatcher, Arthur 'Statistics of Unemployment in the UK'. In *The Concept and Measurement of Involuntary Unemployment*, edited by David Worswick (1976), pp. 83–94.

Thatcher, Margaret *The Path to Power* (1985).

Thirlwall, Anthony and Heather Gibson *Balance of Payments Theory and the UK Experience* (1991).

Thomas, Hugh (editor) *The Establishment* (1959).

Thompson, Helen *British Conservative Governments and the European Exchange Rate Mechanism 1979–1994* (1996).

Thompson, Helen 'The Nation-State and International Capital Flows In Historical Perspective', *Government and Opposition* 32, no. 1 (1997), pp. 84–113.

Thompson, Helen 'The Thatcherite Economic Legacy'. In *The Legacy of Thatcherism*, edited by Stephen Farrall and Colin Hay (2014), pp. 33–68.

Thompson, Noel 'Hollowing Out the State: Public Choice Theory and the Critique of Keynesian Social Democracy', *CBH* 22, no. 3 (2008), pp. 355–82.

Thompson, Noel 'Conceptualising the Consumer: British Socialist Democratic Political Economy in the Golden Age of Capitalisms', *CBH* 25, no. 2 (2011), pp. 297–321.

Tiratsoo, Nick *Reconstruction, Affluence and Labour Politics: Coventry 1945–1960* (1990).

Tiratsoo, Nick and Jim Tomlinson *Industrial Efficiency and State Intervention: Labour 1939–51* (1993).

Todd, Selina *The People: The Rise and Fall of the Working Class, 1910–2010* (2014).

Tomlinson, Jim *Problems of British Economic Policy 1870–1945* (1981).

Tomlinson, Jim 'The "Economics of Politics" and Public Expenditure: A Critique', *Economy and Society* 10, no. 4 (1981), pp. 381–402.

Tomlinson, Jim *Employment Policy: The Crucial Years 1939–1955* (1987).

Tomlinson, Jim *Public Policy and the Economy since 1900* (1990).

Tomlinson, Jim 'The Failure of the Anglo-American Council on Productivity', *Business History* 32, no. 1 (1991), pp. 82–92.

Tomlinson, Jim 'The Labour Government and the Trade Unions, 1945–51'. In *The Attlee Years*, edited by Nick Tiratsoo (1991), pp. 90–105.

Tomlinson, Jim 'Mr Attlee's Supply-Side Socialism', *EcHR* 46, no. 1 (1993), pp. 1–22.

Tomlinson, Jim *Government and the Enterprise since 1900: The Changing Problem of Efficiency* (1994).

Tomlinson, Jim 'An Unfortunate Alliance: Keynesianism and the Conservatives, 1951–64', *History of Political Economy* 36, supplement (1995), pp. 61–85.

Tomlinson, Jim 'Inventing "Decline": The Falling Behind of the British Economy in the Post-War Years', *EcHR* 49, no. 4 (1996), pp. 731–57.

Tomlinson, Jim 'Correlli Barnett's History: The Case of Marshall Aid', *TCBH* 7, no. 2 (1997), pp. 222–38.

Tomlinson, Jim *Democratic Socialism and Economic Policy: The Attlee Years 1945–1951* (1997).

Tomlinson, Jim 'Why So Austere? The British Welfare State of the 1940s', *JSP* 27, no. 1 (1998), pp. 63–77.

Tomlinson, Jim 'Labour and the Economy'. In *Labour's First Century*, edited by Duncan Tanner, Pat Thane, and Nick Tiratsoo (2001), pp. 46–79.

Tomlinson, Jim, 'The "Productivity Problem" in the 1960s', *Past and Present* no. 175 (2002), pp. 188–210.

Tomlinson, Jim 'The Commonwealth, the Balance of Payments and the Politics of International Poverty: British Aid Policy, 1958–1971', *Contemporary European History* 12, no. 3 (2003), pp. 417–22.

Tomlinson, Jim *The Labour Governments, 1964–1970, vol. III: Economic Policy* (2004).

Tomlinson, Jim 'The Labour Party and the City, 1945–1970'. In *British Government and the City of London in the Twentieth Century*, edited by Ranald Michie and Philip Williamson (2004), pp. 174–92.

Tomlinson, Jim 'Managing the Economy, Managing the People: Britain circa 1931–1970', *EcHR* 58, no. 3 (2005), pp. 555–85.

Tomlinson, Jim 'Mrs Thatcher's Economic Adventurism', *British Politics* 2, no. 1 (2007), pp. 3–19.

Tomlinson, Jim 'A "Failed Experiment"? Public Ownership and the Narratives of Post-War Britain', *Labour History Review* 73, no. 2 (2008), pp. 199–214.

Tomlinson, Jim 'History as Political Rhetoric', *Political Studies Review* 6, no. 3 (2008), pp. 297–307.

Tomlinson, Jim 'Balanced Accounts? Constructing the Balance of Payments Problem in Post-War Britain', *EHR* 104, no. 509 (2009), pp. 863–84.

Tomlinson, Jim 'Not "Decline and Revival": An Alternative Narrative on British Post-War Productivity'. In *Business in Britain in the Twentieth Century*, edited by Richard Coopey and Peter Lyth (2009), pp. 153–67.

Tomlinson, Jim 'Re-Inventing the "Moral Economy" in Post-War Britain', *Historical Research* 84, no. 224 (2010), pp. 356–73.

Tomlinson, Jim 'From "Distribution of Industry" to "Local Keynesianism": An Unacknowledged Policy Revolution?', *British Politics* 7, no. 3 (2012), pp. 204–23.

Tomlinson, Jim 'Thatcher, monetarism, and the Politics of Inflation'. In *Making Thatcher's Britain*, edited by Ben Jackson and Robert Saunders (2012), pp. 62–77.

Tomlinson, Jim 'The Politics of Declinism'. In *Reassessing 1970s Britain*, edited by Lawrence Black, Hugh Pemberton, and Pat Thane (2013), pp. 41–60.

Tomlinson, Jim 'Distributional Politics: The Search for Equality in Britain since the First World War'. In *The Contradictions of Capital in the Twenty-first Century*, edited by Pat Hudson and Keith Tribe (2016), pp. 167–91.

Toniolo, Gianni and Piet Clement *Central Bank Co-operation at the Bank for International Settlements, 1930–1973* (2005).

Tooze, Adam 'Imagining National Economies: National and International Economic Statistics, 1900–1950'. In *Imagining Nations*, edited by Geoffrey Cubitt (1998), pp. 212–28.

Tooze, Adam *Statistics and the German State, 1900–1945: The Making of Modern Economic Knowledge* (2001).

Toye, Richard 'The Attlee Government, the Imperial Preference System and the Creation of the GATT', *EHR* 118, no. 478 (2003), pp. 912–39.

Toye, Richard *The Labour Party and the Planned Economy 1931–1951* (2003).

Trentmann, Frank 'The Strange Death of Free Trade: The Erosion of "Liberal Consensus" in Great Britain, *c.*1903–1932'. In *Citizenship and Community: Liberals, Radicals and Collective Identities in the British Isles 1865–1931*, edited by Eugenio Biagini (1996), pp. 219–50.

Trentmann, Frank 'Wealth and Welfare: The British Left between Free Trade and National Political Economy before the First World War', *Historical Research* 70, no. 1 (1997), pp. 70–98.

Trentmann, Frank 'Bread, Milk and Democracy: Consumption and Citizenship in Twentieth Century Britain'. In *The Politics of Consumption*, edited by Martin Daunton and Matthew Hilton (2001), pp. 129–64.

Trentmann, Frank *Free Trade Nation* (2008).

Trevithick, James and Charles Mulvay *The Economics of Inflation* (1975).

Tribe, Keith *The Economy of the Word: History, Language and Economics* (2015).

TUC 'Productivity: Report of Special Conference of TU Executive Committees, 18 November 1948' (1948).

TUC *Trade Unions and Productivity* (1951).

Turner, Henry 'Wages: Industry Rates, Workplace Rates and the Wage Drift', *Manchester School* 24, no. 1 (1954), pp. 95–123.

Tyszynski, Henry 'World Trade in Manufactured Commodities', *Manchester School* 19, no. 3 (1951), pp. 272–304.

UN *Economic Bulletin for Europe* (1949).

UNECE *Economic Survey of Europe in 1949* (1950).

UNECE *Economic Survey of Europe in 1957* (1958).

UNECE *Economic Commissioner for Europe: The first 10 years, 1947–57* (1958).

Ussher, Kitty 'Labour's Record on the Economy'. In *Reassessing New Labour*, edited by Peter Diamond and Michael Kenny (2011), ss. 108–22.

Vaizey, John *In Breach of Promise* (1983).

Van Horn, Robert 'Reinventing Monopoly and the Role of Corporations: The Roots of Chicago Law and Economics'. In *The Road from Mont Pelerin*, edited by Philip Mirowski and Dieter Plehwe (2009) pp. 204–37.

Varoufakis, Yanis *The Global Minotaur: America, Europe and the Future of the Global Economy* (3rd edn, 2015).

Vernon Raymond *Sovereignty at Bay* (1971).

Wadsworth, Jonathan 'Eyes Down for a Full House: Labour Market Polarisation and the Housing Market in Britain', *SJPE* 45, no. 4 (1998), pp. 376–92.

Walker, Carol '"Don't Cut Down the Tall Poppies": Thatcherism and the Strategy of Inequality'. In *The Legacy of Thatcherism*, edited by Stephen Farrall and Colin Hay (2014), pp. 282–305.

Walsh, James 'When Do Ideas Matter? The Success and Failure of Thatcherite Ideas', *Comparative Political Studies* 33, no. 4 (2000), pp. 483–516.

Walters, William 'The "Discovery" of Unemployment: New Forms for the Government of Poverty', *Economy and Society* 23, no. 3 (1994), pp. 265–90.

White, Michael and Kurt Schuler 'Who Said "Debase the Currency": Keynes or Lenin?', *Journal of Economic Perspectives* 23, no. 3 (2009), pp. 213–22.

Whiteside, Noel 'Creating the Welfare State in Britain, 1945–1960', *JSP* 25, no. 1 (1996), pp. 83–103.

Whiting, Richard *The Labour Party and Taxation* (2000).

Wickham-Jones Mark 'New Labour in the Global Economy: Partisan Politics and the Social Democratic Model', *BJPIR* 2, no. 1 (2000), pp. 1–25.

Wilding, Paul 'The Welfare State and the Conservatives', *PS* 45, no. 4 (1997), pp. 716–26.

Wildy, Tom 'From the MOI to the COI—Publicity and Propaganda in Britain, 1945–1951: The NHS and Insurance Campaigns of 1948', *Historical Journal of Film, Radio and Television* 6, no. 1 (1986), pp. 3–17.

Wiles, Peter 'Notes on the Efficiency of Labour', *Oxford Economic Papers* 3, no. 1 (1951), pp. 173–9.

Williamson, Adrian *Conservative Economic Policymaking and the Birth of Thatcherism, 1964–1979* (2015).

Wilson, Harold *Post-war Economic Policies in Britain* (1957).

Wilson, Harold *Purpose in Politics: Selected Speeches* (1964).

Wilson, Harold 'Statistics and Decision-Making in Government—Bradshaw Revisited', *JRSS, Series A* 136 (1973), pp. 1–16.

Winch, Donald *Economics and Policy* (1972).

Winch, Donald 'Economic Knowledge and Government in Britain'. In *The State and Economic Knowledge*, edited by Mary Furner and Barry Supple (1990), pp. 40–70.

Wood, Adrian 'How Trade Hurt Unskilled Workers', *Journal of Economic Perspectives* 9, no. 1 (1995), pp. 57–80.
Wood, John *How Much Unemployment?* (1972).
Wood, John *How Little Unemployment?* (1975).
Wootton, Barbara *The Social Foundations of Wages Policy* (2nd edn, 1962).
Wootton, Barbara *Incomes Policy: An Inquest and a Proposal* (1974).
Worswick, David 'Introduction' to *The Concept and Measurement of Involuntary Unemployment*, edited by David Worswick (1976), pp. 13–16.
Wren-Lewis, Simon 'Lessons from Failure: Fiscal Policy, Indulgence and Ideology', *NIER* no. 217 (2011), RR. 31–46.
Wren-Lewis, Simon 'Aggregate Fiscal Policy under the Labour Government', *OREP* 29, no. 1 (2013), pp. 25–46.
Wring, Dominic *The Politics of Marketing the Labour Party* (2005).
Wysploz, Charles 'Fiscal Discipline: Rules rather than Institutions', *NIER* no. 217 (2011), RR. 19–30.
Zis, George 'The Elusive Case for Flexible Exchange Rates'. In *Exchange Rates and Economic Policy in the Twentieth Century*, edited by Ross Catterall and Derek Aldcroft (2004), pp. 254–95.
Zweiniger-Bargielowska, Ina *Austerity in Britain: Rationing, Controls, and Consumption 1939–1955* (2000).

Index